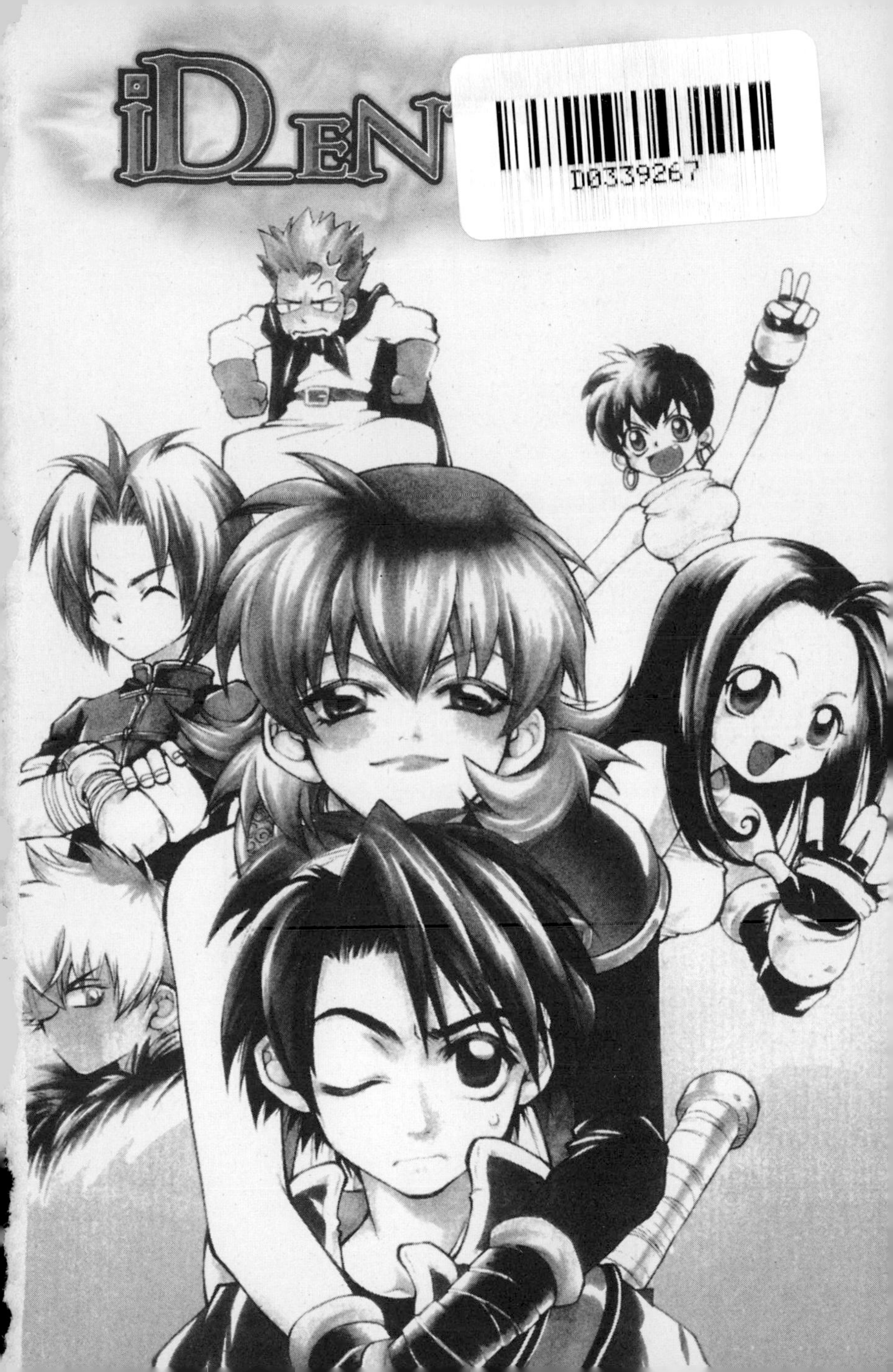

iD_eNTITY Vol. 3
Written by Hee-Joon Son
Illustrated by Youn-Kyung Kim

Translation - Sarah Kim
English Adaptation - Jason Dietrich
Copy Editor - Wendy Hunter
Retouch and Lettering - Lucas Rivera
Production Artist - Jason Milligan
Cover Design - Jorge Negrete

Editor - Tim Beedle
Digital Imaging Manager - Chris Buford
Production Managers - Jennifer Miller and Mutsumi Miyazaki
Managing Editor - Jill Freshney
VP of Production - Ron Klamert
Publisher and E.I.C. - Mike Kiley
President and C.O.O. - John Parker
C.E.O. - Stuart Levy

A 🔘 **TOKYOPOP**® Manga

TOKYOPOP Inc.
5900 Wilshire Blvd. Suite 2000
Los Angeles, CA 90036

E-mail: info@TOKYOPOP.com
Come visit us online at www.TOKYOPOP.com

ISBN: 1-59532-347-3

First TOKYOPOP printing: September 2005

10 9 8 7 6 5 4 3 2 1

Printed in the USA

vOL. 3

wRITTEN bY hEE-jOON sON
iLLUSTRATED bY yOUN-kYUNG kIM

HAMBURG // LONDON // LOS ANGELES // TOKYO

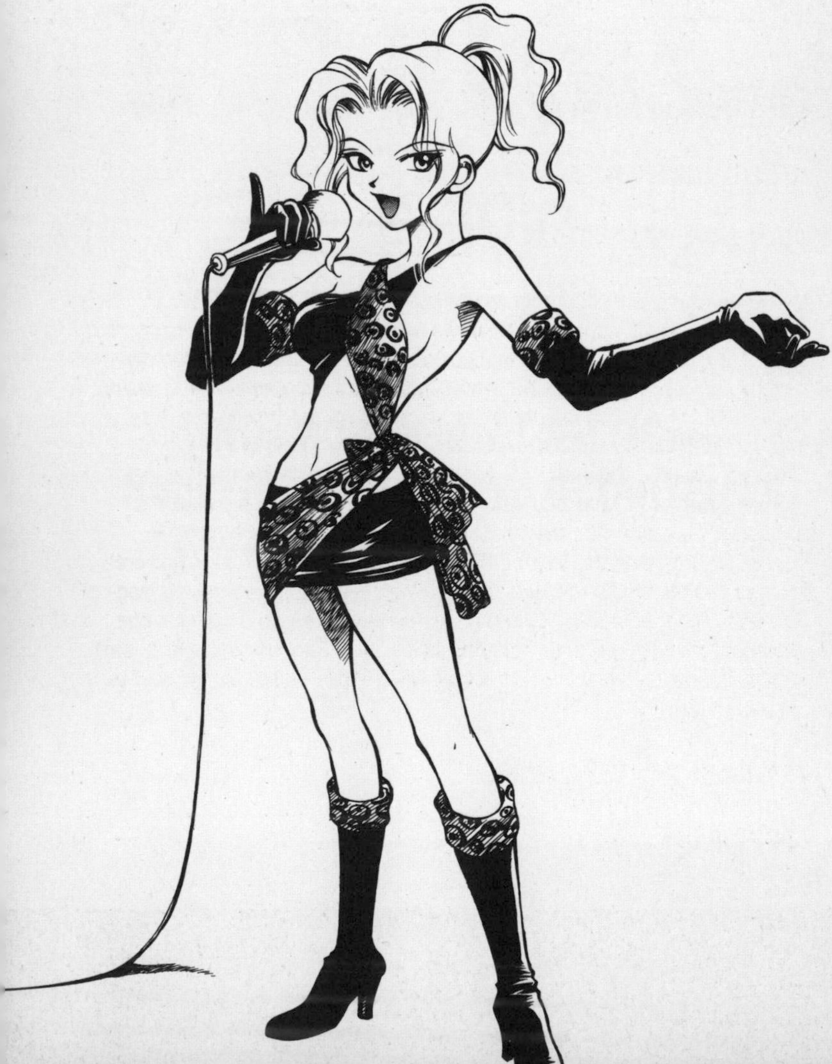

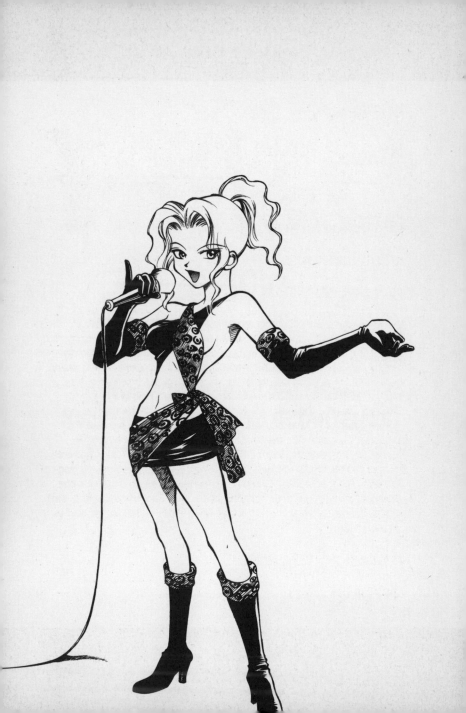

pREVIOUSLY iN

iDENTITY™

PASSWORD RECOGNIZED...

IDENTITY CONFIRMED...

ACCESSING PAST VOLUME FILE...

In real life, Jang-Gun, Kwan-Su and Woon-Suk are average kids with average problems, but in the virtual world of Lost Saga, they're Team Triple Threat. Using the screen names Roto, Boromid and Ah-Dol, they've become heroes to countless NPCs and legends among gamers everywhere. However, this tight-knit little team has received quite a shakeup by way of a hot little warrior named Yureka. Mysterious and powerful, Yureka is everything Jang-Gun has ever wanted in a woman. There's just one problem, Yureka IS Jang-Gun. After his previous ID card expires, he temporarily assumes the identity of Yureka after finding an unclaimed, fully valid ID card on the floor of his favorite gaming shop. However, there's more to this identity than meets the eye. After renewing his Roto ID, Jang-Gun was prepared to drop his feminine alter ego. The only problem is she doesn't seem willing to drop him. And when Jang-Gun logs on as Roto, only to have Yureka show up with the rest of Team Triple Threat, things start to get a little weird...

TRANSMISSION COMPLETE...

LOGGING OFF...

rOGUE'S gALLERY

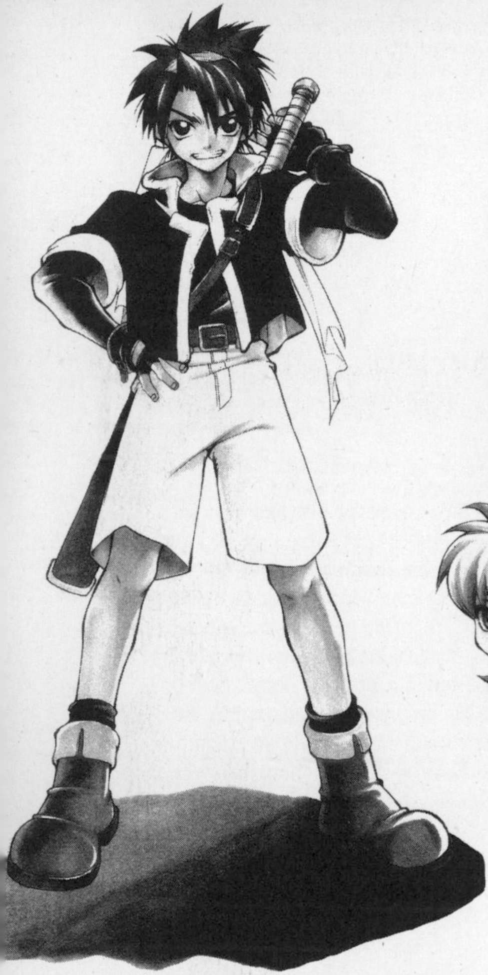

iD_ROTO *Offline: Jang-Gun*

Class:	Level:	Sub-class:
Sorcerer	Master	Warrior

The pint-sized pointman of Team Triple Threat, Roto pushes himself near the breaking point, playing video games all night, every night, and somehow still managing to make the grade as an "A" student. Having lost his father, and barely tall enough to see over shop counters, Roto's got a thing or two to try and compensate for. In Korean, Roto's offline name, Jang-Gun literally means "General" and Roto bears more than a passing similarity to another general with an inferiority complex, Napoleon. And like Napoleon, the only thing shorter than his temper is, well, him.

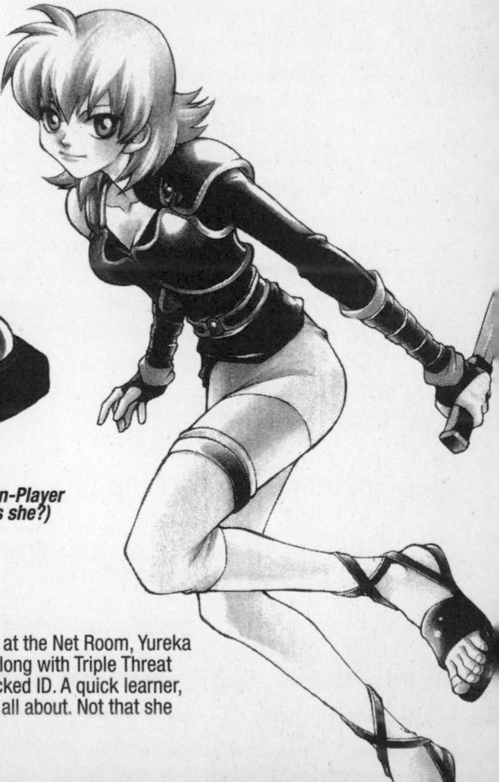

iD_YUREKA *Offline: None, Non-Player Character (or is she?)*

Class:	Level:	Sub-class:
Warrior	Novice (But with her through-the-roof stats, she's effectively master level...)	?

The spitting image of a babe Roto walked in on at the Net Room, Yureka is an Artificial Intelligence that's been tagging along with Triple Threat ever since Roto mistakenly logged in with a hacked ID. A quick learner, she's still trying to figure out what Lost Saga is all about. Not that she has the best teachers.

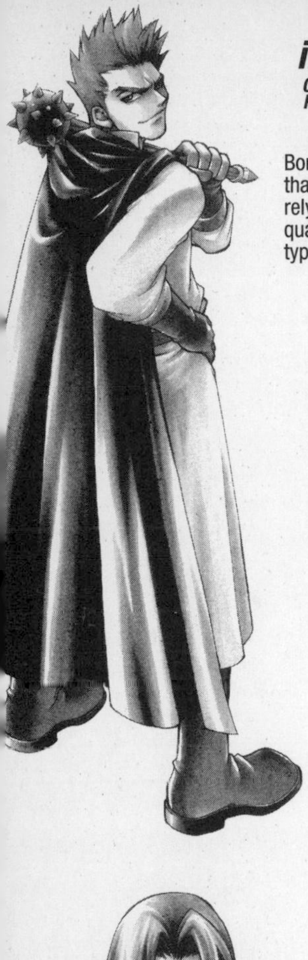

iD_BOROMID *Offline: Kwan-Su Pan*

Class: Priest **Level:** Master **Sub-class:** Warrior

Boromid is deep as a puddle, sharp as a bowling ball and flakier than oven-fresh baklava. When the going gets tough, you can rely on Boromid…to be running the other way. Not exactly the qualities you're after when interviewing for a priest, who are typically the party's backup plan if they get in over their heads.

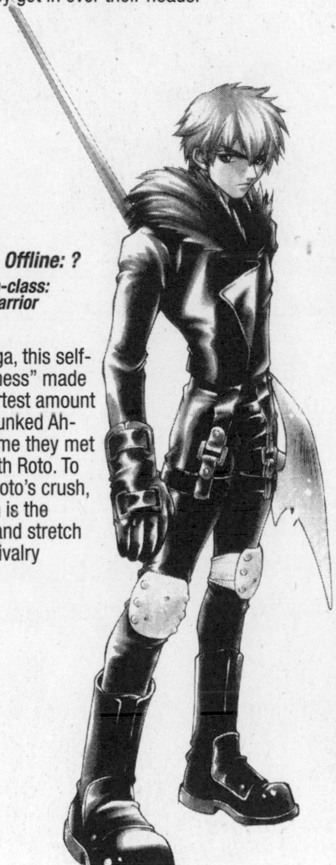

iD_ARADON *Offline: ?*

Class: Sorcerer **Level:** Master **Sub-class:** Warrior

A rising star in Lost Saga, this self-styled "Master of Darkness" made master level in the shortest amount of time, ever. He also punked Ah-Dol and Boromid last time they met and went toe-to-toe with Roto. To make matters worse, Roto's crush, Miss Piri, thinks Aradon is the hottest thing in shorts and stretch pants. Could this be a rivalry brewing? Naah…

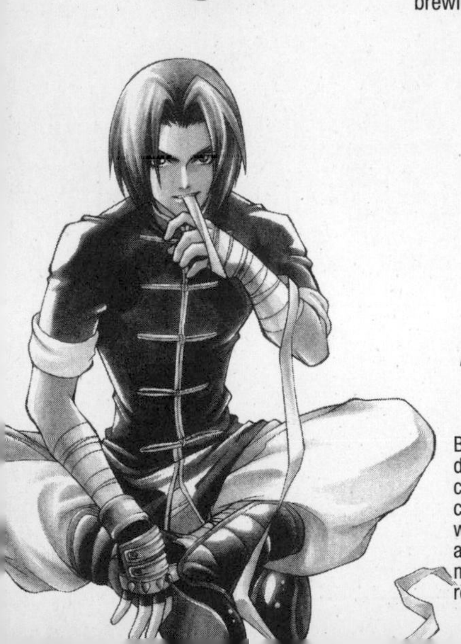

iD_AH-DOL *Offline: Woon-Suk Sung*

Class: Warrior **Level:** Master **Sub-class:** Sorcerer

Both the brains and the brawn behind the Triple Threat, Ah-Dol doesn't say much. When he does, it's usually followed by the crunch of breaking bones. Taking a hands-on approach to combat, he prefers to pummel his opponents into submission with his spiked knuckledusters rather than use a sword or a club. Despite all that, Ah-Dol is easily the most grounded member of Triple Threat, able to relate to the offline world in a relatively normal fashion.

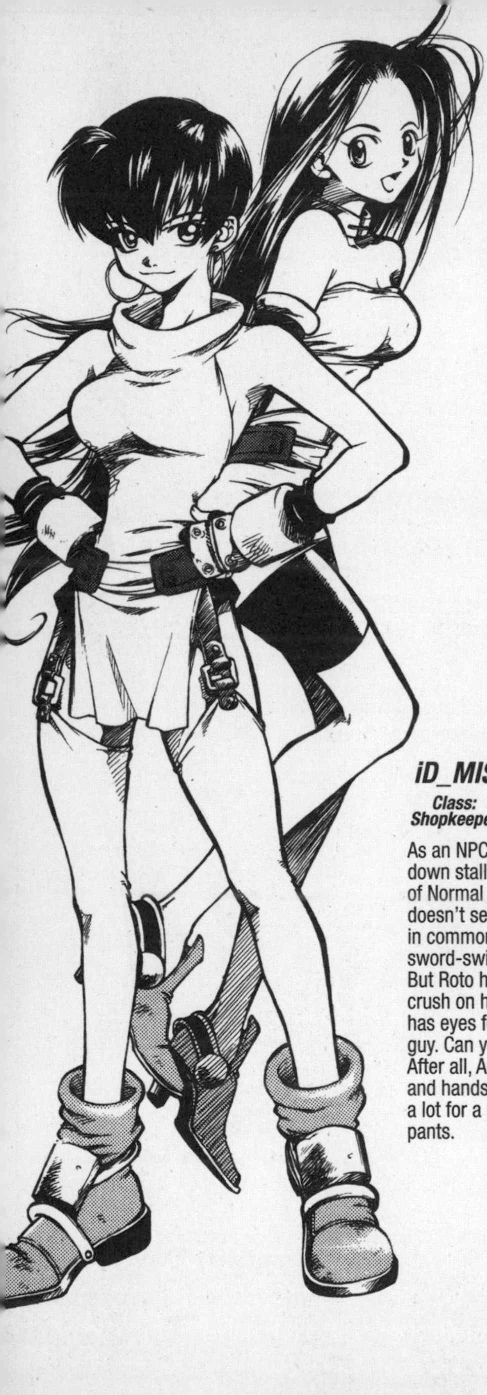

iD_FALLEN ANGELS, K.C and JULIE

Offline: Pop Idols the Lovely Angels, Jin-Mee Kang and Gina Kang

Class: *Thief* ***Level:*** *Master* ***Sub-class:*** *?*

Offline, they're squeaky-clean pop singers the Lovely Angels. But down in the game they indulge their inner bad girls as the thief duo the Fallen Angels. After a run-in with Triple Threat, they've ostensibly gone straight. But will the thrill of breaking the rules get the better of these two cat burglars?

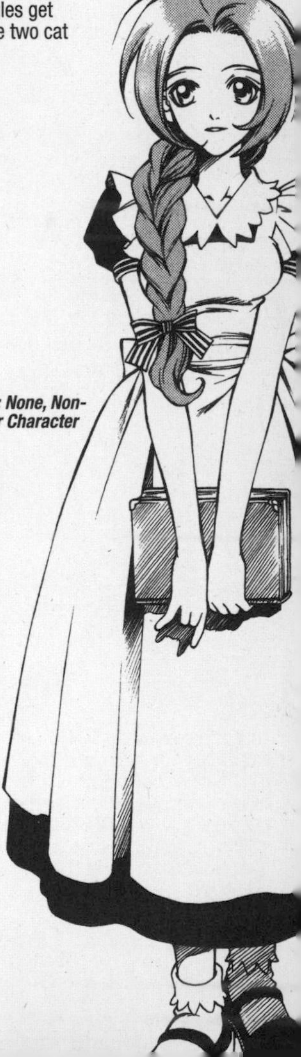

iD_MISS PIRI

Offline: None, Non-Player Character

Class: *Shopkeeper*

As an NPC keeping a run-down stall in a seedy corner of Normal City, Miss Piri doesn't seem to have much in common with the other sword-swingers in our story. But Roto has a super-sized crush on her, and she…only has eyes for that Aradon guy. Can you blame her? After all, Aradon is tall, dark and handsome…and does a lot for a pair of stretch pants.

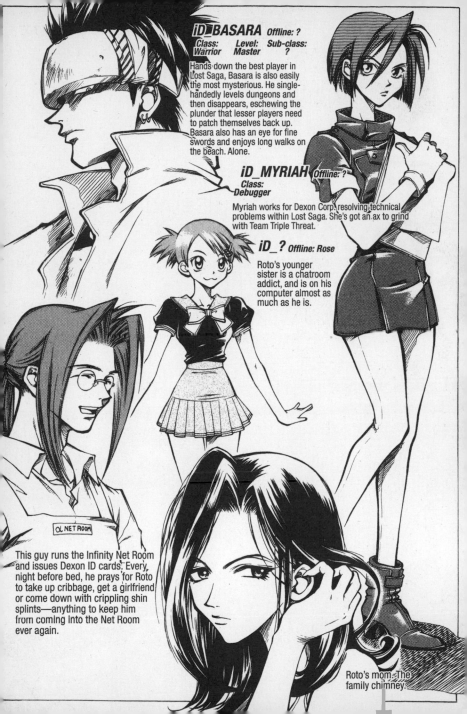

iD_BASARA
Offline: ?

Class:	Level:	Sub-class:
Warrior	Master	?

Hands down the best player in Lost Saga, Basara is also easily the most mysterious. He single-handedly levels dungeons and then disappears, eschewing the plunder that lesser players need to patch themselves back up. Basara also has an eye for fine swords and enjoys long walks on the beach. Alone.

iD_MYRIAH
Offline: ?

**Class:
Debugger**

Myriah works for Dexon Corp, resolving technical problems within Lost Saga. She's got an ax to grind with Team Triple Threat.

iD_?
Offline: Rose

Roto's younger sister is a chatroom addict, and is on his computer almost as much as he is.

This guy runs the Infinity Net Room and issues Dexon ID cards. Every night before bed, he prays for Roto to take up cribbage, get a girlfriend or come down with crippling shin splints—anything to keep him from coming into the Net Room ever again.

Roto's mom. The family chimney.

CONTENTS

STAGE 15
DOUBLE JEOPARDY

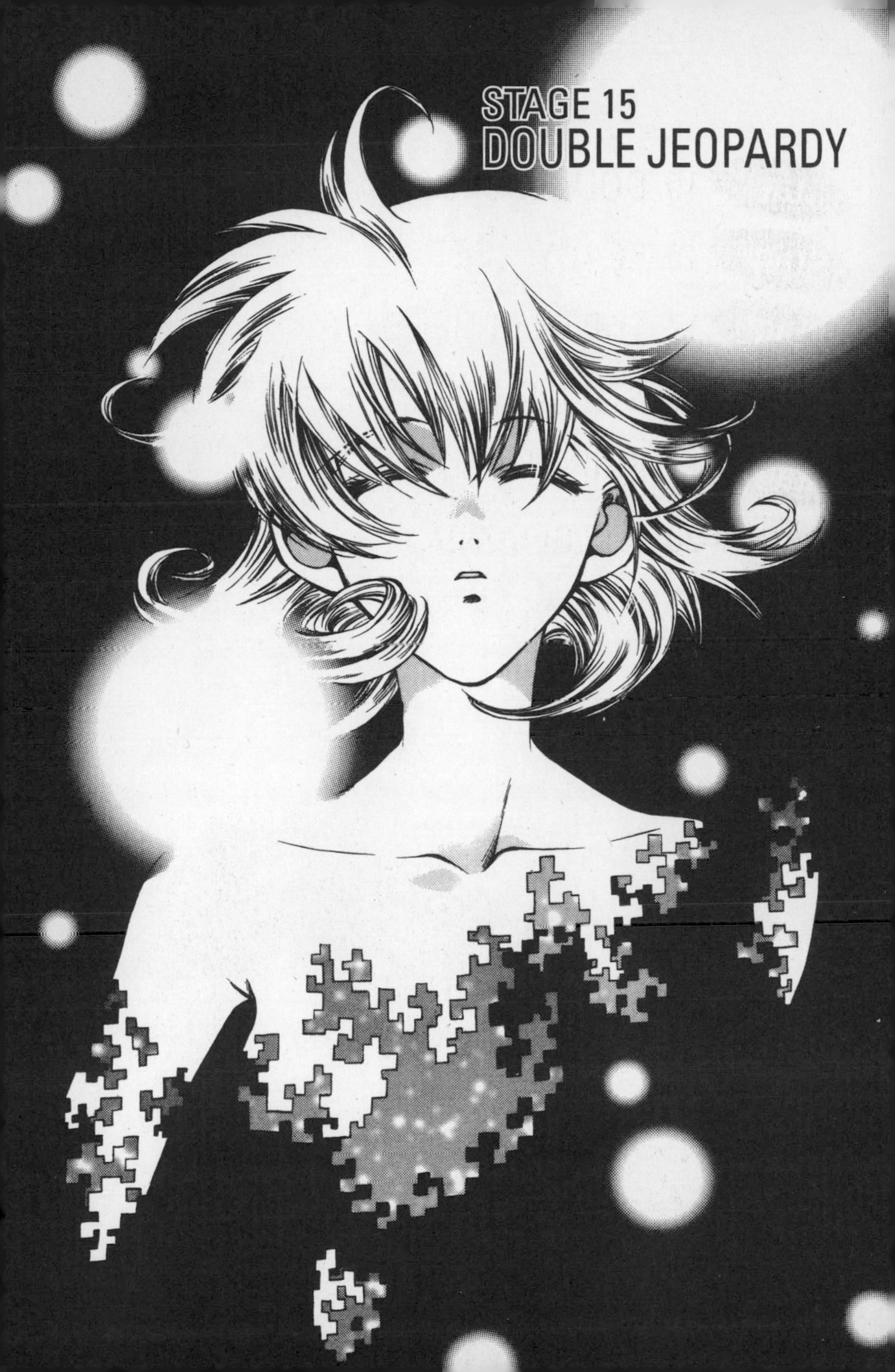

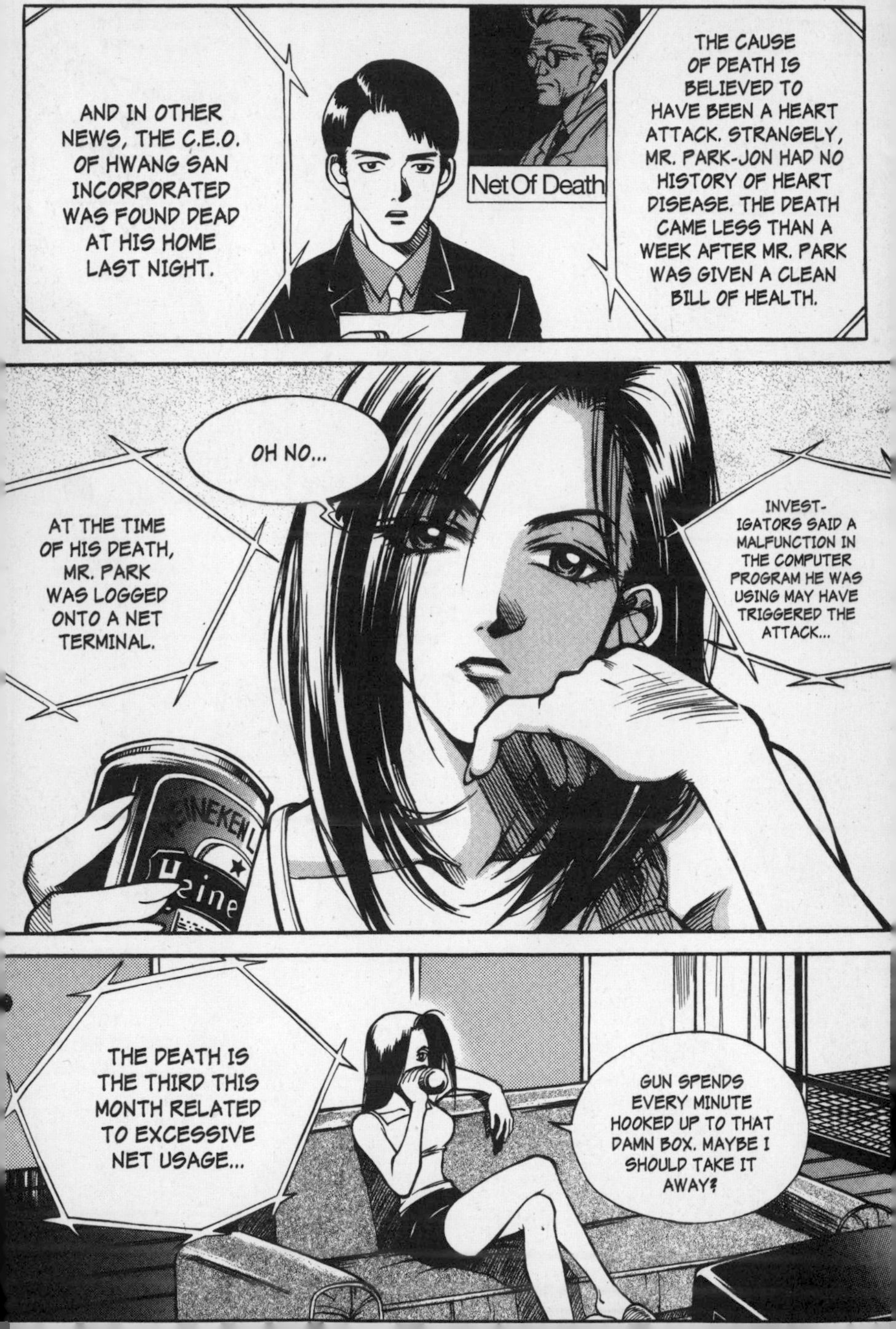
AND IN OTHER NEWS, THE C.E.O. OF HWANG SAN INCORPORATED WAS FOUND DEAD AT HIS HOME LAST NIGHT.
Net Of Death
THE CAUSE OF DEATH IS BELIEVED TO HAVE BEEN A HEART ATTACK. STRANGELY, MR. PARK-JON HAD NO HISTORY OF HEART DISEASE. THE DEATH CAME LESS THAN A WEEK AFTER MR. PARK WAS GIVEN A CLEAN BILL OF HEALTH.
OH NO...
AT THE TIME OF HIS DEATH, MR. PARK WAS LOGGED ONTO A NET TERMINAL.
INVEST-IGATORS SAID A MALFUNCTION IN THE COMPUTER PROGRAM HE WAS USING MAY HAVE TRIGGERED THE ATTACK...
THE DEATH IS THE THIRD THIS MONTH RELATED TO EXCESSIVE NET USAGE...
GUN SPENDS EVERY MINUTE HOOKED UP TO THAT DAMN BOX. MAYBE I SHOULD TAKE IT AWAY?

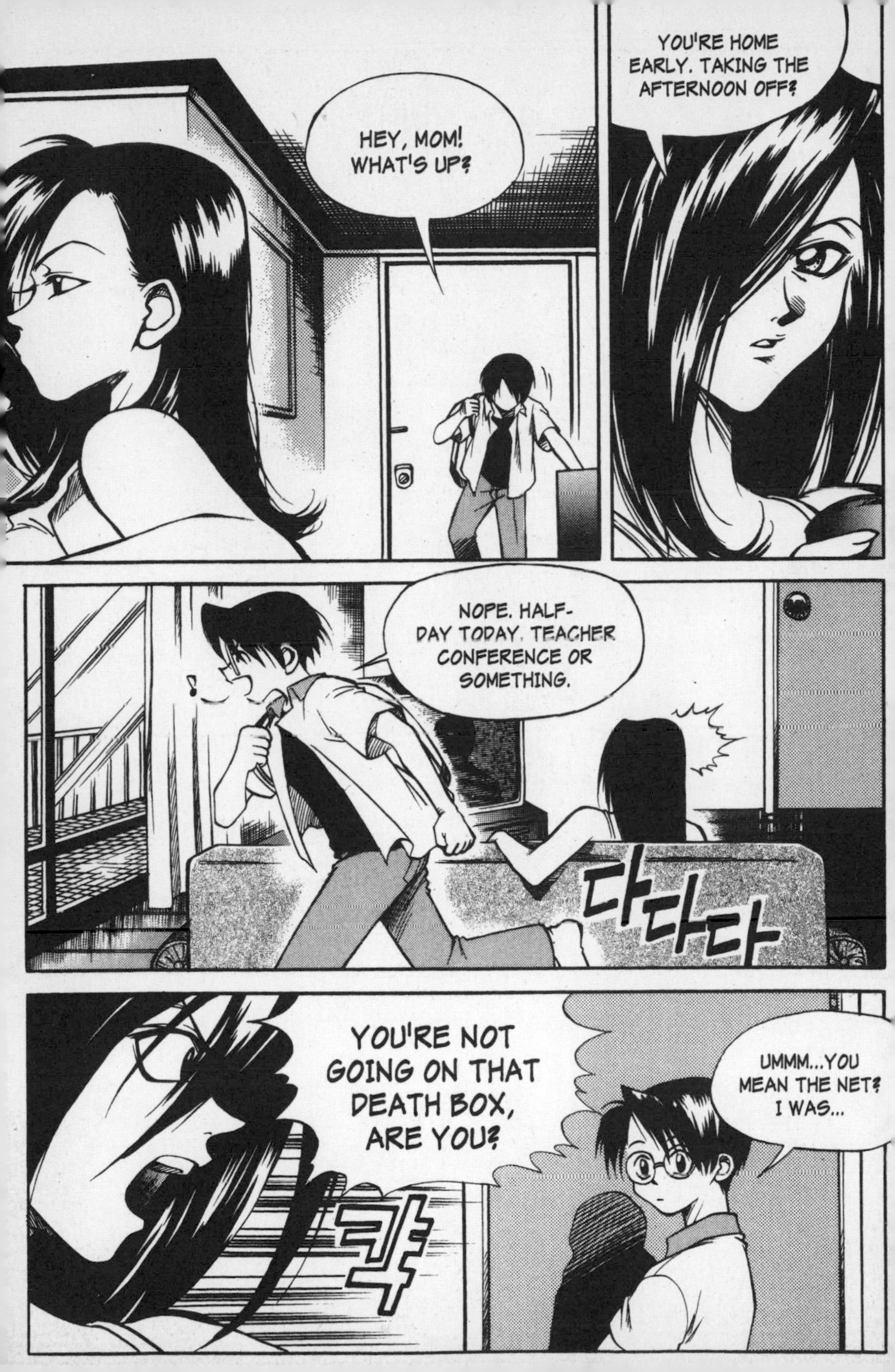
HEY, MOM! WHAT'S UP?
YOU'RE HOME EARLY. TAKING THE AFTERNOON OFF?
NOPE. HALF-DAY TODAY. TEACHER CONFERENCE OR SOMETHING.
다다다
YOU'RE NOT GOING ON THAT DEATH BOX, ARE YOU?
콱
UMMM...YOU MEAN THE NET? I WAS...

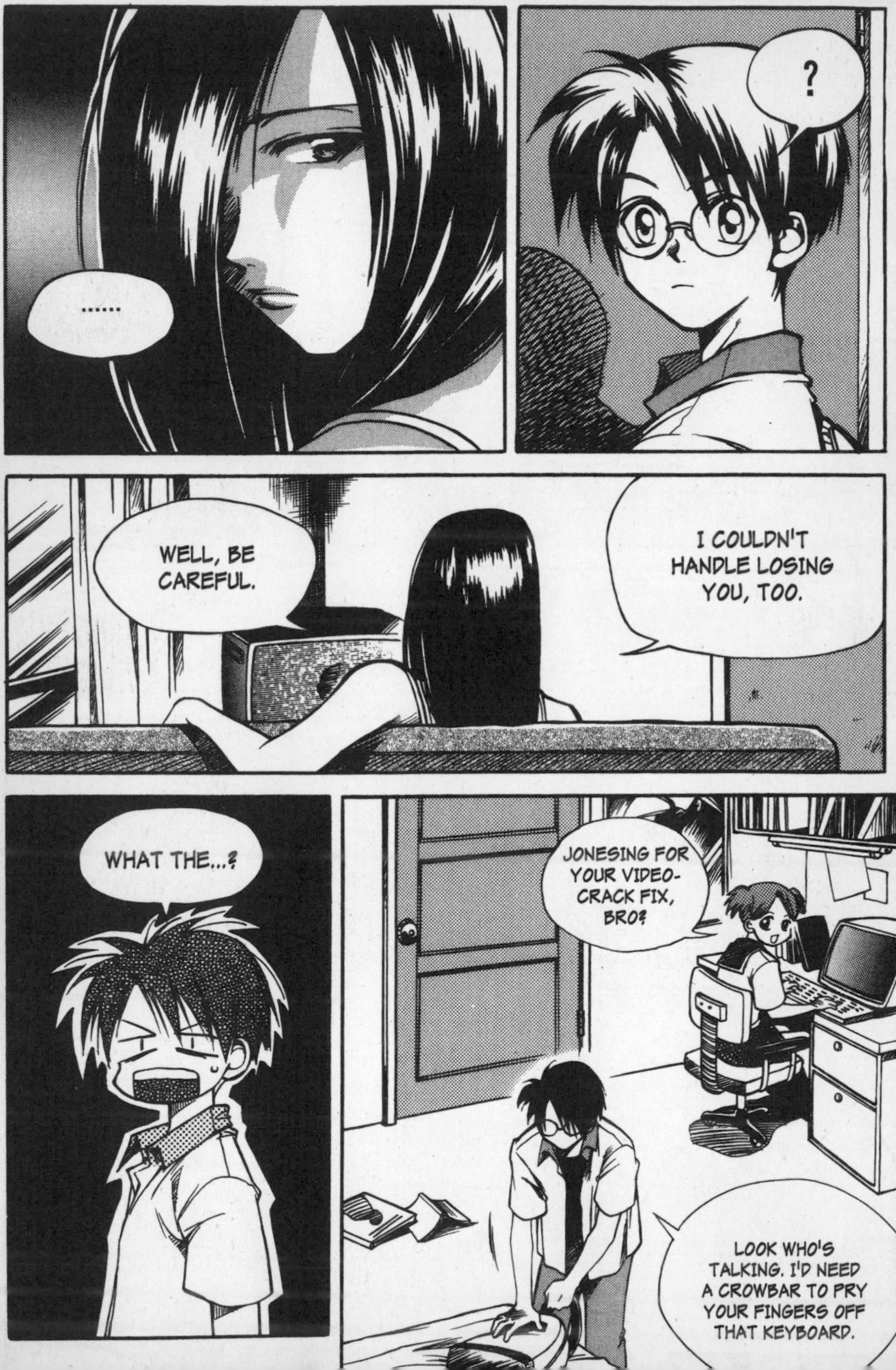
......
?
WELL, BE CAREFUL.
I COULDN'T HANDLE LOSING YOU, TOO.
WHAT THE...?
JONESING FOR YOUR VIDEO-CRACK FIX, BRO?
LOOK WHO'S TALKING. I'D NEED A CROWBAR TO PRY YOUR FINGERS OFF THAT KEYBOARD.

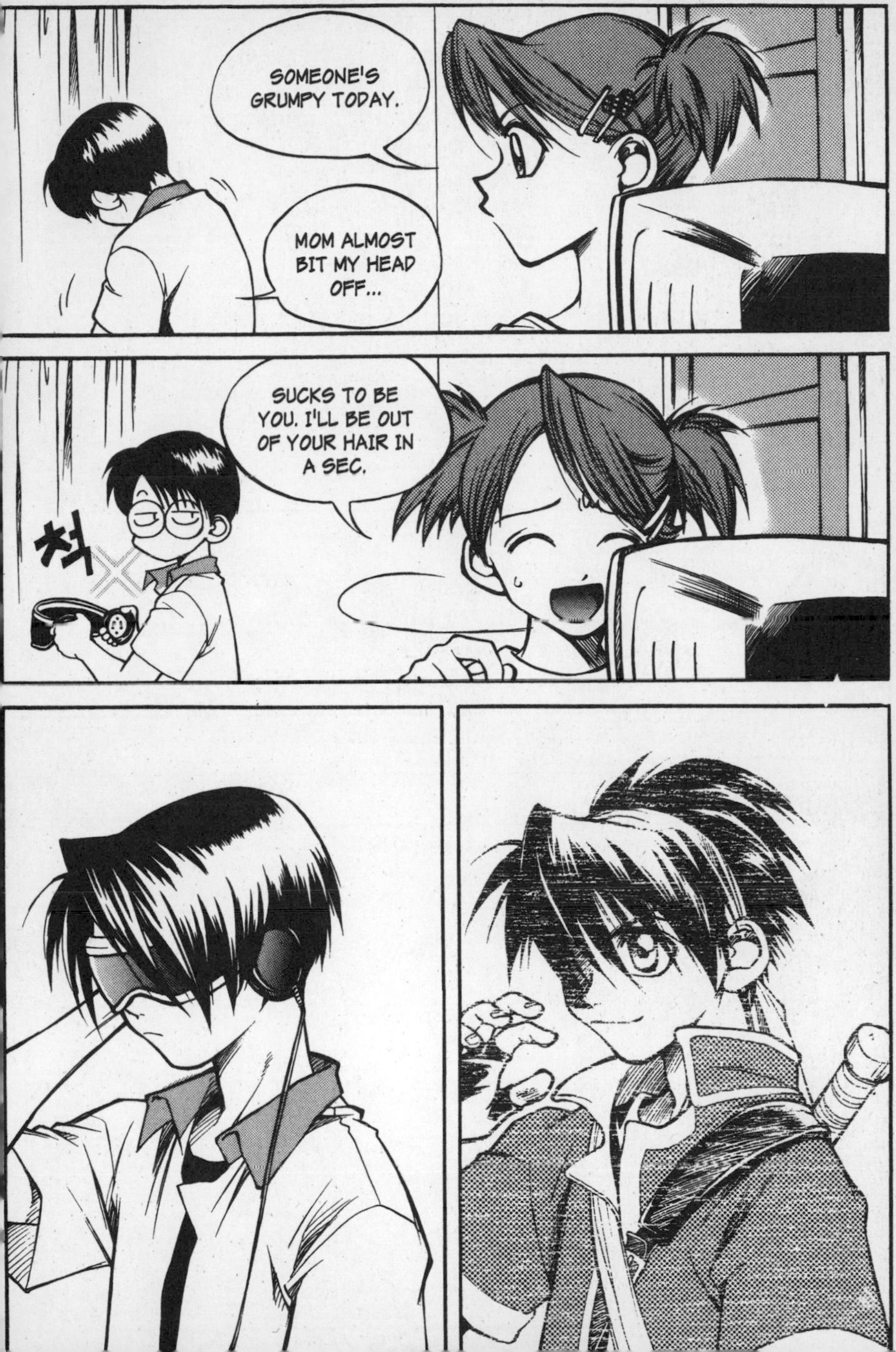
SOMEONE'S GRUMPY TODAY.
MOM ALMOST BIT MY HEAD OFF...
SUCKS TO BE YOU. I'LL BE OUT OF YOUR HAIR IN A SEC.
척

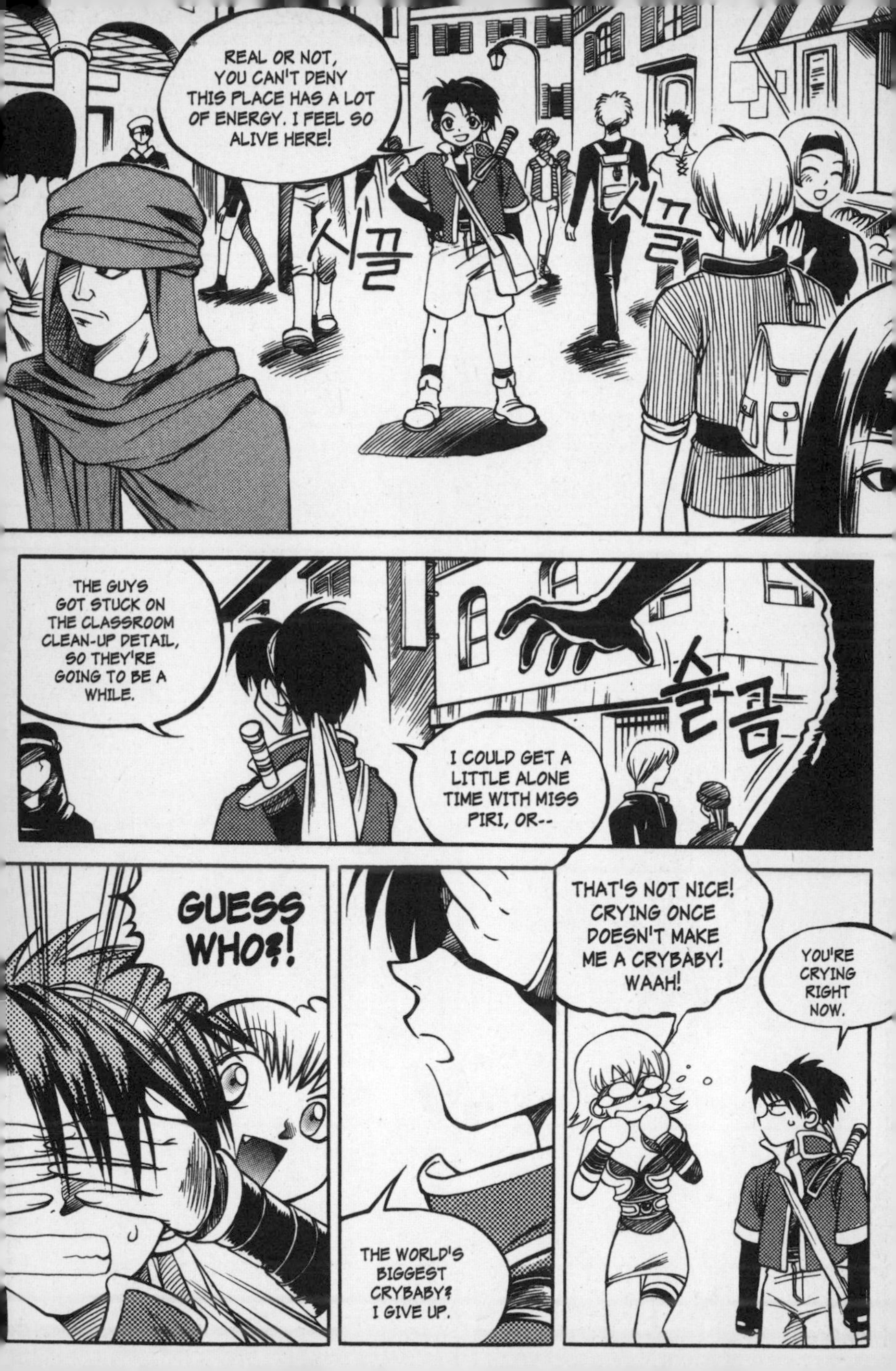
REAL OR NOT, YOU CAN'T DENY THIS PLACE HAS A LOT OF ENERGY. I FEEL SO ALIVE HERE!
시끌
시끌
THE GUYS GOT STUCK ON THE CLASSROOM CLEAN-UP DETAIL, SO THEY'RE GOING TO BE A WHILE.
슬금
I COULD GET A LITTLE ALONE TIME WITH MISS PIRI, OR--
GUESS WHO?!
THE WORLD'S BIGGEST CRYBABY? I GIVE UP.
THAT'S NOT NICE! CRYING ONCE DOESN'T MAKE ME A CRYBABY! WAAH!
YOU'RE CRYING RIGHT NOW.

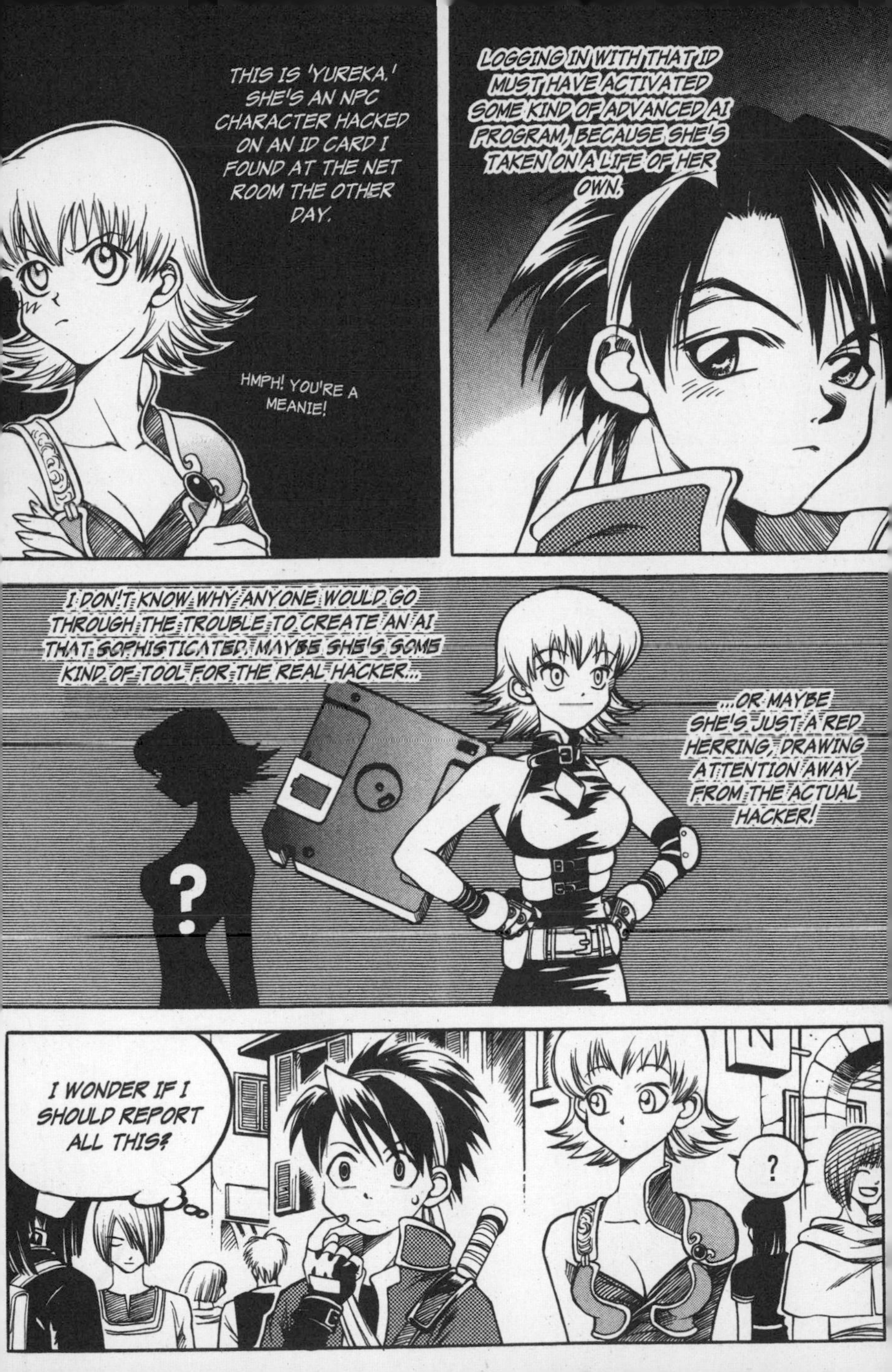
THIS IS 'YUREKA.' SHE'S AN NPC CHARACTER HACKED ON AN ID CARD I FOUND AT THE NET ROOM THE OTHER DAY.
HMPH! YOU'RE A MEANIE!
LOGGING IN WITH THAT ID MUST HAVE ACTIVATED SOME KIND OF ADVANCED AI PROGRAM, BECAUSE SHE'S TAKEN ON A LIFE OF HER OWN.
I DON'T KNOW WHY ANYONE WOULD GO THROUGH THE TROUBLE TO CREATE AN AI THAT SOPHISTICATED. MAYBE SHE'S SOME KIND OF TOOL FOR THE REAL HACKER...
...OR MAYBE SHE'S JUST A RED HERRING, DRAWING ATTENTION AWAY FROM THE ACTUAL HACKER!
?
I WONDER IF I SHOULD REPORT ALL THIS?
?

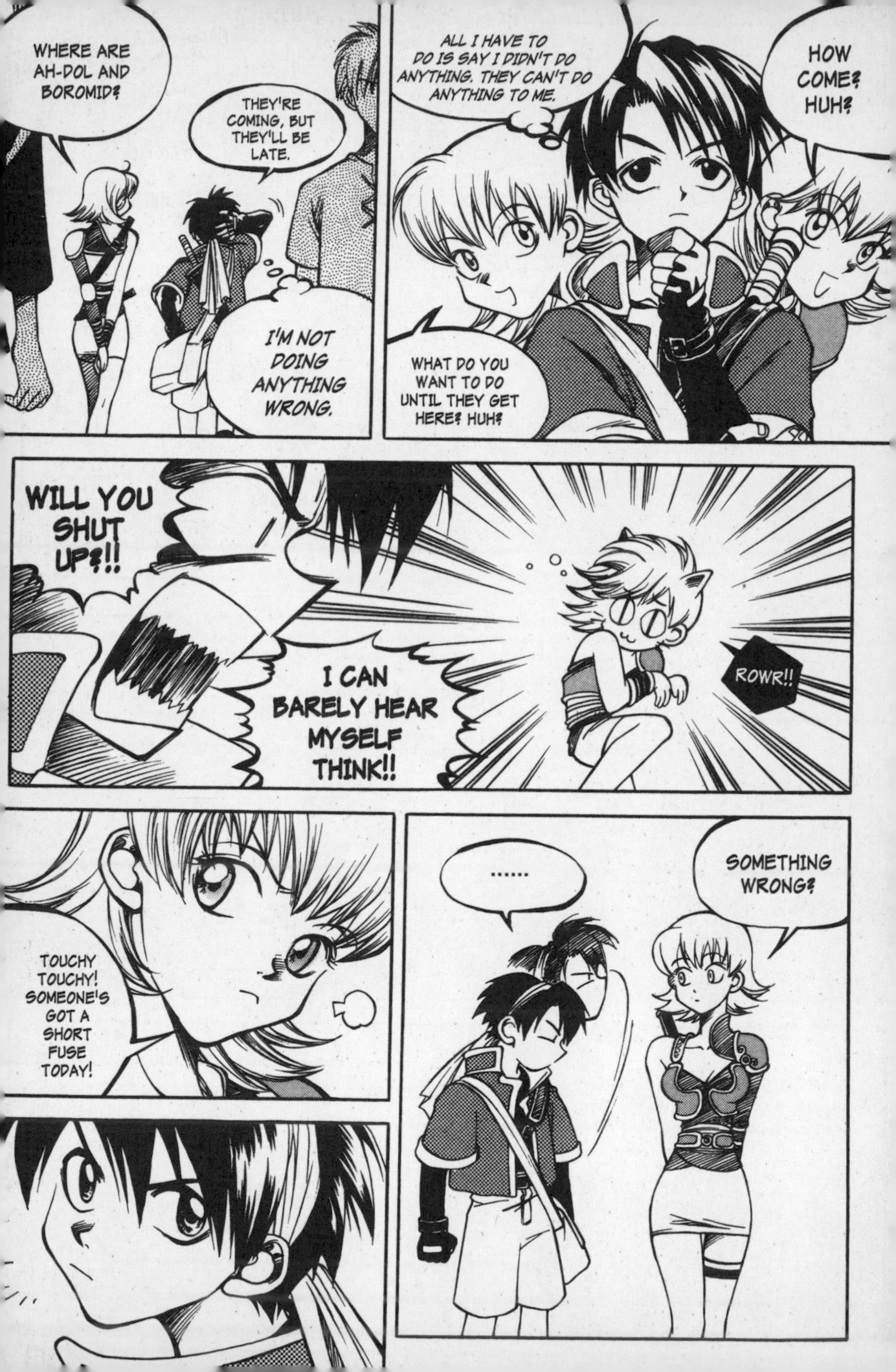
WHERE ARE AH-DOL AND BOROMID?
THEY'RE COMING, BUT THEY'LL BE LATE.
I'M NOT DOING ANYTHING WRONG.
ALL I HAVE TO DO IS SAY I DIDN'T DO ANYTHING. THEY CAN'T DO ANYTHING TO ME.
HOW COME? HUH?
WHAT DO YOU WANT TO DO UNTIL THEY GET HERE? HUH?
WILL YOU SHUT UP?!!
I CAN BARELY HEAR MYSELF THINK!!
ROWR!!
TOUCHY TOUCHY! SOMEONE'S GOT A SHORT FUSE TODAY!
......
SOMETHING WRONG?

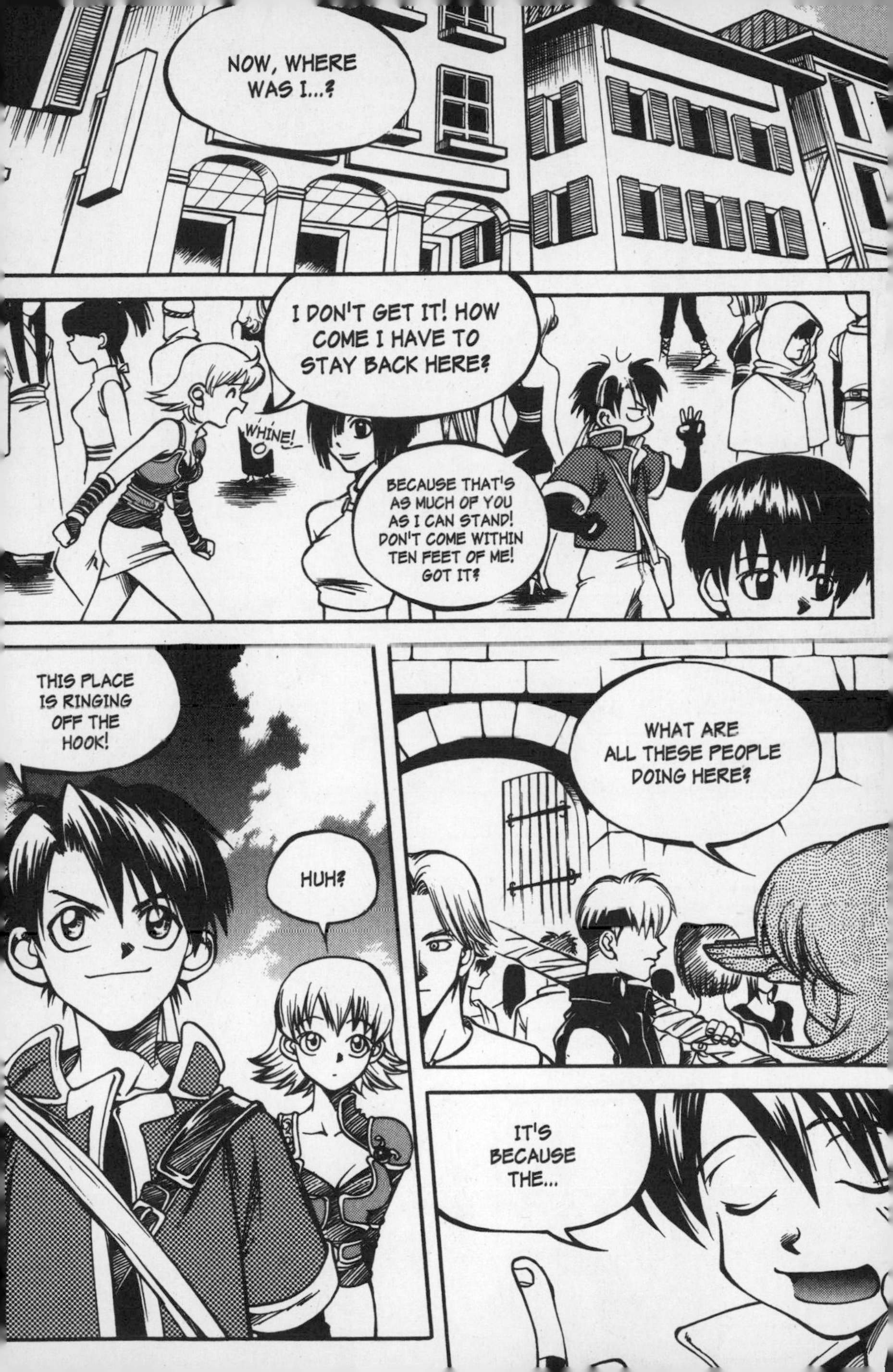
NOW, WHERE WAS I...?
I DON'T GET IT! HOW COME I HAVE TO STAY BACK HERE?
WHINE!
BECAUSE THAT'S AS MUCH OF YOU AS I CAN STAND! DON'T COME WITHIN TEN FEET OF ME! GOT IT?
THIS PLACE IS RINGING OFF THE HOOK!
HUH?
WHAT ARE ALL THESE PEOPLE DOING HERE?
IT'S BECAUSE THE...

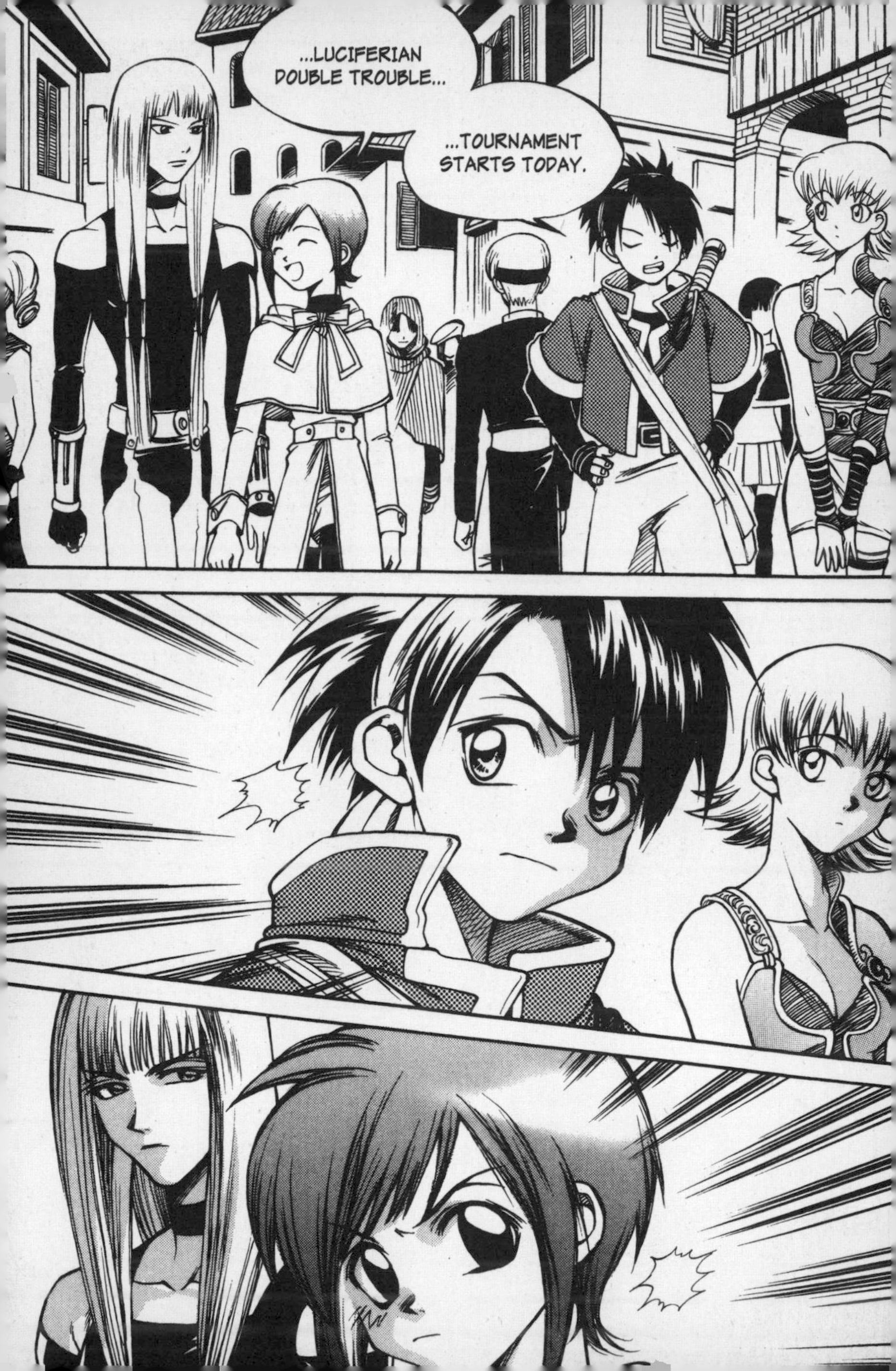
...LUCIFERIAN DOUBLE TROUBLE...
...TOURNAMENT STARTS TODAY.

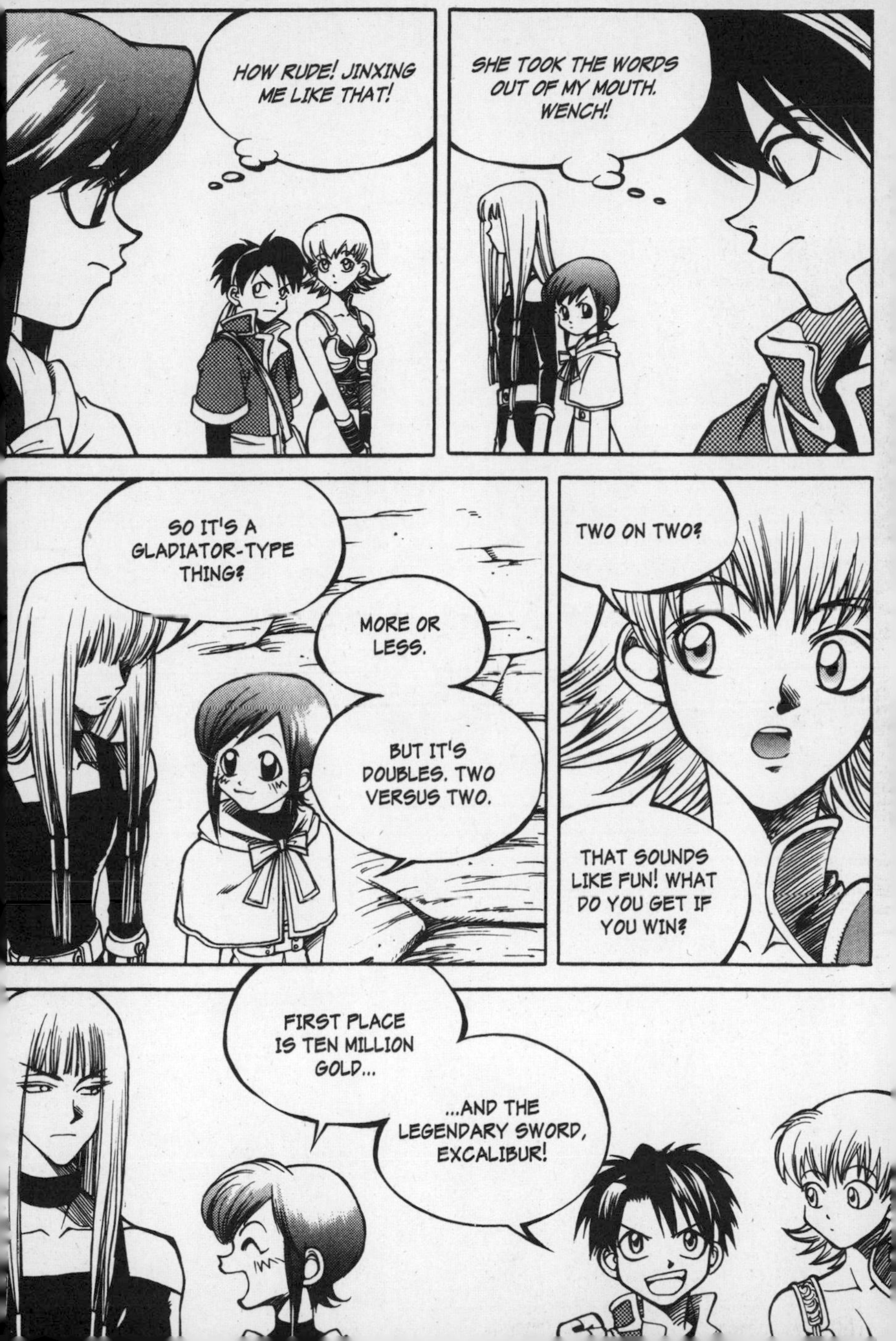
HOW RUDE! JINXING ME LIKE THAT!
SHE TOOK THE WORDS OUT OF MY MOUTH. WENCH!
SO IT'S A GLADIATOR-TYPE THING?
MORE OR LESS.
BUT IT'S DOUBLES. TWO VERSUS TWO.
TWO ON TWO?
THAT SOUNDS LIKE FUN! WHAT DO YOU GET IF YOU WIN?
FIRST PLACE IS TEN MILLION GOLD...
...AND THE LEGENDARY SWORD, EXCALIBUR!

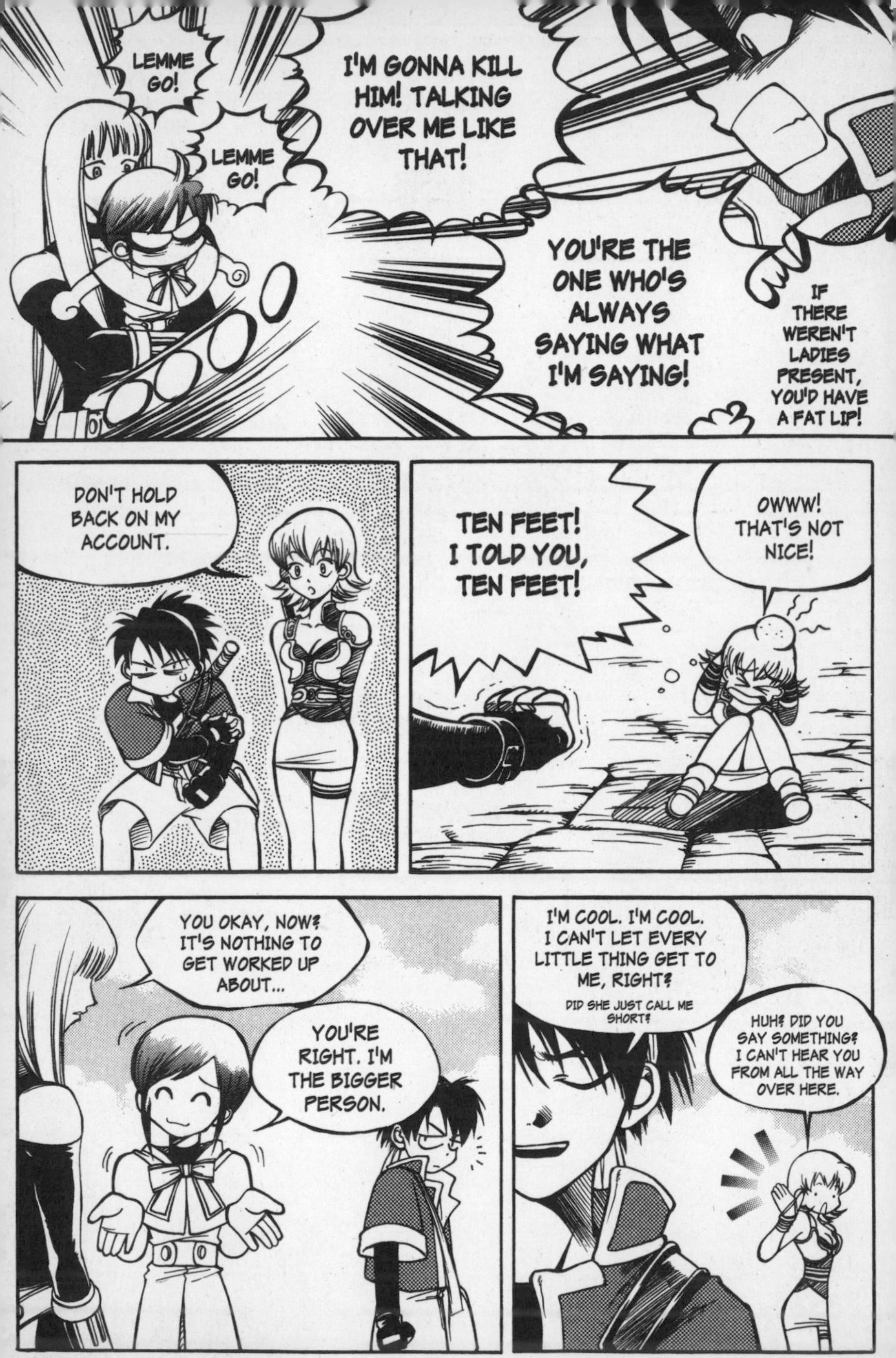
LEMME GO!
LEMME GO!
I'M GONNA KILL HIM! TALKING OVER ME LIKE THAT!
YOU'RE THE ONE WHO'S ALWAYS SAYING WHAT I'M SAYING!
IF THERE WEREN'T LADIES PRESENT, YOU'D HAVE A FAT LIP!
DON'T HOLD BACK ON MY ACCOUNT.
TEN FEET! I TOLD YOU, TEN FEET!
OWWW! THAT'S NOT NICE!
YOU OKAY, NOW? IT'S NOTHING TO GET WORKED UP ABOUT...
YOU'RE RIGHT. I'M THE BIGGER PERSON.
I'M COOL. I'M COOL. I CAN'T LET EVERY LITTLE THING GET TO ME, RIGHT?
DID SHE JUST CALL ME SHORT?
HUH? DID YOU SAY SOMETHING? I CAN'T HEAR YOU FROM ALL THE WAY OVER HERE.

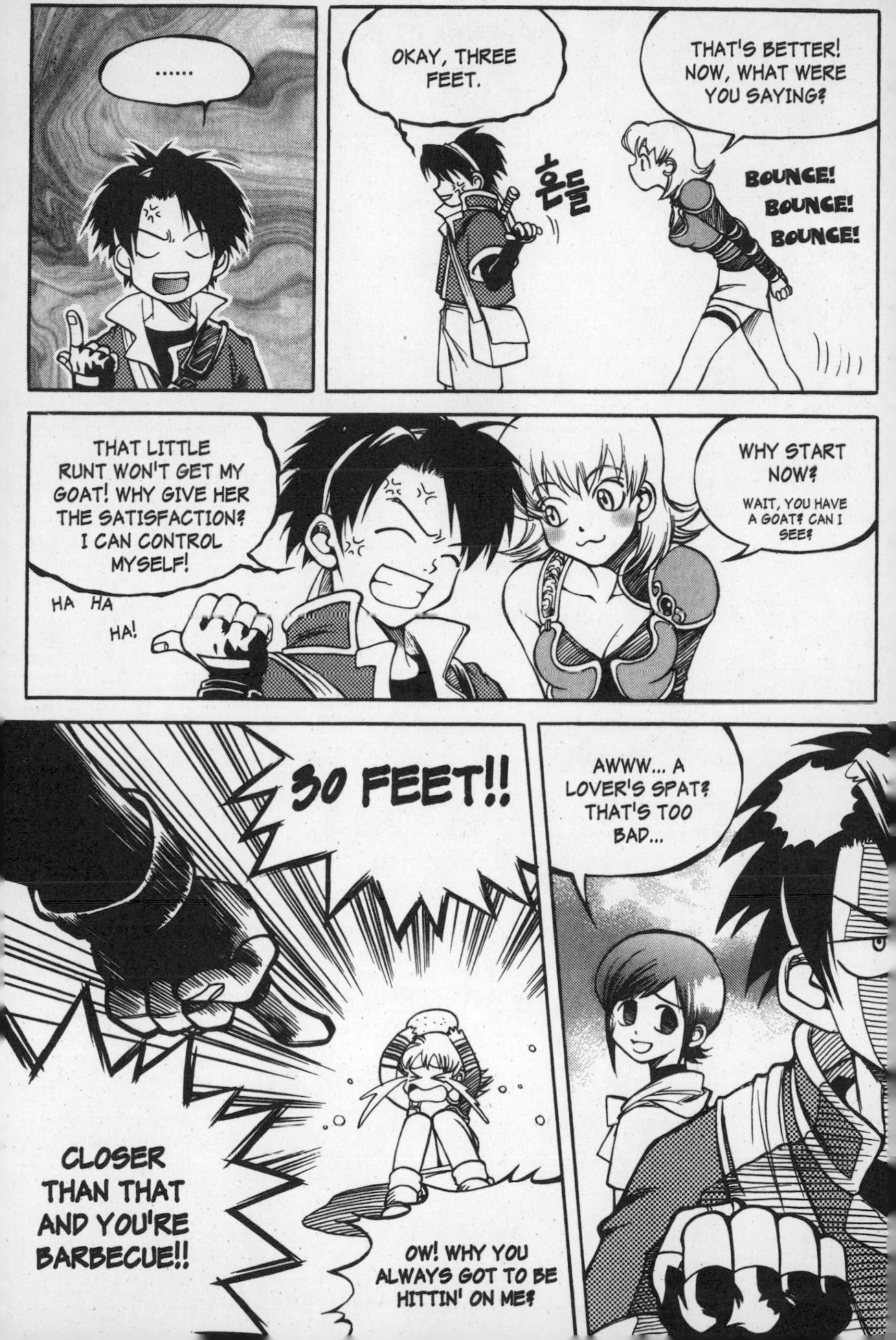

......
OKAY, THREE FEET.
혼들
THAT'S BETTER! NOW, WHAT WERE YOU SAYING?
BOUNCE! BOUNCE! BOUNCE!
THAT LITTLE RUNT WON'T GET MY GOAT! WHY GIVE HER THE SATISFACTION? I CAN CONTROL MYSELF!
HA HA HA!
WHY START NOW?
WAIT, YOU HAVE A GOAT? CAN I SEE?
30 FEET!!
CLOSER THAN THAT AND YOU'RE BARBECUE!!
OW! WHY YOU ALWAYS GOT TO BE HITTIN' ON ME?
AWWW... A LOVER'S SPAT? THAT'S TOO BAD...

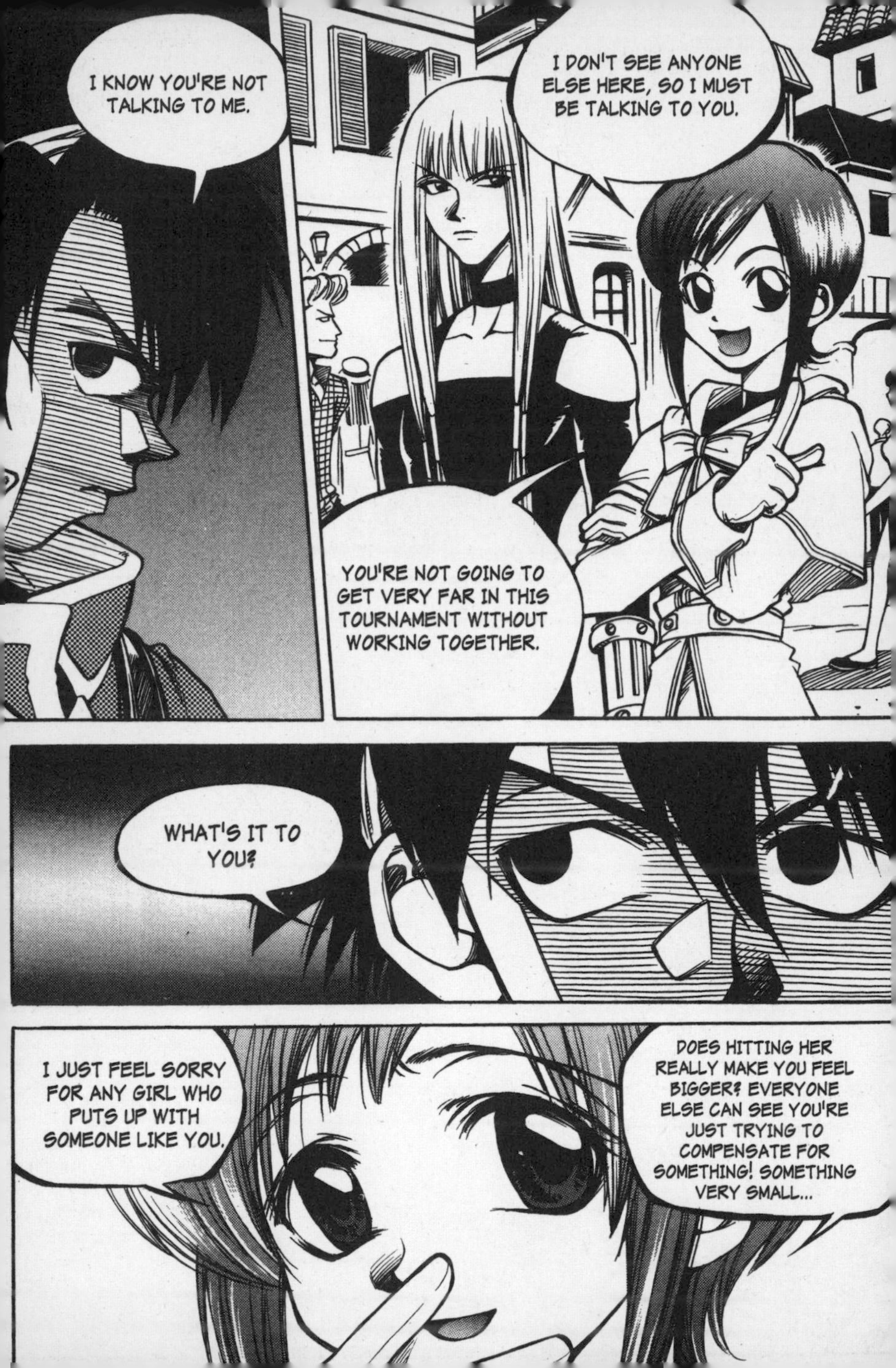
I KNOW YOU'RE NOT TALKING TO ME.
I DON'T SEE ANYONE ELSE HERE, SO I MUST BE TALKING TO YOU.
YOU'RE NOT GOING TO GET VERY FAR IN THIS TOURNAMENT WITHOUT WORKING TOGETHER.
WHAT'S IT TO YOU?
I JUST FEEL SORRY FOR ANY GIRL WHO PUTS UP WITH SOMEONE LIKE YOU.
DOES HITTING HER REALLY MAKE YOU FEEL BIGGER? EVERYONE ELSE CAN SEE YOU'RE JUST TRYING TO COMPENSATE FOR SOMETHING! SOMETHING VERY SMALL...

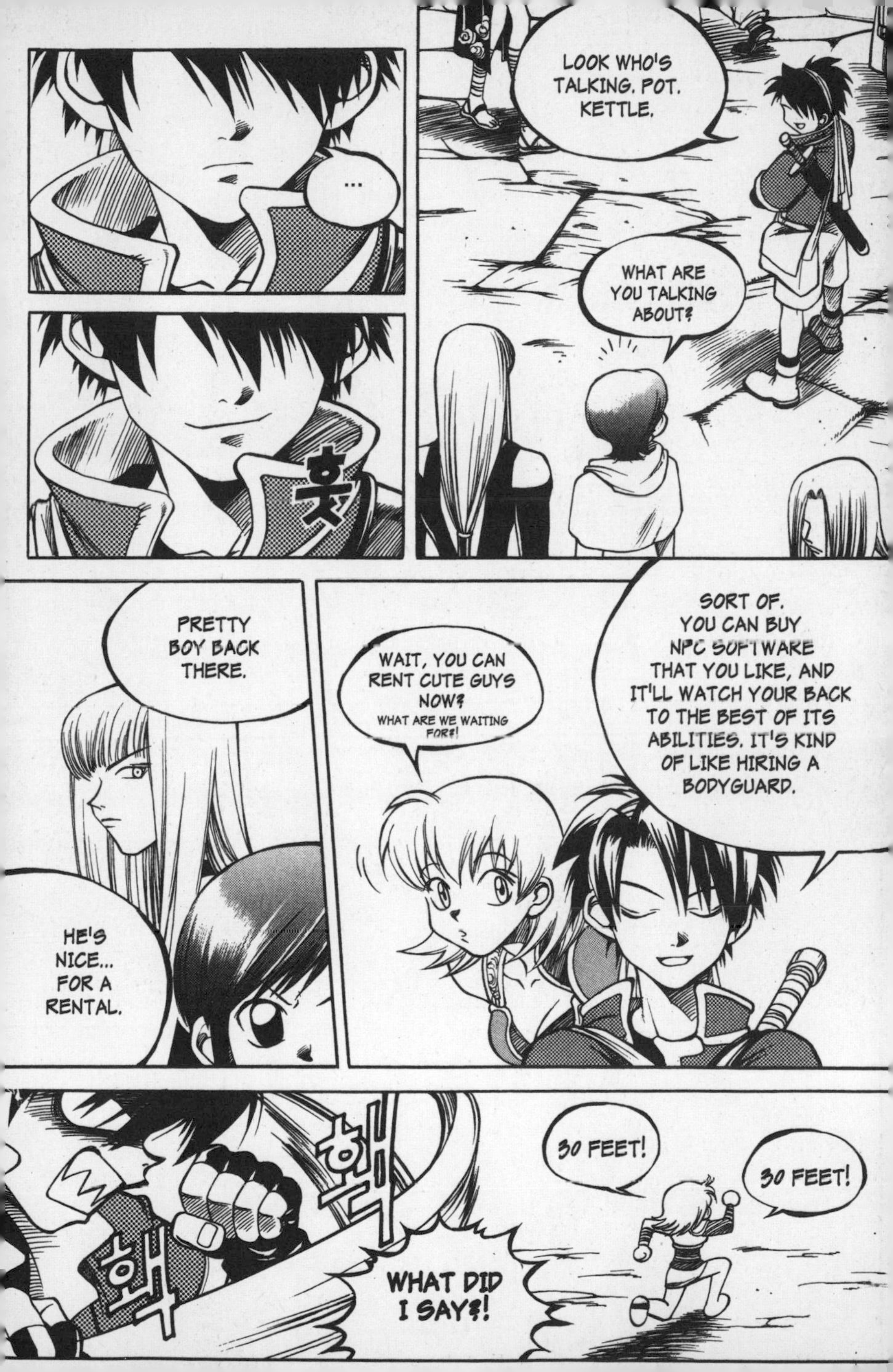
...
LOOK WHO'S TALKING. POT. KETTLE.
WHAT ARE YOU TALKING ABOUT?
PRETTY BOY BACK THERE.
HE'S NICE... FOR A RENTAL.
WAIT, YOU CAN RENT CUTE GUYS NOW? WHAT ARE WE WAITING FOR?!
SORT OF. YOU CAN BUY NPC SOFTWARE THAT YOU LIKE, AND IT'LL WATCH YOUR BACK TO THE BEST OF ITS ABILITIES. IT'S KIND OF LIKE HIRING A BODYGUARD.
30 FEET!
30 FEET!
WHAT DID I SAY?!

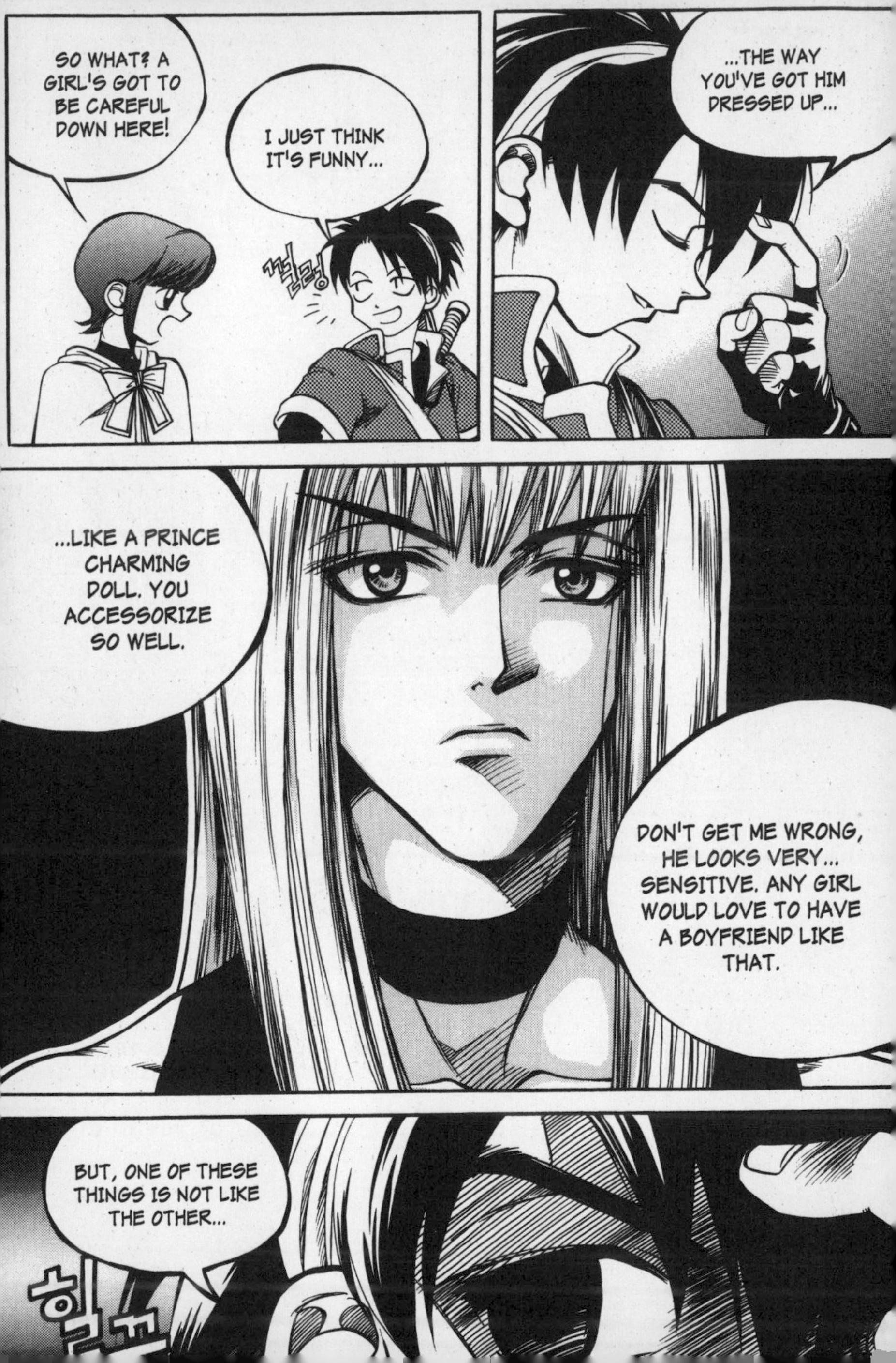
SO WHAT? A GIRL'S GOT TO BE CAREFUL DOWN HERE!
I JUST THINK IT'S FUNNY...
...THE WAY YOU'VE GOT HIM DRESSED UP...
...LIKE A PRINCE CHARMING DOLL. YOU ACCESSORIZE SO WELL.
DON'T GET ME WRONG, HE LOOKS VERY... SENSITIVE. ANY GIRL WOULD LOVE TO HAVE A BOYFRIEND LIKE THAT.
BUT, ONE OF THESE THINGS IS NOT LIKE THE OTHER...

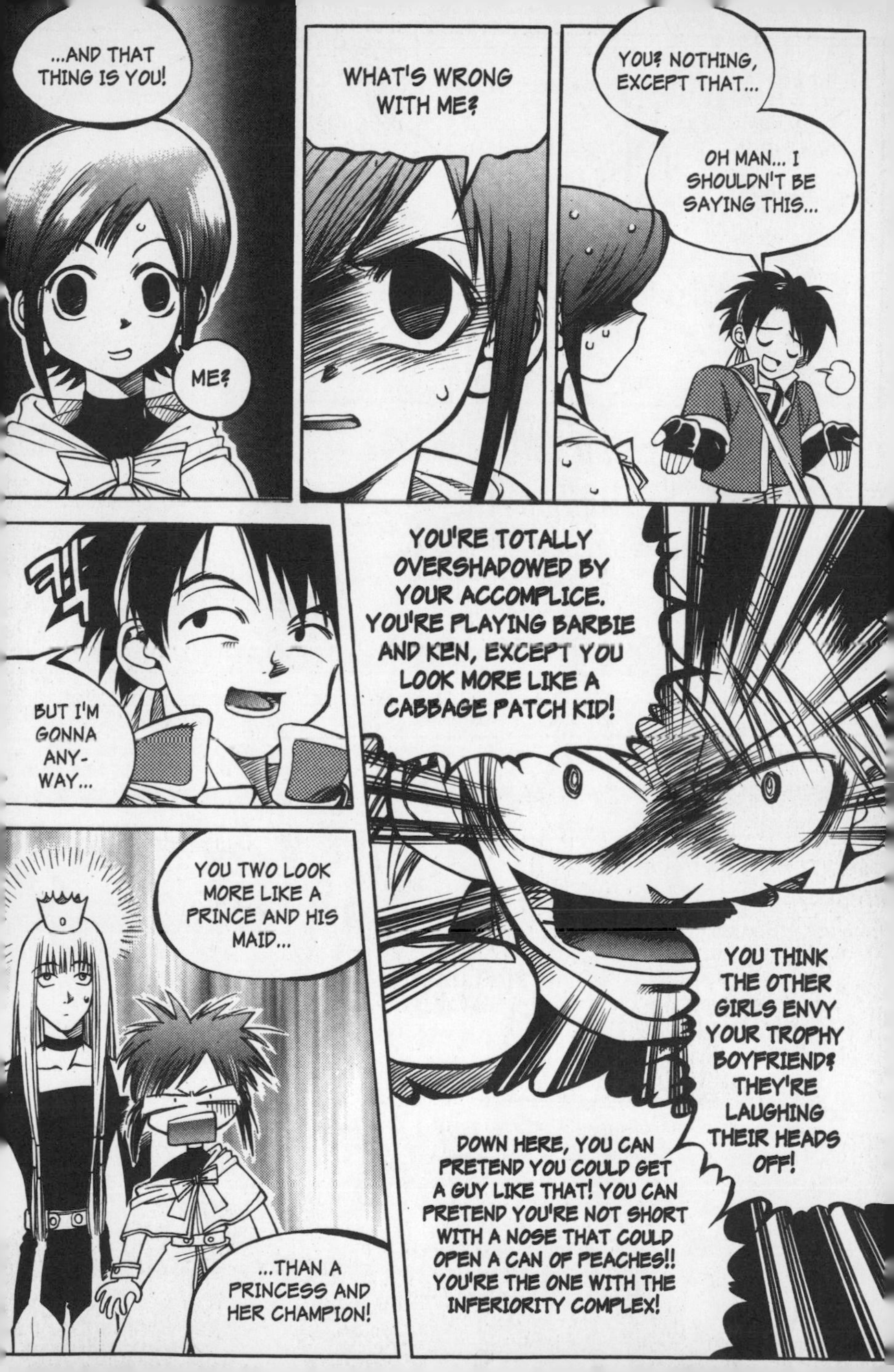

...AND THAT THING IS YOU!
ME?
WHAT'S WRONG WITH ME?
YOU? NOTHING, EXCEPT THAT...
OH MAN... I SHOULDN'T BE SAYING THIS...
BUT I'M GONNA ANY-WAY...
YOU'RE TOTALLY OVERSHADOWED BY YOUR ACCOMPLICE. YOU'RE PLAYING BARBIE AND KEN, EXCEPT YOU LOOK MORE LIKE A CABBAGE PATCH KID!
YOU TWO LOOK MORE LIKE A PRINCE AND HIS MAID...
...THAN A PRINCESS AND HER CHAMPION!
YOU THINK THE OTHER GIRLS ENVY YOUR TROPHY BOYFRIEND? THEY'RE LAUGHING THEIR HEADS OFF!
DOWN HERE, YOU CAN PRETEND YOU COULD GET A GUY LIKE THAT! YOU CAN PRETEND YOU'RE NOT SHORT WITH A NOSE THAT COULD OPEN A CAN OF PEACHES!! YOU'RE THE ONE WITH THE INFERIORITY COMPLEX!

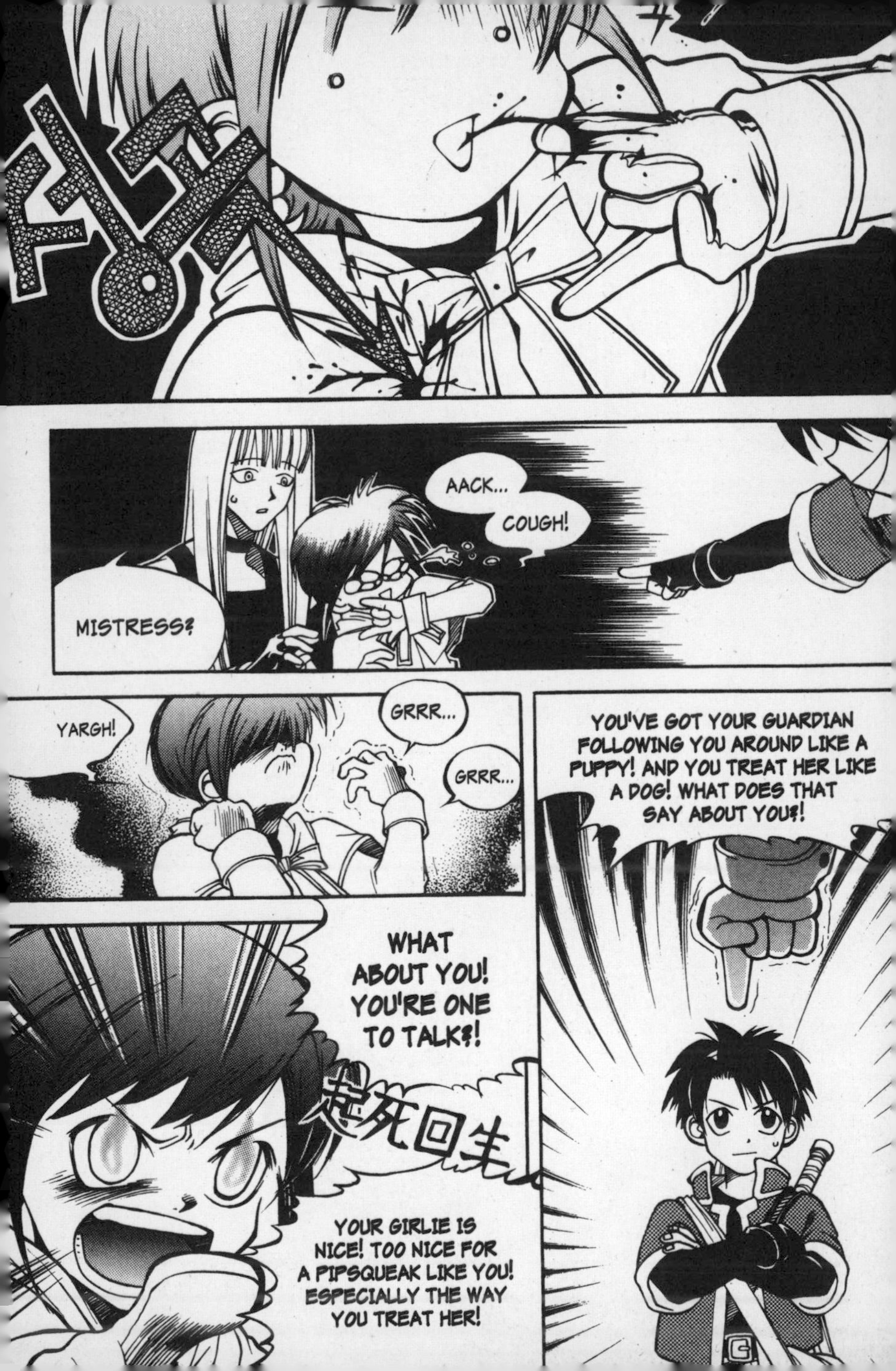
MISTRESS?
AACK...
COUGH!
YARGH!
GRRR...
GRRR...
WHAT ABOUT YOU! YOU'RE ONE TO TALK?!
起死回生
YOUR GIRLIE IS NICE! TOO NICE FOR A PIPSQUEAK LIKE YOU! ESPECIALLY THE WAY YOU TREAT HER!
YOU'VE GOT YOUR GUARDIAN FOLLOWING YOU AROUND LIKE A PUPPY! AND YOU TREAT HER LIKE A DOG! WHAT DOES THAT SAY ABOUT YOU?!

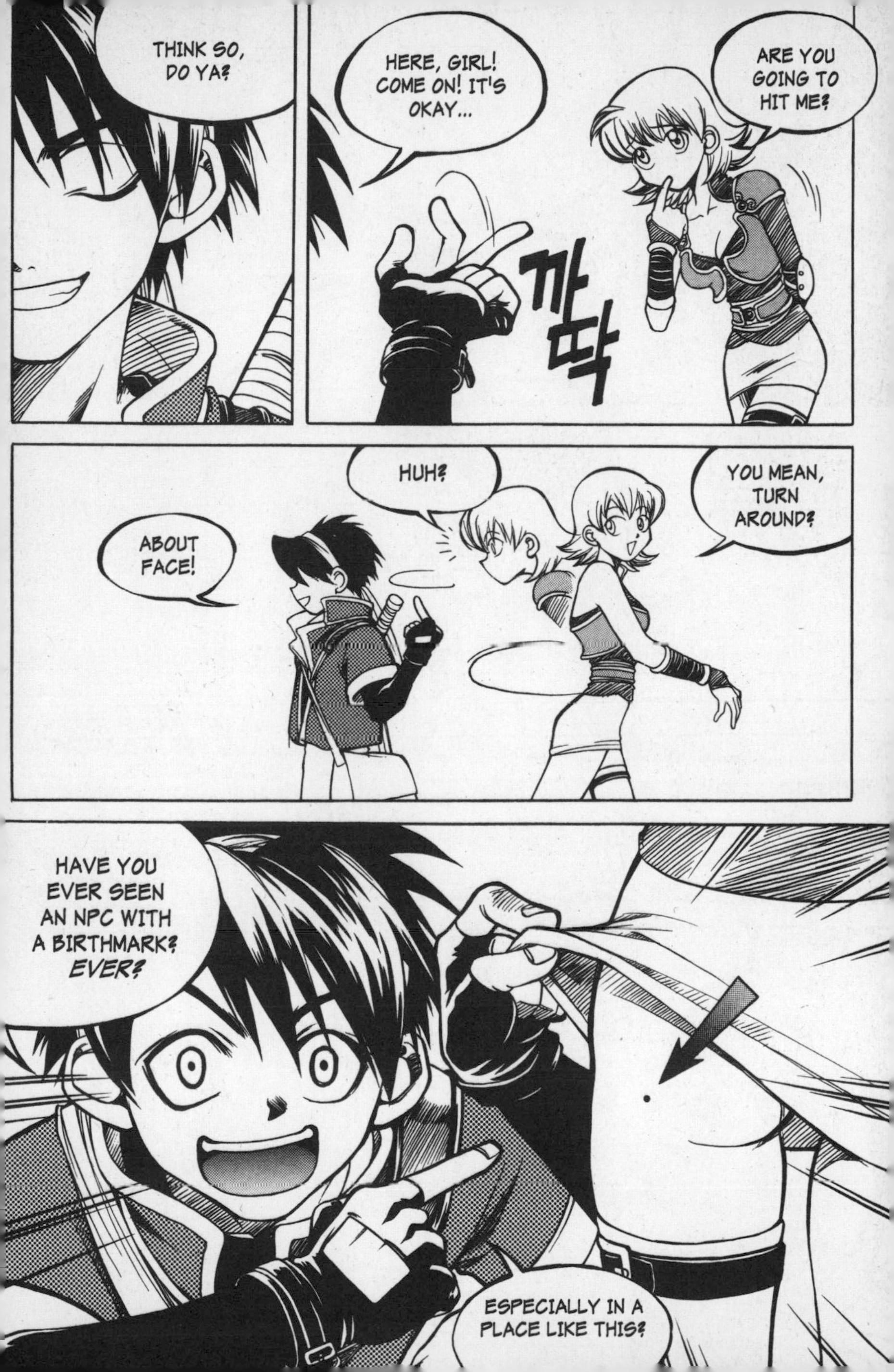
THINK SO, DO YA?
HERE, GIRL! COME ON! IT'S OKAY...
까딱
ARE YOU GOING TO HIT ME?
ABOUT FACE!
HUH?
YOU MEAN, TURN AROUND?
HAVE YOU EVER SEEN AN NPC WITH A BIRTHMARK? *EVER?*
ESPECIALLY IN A PLACE LIKE THIS?

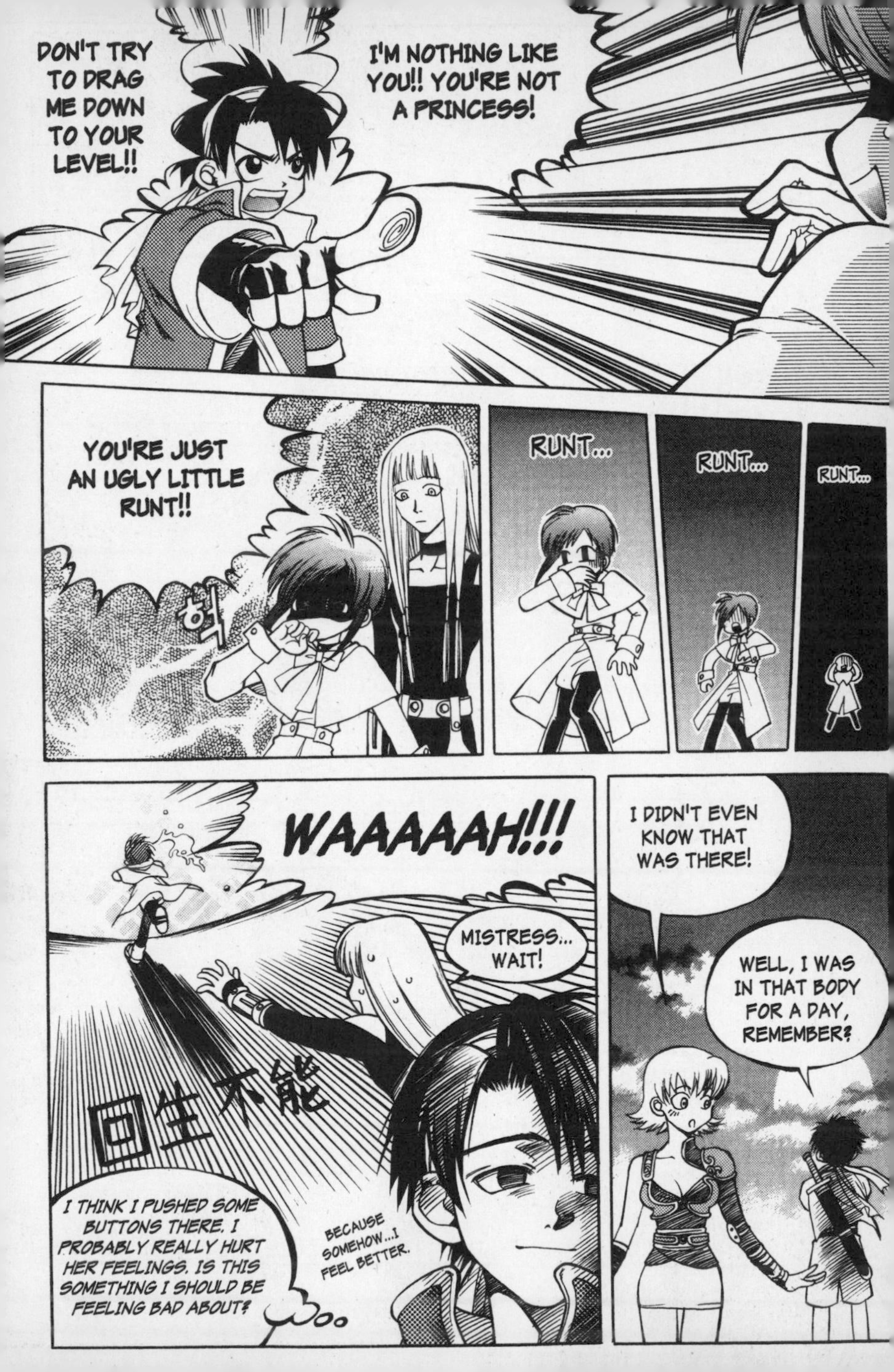
DON'T TRY TO DRAG ME DOWN TO YOUR LEVEL!!
I'M NOTHING LIKE YOU!! YOU'RE NOT A PRINCESS!
YOU'RE JUST AN UGLY LITTLE RUNT!!
헉
RUNT...
RUNT...
RUNT...
WAAAAAH!!!
MISTRESS... WAIT!
回生不能
I THINK I PUSHED SOME BUTTONS THERE. I PROBABLY REALLY HURT HER FEELINGS. IS THIS SOMETHING I SHOULD BE FEELING BAD ABOUT?
BECAUSE SOMEHOW...I FEEL BETTER.
I DIDN'T EVEN KNOW THAT WAS THERE!
WELL, I WAS IN THAT BODY FOR A DAY, REMEMBER?

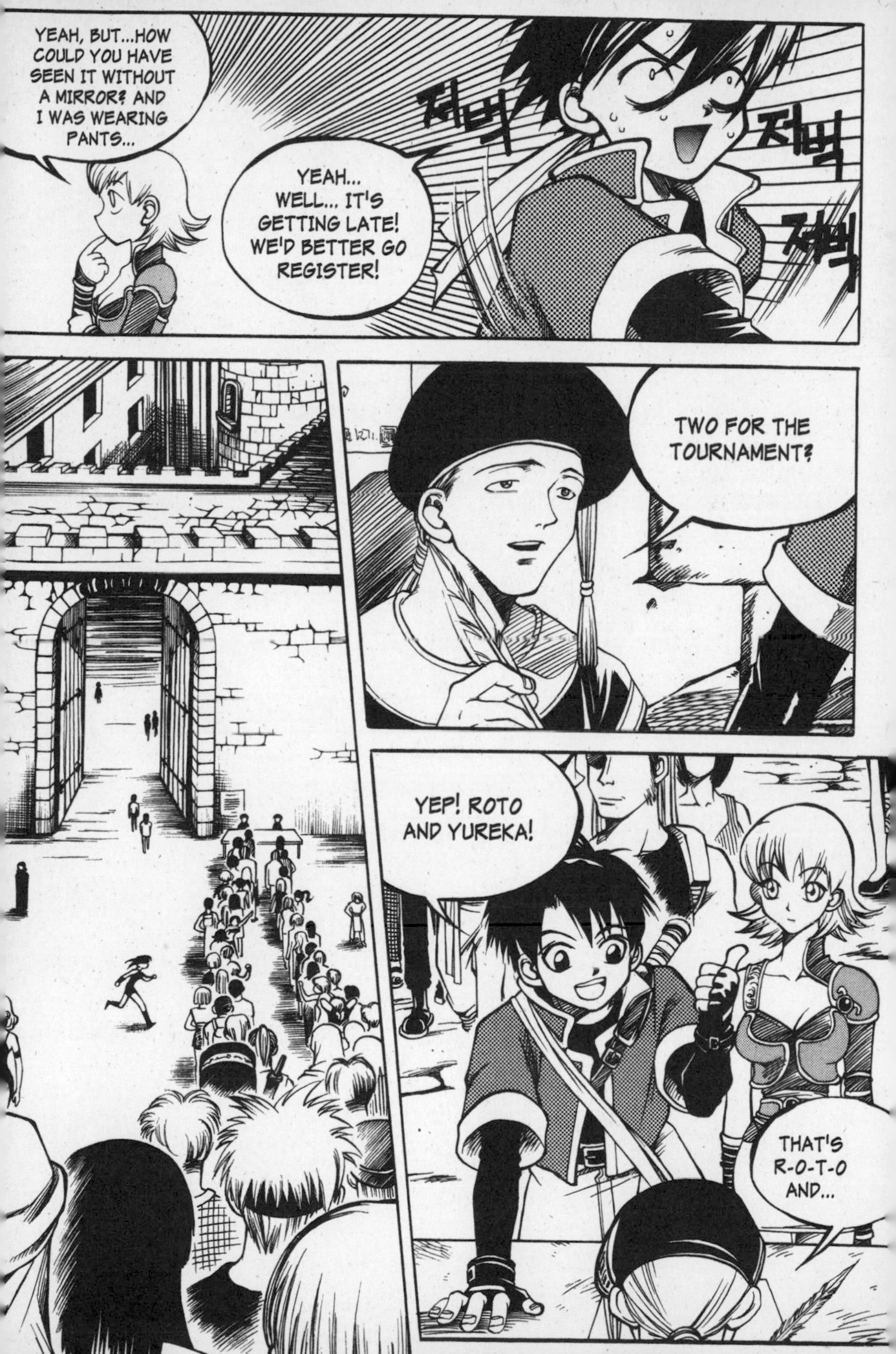
YEAH, BUT...HOW COULD YOU HAVE SEEN IT WITHOUT A MIRROR? AND I WAS WEARING PANTS...
YEAH... WELL... IT'S GETTING LATE! WE'D BETTER GO REGISTER!
저벅
저벅
저벅
TWO FOR THE TOURNAMENT?
YEP! ROTO AND YUREKA!
THAT'S R-O-T-O AND...

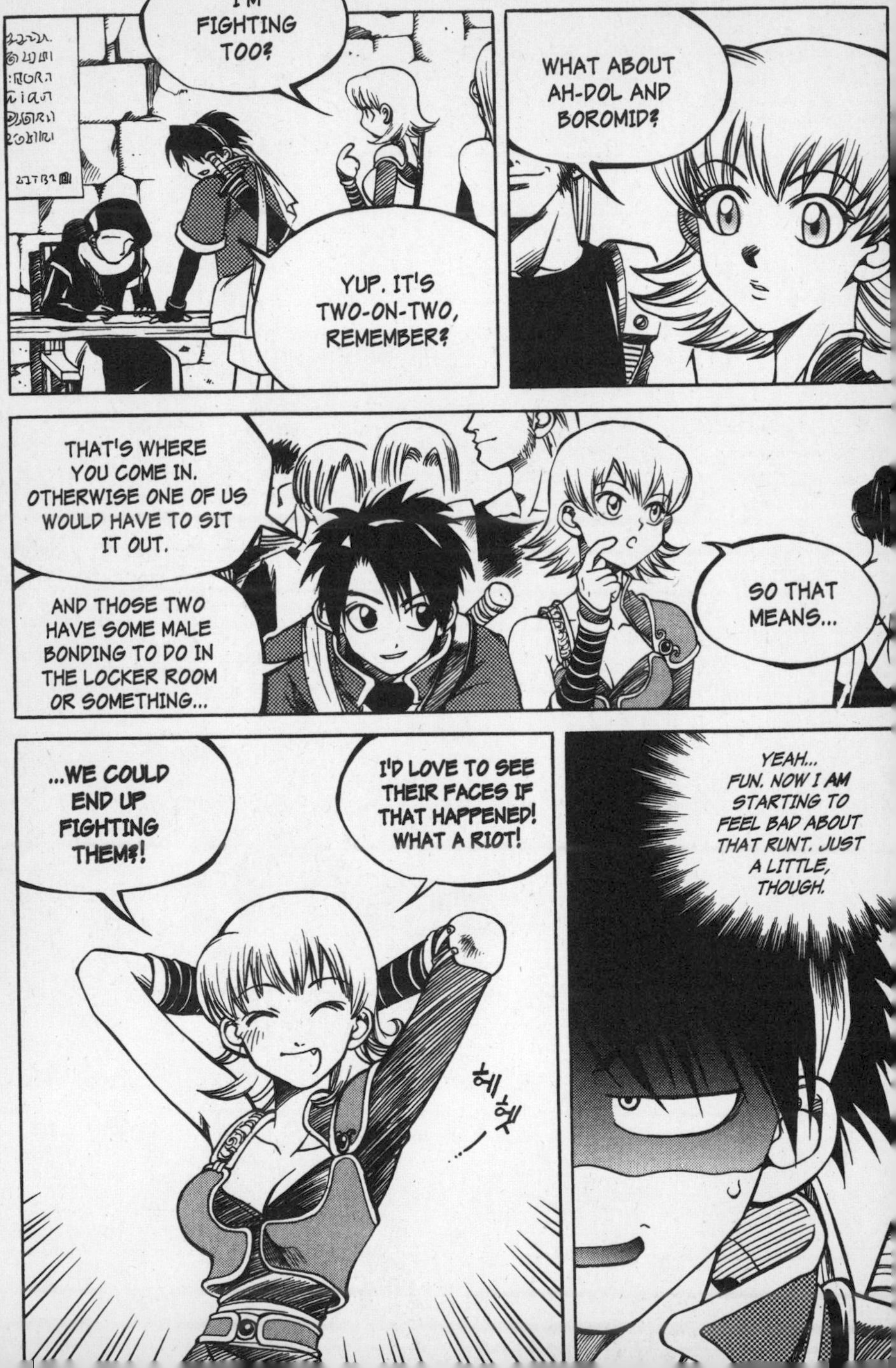
I'M FIGHTING TOO?
YUP. IT'S TWO-ON-TWO, REMEMBER?
WHAT ABOUT AH-DOL AND BOROMID?
THAT'S WHERE YOU COME IN. OTHERWISE ONE OF US WOULD HAVE TO SIT IT OUT.
AND THOSE TWO HAVE SOME MALE BONDING TO DO IN THE LOCKER ROOM OR SOMETHING...
SO THAT MEANS...
...WE COULD END UP FIGHTING THEM?!
I'D LOVE TO SEE THEIR FACES IF THAT HAPPENED! WHAT A RIOT!
헤헷
YEAH... FUN. NOW I AM STARTING TO FEEL BAD ABOUT THAT RUNT. JUST A LITTLE, THOUGH.

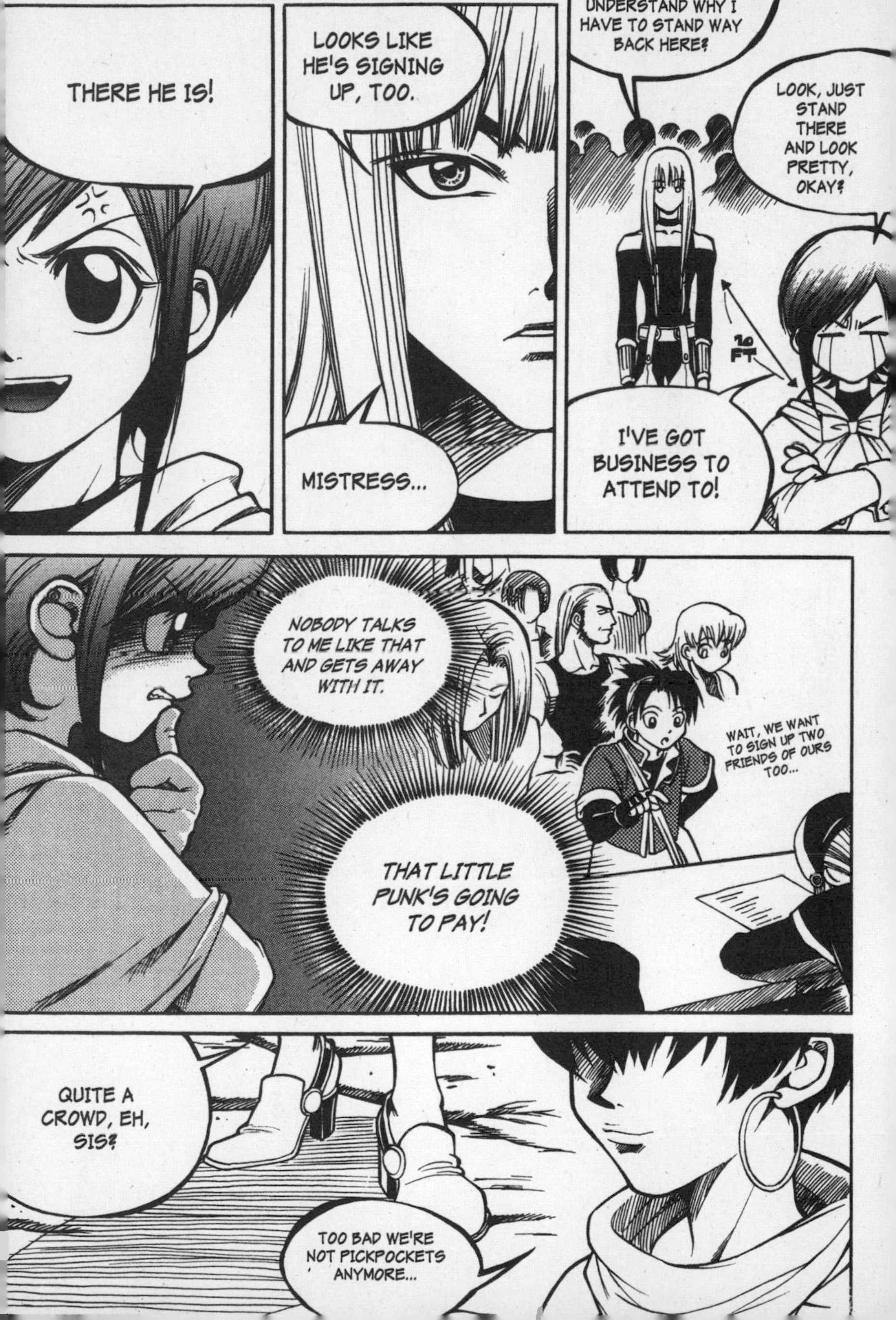
THERE HE IS!
LOOKS LIKE HE'S SIGNING UP, TOO.
MISTRESS...
...I STILL DON'T UNDERSTAND WHY I HAVE TO STAND WAY BACK HERE?
LOOK, JUST STAND THERE AND LOOK PRETTY, OKAY?
10 FT
I'VE GOT BUSINESS TO ATTEND TO!
NOBODY TALKS TO ME LIKE THAT AND GETS AWAY WITH IT.
THAT LITTLE PUNK'S GOING TO PAY!
WAIT, WE WANT TO SIGN UP TWO FRIENDS OF OURS TOO...
QUITE A CROWD, EH, SIS?
TOO BAD WE'RE NOT PICKPOCKETS ANYMORE...

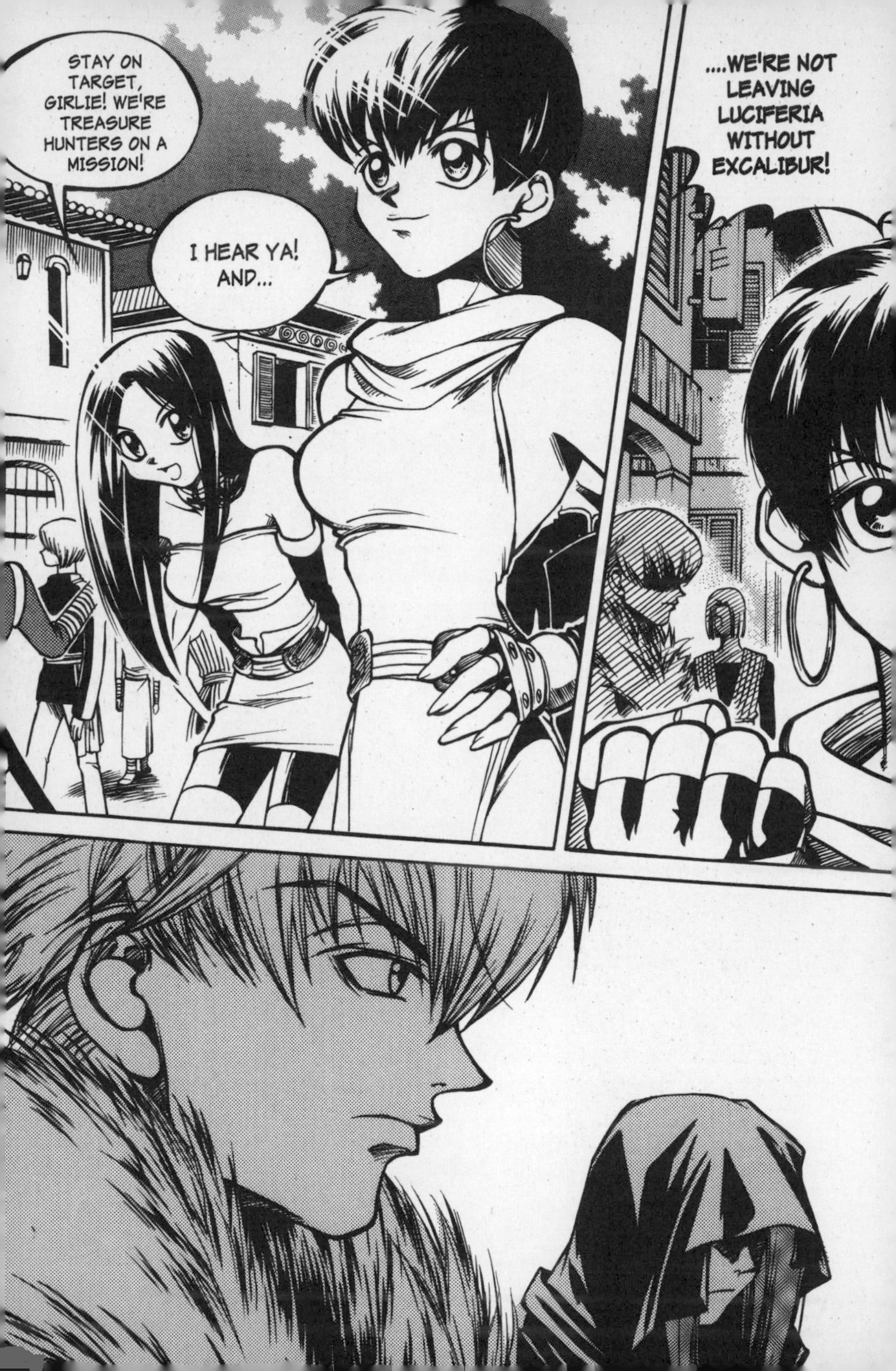

STAY ON TARGET, GIRLIE! WE'RE TREASURE HUNTERS ON A MISSION!
I HEAR YA! AND...
....WE'RE NOT LEAVING LUCIFERIA WITHOUT EXCALIBUR!

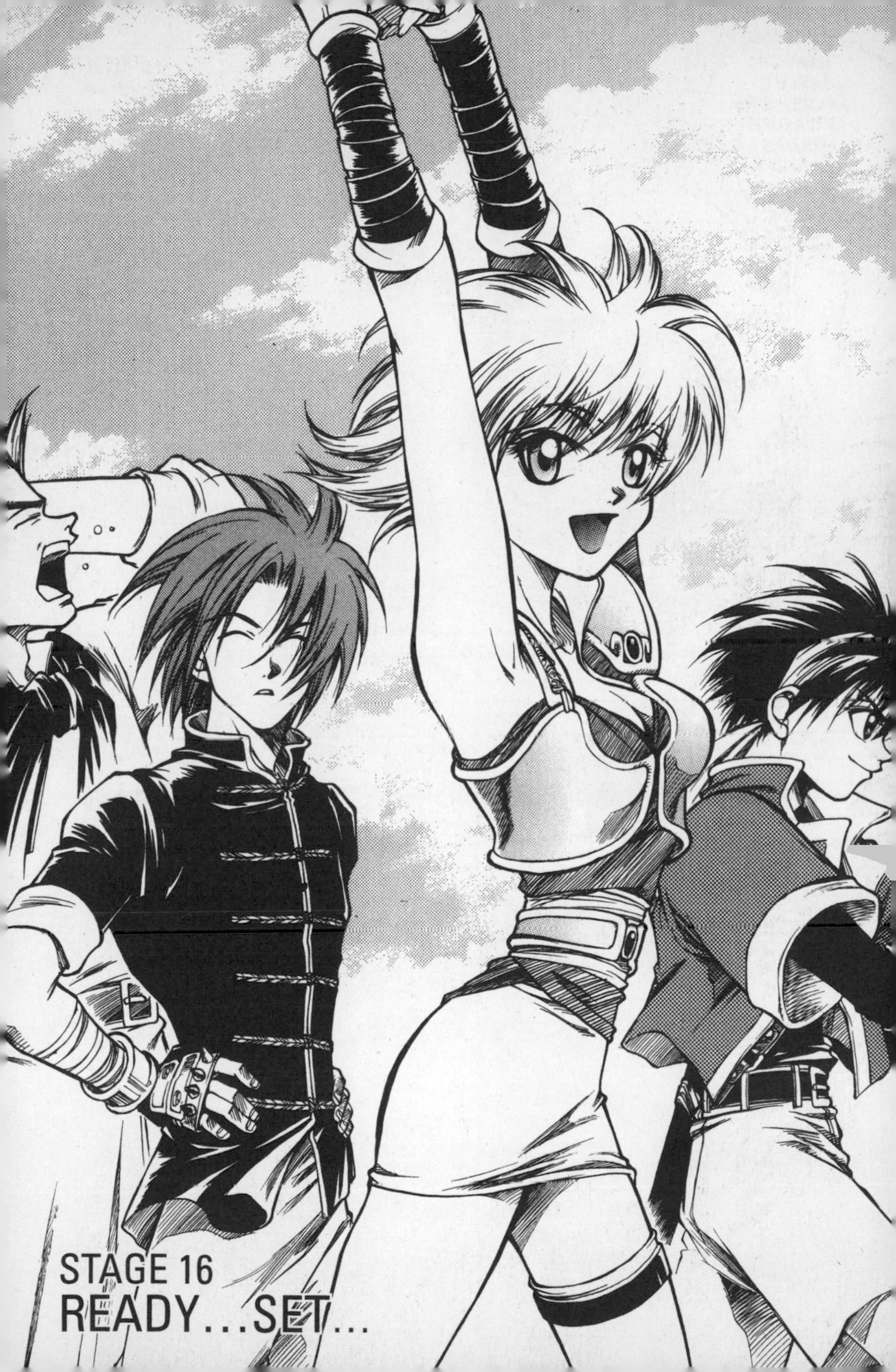
STAGE 16
READY...SET...

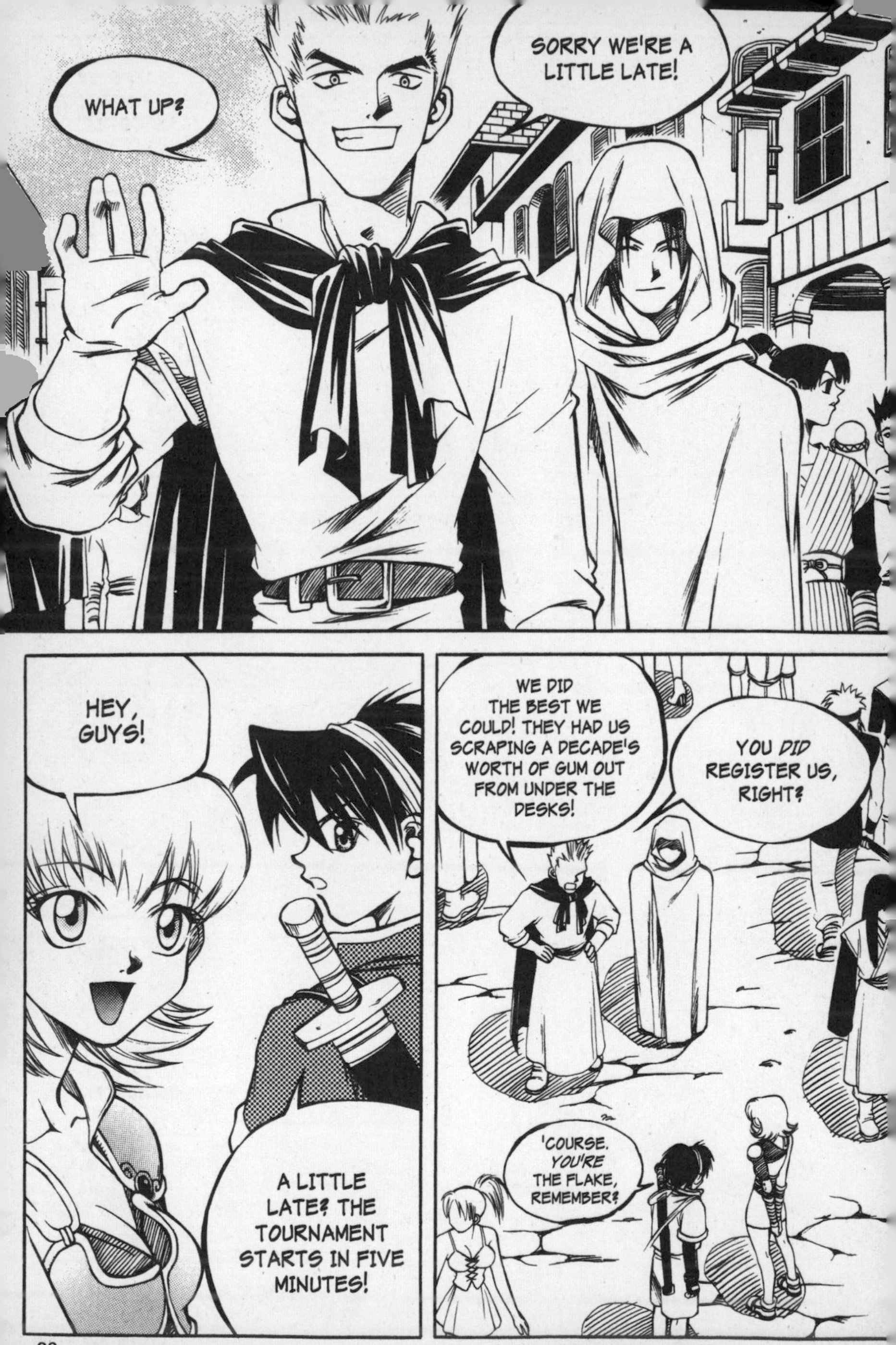

WHAT UP?
SORRY WE'RE A LITTLE LATE!
HEY, GUYS!
A LITTLE LATE? THE TOURNAMENT STARTS IN FIVE MINUTES!
WE DID THE BEST WE COULD! THEY HAD US SCRAPING A DECADE'S WORTH OF GUM OUT FROM UNDER THE DESKS!
YOU *DID* REGISTER US, RIGHT?
'COURSE. *YOU'RE* THE FLAKE, REMEMBER?

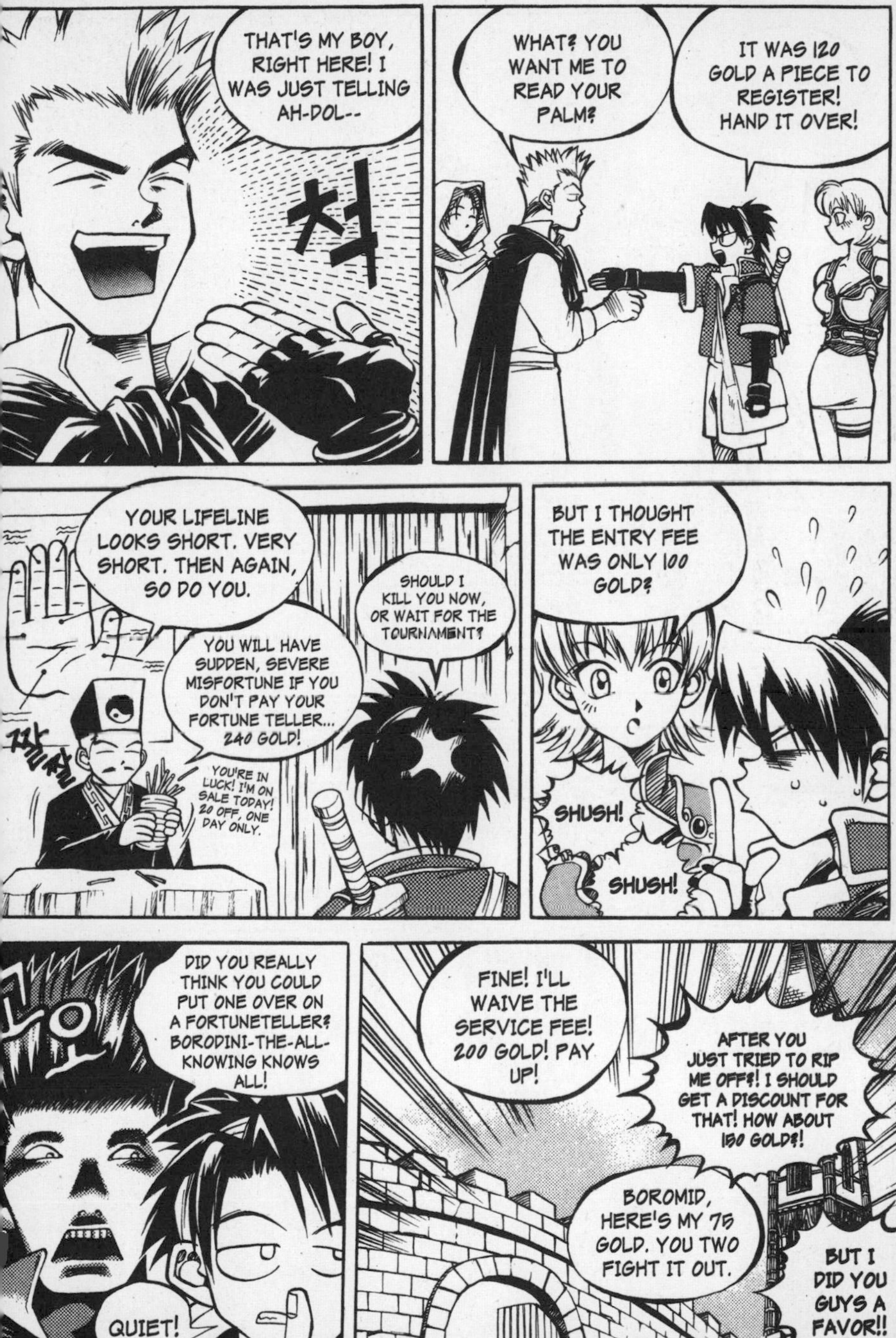
THAT'S MY BOY, RIGHT HERE! I WAS JUST TELLING AH-DOL--
척
WHAT? YOU WANT ME TO READ YOUR PALM?
IT WAS 120 GOLD A PIECE TO REGISTER! HAND IT OVER!
YOUR LIFELINE LOOKS SHORT. VERY SHORT. THEN AGAIN, SO DO YOU.
YOU WILL HAVE SUDDEN, SEVERE MISFORTUNE IF YOU DON'T PAY YOUR FORTUNE TELLER... 240 GOLD!
YOU'RE IN LUCK! I'M ON SALE TODAY! 20 OFF, ONE DAY ONLY.
SHOULD I KILL YOU NOW, OR WAIT FOR THE TOURNAMENT?
BUT I THOUGHT THE ENTRY FEE WAS ONLY 100 GOLD?
SHUSH!
SHUSH!
DID YOU REALLY THINK YOU COULD PUT ONE OVER ON A FORTUNETELLER? BORODINI-THE-ALL-KNOWING KNOWS ALL!
QUIET!
FINE! I'LL WAIVE THE SERVICE FEE! 200 GOLD! PAY UP!
AFTER YOU JUST TRIED TO RIP ME OFF?! I SHOULD GET A DISCOUNT FOR THAT! HOW ABOUT 150 GOLD?!
BOROMID, HERE'S MY 75 GOLD. YOU TWO FIGHT IT OUT.
BUT I DID YOU GUYS A FAVOR!!

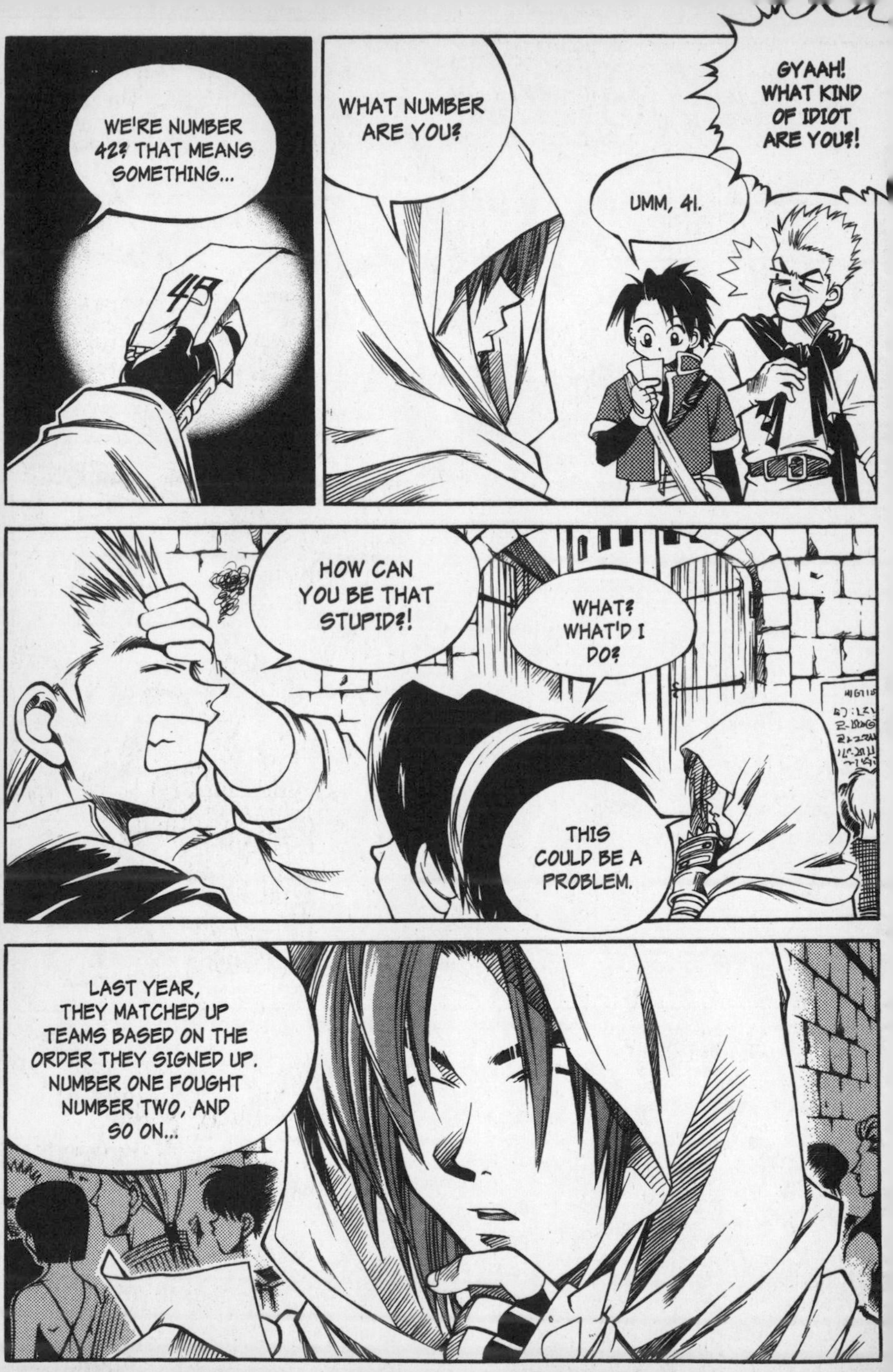
WE'RE NUMBER 42? THAT MEANS SOMETHING...
WHAT NUMBER ARE YOU?
UMM, 41.
GYAAH! WHAT KIND OF IDIOT ARE YOU?!
HOW CAN YOU BE THAT STUPID?!
WHAT? WHAT'D I DO?
THIS COULD BE A PROBLEM.
LAST YEAR, THEY MATCHED UP TEAMS BASED ON THE ORDER THEY SIGNED UP. NUMBER ONE FOUGHT NUMBER TWO, AND SO ON...

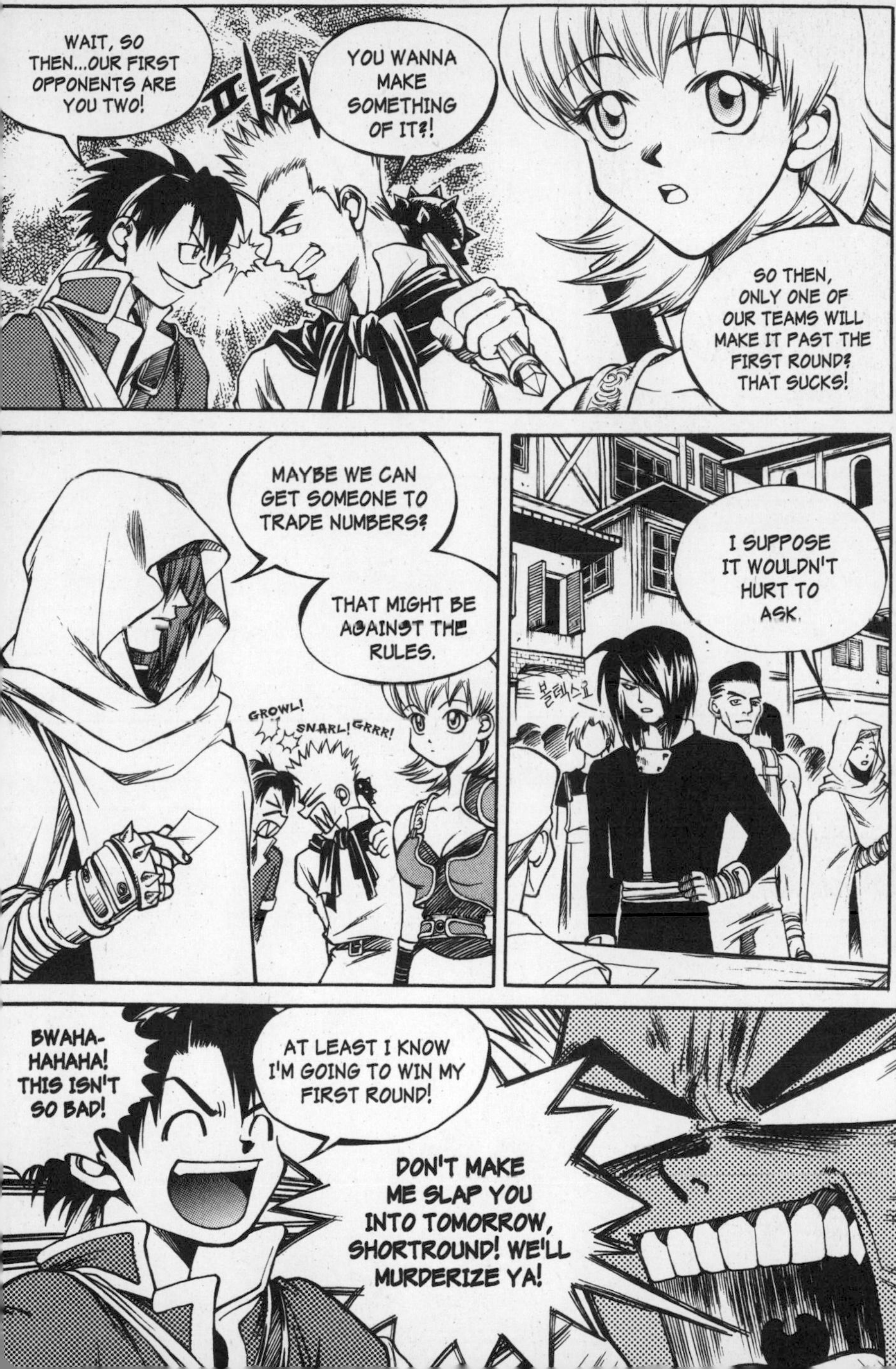
WAIT, SO THEN...OUR FIRST OPPONENTS ARE YOU TWO!
YOU WANNA MAKE SOMETHING OF IT?!
SO THEN, ONLY ONE OF OUR TEAMS WILL MAKE IT PAST THE FIRST ROUND? THAT SUCKS!
MAYBE WE CAN GET SOMEONE TO TRADE NUMBERS?
THAT MIGHT BE AGAINST THE RULES.
GROWL!
SNARL!
GRRR!
I SUPPOSE IT WOULDN'T HURT TO ASK.
BWAHA-HAHAHA! THIS ISN'T SO BAD!
AT LEAST I KNOW I'M GOING TO WIN MY FIRST ROUND!
DON'T MAKE ME SLAP YOU INTO TOMORROW, SHORTROUND! WE'LL MURDERIZE YA!

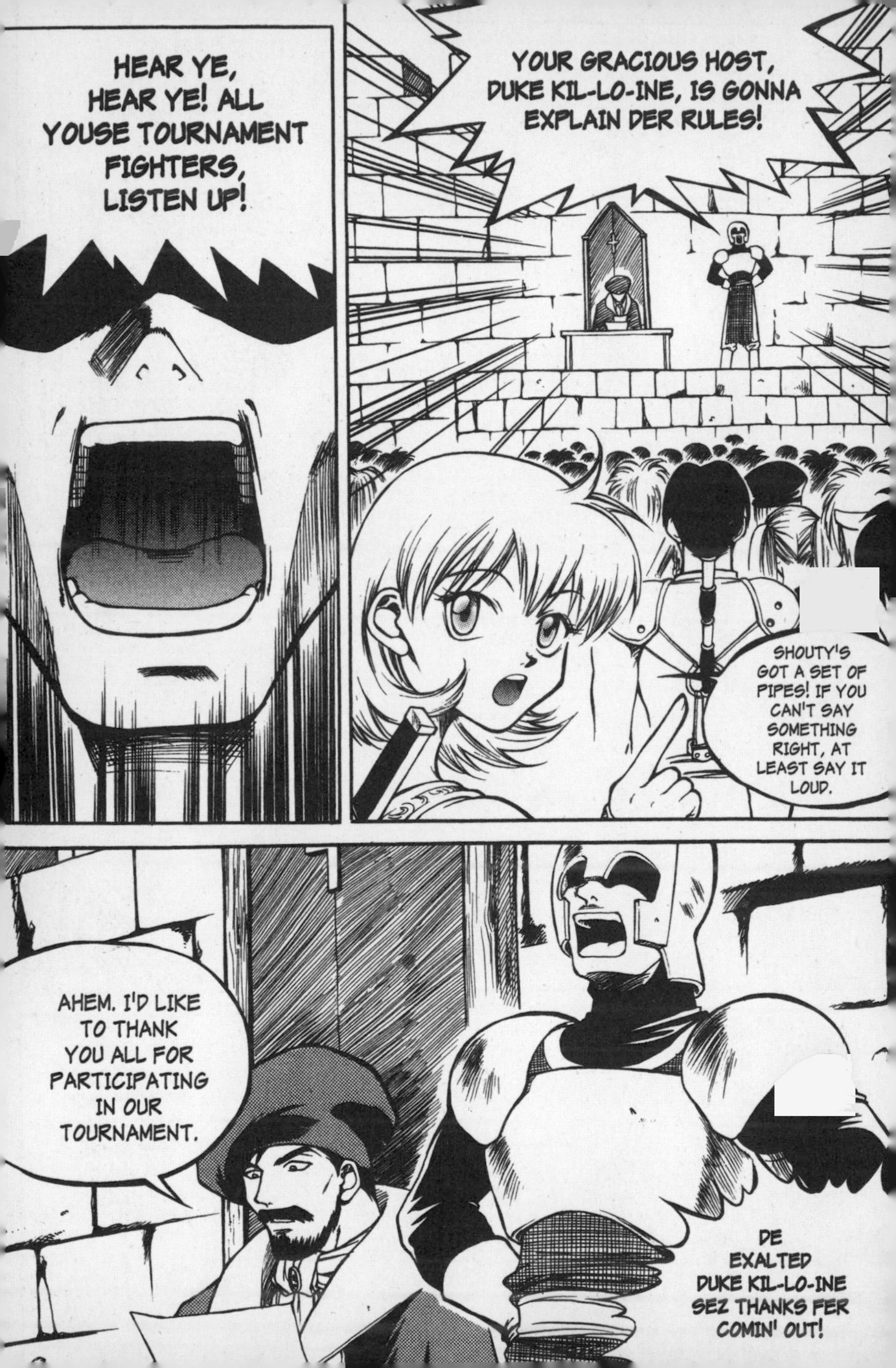
HEAR YE, HEAR YE! ALL YOUSE TOURNAMENT FIGHTERS, LISTEN UP!
YOUR GRACIOUS HOST, DUKE KIL-LO-INE, IS GONNA EXPLAIN DER RULES!
SHOUTY'S GOT A SET OF PIPES! IF YOU CAN'T SAY SOMETHING RIGHT, AT LEAST SAY IT LOUD.
AHEM. I'D LIKE TO THANK YOU ALL FOR PARTICIPATING IN OUR TOURNAMENT.
DE EXALTED DUKE KIL-LO-INE SEZ THANKS FER COMIN' OUT!

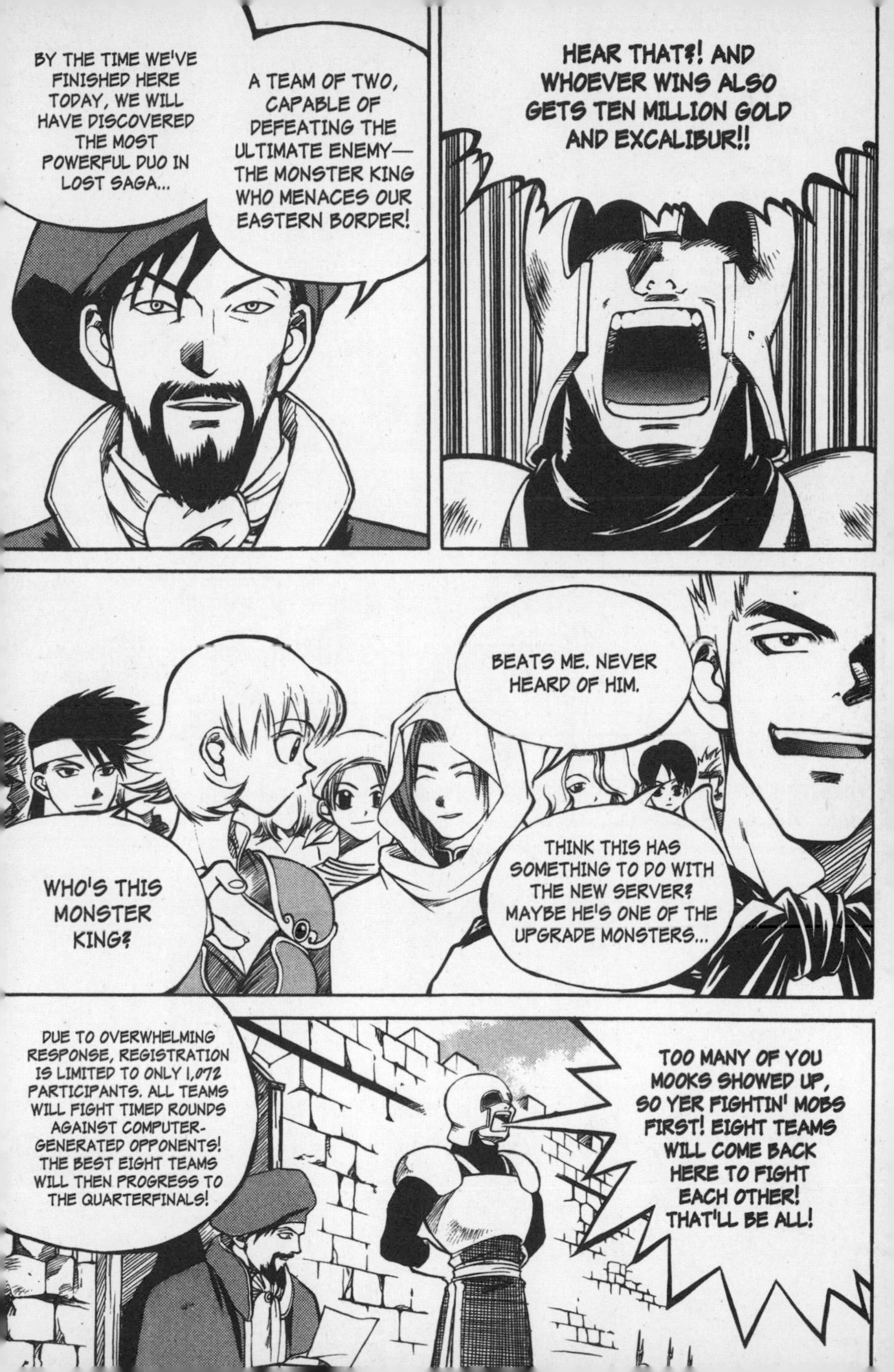
BY THE TIME WE'VE FINISHED HERE TODAY, WE WILL HAVE DISCOVERED THE MOST POWERFUL DUO IN LOST SAGA...
A TEAM OF TWO, CAPABLE OF DEFEATING THE ULTIMATE ENEMY—THE MONSTER KING WHO MENACES OUR EASTERN BORDER!
HEAR THAT?! AND WHOEVER WINS ALSO GETS TEN MILLION GOLD AND EXCALIBUR!!
WHO'S THIS MONSTER KING?
BEATS ME. NEVER HEARD OF HIM.
THINK THIS HAS SOMETHING TO DO WITH THE NEW SERVER? MAYBE HE'S ONE OF THE UPGRADE MONSTERS...
DUE TO OVERWHELMING RESPONSE, REGISTRATION IS LIMITED TO ONLY 1,072 PARTICIPANTS. ALL TEAMS WILL FIGHT TIMED ROUNDS AGAINST COMPUTER-GENERATED OPPONENTS! THE BEST EIGHT TEAMS WILL THEN PROGRESS TO THE QUARTERFINALS!
TOO MANY OF YOU MOOKS SHOWED UP, SO YER FIGHTIN' MOBS FIRST! EIGHT TEAMS WILL COME BACK HERE TO FIGHT EACH OTHER! THAT'LL BE ALL!

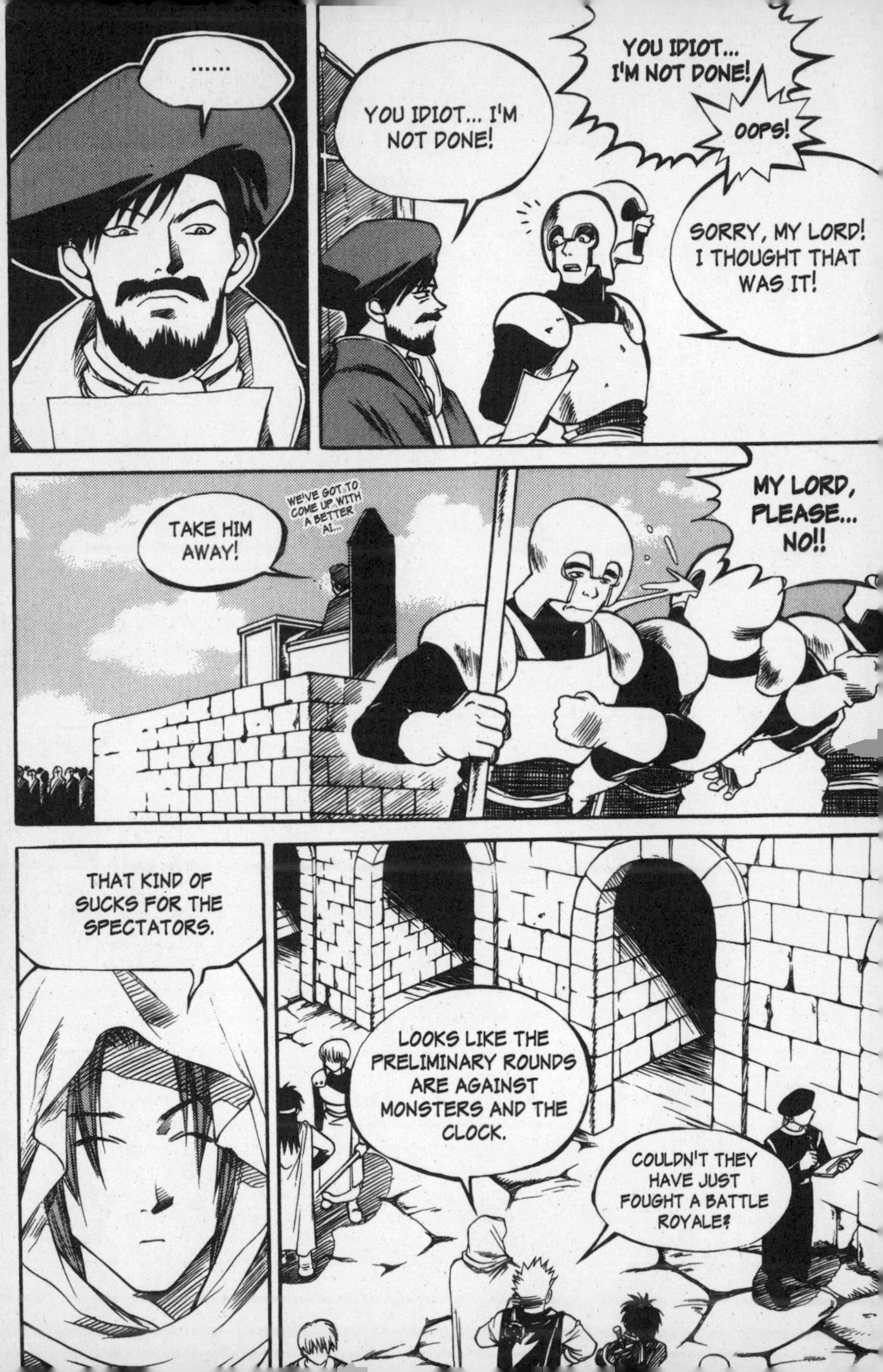
......
YOU IDIOT... I'M NOT DONE!
YOU IDIOT... I'M NOT DONE!
OOPS!
SORRY, MY LORD! I THOUGHT THAT WAS IT!
TAKE HIM AWAY!
WE'VE GOT TO COME UP WITH A BETTER AI...
MY LORD, PLEASE... NO!!
THAT KIND OF SUCKS FOR THE SPECTATORS.
LOOKS LIKE THE PRELIMINARY ROUNDS ARE AGAINST MONSTERS AND THE CLOCK.
COULDN'T THEY HAVE JUST FOUGHT A BATTLE ROYALE?

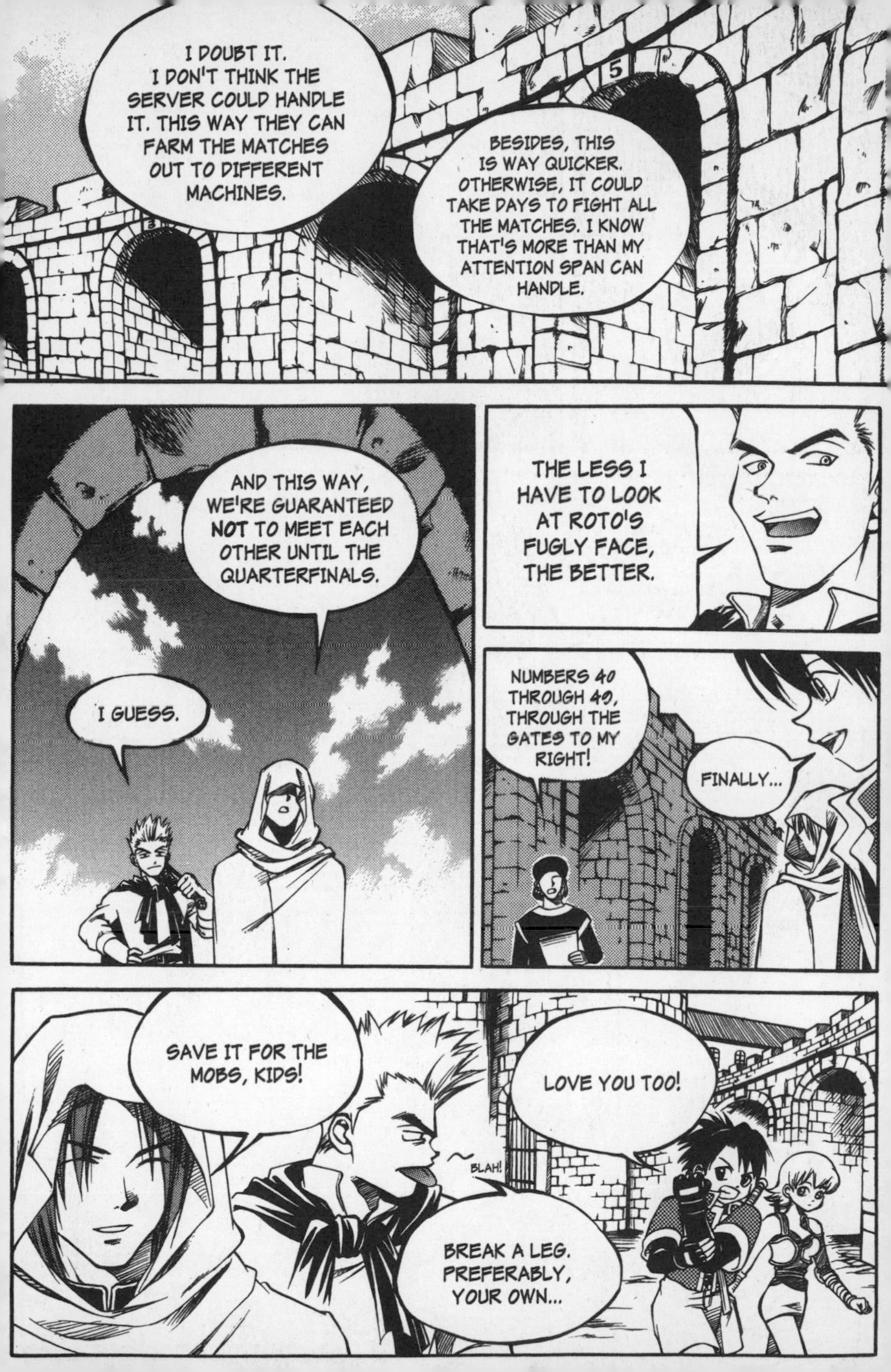
I DOUBT IT. I DON'T THINK THE SERVER COULD HANDLE IT. THIS WAY THEY CAN FARM THE MATCHES OUT TO DIFFERENT MACHINES.
5
BESIDES, THIS IS WAY QUICKER. OTHERWISE, IT COULD TAKE DAYS TO FIGHT ALL THE MATCHES. I KNOW THAT'S MORE THAN MY ATTENTION SPAN CAN HANDLE.
AND THIS WAY, WE'RE GUARANTEED NOT TO MEET EACH OTHER UNTIL THE QUARTERFINALS.
I GUESS.
THE LESS I HAVE TO LOOK AT ROTO'S FUGLY FACE, THE BETTER.
NUMBERS 40 THROUGH 49, THROUGH THE GATES TO MY RIGHT!
FINALLY...
SAVE IT FOR THE MOBS, KIDS!
BLAH!
LOVE YOU TOO!
BREAK A LEG. PREFERABLY, YOUR OWN...

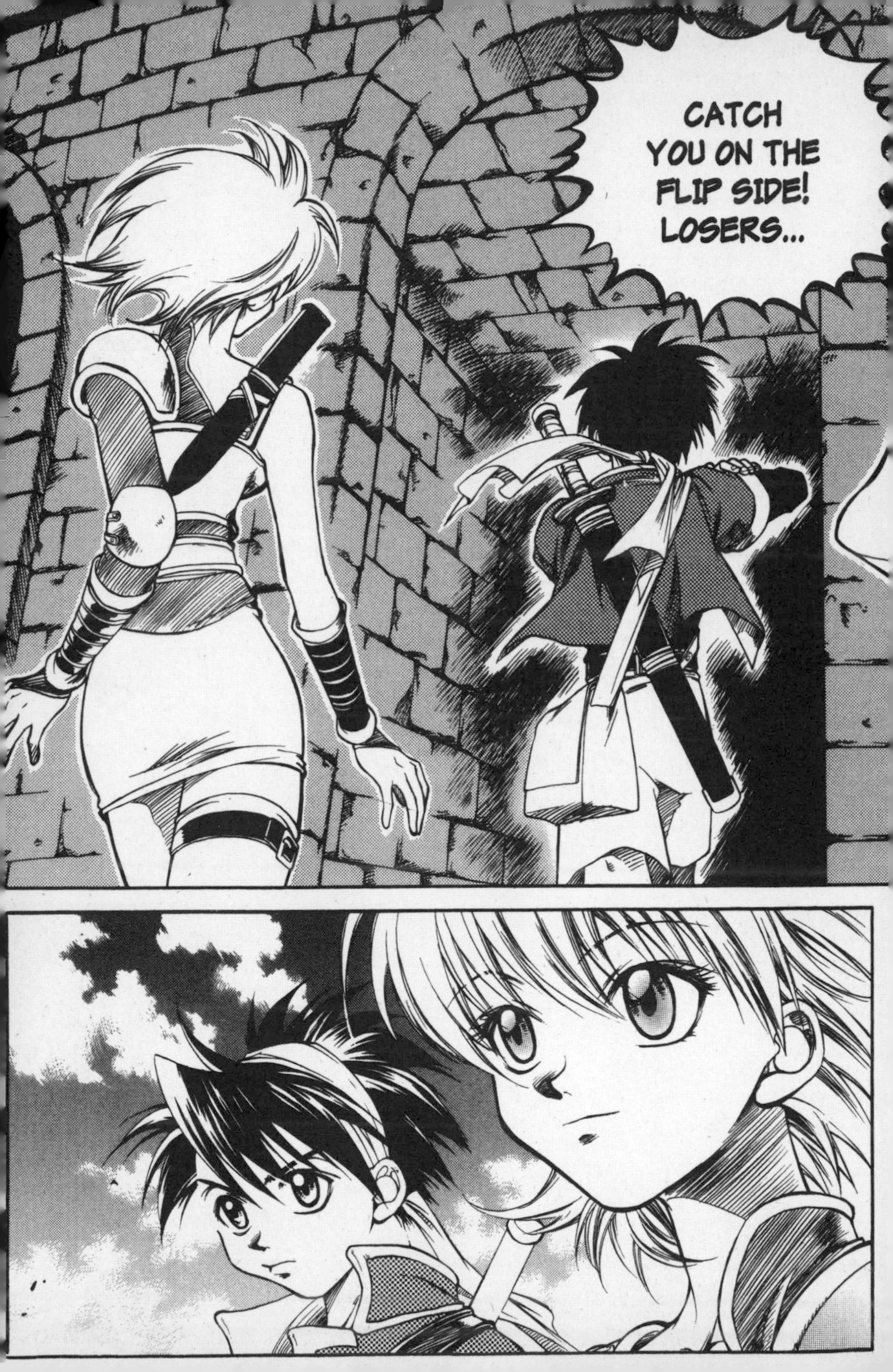
CATCH YOU ON THE FLIP SIDE! LOSERS...

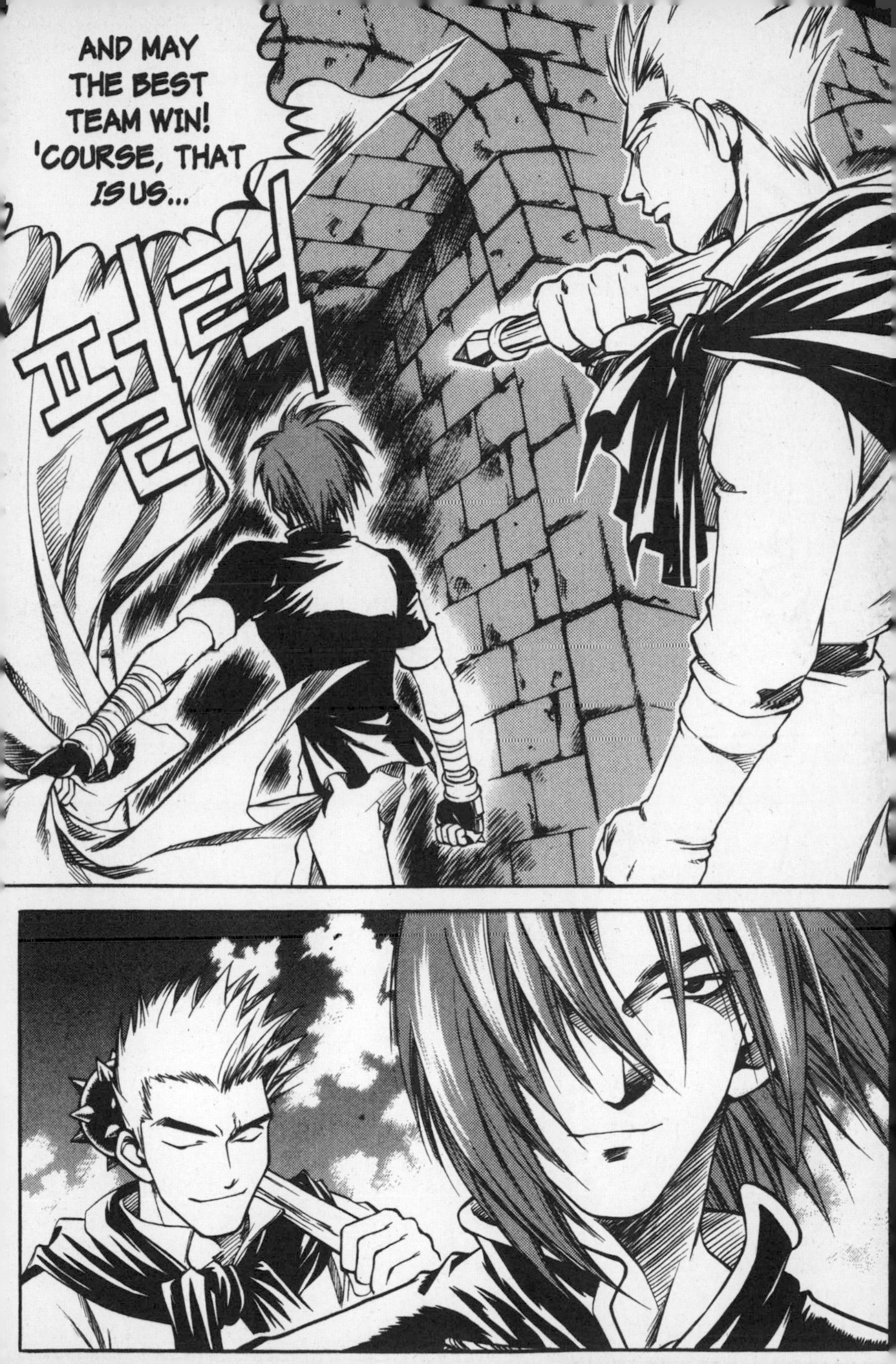
AND MAY THE BEST TEAM WIN! 'COURSE, THAT *IS* US...
펄럭

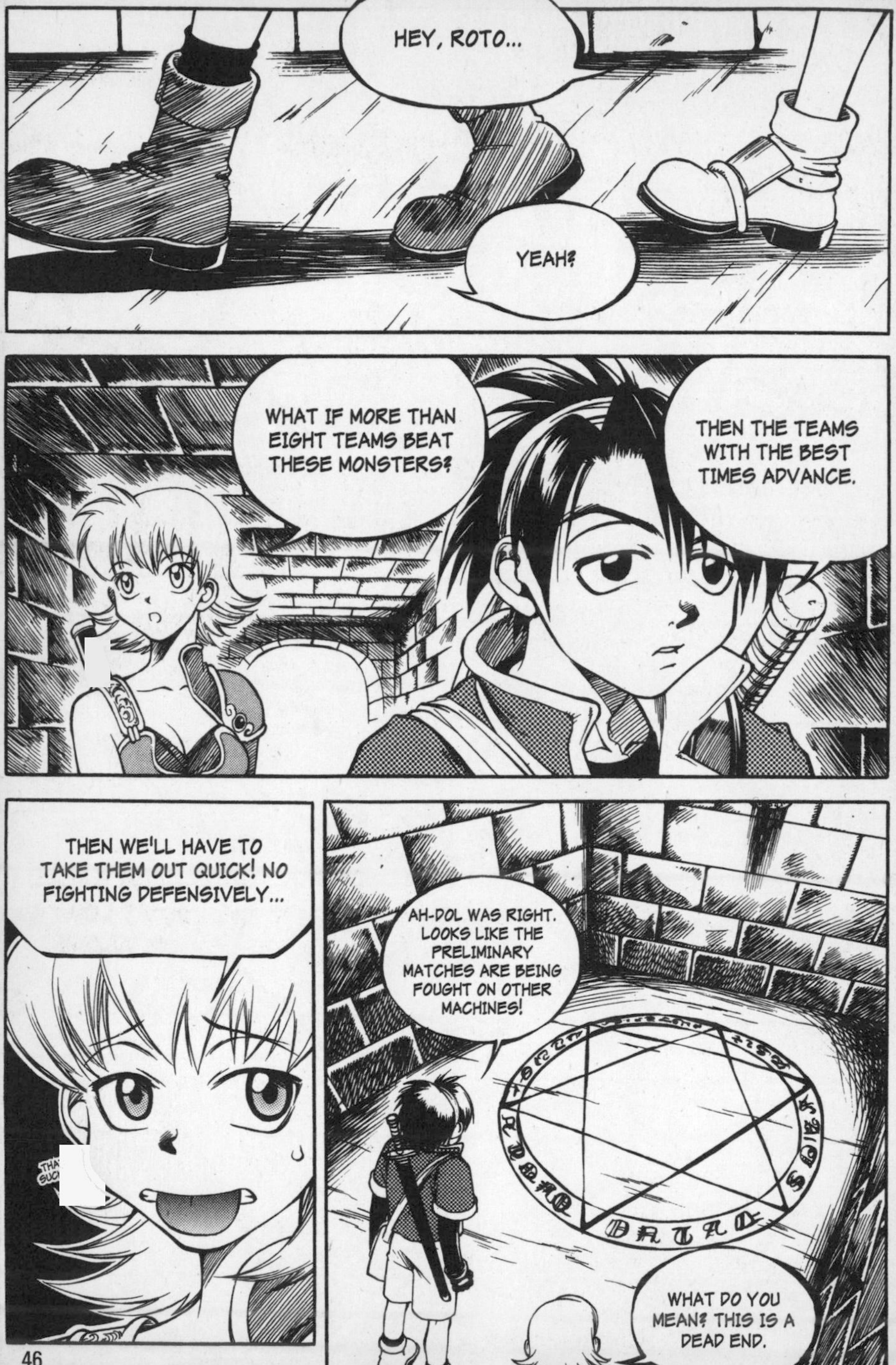
HEY, ROTO...
YEAH?
WHAT IF MORE THAN EIGHT TEAMS BEAT THESE MONSTERS?
THEN THE TEAMS WITH THE BEST TIMES ADVANCE.
THEN WE'LL HAVE TO TAKE THEM OUT QUICK! NO FIGHTING DEFENSIVELY...
AH-DOL WAS RIGHT. LOOKS LIKE THE PRELIMINARY MATCHES ARE BEING FOUGHT ON OTHER MACHINES!
WHAT DO YOU MEAN? THIS IS A DEAD END.

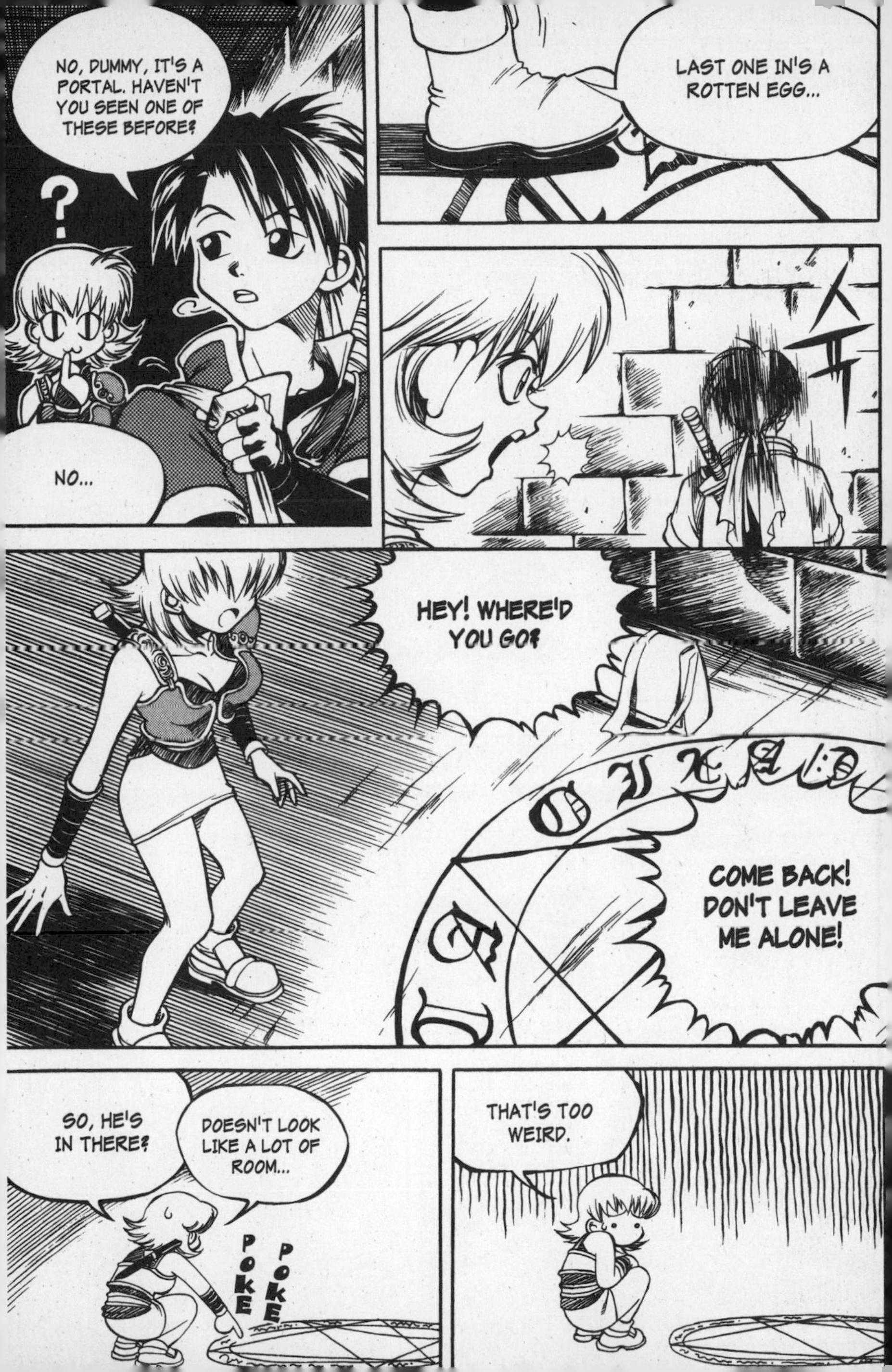
NO, DUMMY, IT'S A PORTAL. HAVEN'T YOU SEEN ONE OF THESE BEFORE?
?
NO...
LAST ONE IN'S A ROTTEN EGG...
HEY! WHERE'D YOU GO?
COME BACK! DON'T LEAVE ME ALONE!
SO, HE'S IN THERE?
DOESN'T LOOK LIKE A LOT OF ROOM...
POKE
POKE
THAT'S TOO WEIRD.

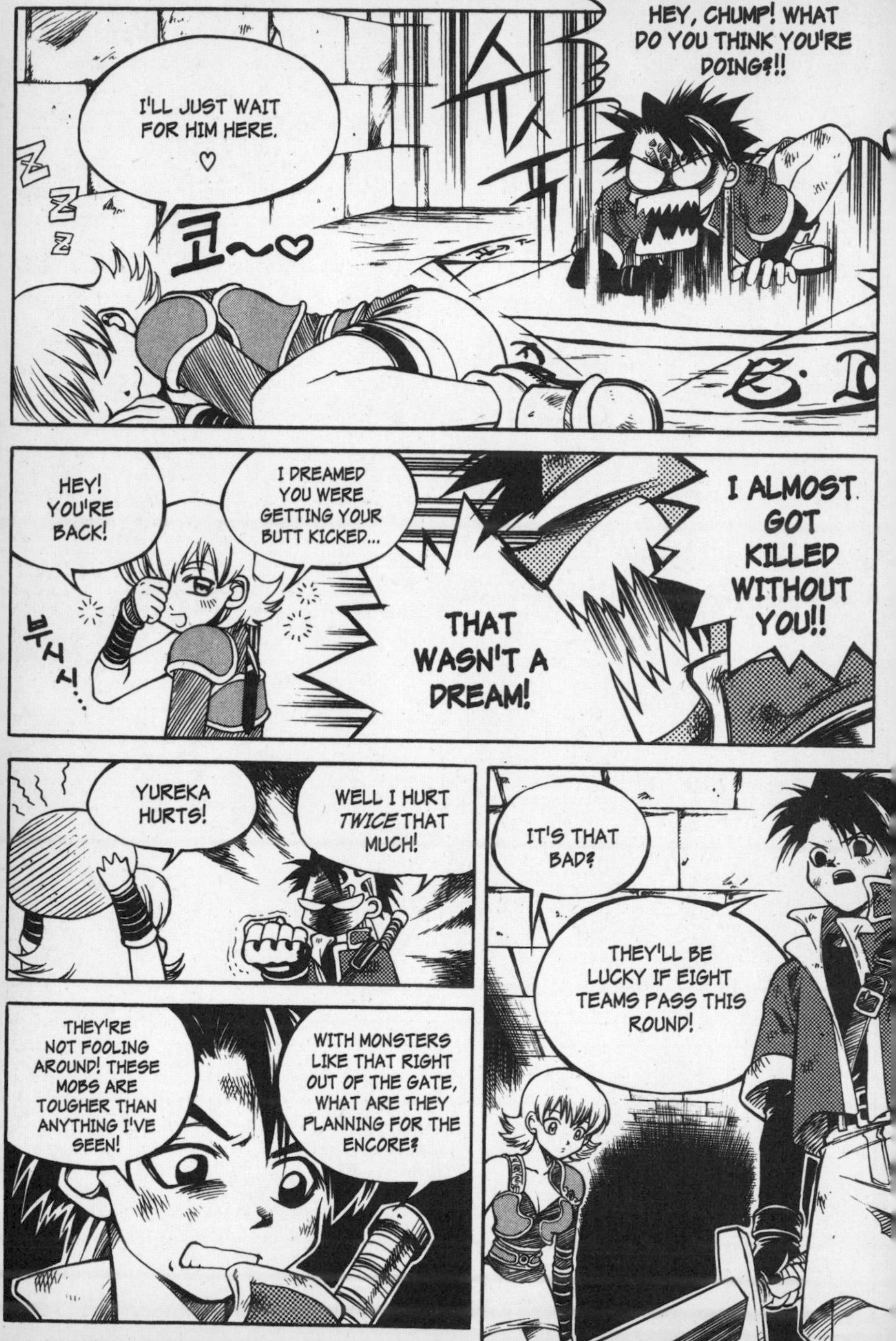

Z Z Z
I'LL JUST WAIT FOR HIM HERE. ♡
코~♡
HEY, CHUMP! WHAT DO YOU THINK YOU'RE DOING?!!
HEY! YOU'RE BACK!
I DREAMED YOU WERE GETTING YOUR BUTT KICKED...
부시시...
THAT WASN'T A DREAM!
I ALMOST GOT KILLED WITHOUT YOU!!
YUREKA HURTS!
WELL I HURT *TWICE* THAT MUCH!
THEY'RE NOT FOOLING AROUND! THESE MOBS ARE TOUGHER THAN ANYTHING I'VE SEEN!
WITH MONSTERS LIKE THAT RIGHT OUT OF THE GATE, WHAT ARE THEY PLANNING FOR THE ENCORE?
IT'S THAT BAD?
THEY'LL BE LUCKY IF EIGHT TEAMS PASS THIS ROUND!

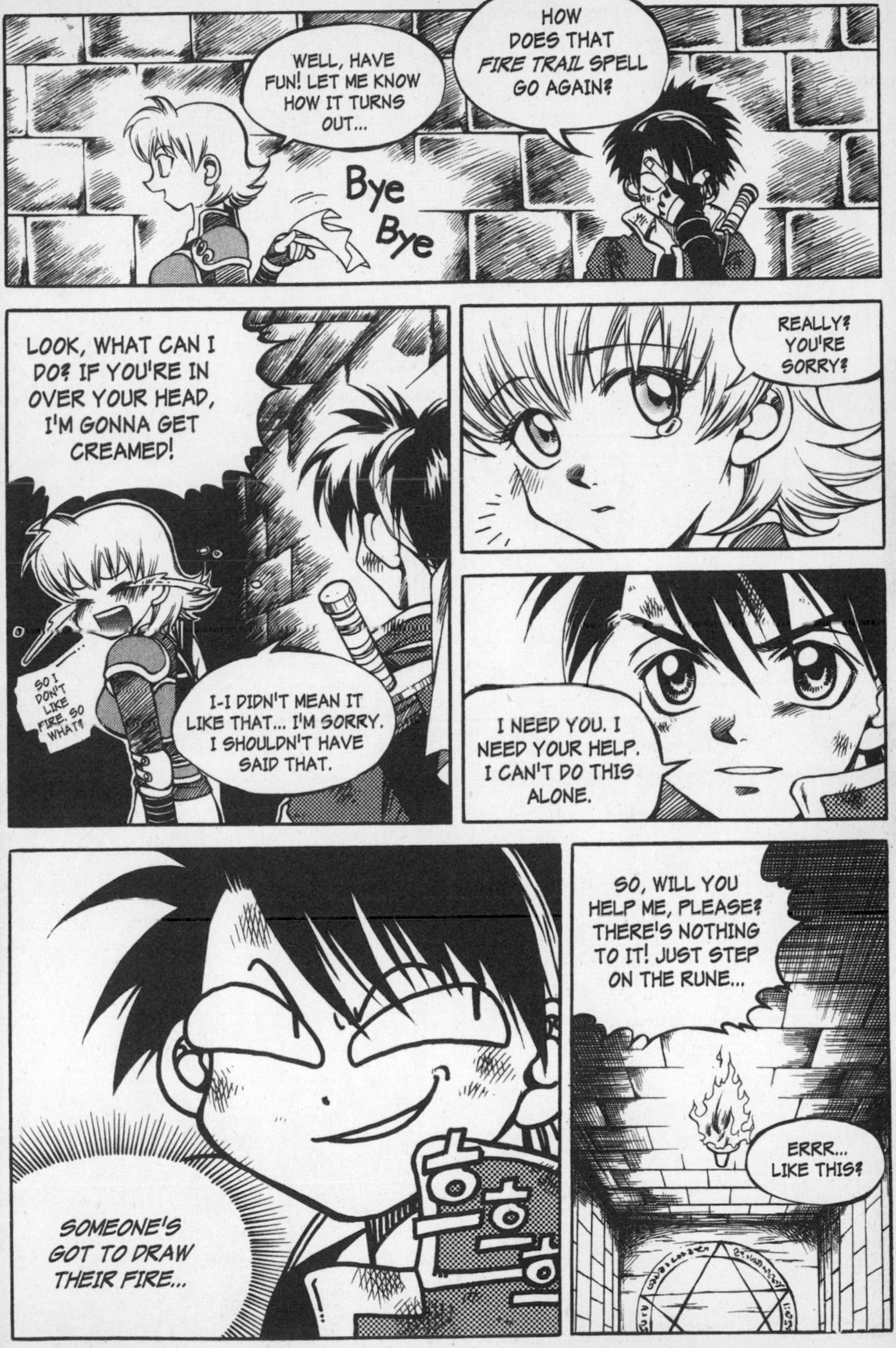
WELL, HAVE FUN! LET ME KNOW HOW IT TURNS OUT...
Bye Bye
HOW DOES THAT FIRE TRAIL SPELL GO AGAIN?
LOOK, WHAT CAN I DO? IF YOU'RE IN OVER YOUR HEAD, I'M GONNA GET CREAMED!
SO I DON'T LIKE FIRE. SO WHAT?
I-I DIDN'T MEAN IT LIKE THAT... I'M SORRY. I SHOULDN'T HAVE SAID THAT.
REALLY? YOU'RE SORRY?
I NEED YOU. I NEED YOUR HELP. I CAN'T DO THIS ALONE.
SOMEONE'S GOT TO DRAW THEIR FIRE...
SO, WILL YOU HELP ME, PLEASE? THERE'S NOTHING TO IT! JUST STEP ON THE RUNE...
ERRR... LIKE THIS?

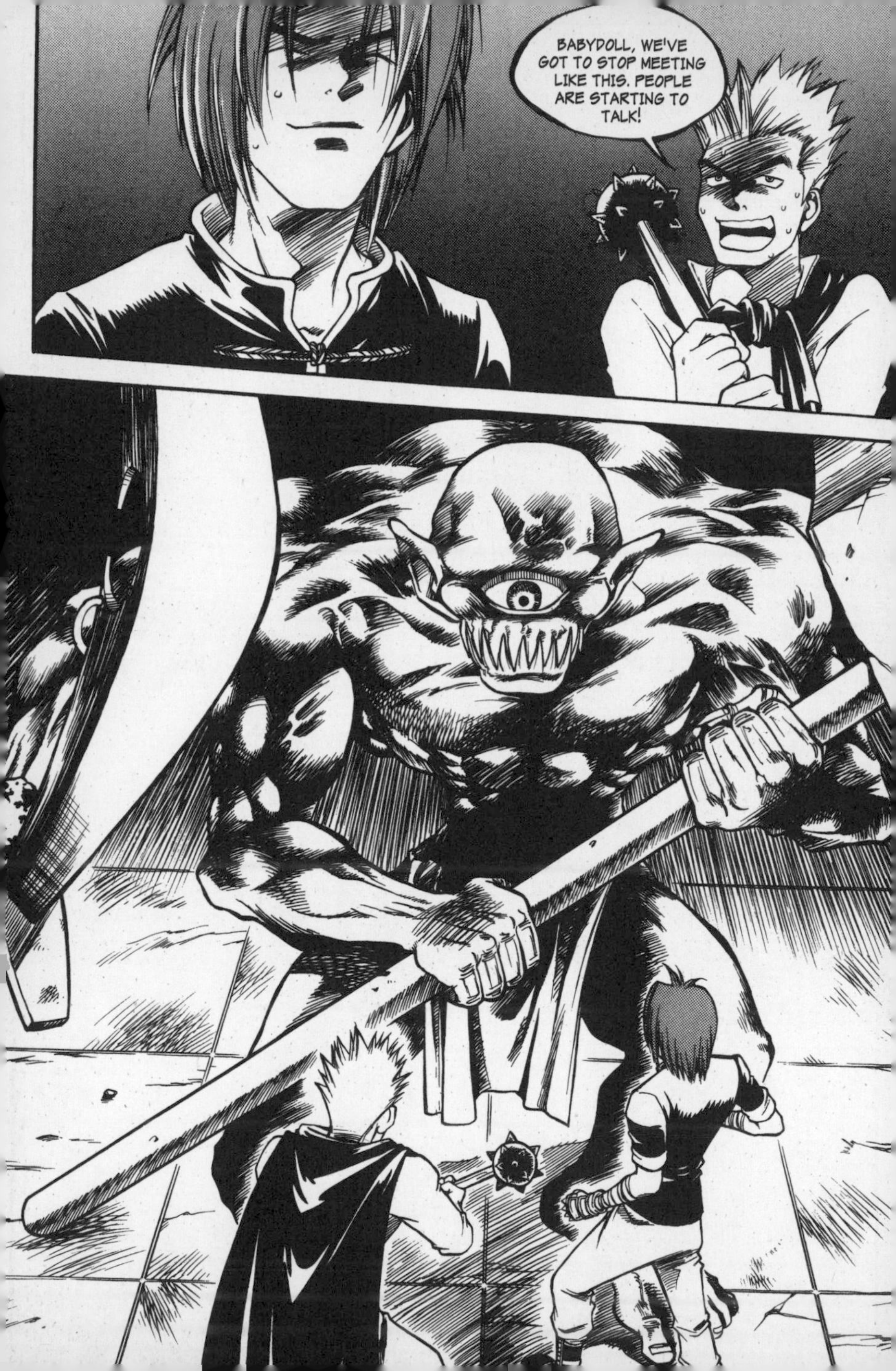
BABYDOLL, WE'VE GOT TO STOP MEETING LIKE THIS. PEOPLE ARE STARTING TO TALK!

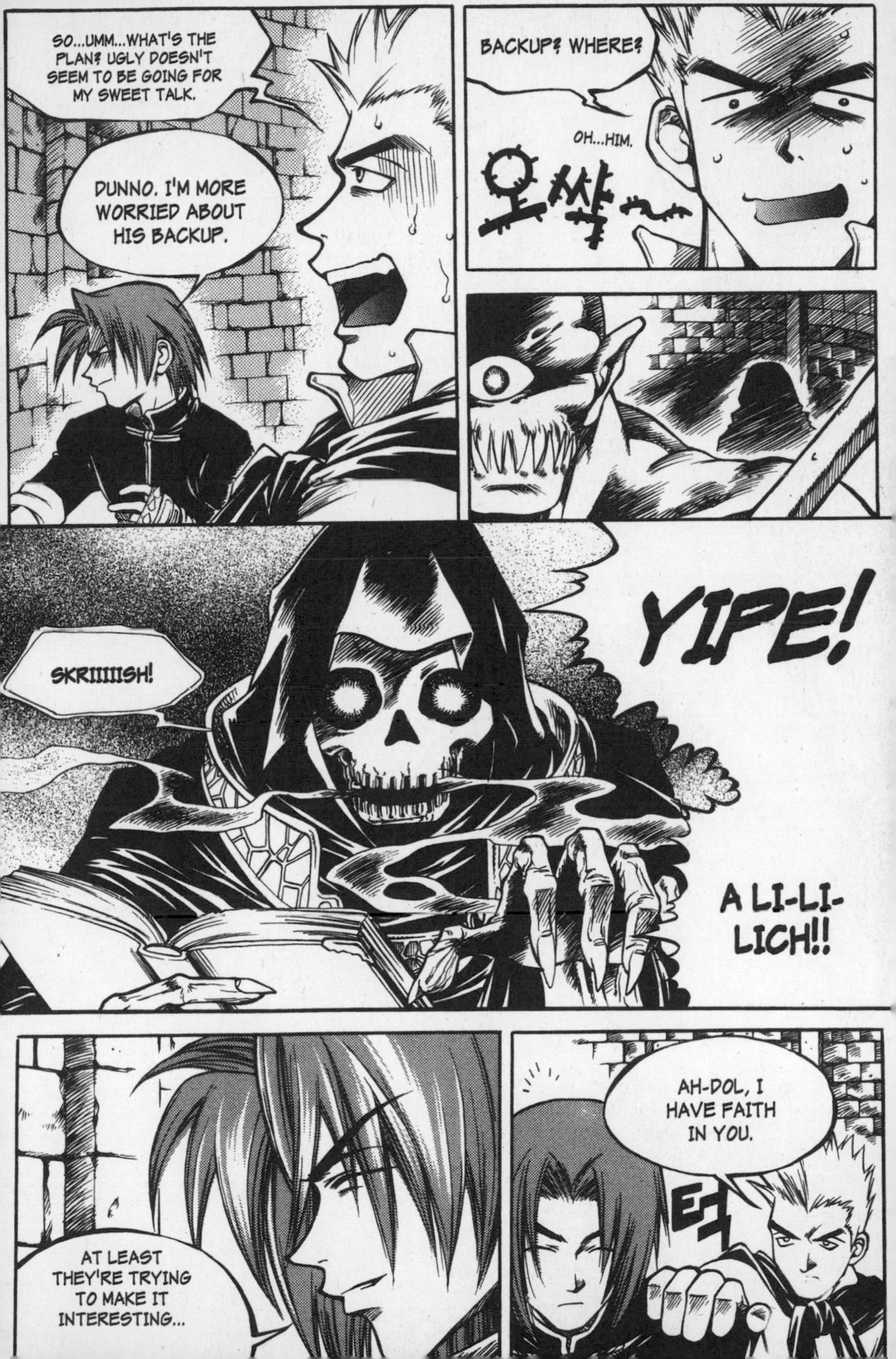
SO...UMM...WHAT'S THE PLAN? UGLY DOESN'T SEEM TO BE GOING FOR MY SWEET TALK.
DUNNO. I'M MORE WORRIED ABOUT HIS BACKUP.
BACKUP? WHERE?
OH...HIM.
오싹
SKRIIIIISH!
YIPE!
A LI-LI-LICH!!
AT LEAST THEY'RE TRYING TO MAKE IT INTERESTING...
AH-DOL, I HAVE FAITH IN YOU.

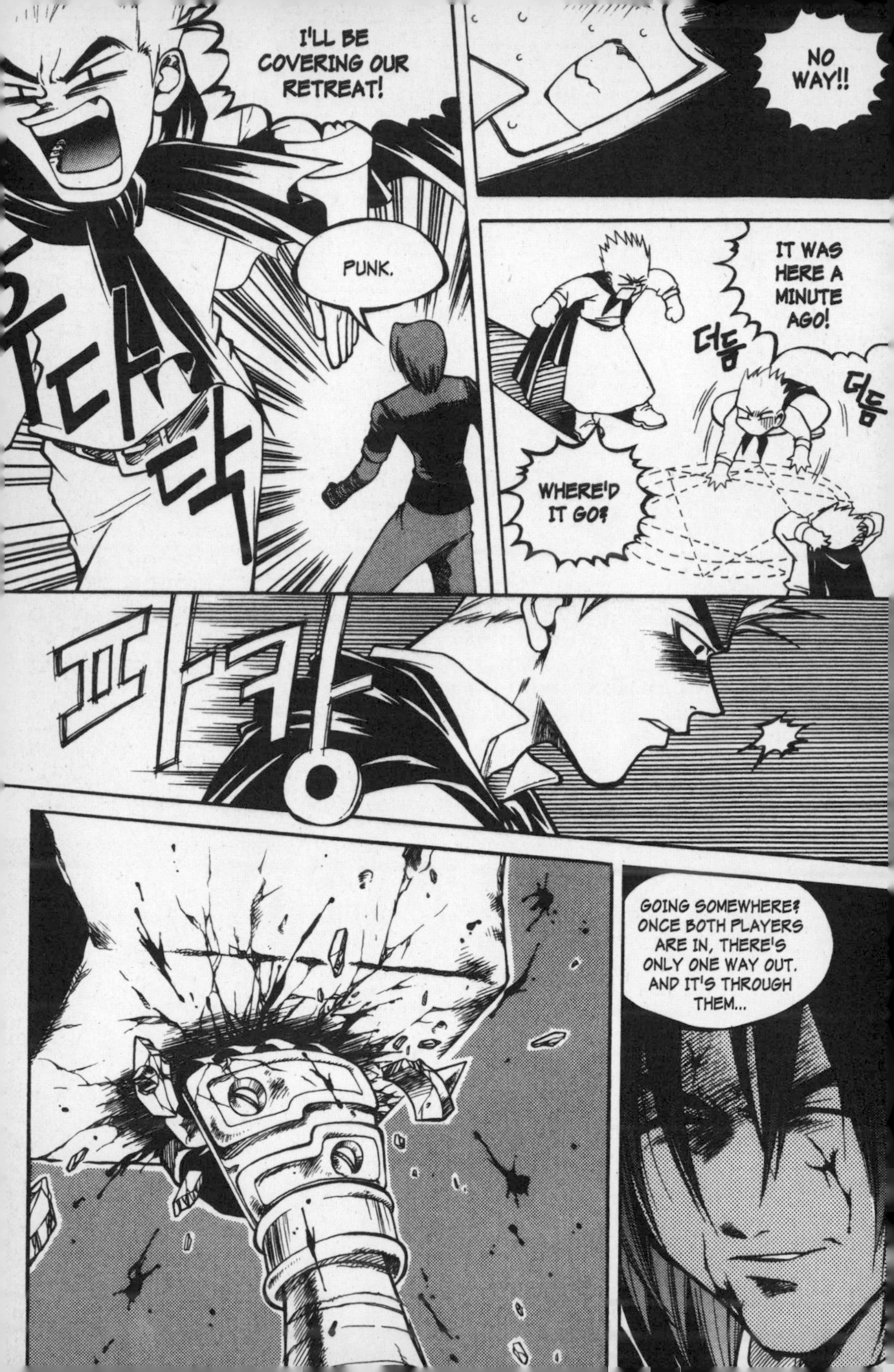
I'LL BE COVERING OUR RETREAT!
PUNK.
NO WAY!!
IT WAS HERE A MINUTE AGO!
더듬
더듬
WHERE'D IT GO?
GOING SOMEWHERE? ONCE BOTH PLAYERS ARE IN, THERE'S ONLY ONE WAY OUT. AND IT'S THROUGH THEM...

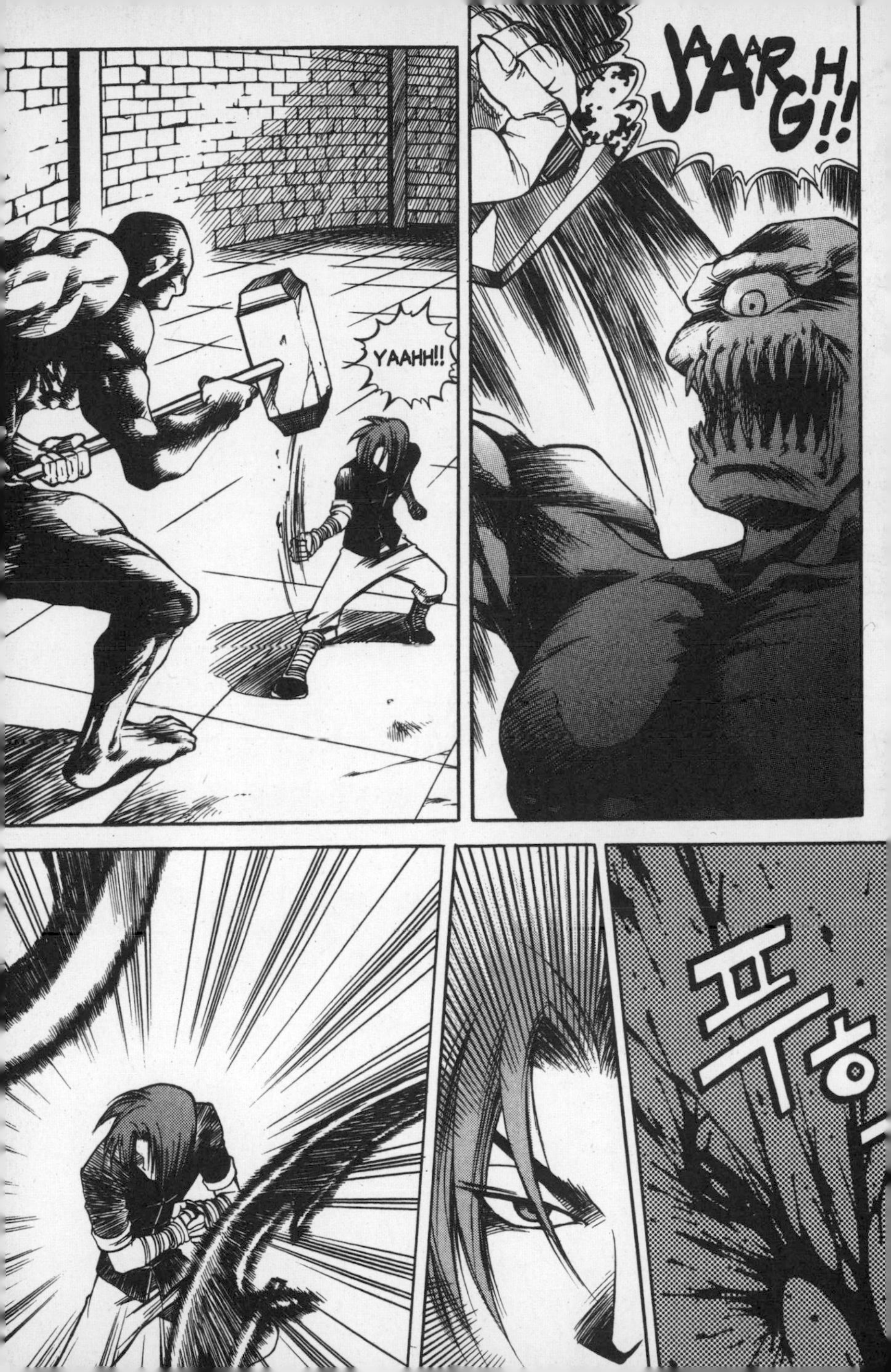
YAAHH!!
JAAARGH!!
푸ㅎ

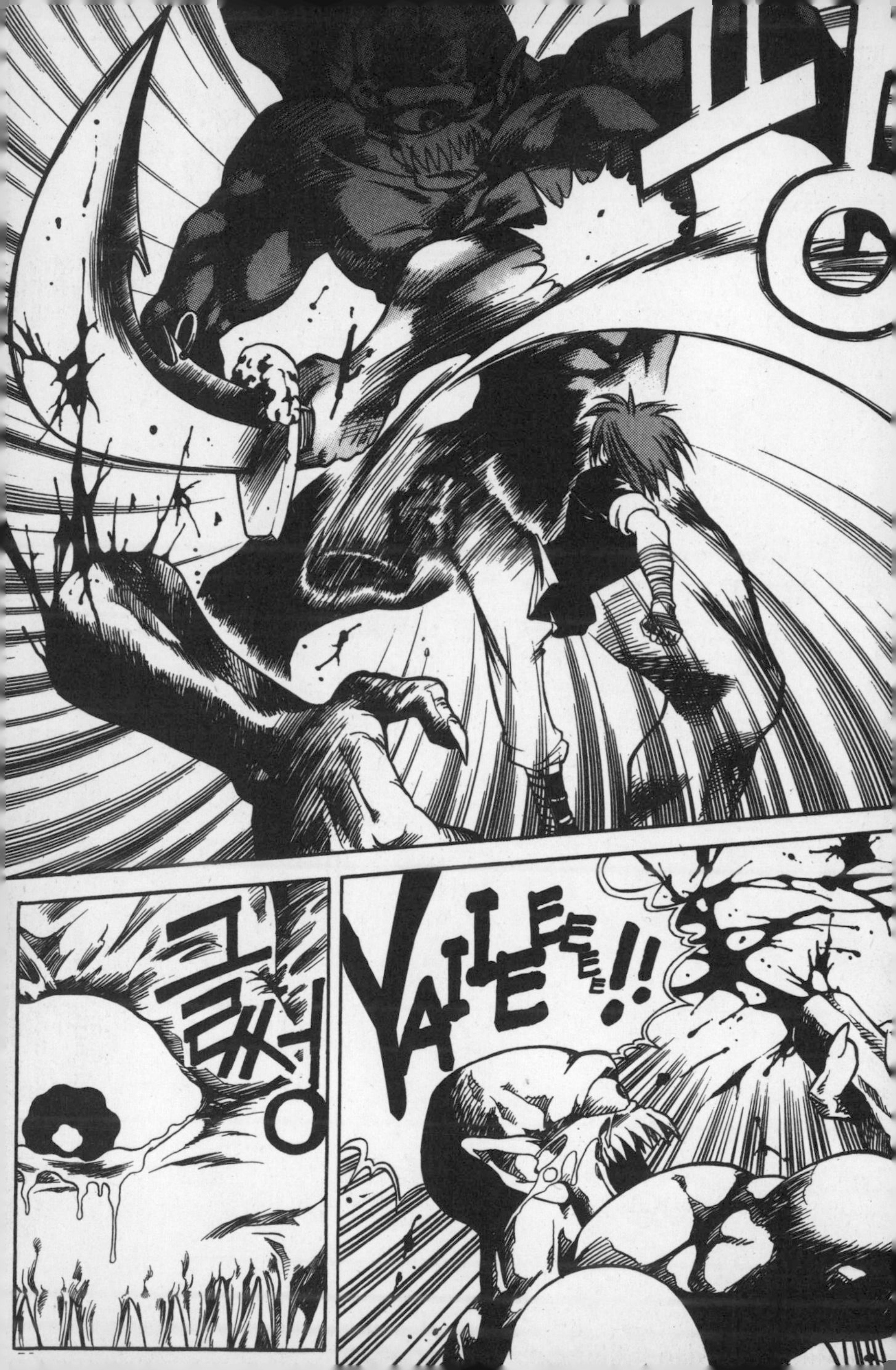
YAIIEEEEE!!

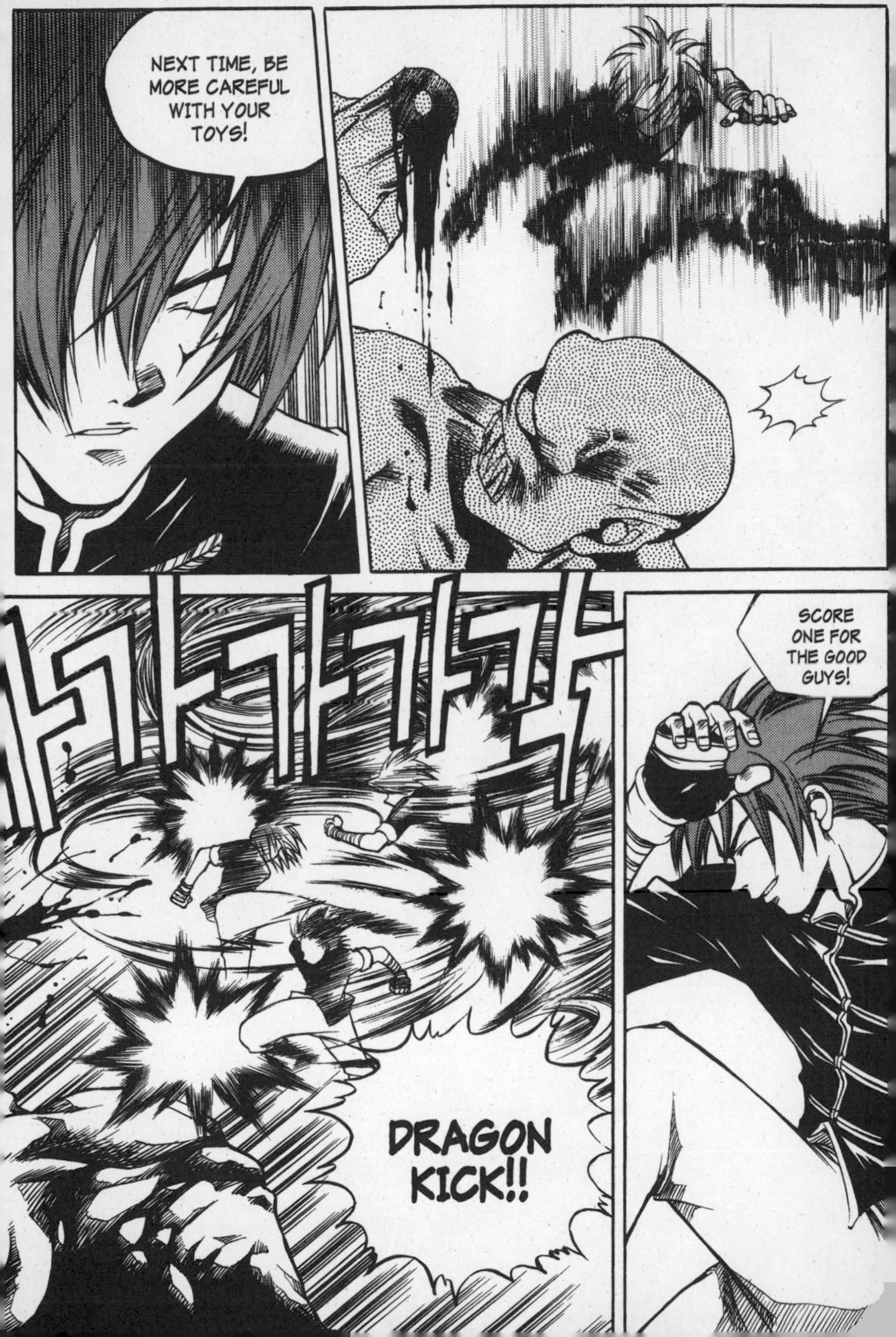
NEXT TIME, BE MORE CAREFUL WITH YOUR TOYS!
DRAGON KICK!!
SCORE ONE FOR THE GOOD GUYS!

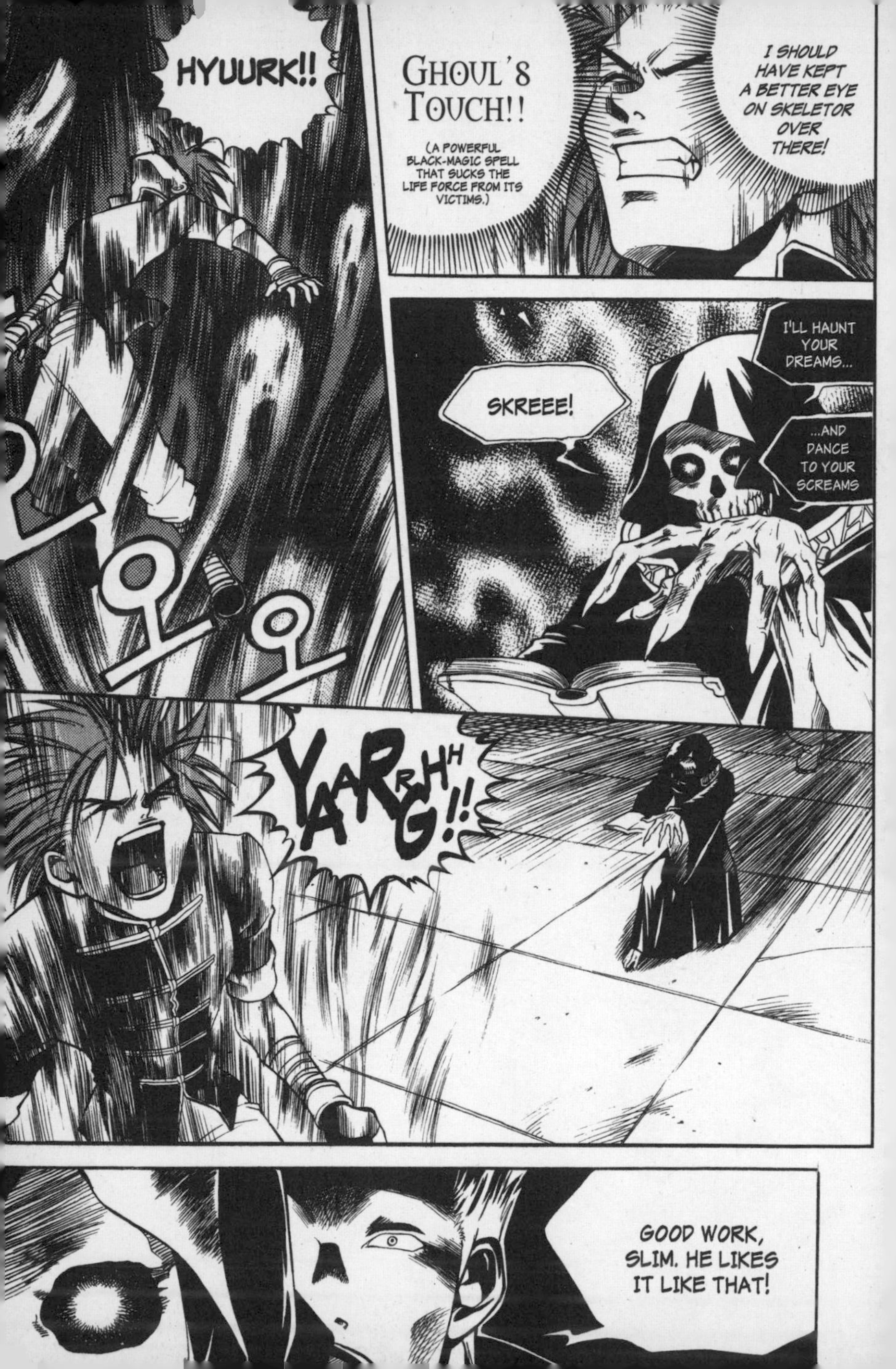
HYUURK!!
GHOUL'S TOUCH!!
(A POWERFUL BLACK-MAGIC SPELL THAT SUCKS THE LIFE FORCE FROM ITS VICTIMS.)
I SHOULD HAVE KEPT A BETTER EYE ON SKELETOR OVER THERE!
SKREEE!
I'LL HAUNT YOUR DREAMS...
...AND DANCE TO YOUR SCREAMS
YAARRGHH!!
GOOD WORK, SLIM. HE LIKES IT LIKE THAT!

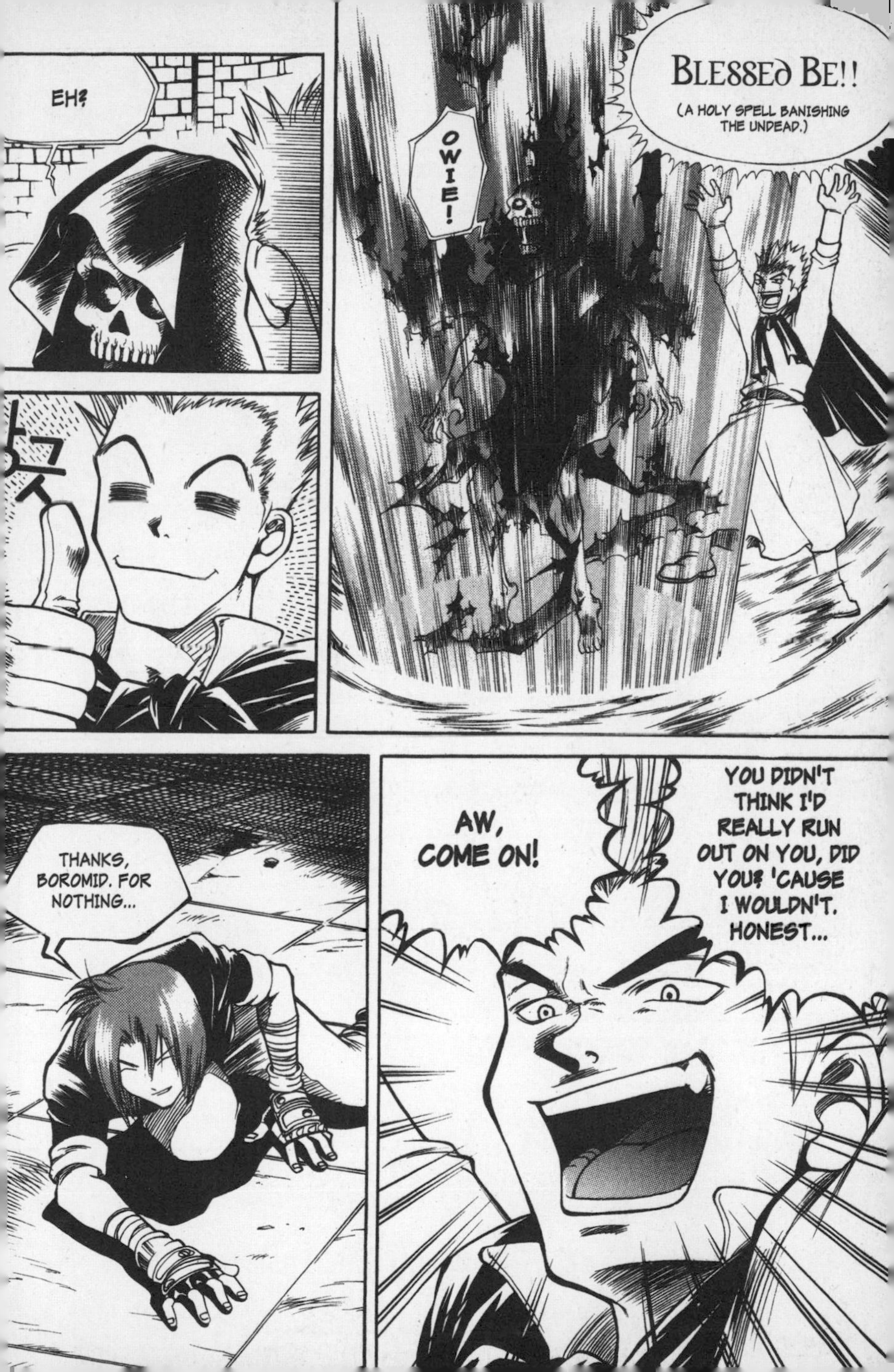
EH?
OWIE!
BLESSED BE!!
(A HOLY SPELL BANISHING THE UNDEAD.)
THANKS, BOROMID. FOR NOTHING...
AW, COME ON!
YOU DIDN'T THINK I'D REALLY RUN OUT ON YOU, DID YOU? 'CAUSE I WOULDN'T. HONEST...

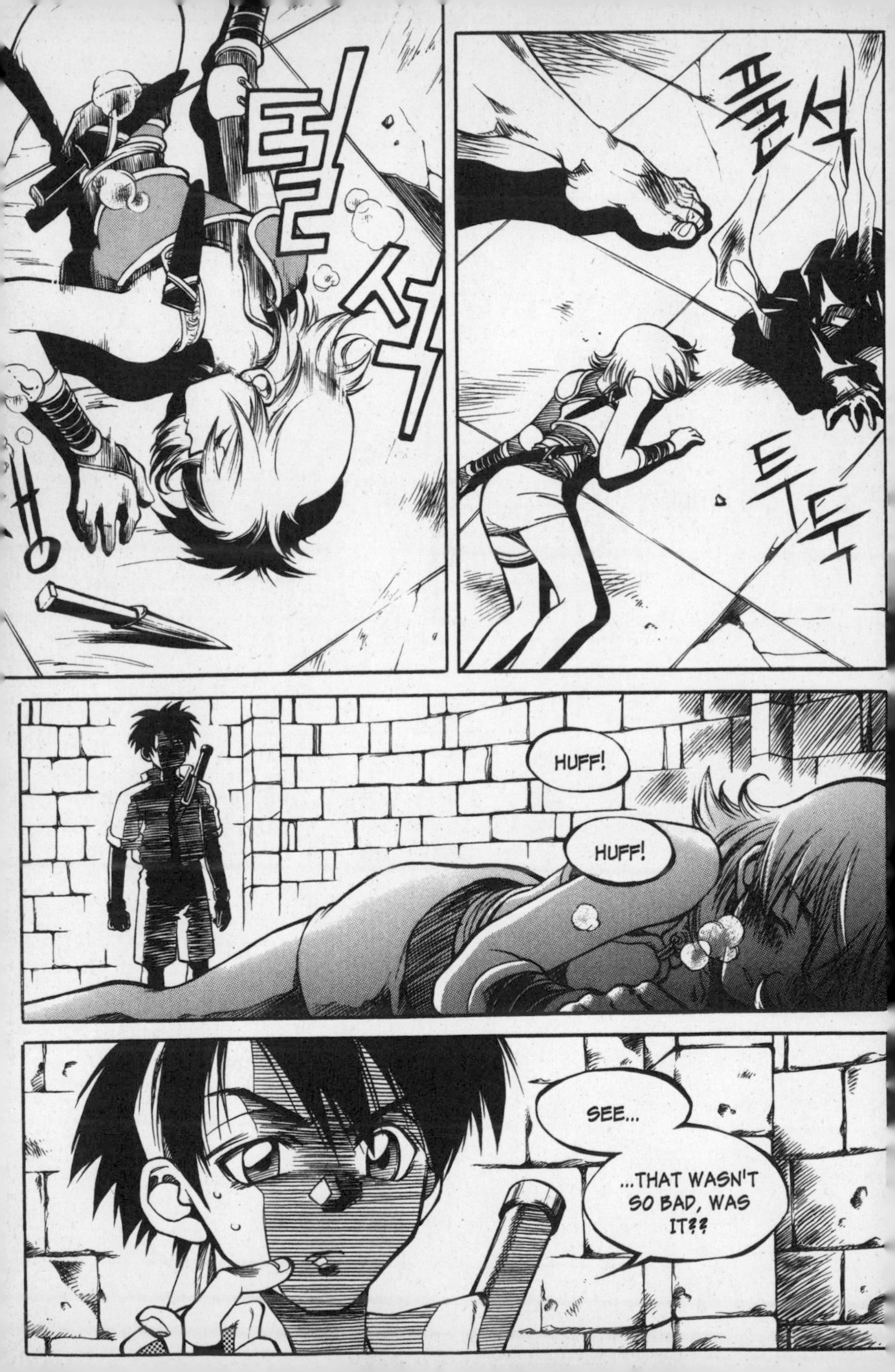
털석
풀석
투둑
HUFF!
HUFF!
SEE...
...THAT WASN'T SO BAD, WAS IT??

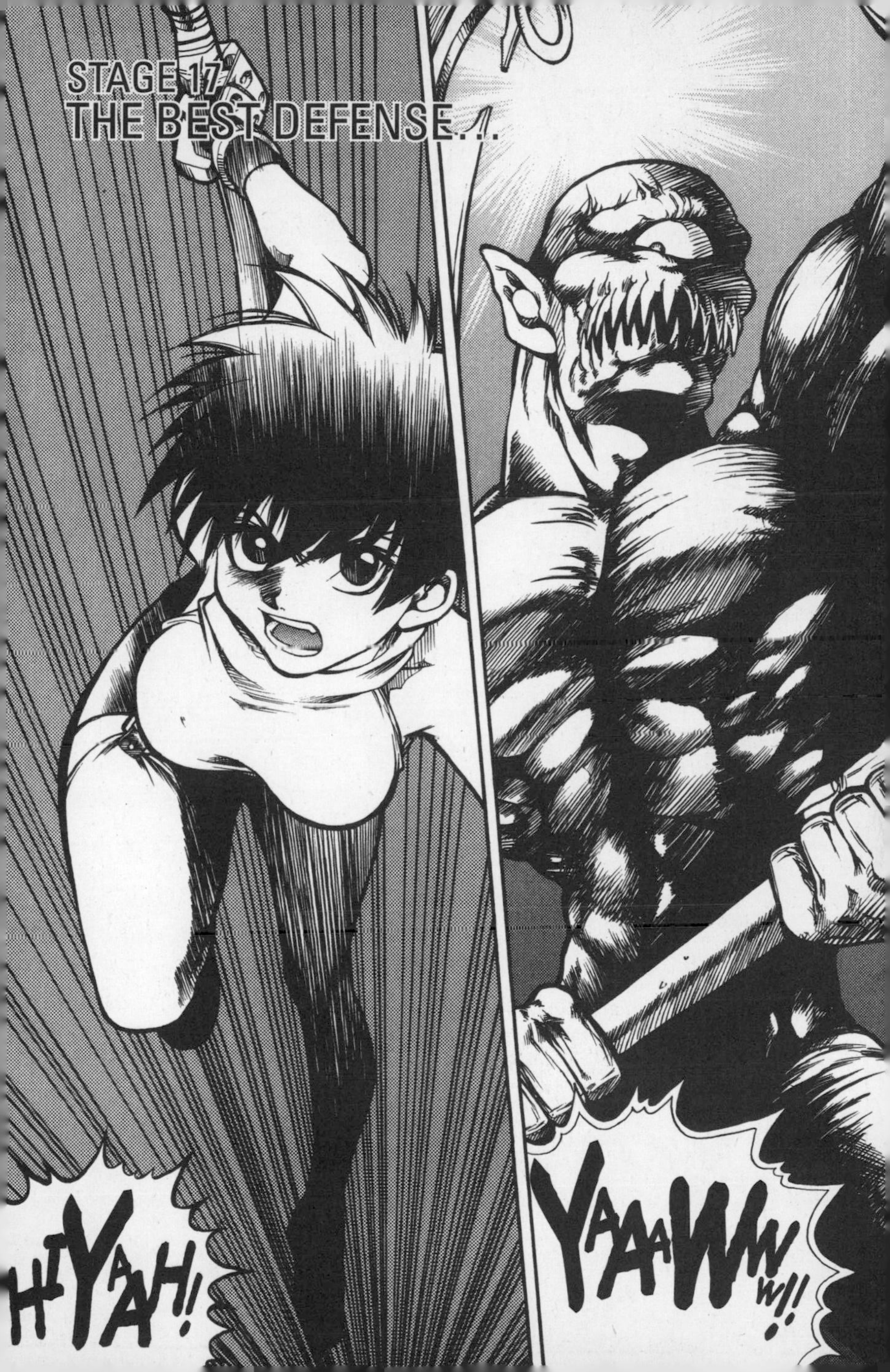
STAGE 17
THE BEST DEFENSE. . .
HIYAAH!!
YAAAWWWW!!

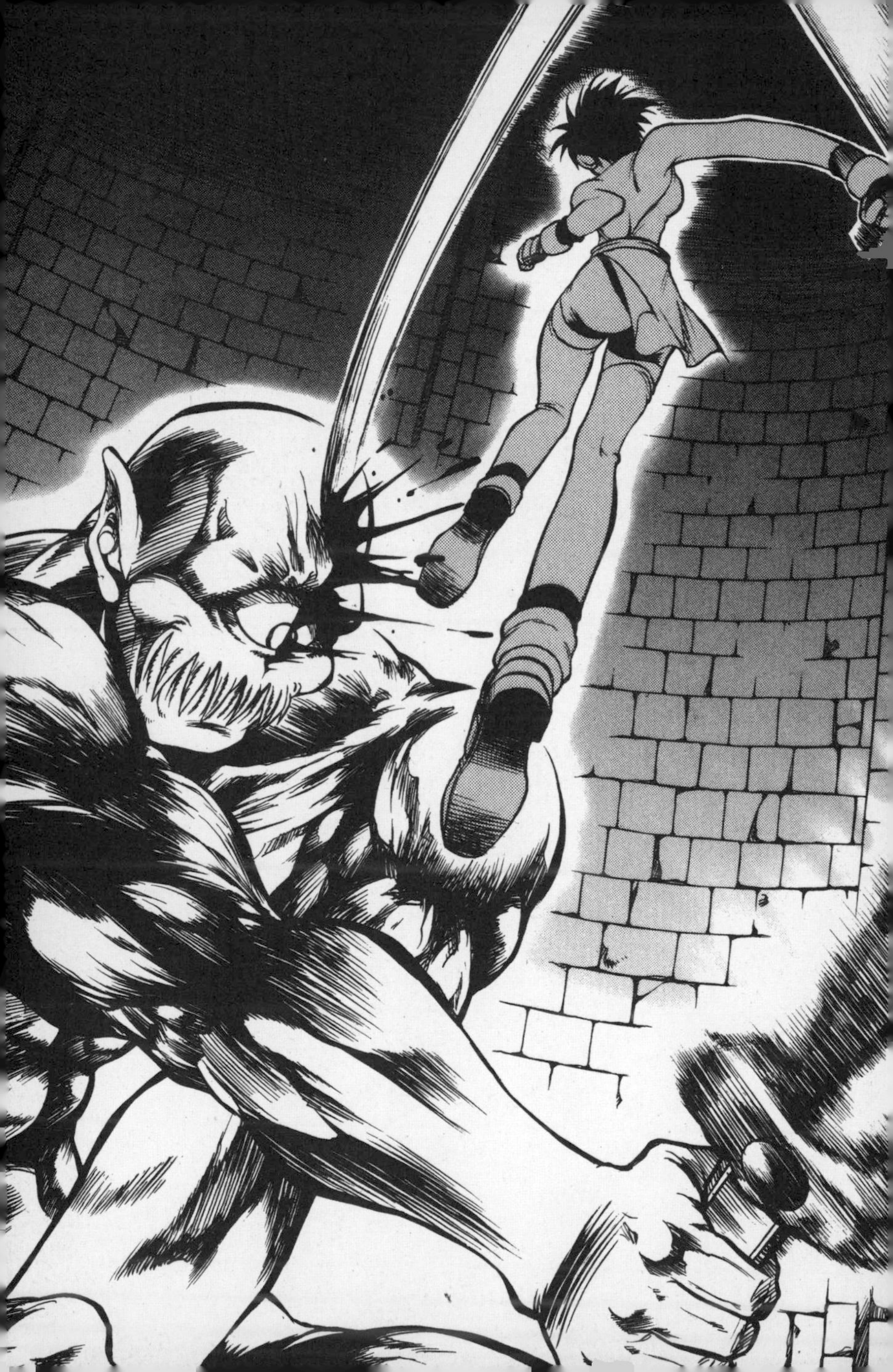

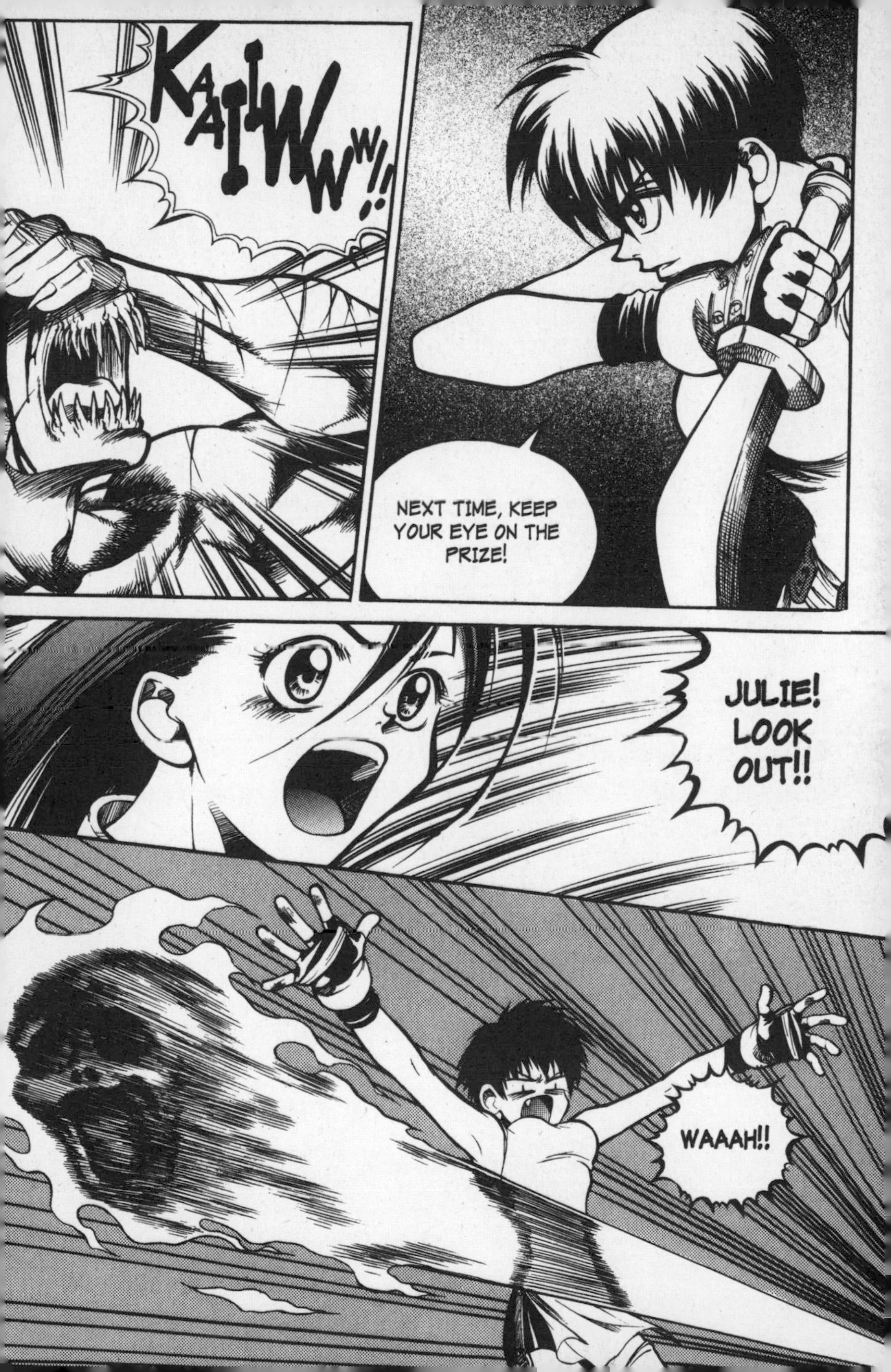
KAAIIWWW!!
NEXT TIME, KEEP YOUR EYE ON THE PRIZE!
JULIE! LOOK OUT!!
WAAAH!!

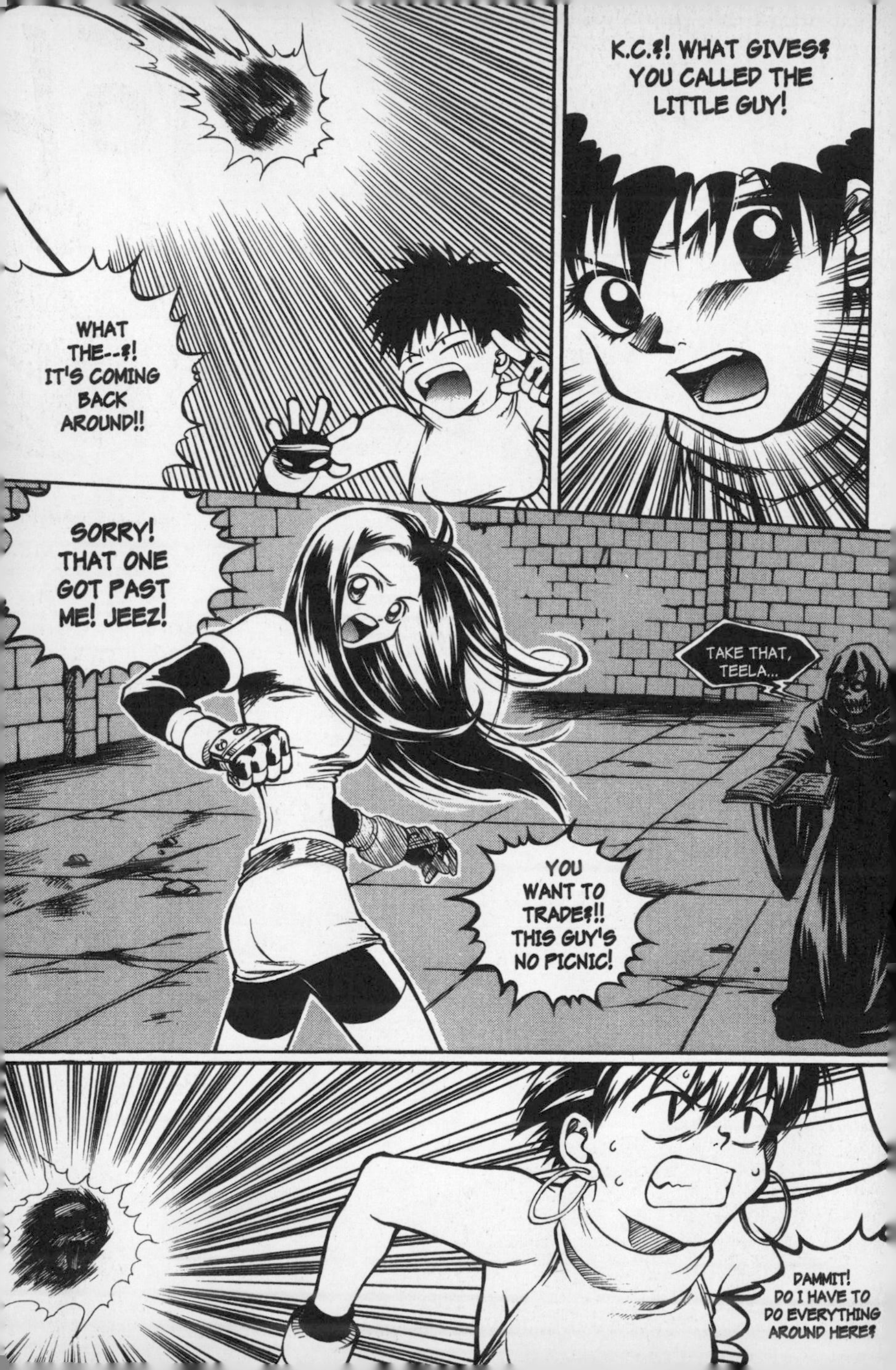
WHAT THE--?! IT'S COMING BACK AROUND!!
K.C.?! WHAT GIVES? YOU CALLED THE LITTLE GUY!
SORRY! THAT ONE GOT PAST ME! JEEZ!
TAKE THAT, TEELA...
YOU WANT TO TRADE?!! THIS GUY'S NO PICNIC!
DAMMIT! DO I HAVE TO DO EVERYTHING AROUND HERE?

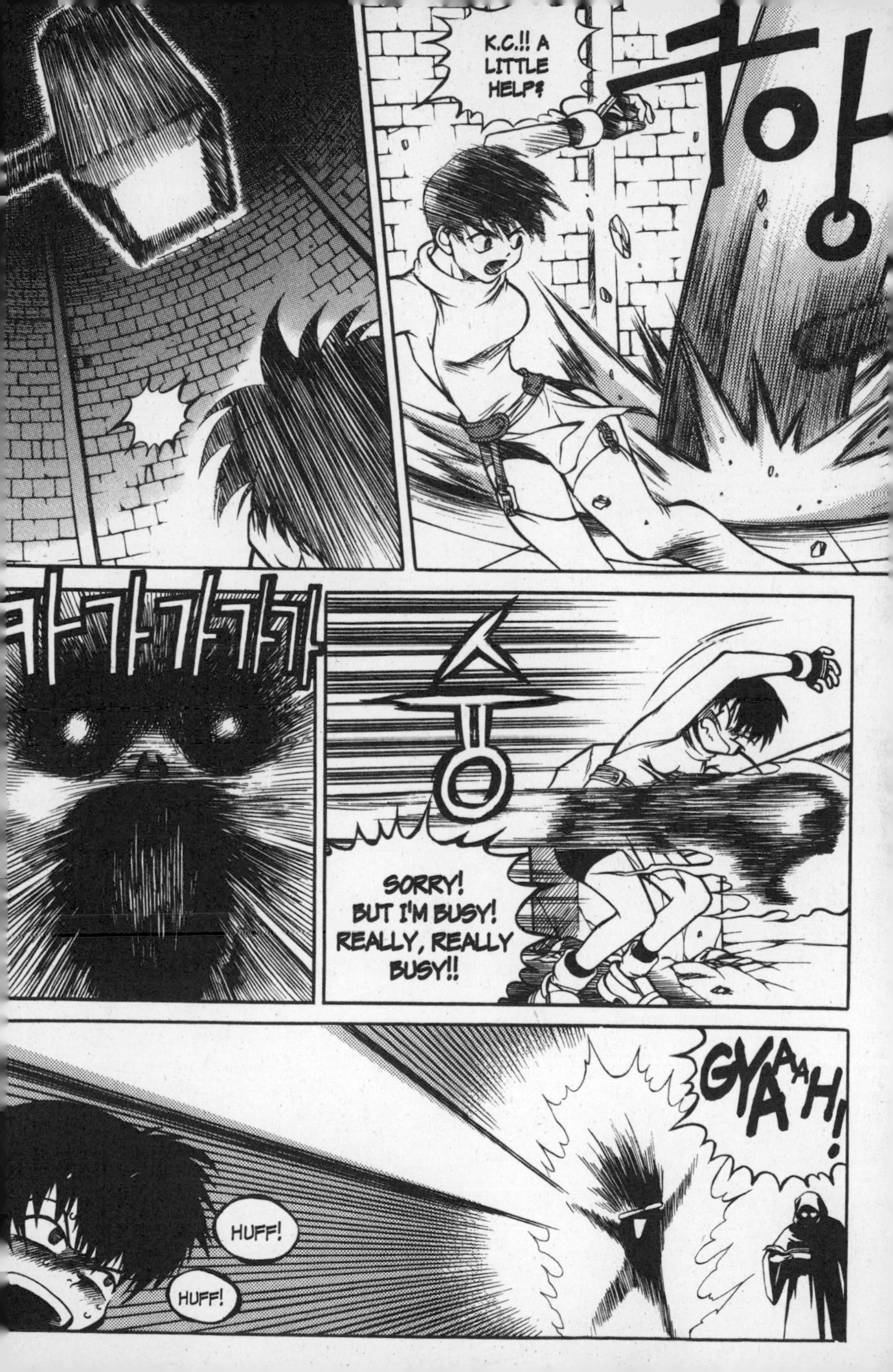
K.C.!! A LITTLE HELP?
SORRY! BUT I'M BUSY! REALLY, REALLY BUSY!!
HUFF!
HUFF!
GYAAAH!

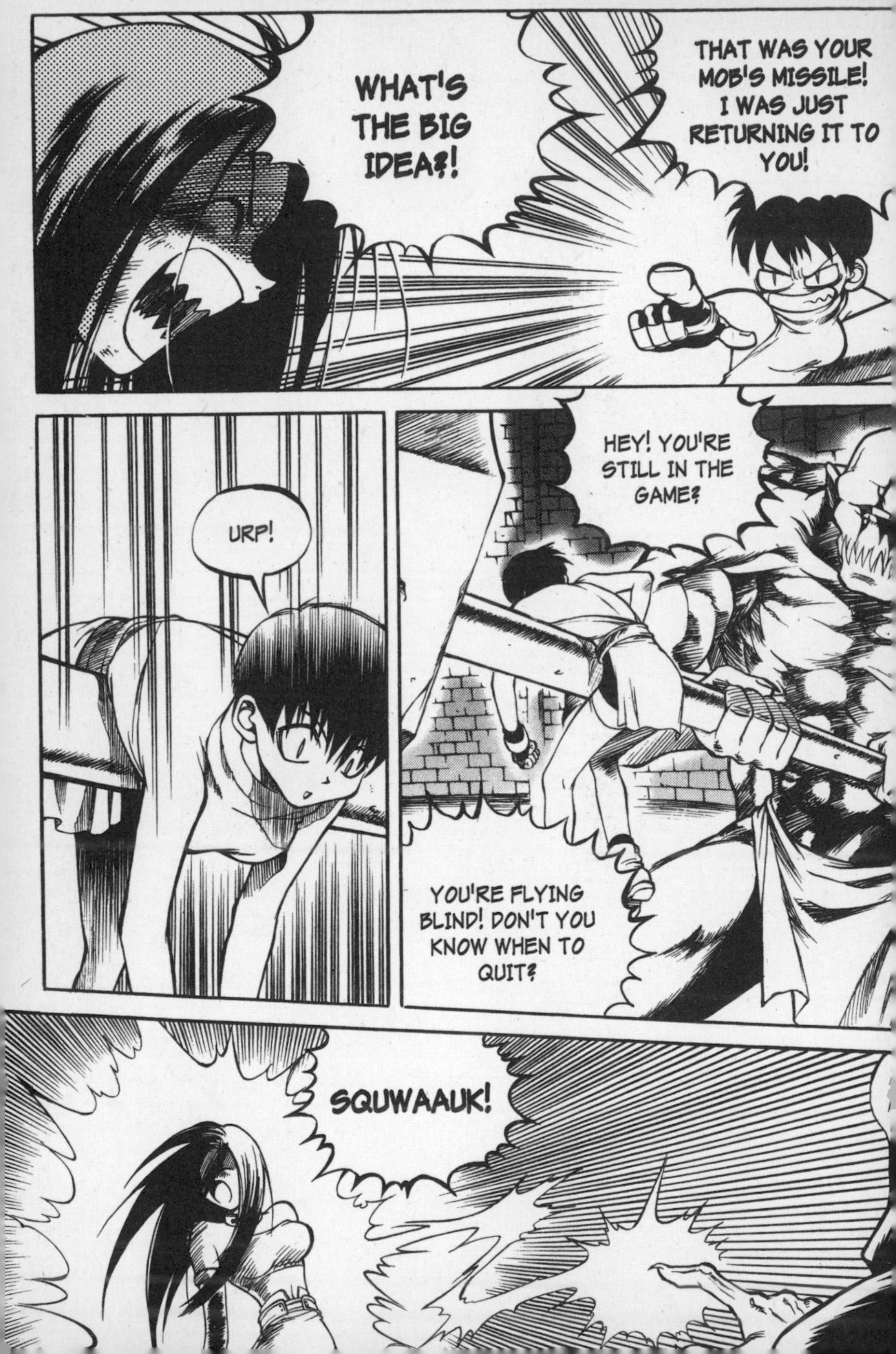
WHAT'S THE BIG IDEA?!
THAT WAS YOUR MOB'S MISSILE! I WAS JUST RETURNING IT TO YOU!
URP!
HEY! YOU'RE STILL IN THE GAME?
YOU'RE FLYING BLIND! DON'T YOU KNOW WHEN TO QUIT?
SQUWAAUK!

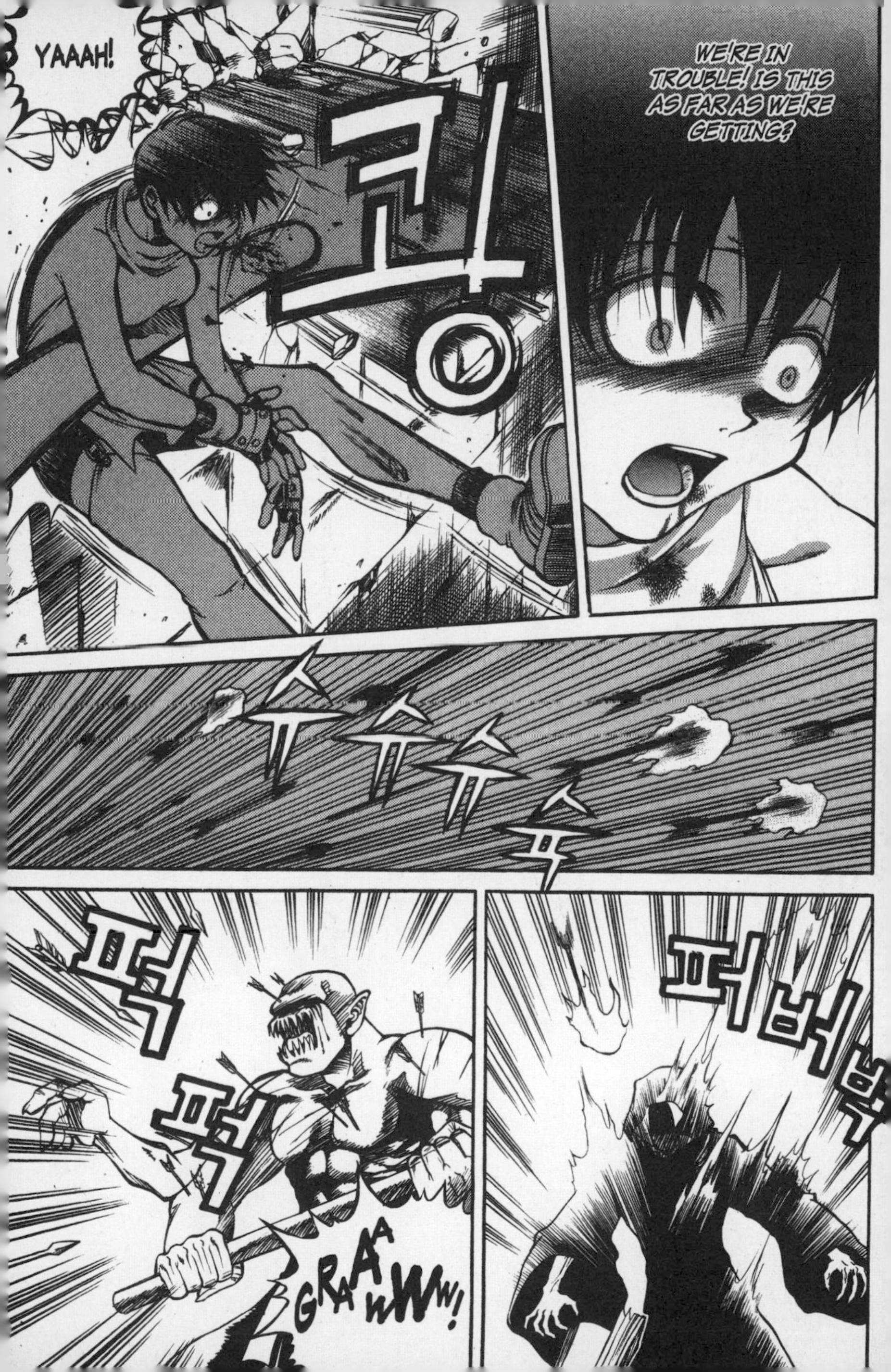
YAAAH!
WE'RE IN TROUBLE! IS THIS AS FAR AS WE'RE GETTING?
GRAAAWWW!

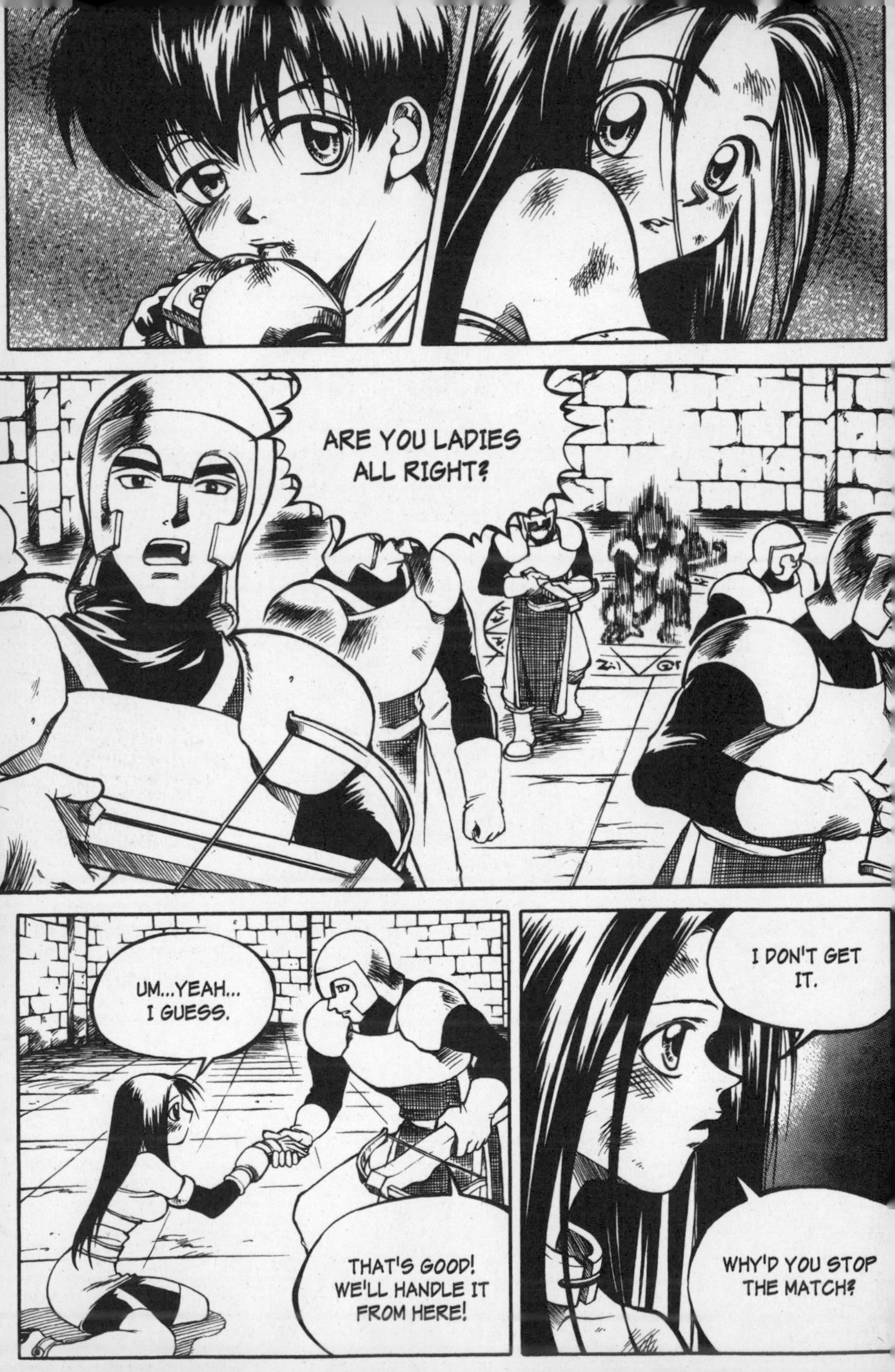
ARE YOU LADIES ALL RIGHT?
UM...YEAH... I GUESS.
THAT'S GOOD! WE'LL HANDLE IT FROM HERE!
I DON'T GET IT.
WHY'D YOU STOP THE MATCH?

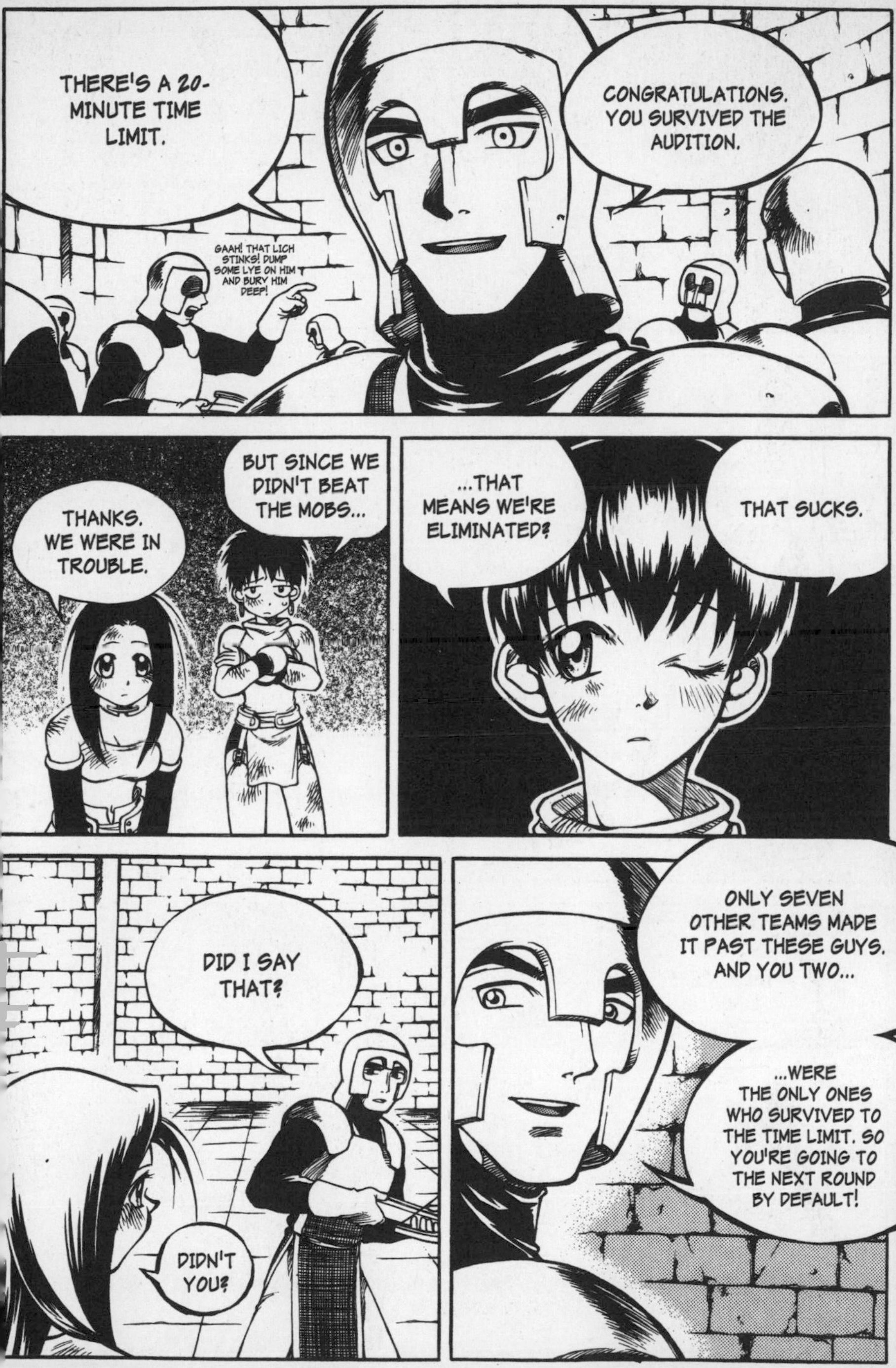
THERE'S A 20-MINUTE TIME LIMIT.
GAAH! THAT LICH STINKS! DUMP SOME LYE ON HIM AND BURY HIM DEEP!
CONGRATULATIONS. YOU SURVIVED THE AUDITION.
THANKS. WE WERE IN TROUBLE.
BUT SINCE WE DIDN'T BEAT THE MOBS...
...THAT MEANS WE'RE ELIMINATED?
THAT SUCKS.
DID I SAY THAT?
DIDN'T YOU?
ONLY SEVEN OTHER TEAMS MADE IT PAST THESE GUYS. AND YOU TWO...
...WERE THE ONLY ONES WHO SURVIVED TO THE TIME LIMIT. SO YOU'RE GOING TO THE NEXT ROUND BY DEFAULT!

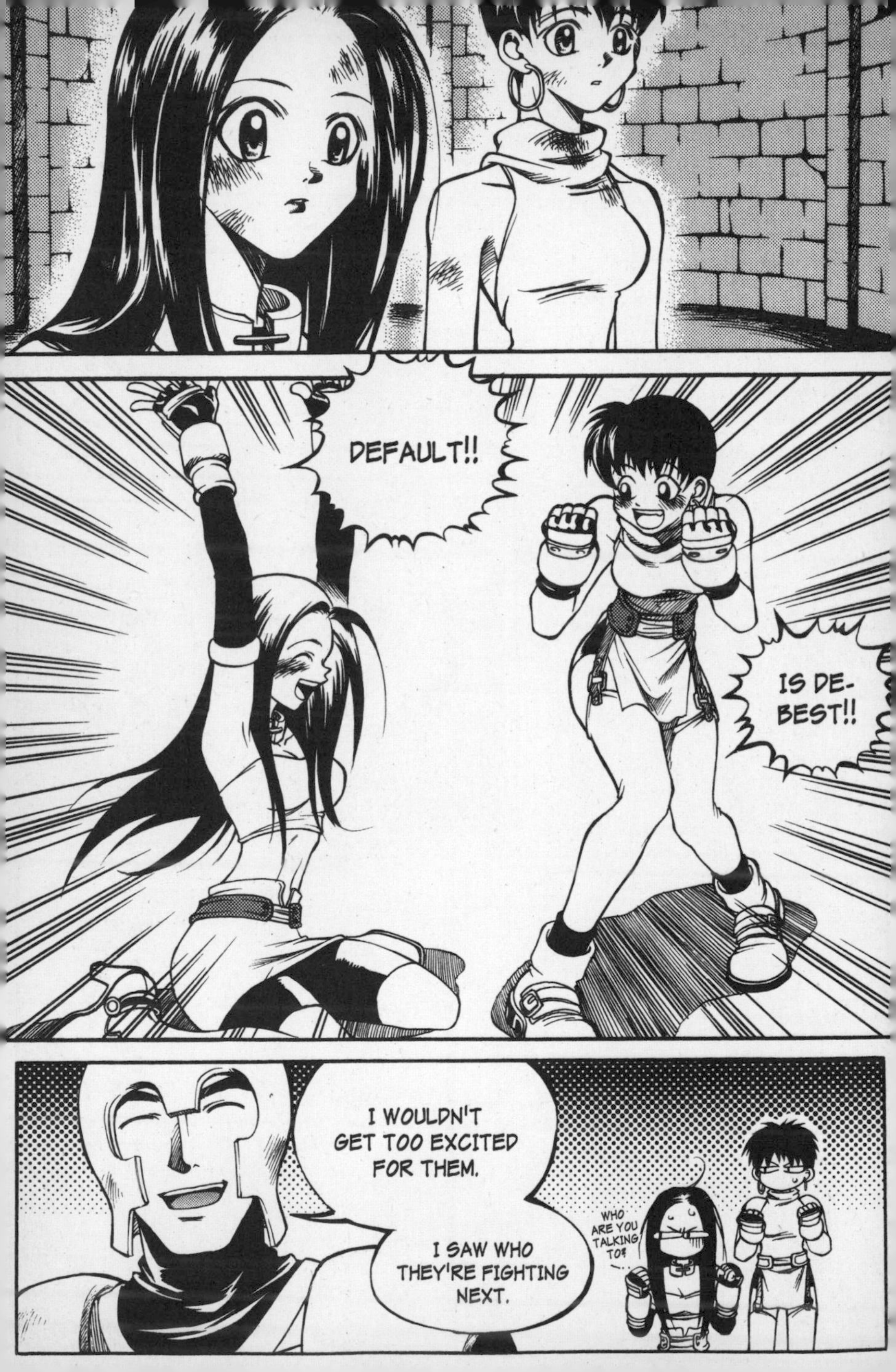
DEFAULT!!
IS DE-BEST!!
I WOULDN'T GET TOO EXCITED FOR THEM.
I SAW WHO THEY'RE FIGHTING NEXT.
WHO ARE YOU TALKING TO?

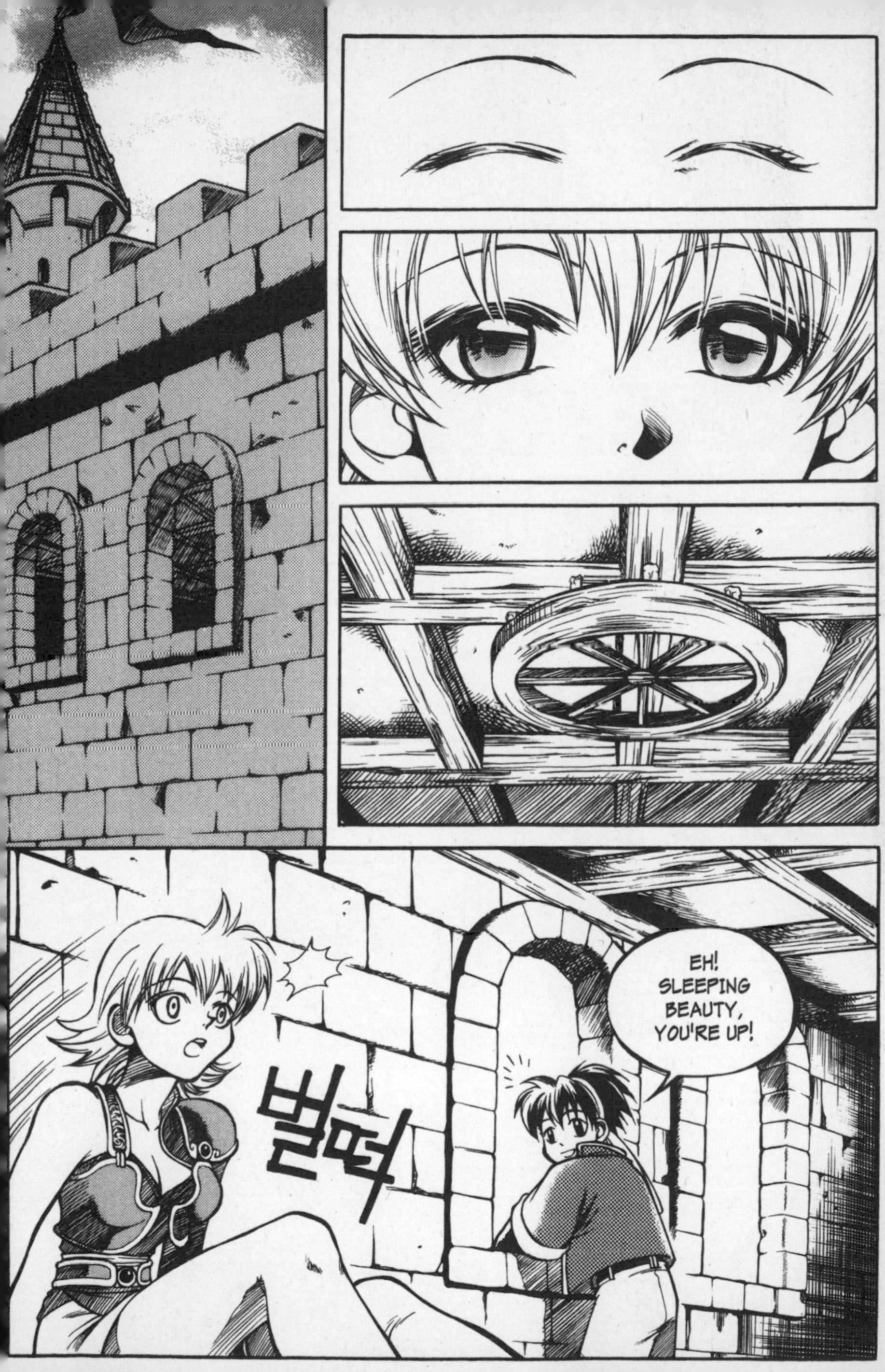
EH! SLEEPING BEAUTY, YOU'RE UP!
벌떡

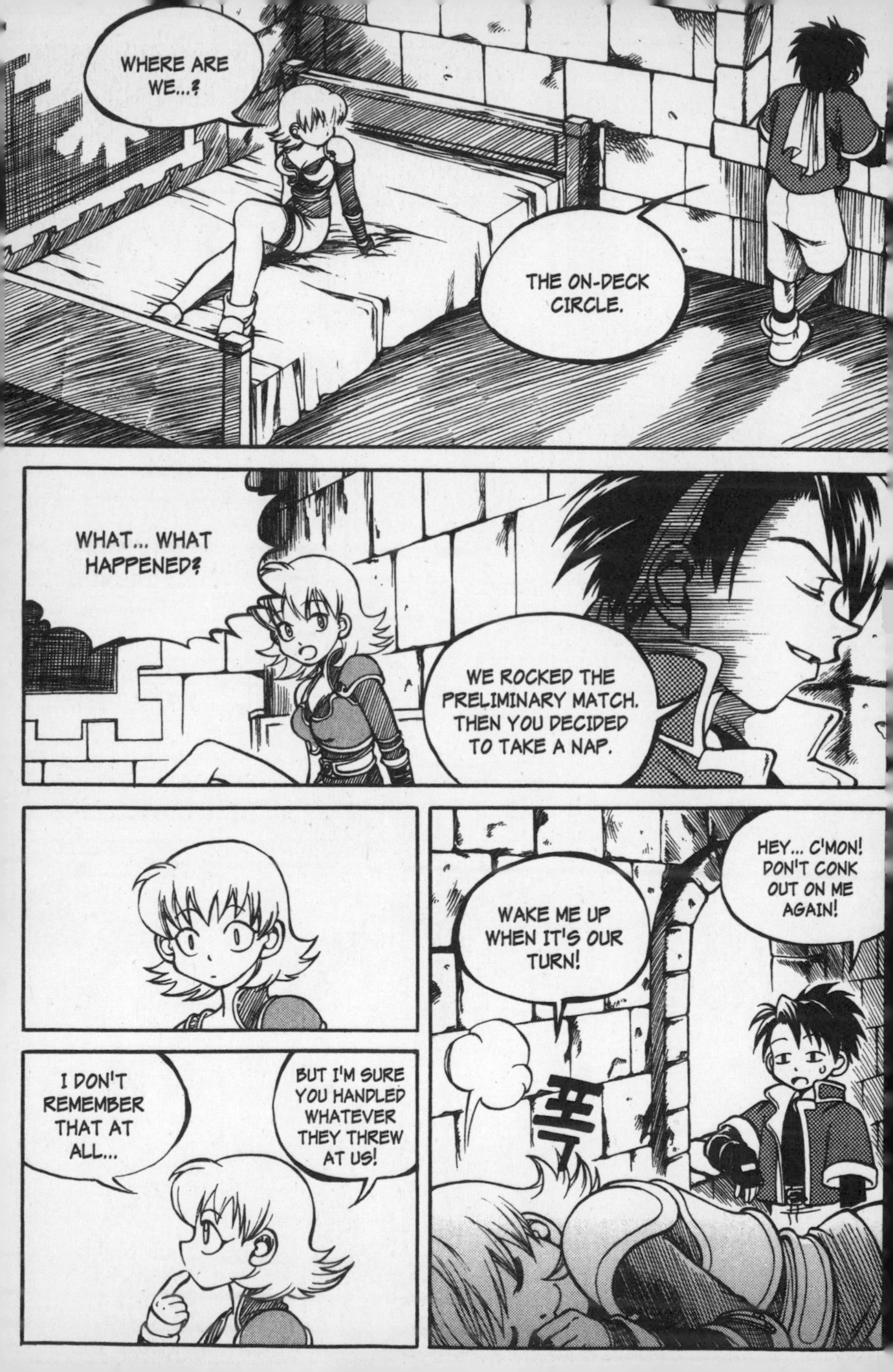
WHERE ARE WE...?
THE ON-DECK CIRCLE.
WHAT... WHAT HAPPENED?
WE ROCKED THE PRELIMINARY MATCH. THEN YOU DECIDED TO TAKE A NAP.
I DON'T REMEMBER THAT AT ALL...
BUT I'M SURE YOU HANDLED WHATEVER THEY THREW AT US!
WAKE ME UP WHEN IT'S OUR TURN!
HEY... C'MON! DON'T CONK OUT ON ME AGAIN!

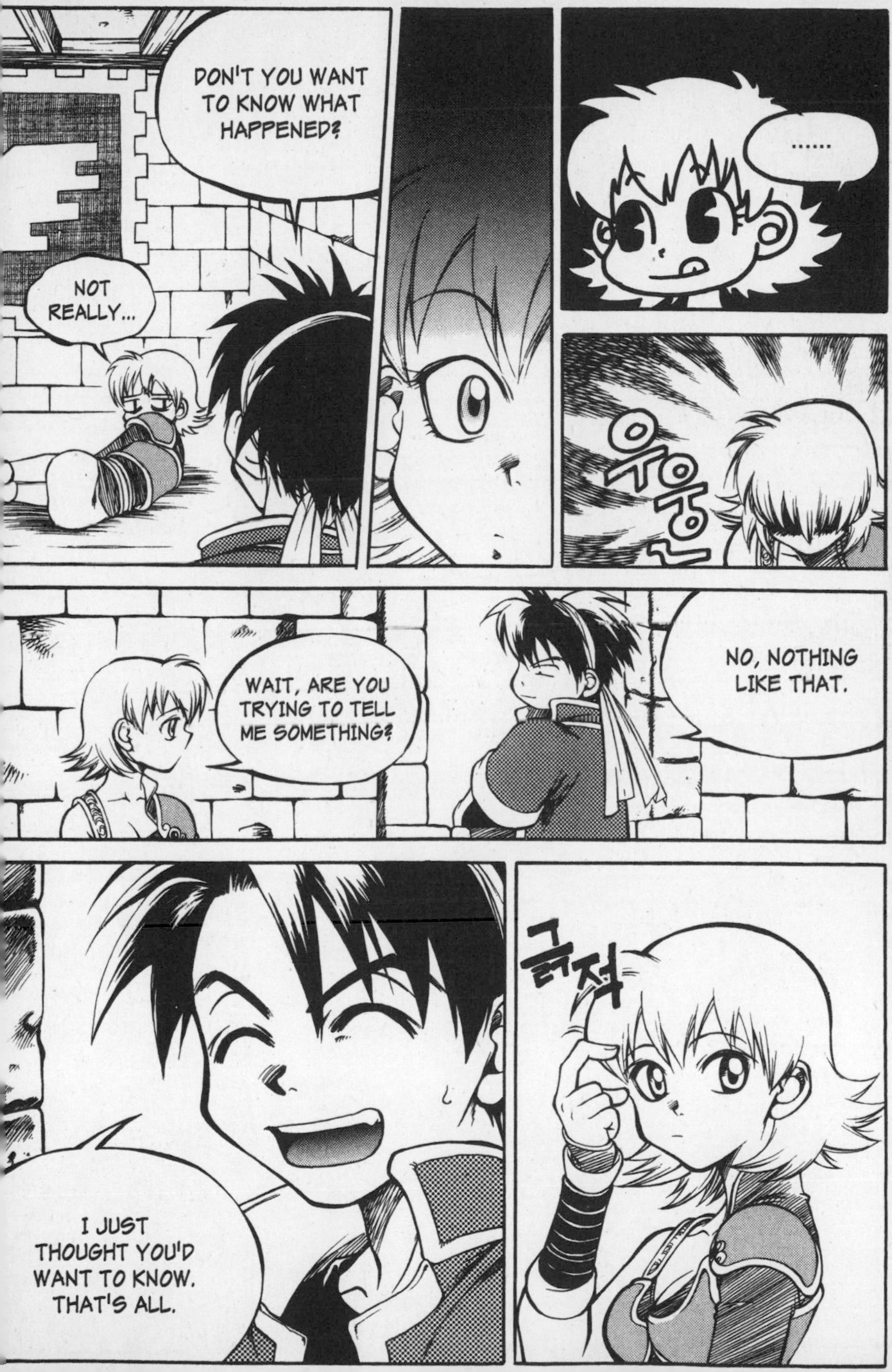
DON'T YOU WANT TO KNOW WHAT HAPPENED?
NOT REALLY...
......
우웅~
WAIT, ARE YOU TRYING TO TELL ME SOMETHING?
NO, NOTHING LIKE THAT.
I JUST THOUGHT YOU'D WANT TO KNOW. THAT'S ALL.
긁적

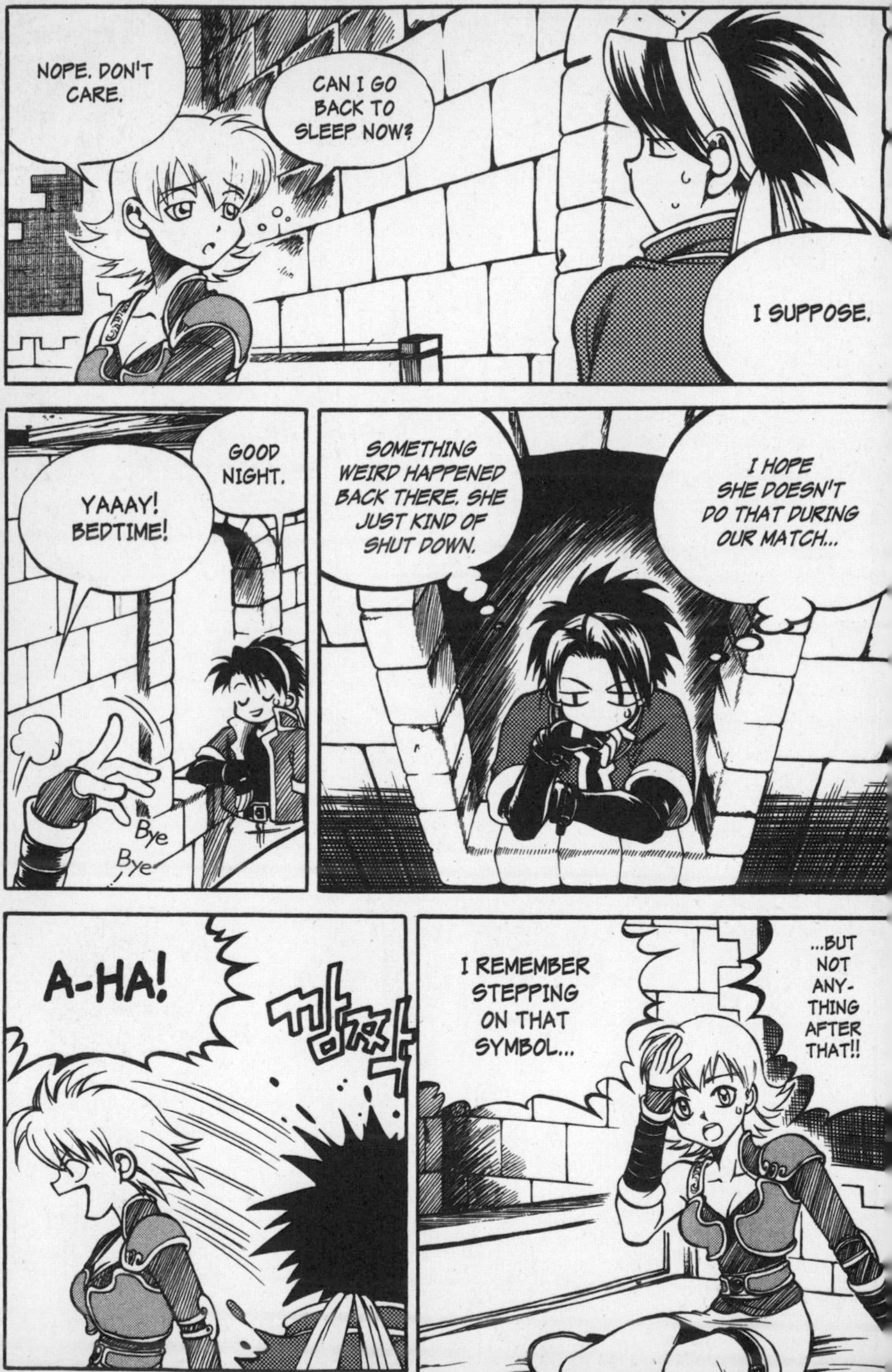
NOPE. DON'T CARE.
CAN I GO BACK TO SLEEP NOW?
I SUPPOSE.
YAAAY! BEDTIME!
GOOD NIGHT.
Bye Bye
SOMETHING WEIRD HAPPENED BACK THERE. SHE JUST KIND OF SHUT DOWN.
I HOPE SHE DOESN'T DO THAT DURING OUR MATCH...
A-HA!
I REMEMBER STEPPING ON THAT SYMBOL...
...BUT NOT ANYTHING AFTER THAT!!

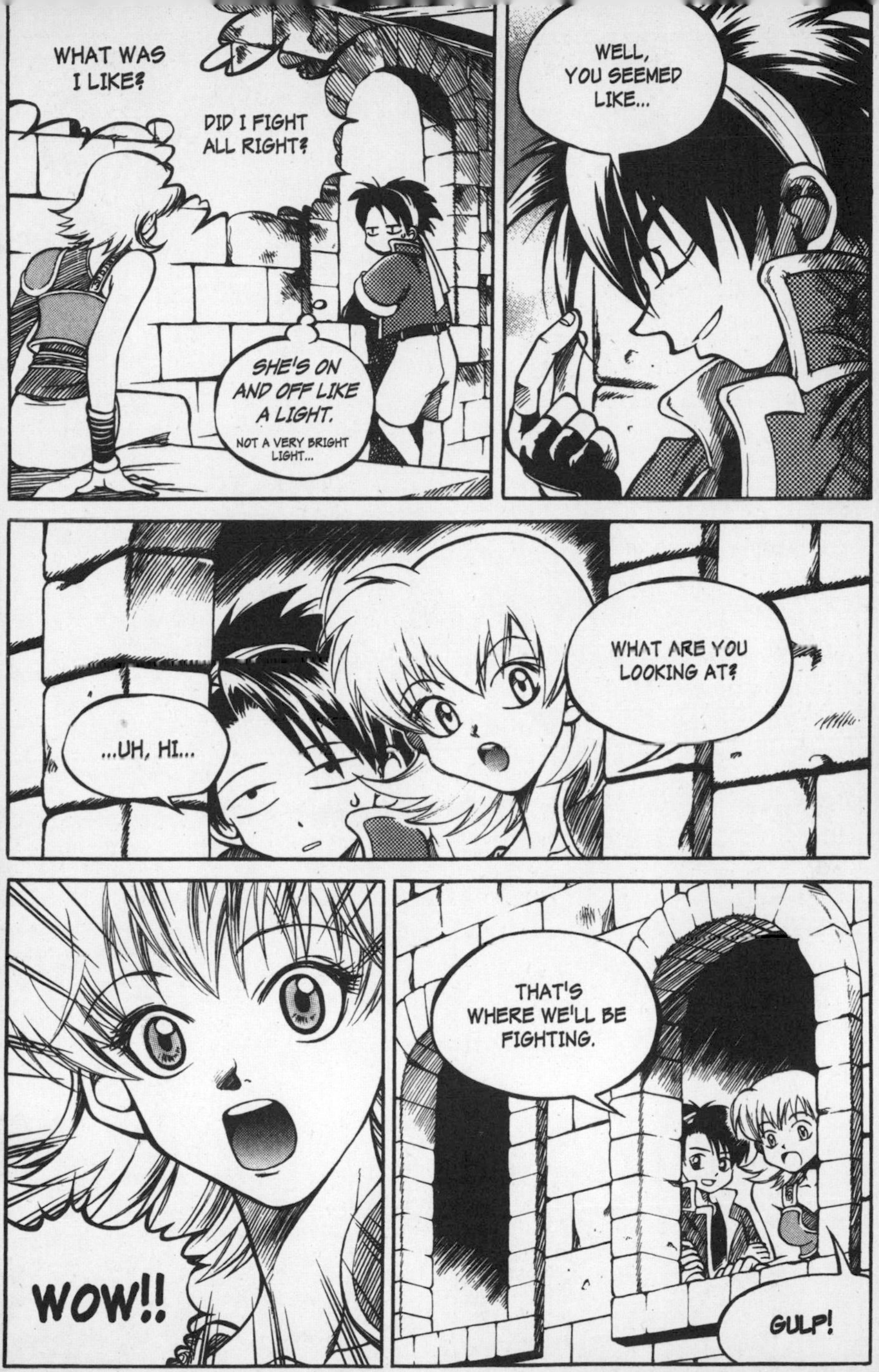
WHAT WAS I LIKE?
DID I FIGHT ALL RIGHT?
SHE'S ON AND OFF LIKE A LIGHT.
NOT A VERY BRIGHT LIGHT...
WELL, YOU SEEMED LIKE...
...UH, HI...
WHAT ARE YOU LOOKING AT?
WOW!!
THAT'S WHERE WE'LL BE FIGHTING.
GULP!

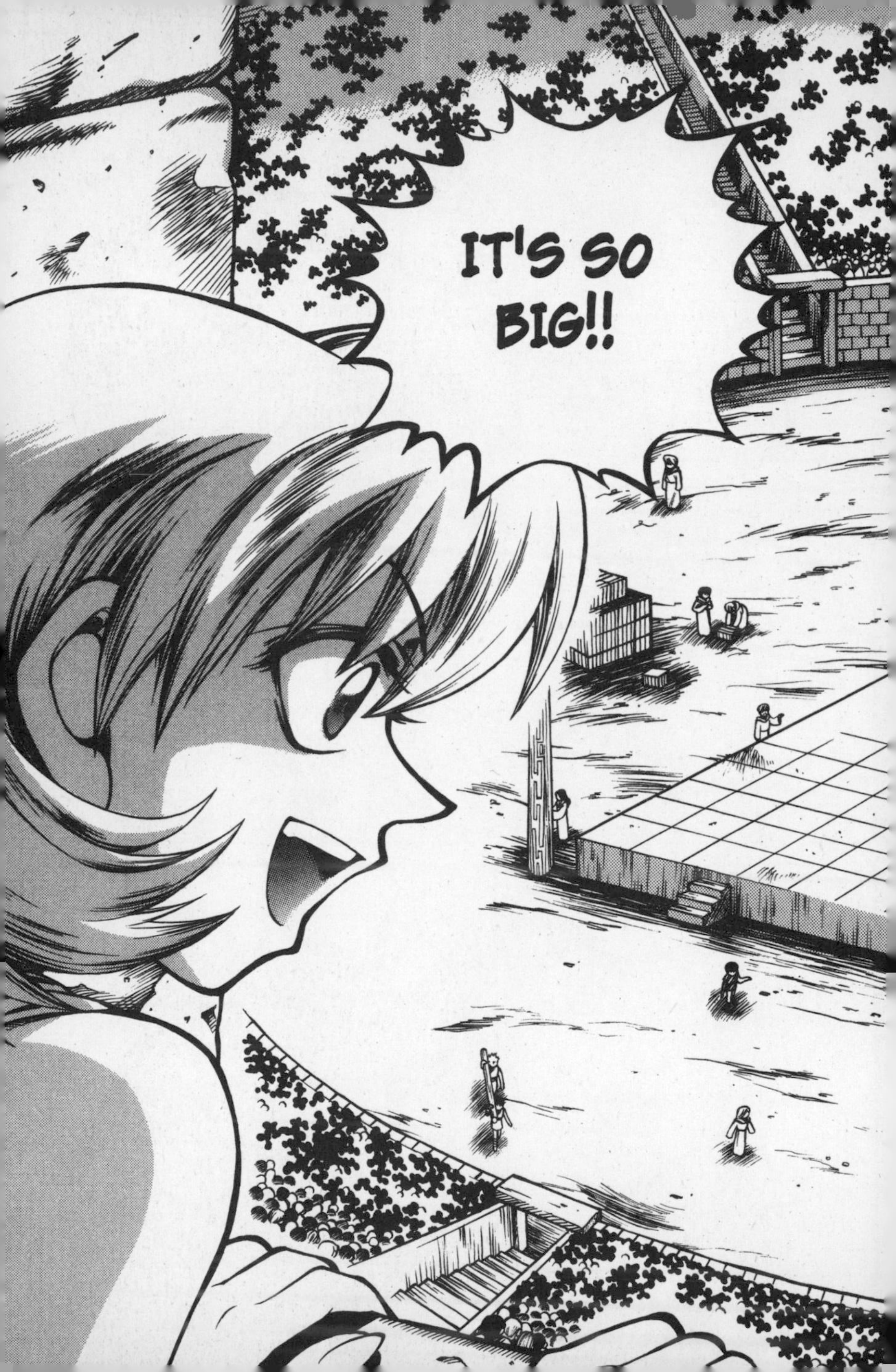
IT'S SO BIG!!

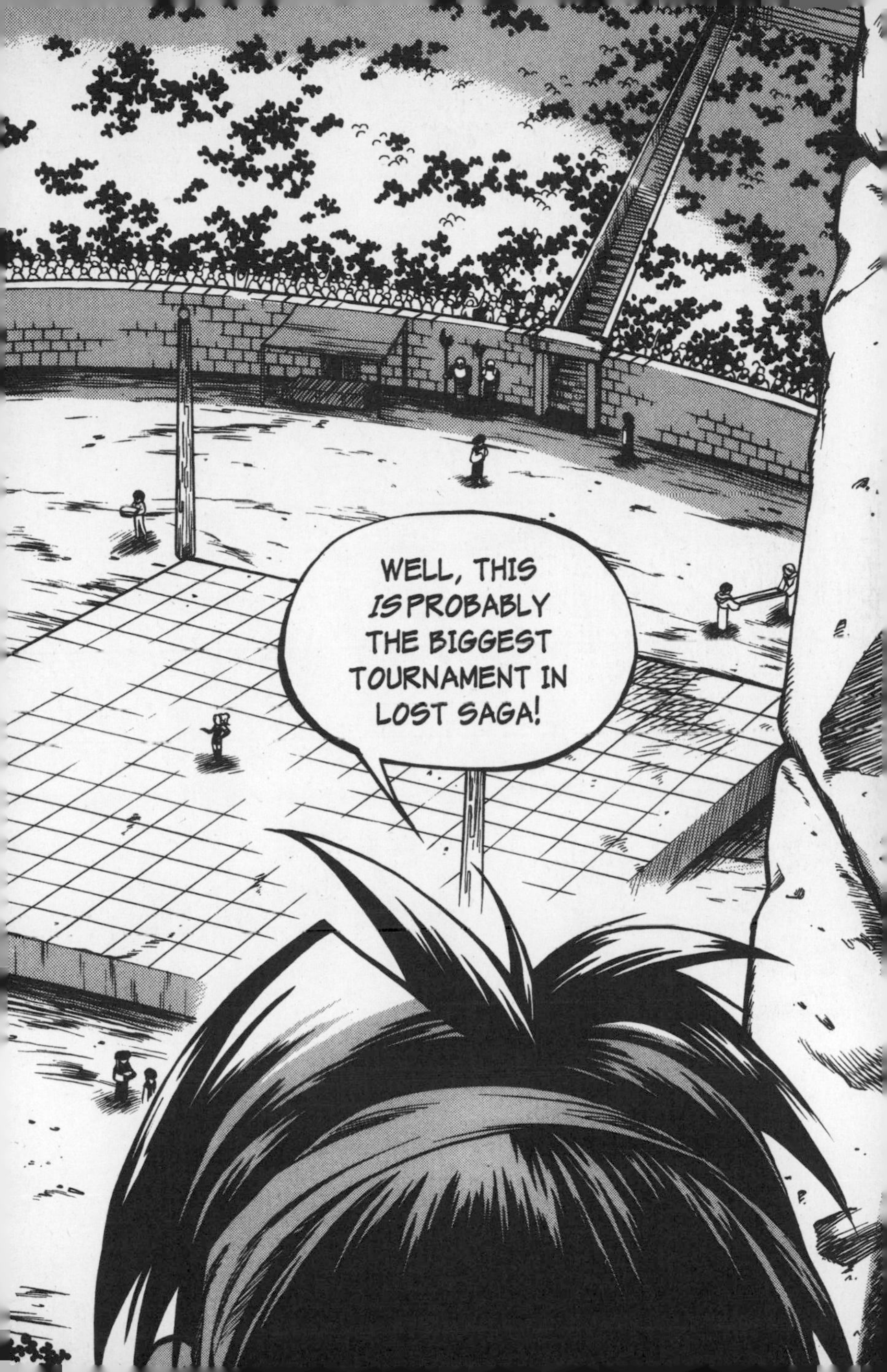
WELL, THIS *IS* PROBABLY THE BIGGEST TOURNAMENT IN LOST SAGA!

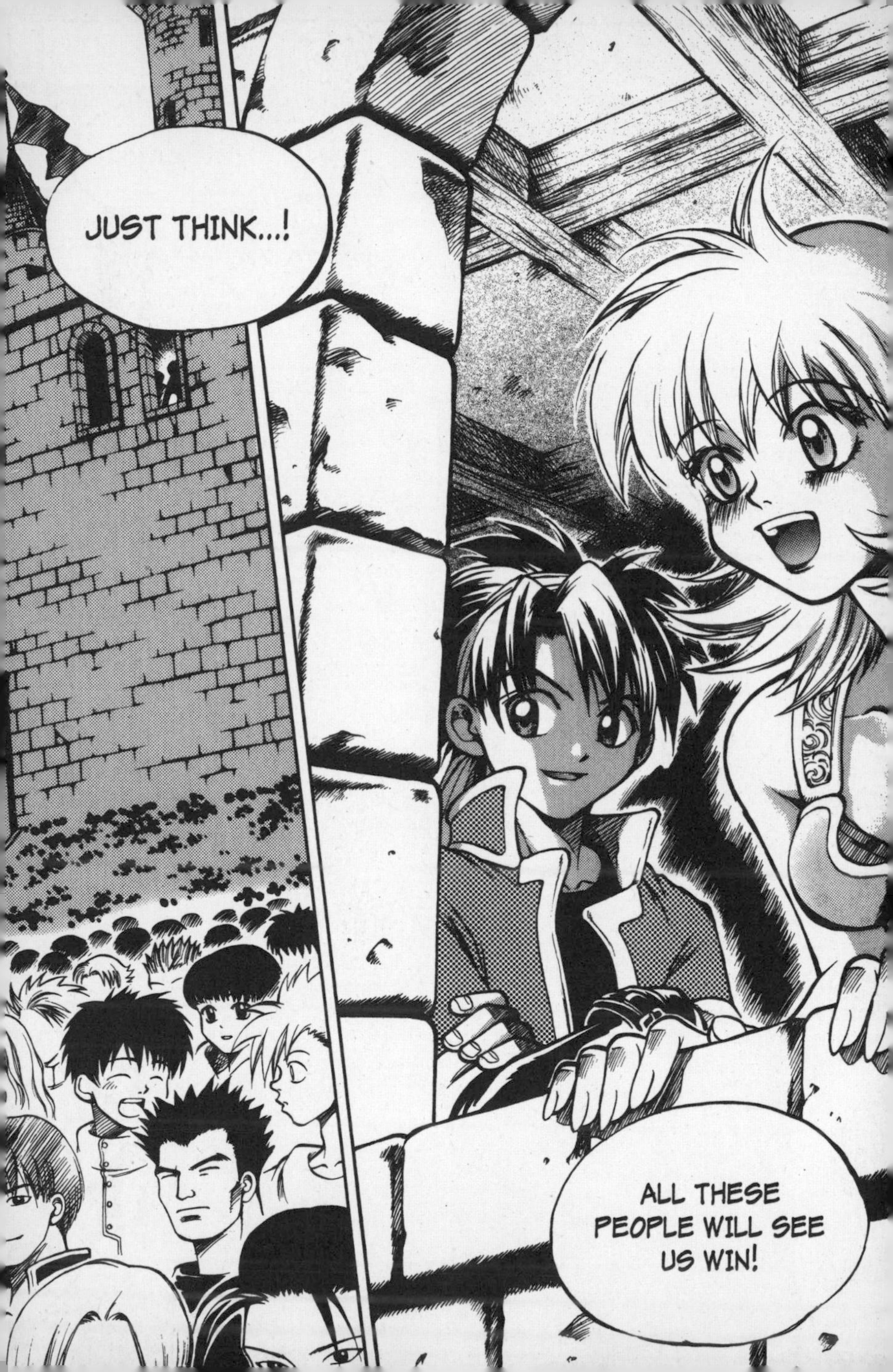
JUST THINK...!
ALL THESE PEOPLE WILL SEE US WIN!

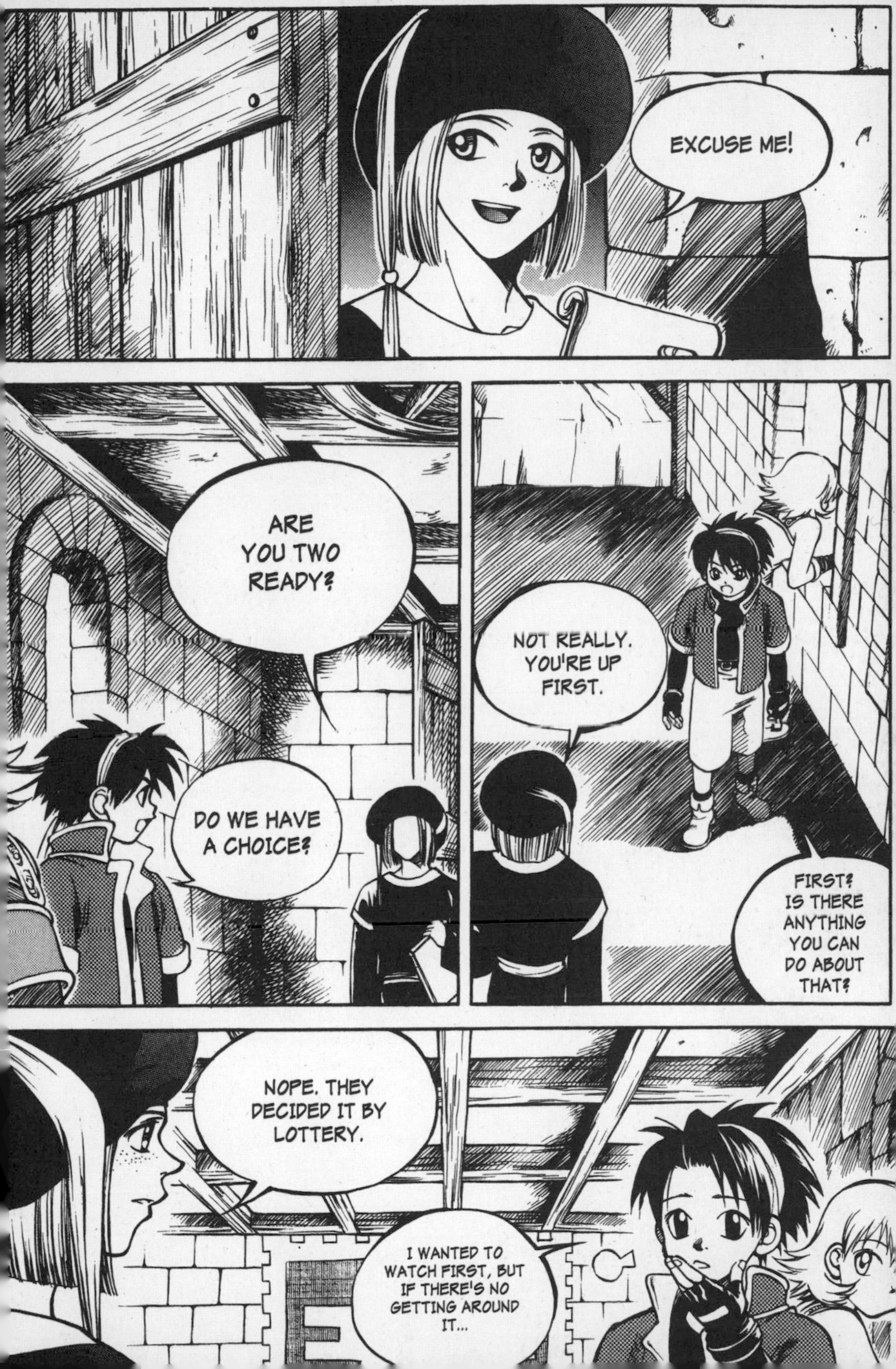
EXCUSE ME!
ARE YOU TWO READY?
DO WE HAVE A CHOICE?
NOT REALLY. YOU'RE UP FIRST.
FIRST? IS THERE ANYTHING YOU CAN DO ABOUT THAT?
NOPE. THEY DECIDED IT BY LOTTERY.
I WANTED TO WATCH FIRST, BUT IF THERE'S NO GETTING AROUND IT...

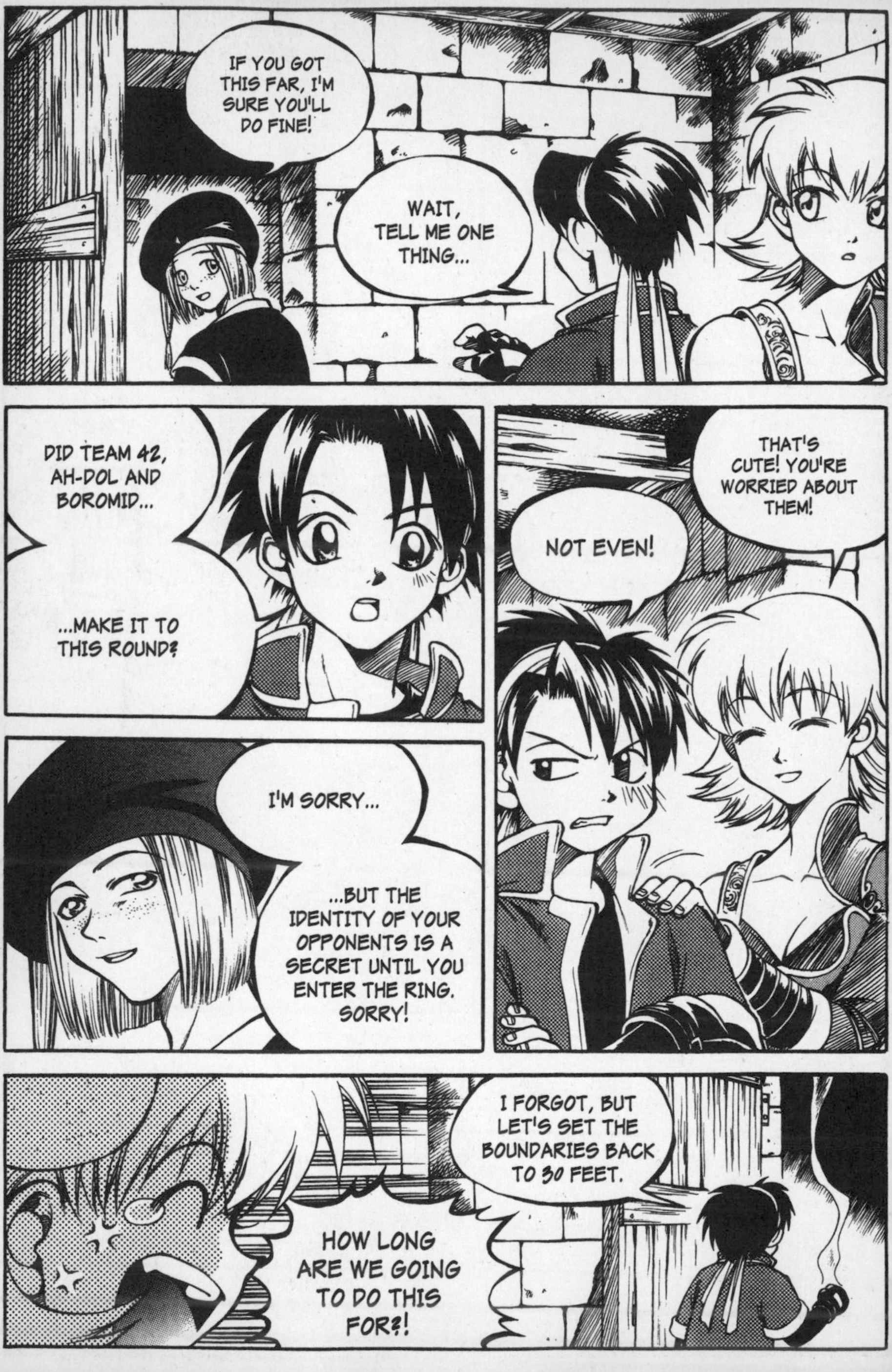
IF YOU GOT THIS FAR, I'M SURE YOU'LL DO FINE!
WAIT, TELL ME ONE THING...
DID TEAM 42, AH-DOL AND BOROMID...
...MAKE IT TO THIS ROUND?
THAT'S CUTE! YOU'RE WORRIED ABOUT THEM!
NOT EVEN!
I'M SORRY...
...BUT THE IDENTITY OF YOUR OPPONENTS IS A SECRET UNTIL YOU ENTER THE RING. SORRY!
HOW LONG ARE WE GOING TO DO THIS FOR?!
I FORGOT, BUT LET'S SET THE BOUNDARIES BACK TO 30 FEET.

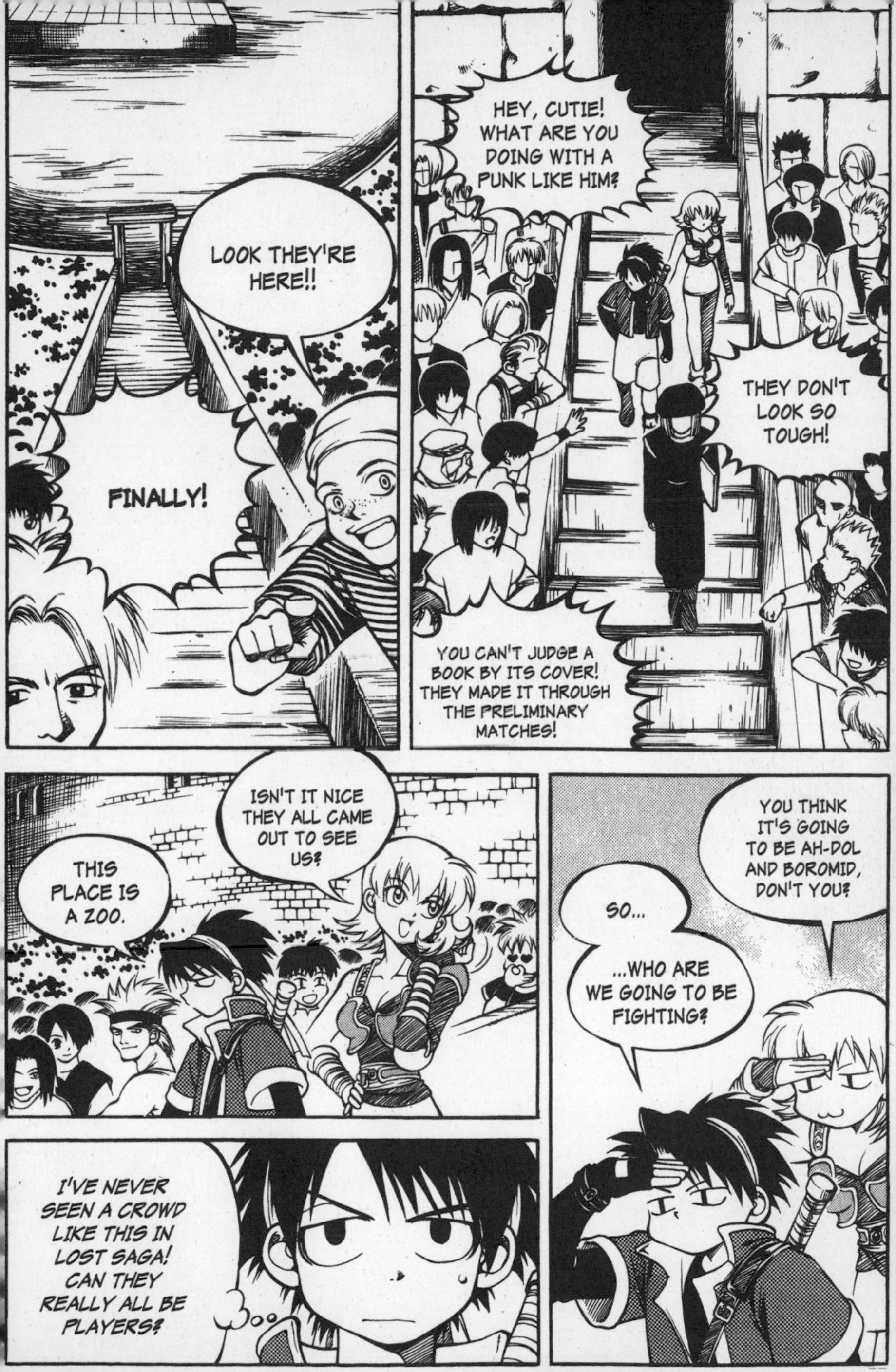
LOOK THEY'RE HERE!!
FINALLY!
HEY, CUTIE! WHAT ARE YOU DOING WITH A PUNK LIKE HIM?
THEY DON'T LOOK SO TOUGH!
YOU CAN'T JUDGE A BOOK BY ITS COVER! THEY MADE IT THROUGH THE PRELIMINARY MATCHES!
THIS PLACE IS A ZOO.
ISN'T IT NICE THEY ALL CAME OUT TO SEE US?
I'VE NEVER SEEN A CROWD LIKE THIS IN LOST SAGA! CAN THEY REALLY ALL BE PLAYERS?
SO...
...WHO ARE WE GOING TO BE FIGHTING?
YOU THINK IT'S GOING TO BE AH-DOL AND BOROMID, DON'T YOU?

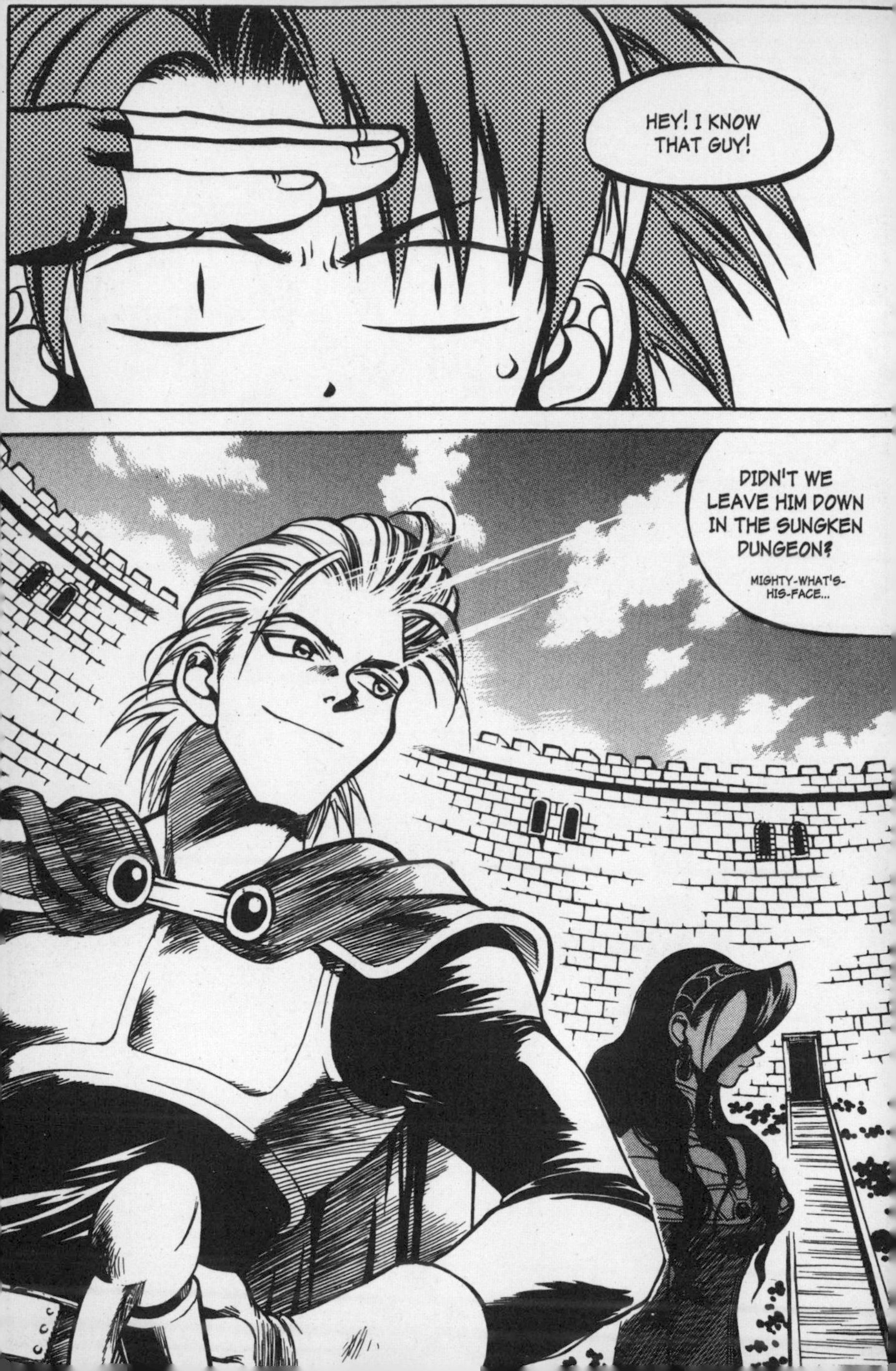
HEY! I KNOW THAT GUY!
DIDN'T WE LEAVE HIM DOWN IN THE SUNGKEN DUNGEON?
MIGHTY-WHAT'S-HIS-FACE...

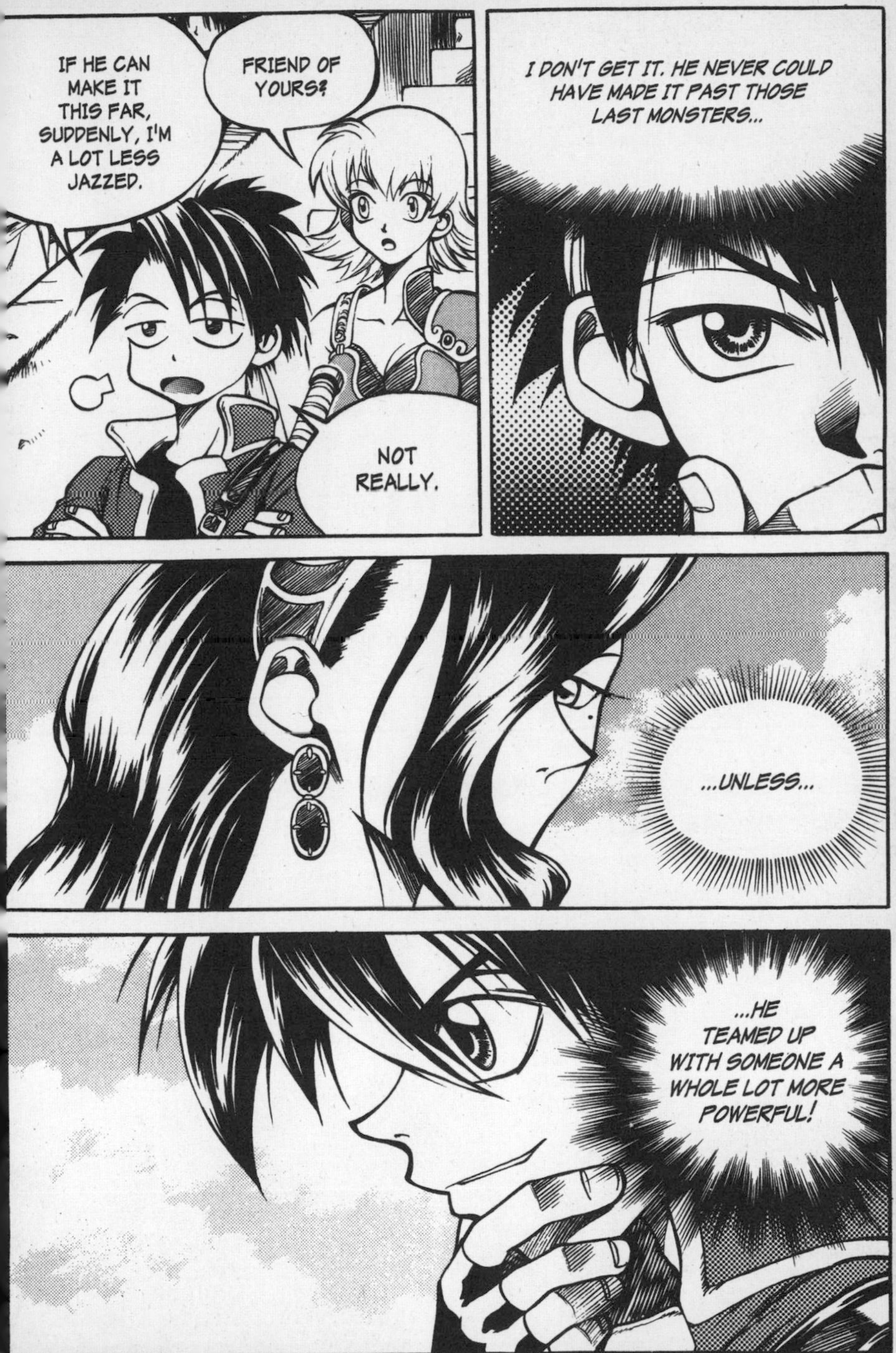
IF HE CAN MAKE IT THIS FAR, SUDDENLY, I'M A LOT LESS JAZZED.
FRIEND OF YOURS?
NOT REALLY.
I DON'T GET IT. HE NEVER COULD HAVE MADE IT PAST THOSE LAST MONSTERS...
...UNLESS...
...HE TEAMED UP WITH SOMEONE A WHOLE LOT MORE POWERFUL!

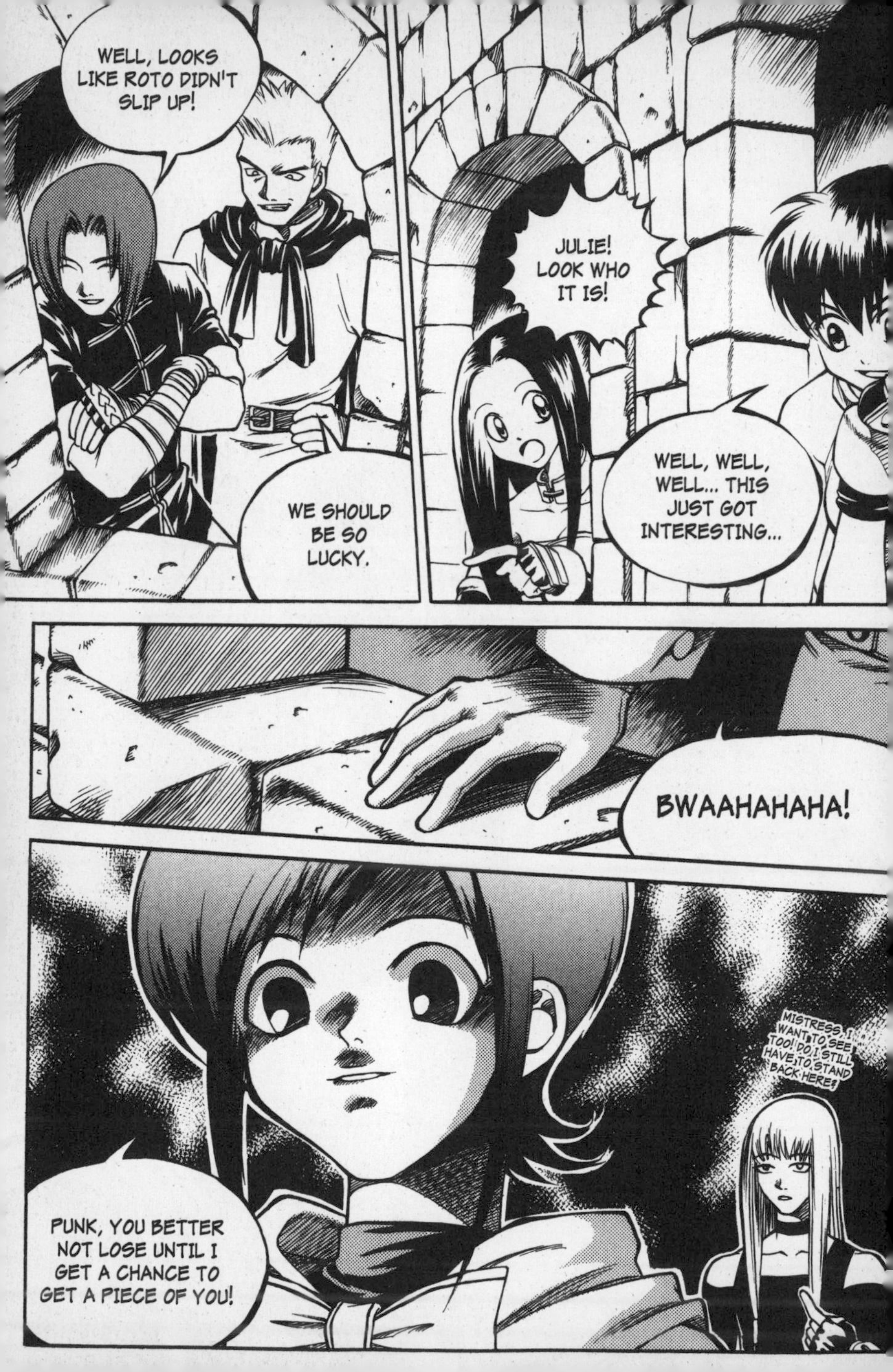
WELL, LOOKS LIKE ROTO DIDN'T SLIP UP!
WE SHOULD BE SO LUCKY.
JULIE! LOOK WHO IT IS!
WELL, WELL, WELL... THIS JUST GOT INTERESTING...
BWAAHAHAHA!
PUNK, YOU BETTER NOT LOSE UNTIL I GET A CHANCE TO GET A PIECE OF YOU!
MISTRESS, I WANT TO SEE TOO! DO I STILL HAVE TO STAND BACK HERE?

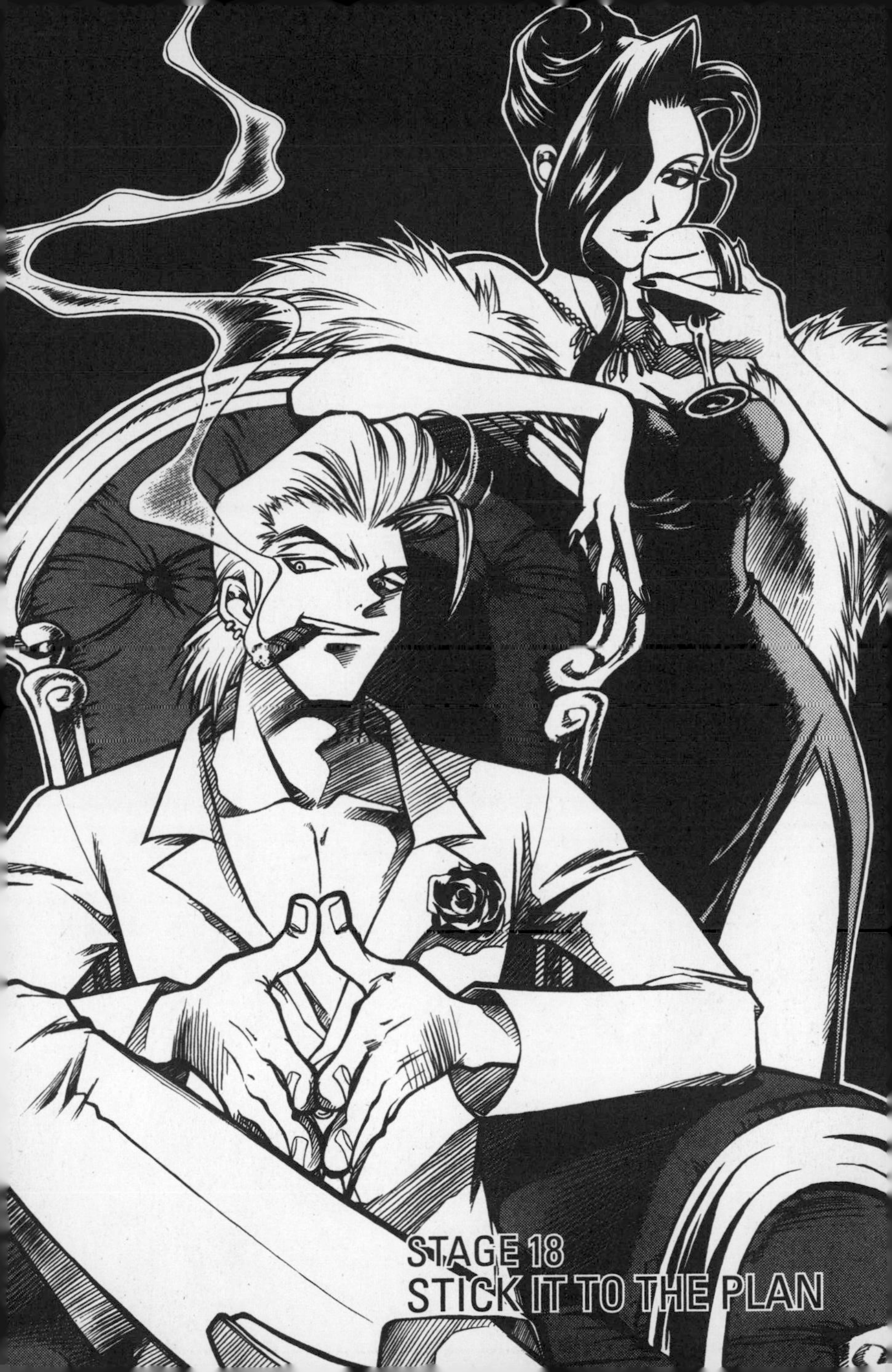
STAGE 18
STICK IT TO THE PLAN

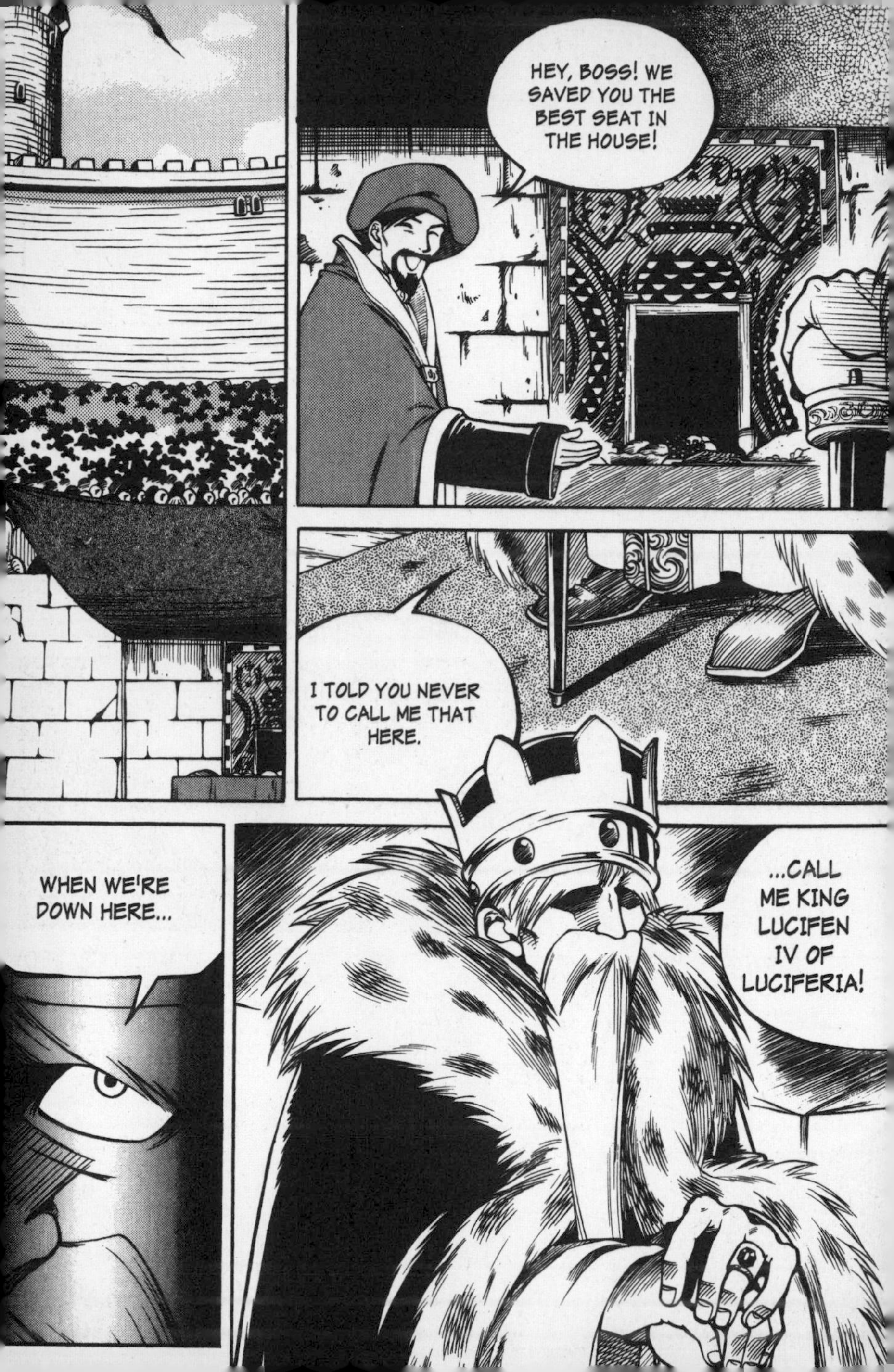
HEY, BOSS! WE SAVED YOU THE BEST SEAT IN THE HOUSE!
I TOLD YOU NEVER TO CALL ME THAT HERE.
WHEN WE'RE DOWN HERE...
...CALL ME KING LUCIFEN IV OF LUCIFERIA!

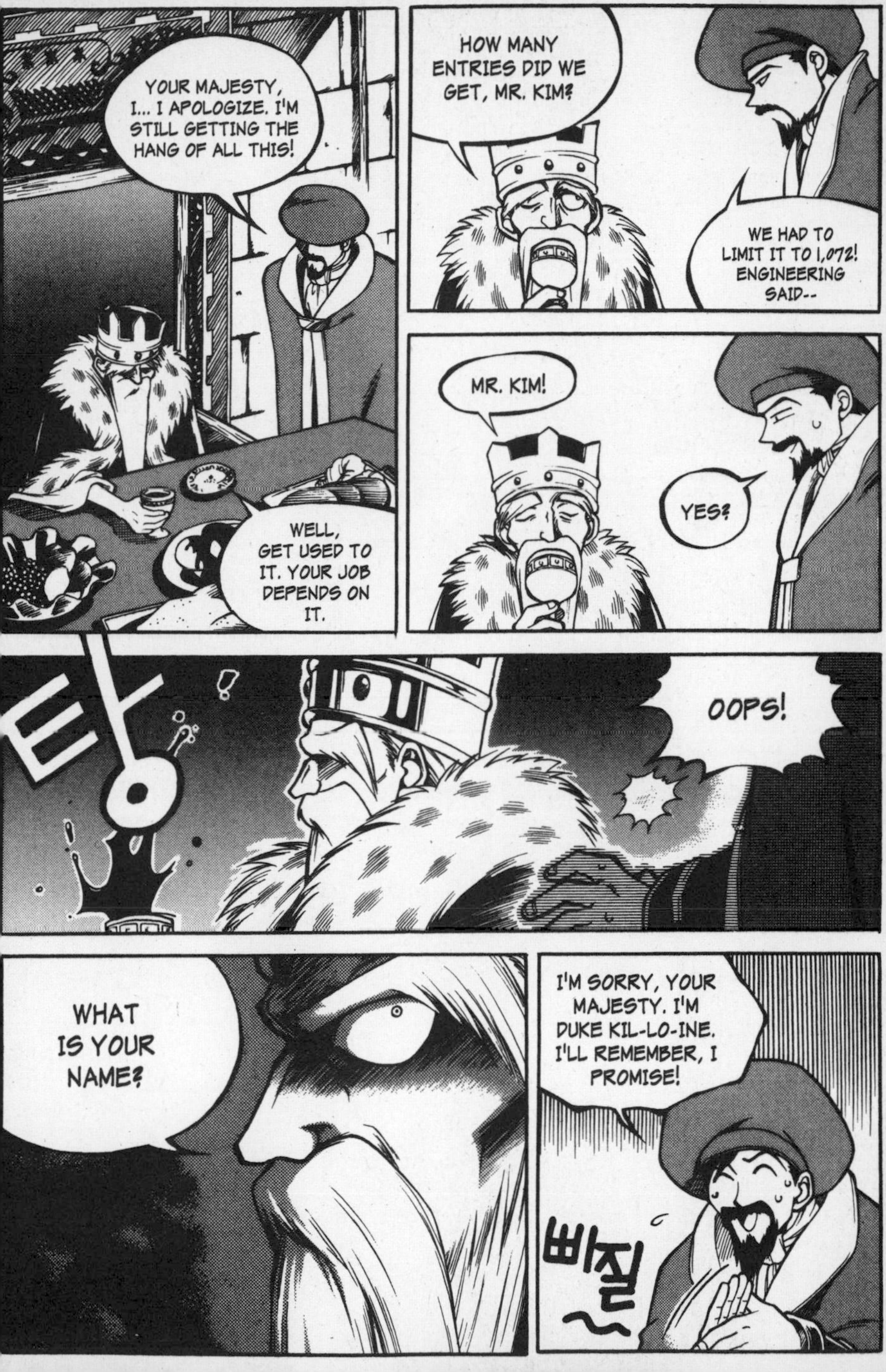
YOUR MAJESTY, I... I APOLOGIZE. I'M STILL GETTING THE HANG OF ALL THIS!
WELL, GET USED TO IT. YOUR JOB DEPENDS ON IT.
HOW MANY ENTRIES DID WE GET, MR. KIM?
WE HAD TO LIMIT IT TO 1,072! ENGINEERING SAID--
MR. KIM!
YES?
OOPS!
WHAT IS YOUR NAME?
I'M SORRY, YOUR MAJESTY. I'M DUKE KIL-LO-INE. I'LL REMEMBER, I PROMISE!
삐질~

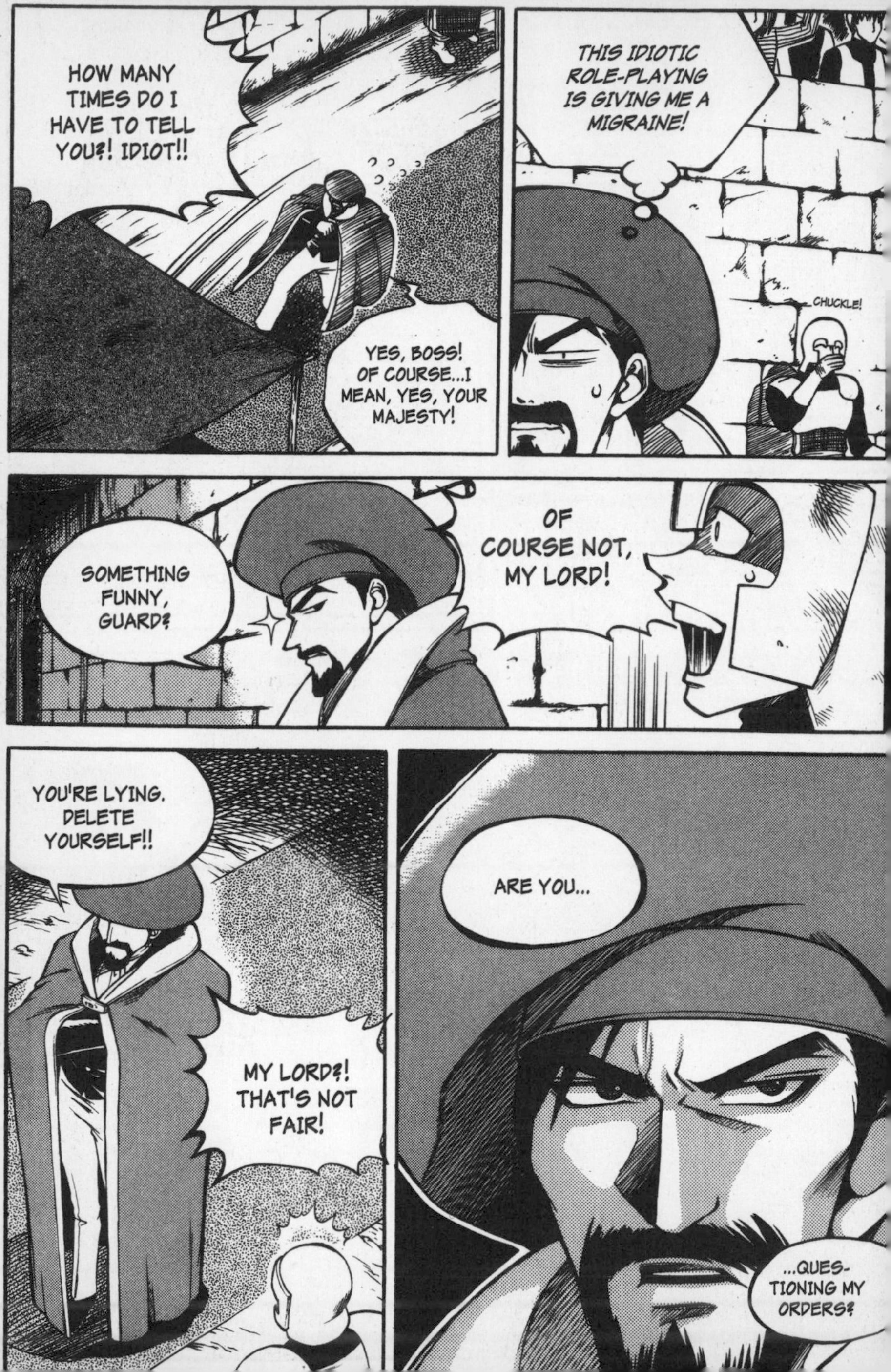
HOW MANY TIMES DO I HAVE TO TELL YOU?! IDIOT!!
YES, BOSS! OF COURSE...I MEAN, YES, YOUR MAJESTY!
THIS IDIOTIC ROLE-PLAYING IS GIVING ME A MIGRAINE!
CHUCKLE!
SOMETHING FUNNY, GUARD?
OF COURSE NOT, MY LORD!
YOU'RE LYING. DELETE YOURSELF!!
MY LORD?! THAT'S NOT FAIR!
ARE YOU...
...QUES-TIONING MY ORDERS?

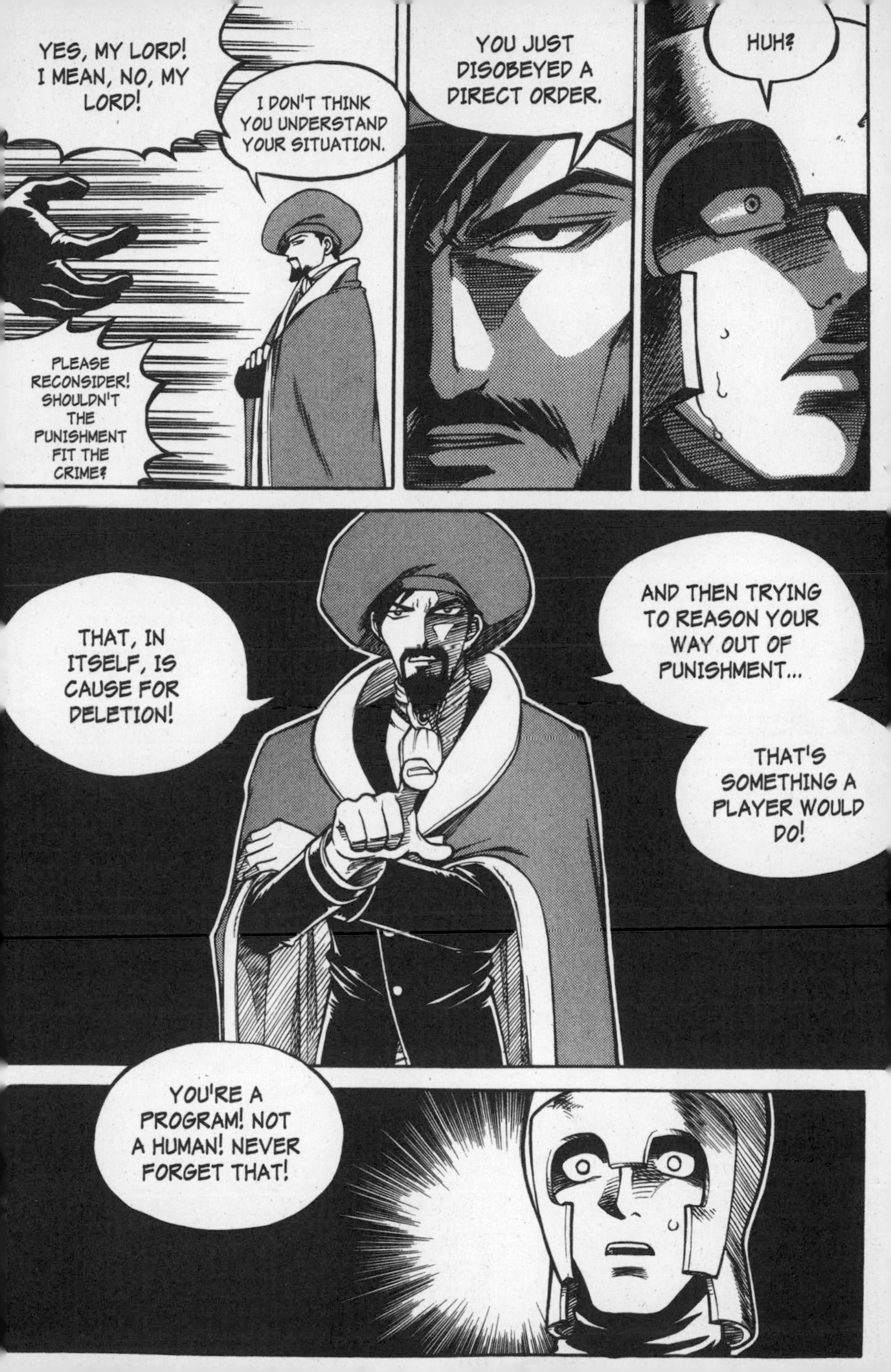
YES, MY LORD! I MEAN, NO, MY LORD!
I DON'T THINK YOU UNDERSTAND YOUR SITUATION.
PLEASE RECONSIDER! SHOULDN'T THE PUNISHMENT FIT THE CRIME?
YOU JUST DISOBEYED A DIRECT ORDER.
HUH?
THAT, IN ITSELF, IS CAUSE FOR DELETION!
AND THEN TRYING TO REASON YOUR WAY OUT OF PUNISHMENT...
THAT'S SOMETHING A PLAYER WOULD DO!
YOU'RE A PROGRAM! NOT A HUMAN! NEVER FORGET THAT!

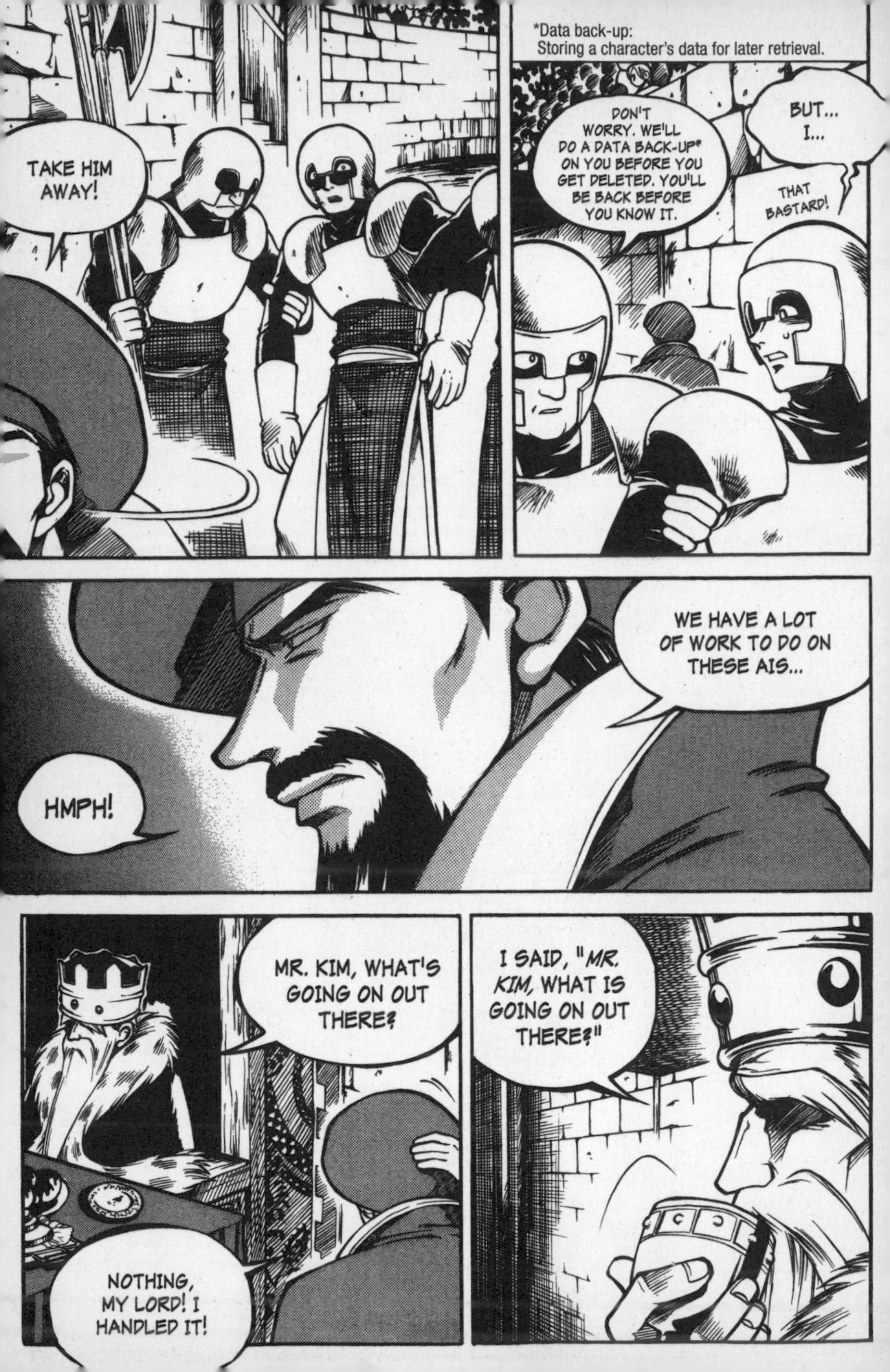
TAKE HIM AWAY!
*Data back-up:
Storing a character's data for later retrieval.
DON'T WORRY. WE'LL DO A DATA BACK-UP* ON YOU BEFORE YOU GET DELETED. YOU'LL BE BACK BEFORE YOU KNOW IT.
BUT... I...
THAT BASTARD!
HMPH!
WE HAVE A LOT OF WORK TO DO ON THESE AIS...
MR. KIM, WHAT'S GOING ON OUT THERE?
NOTHING, MY LORD! I HANDLED IT!
I SAID, "MR. KIM, WHAT IS GOING ON OUT THERE?"

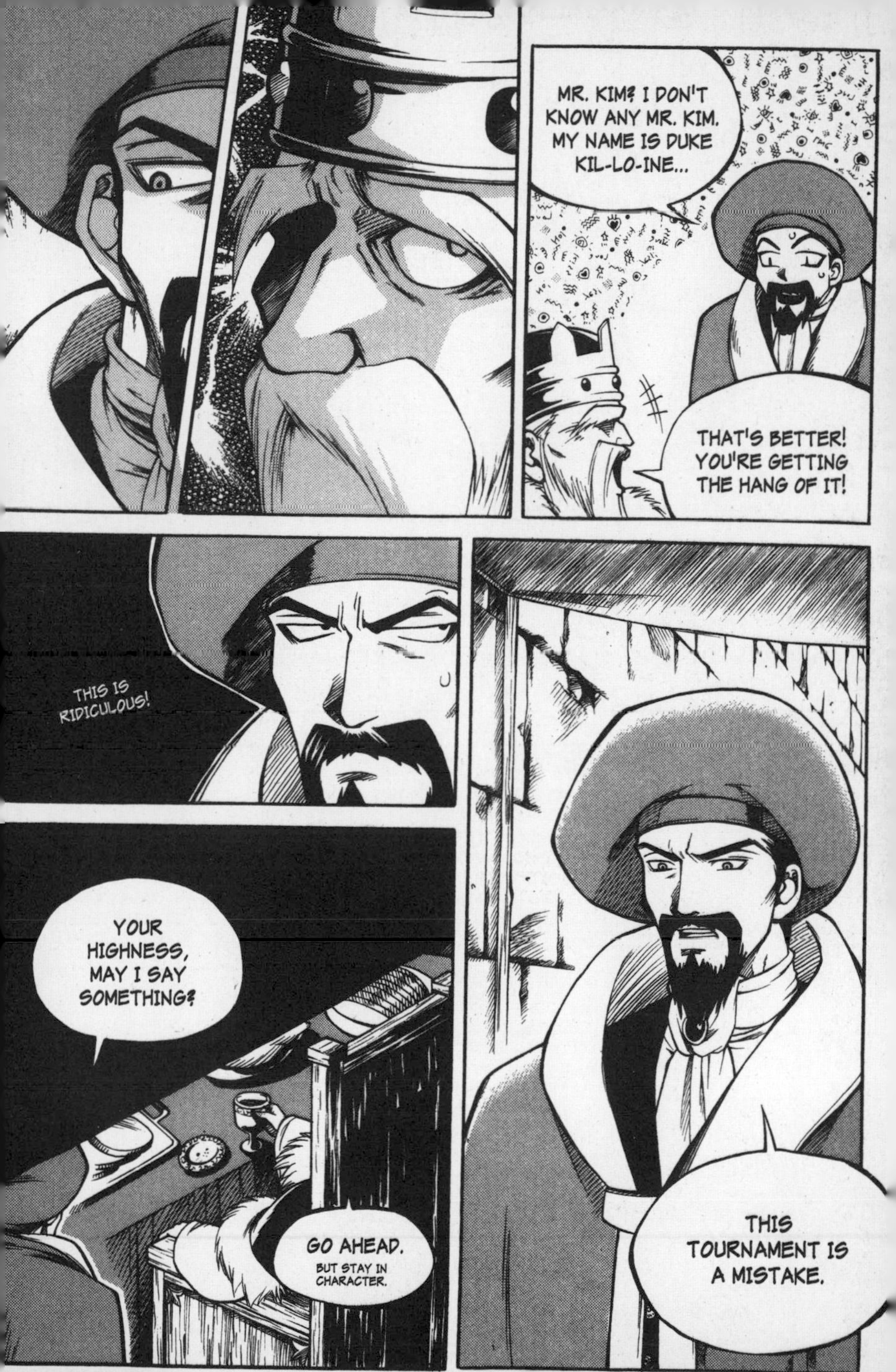
MR. KIM? I DON'T KNOW ANY MR. KIM. MY NAME IS DUKE KIL-LO-INE...
THAT'S BETTER! YOU'RE GETTING THE HANG OF IT!
THIS IS RIDICULOUS!
YOUR HIGHNESS, MAY I SAY SOMETHING?
GO AHEAD.
BUT STAY IN CHARACTER.
THIS TOURNAMENT IS A MISTAKE.

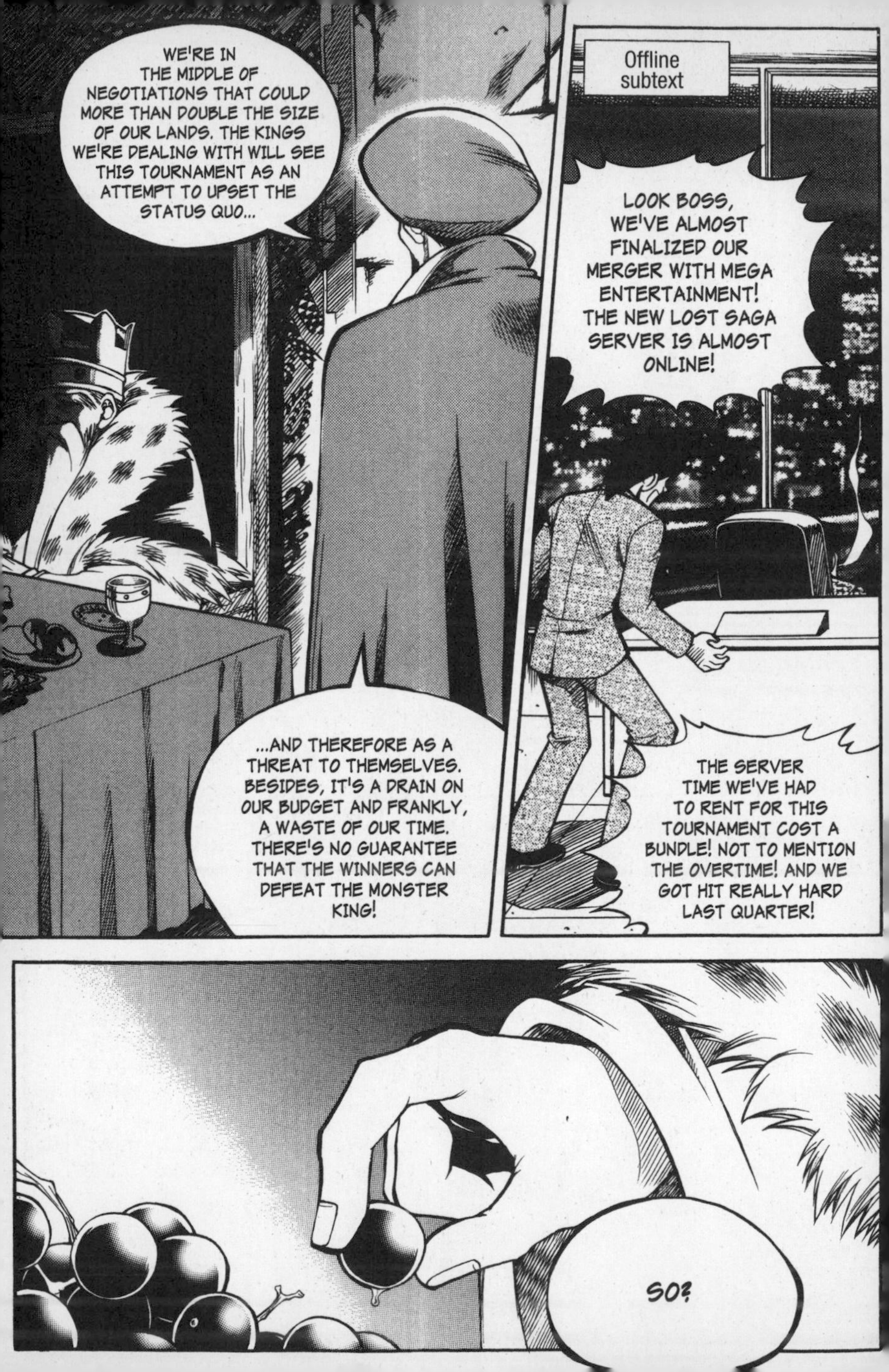
WE'RE IN THE MIDDLE OF NEGOTIATIONS THAT COULD MORE THAN DOUBLE THE SIZE OF OUR LANDS. THE KINGS WE'RE DEALING WITH WILL SEE THIS TOURNAMENT AS AN ATTEMPT TO UPSET THE STATUS QUO...
...AND THEREFORE AS A THREAT TO THEMSELVES. BESIDES, IT'S A DRAIN ON OUR BUDGET AND FRANKLY, A WASTE OF OUR TIME. THERE'S NO GUARANTEE THAT THE WINNERS CAN DEFEAT THE MONSTER KING!
Offline subtext
LOOK BOSS, WE'VE ALMOST FINALIZED OUR MERGER WITH MEGA ENTERTAINMENT! THE NEW LOST SAGA SERVER IS ALMOST ONLINE!
THE SERVER TIME WE'VE HAD TO RENT FOR THIS TOURNAMENT COST A BUNDLE! NOT TO MENTION THE OVERTIME! AND WE GOT HIT REALLY HARD LAST QUARTER!
SO?

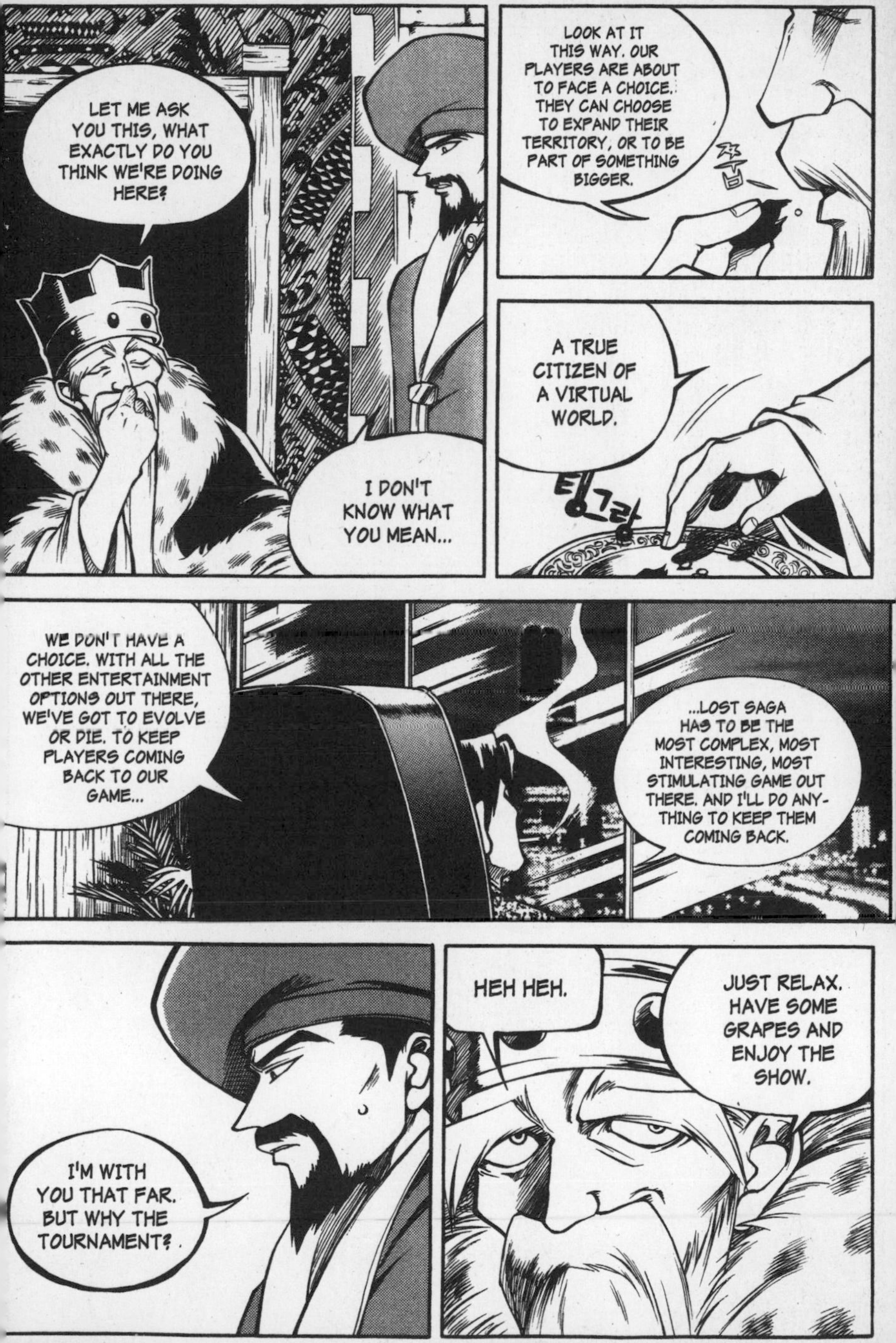
LET ME ASK YOU THIS, WHAT EXACTLY DO YOU THINK WE'RE DOING HERE?
I DON'T KNOW WHAT YOU MEAN...
LOOK AT IT THIS WAY. OUR PLAYERS ARE ABOUT TO FACE A CHOICE. THEY CAN CHOOSE TO EXPAND THEIR TERRITORY, OR TO BE PART OF SOMETHING BIGGER.
A TRUE CITIZEN OF A VIRTUAL WORLD.
WE DON'T HAVE A CHOICE. WITH ALL THE OTHER ENTERTAINMENT OPTIONS OUT THERE, WE'VE GOT TO EVOLVE OR DIE. TO KEEP PLAYERS COMING BACK TO OUR GAME...
...LOST SAGA HAS TO BE THE MOST COMPLEX, MOST INTERESTING, MOST STIMULATING GAME OUT THERE. AND I'LL DO ANY-THING TO KEEP THEM COMING BACK.
I'M WITH YOU THAT FAR. BUT WHY THE TOURNAMENT?
HEH HEH.
JUST RELAX. HAVE SOME GRAPES AND ENJOY THE SHOW.

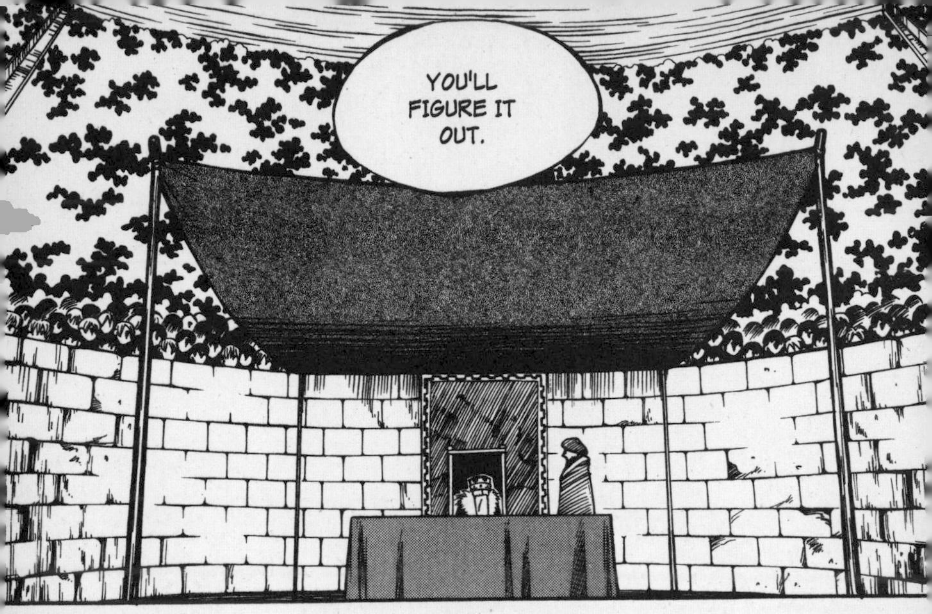
YOU'LL FIGURE IT OUT.

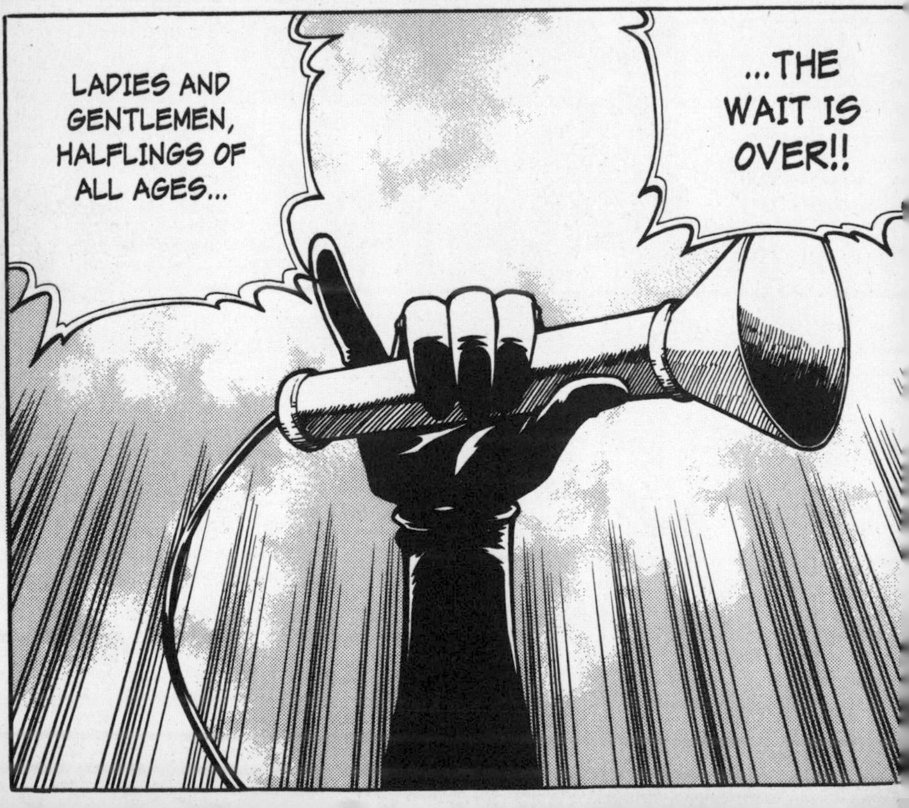
LADIES AND GENTLEMEN, HALFLINGS OF ALL AGES...
...THE WAIT IS OVER!!

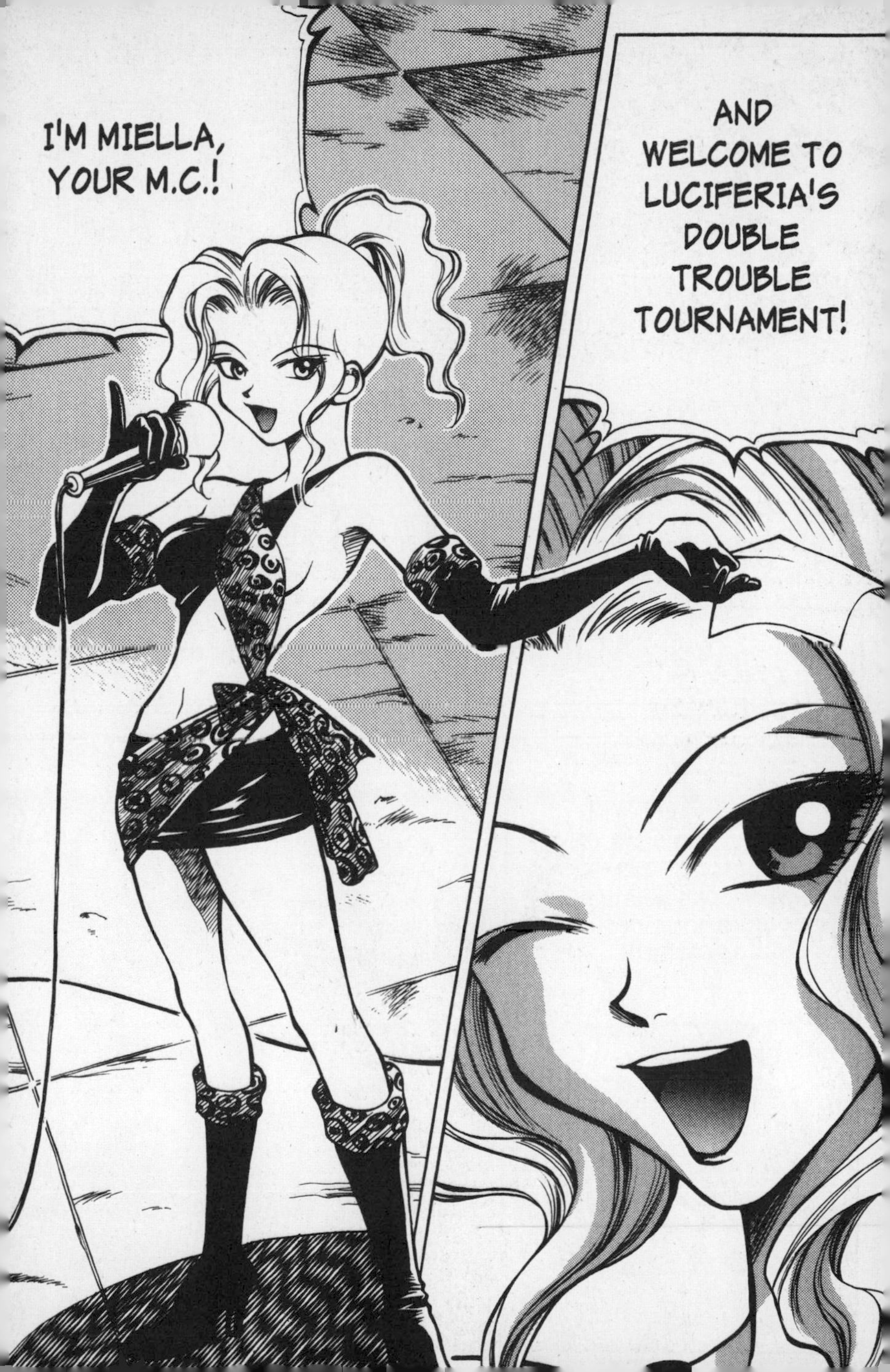
I'M MIELLA, YOUR M.C.!
AND WELCOME TO LUCIFERIA'S DOUBLE TROUBLE TOURNAMENT!

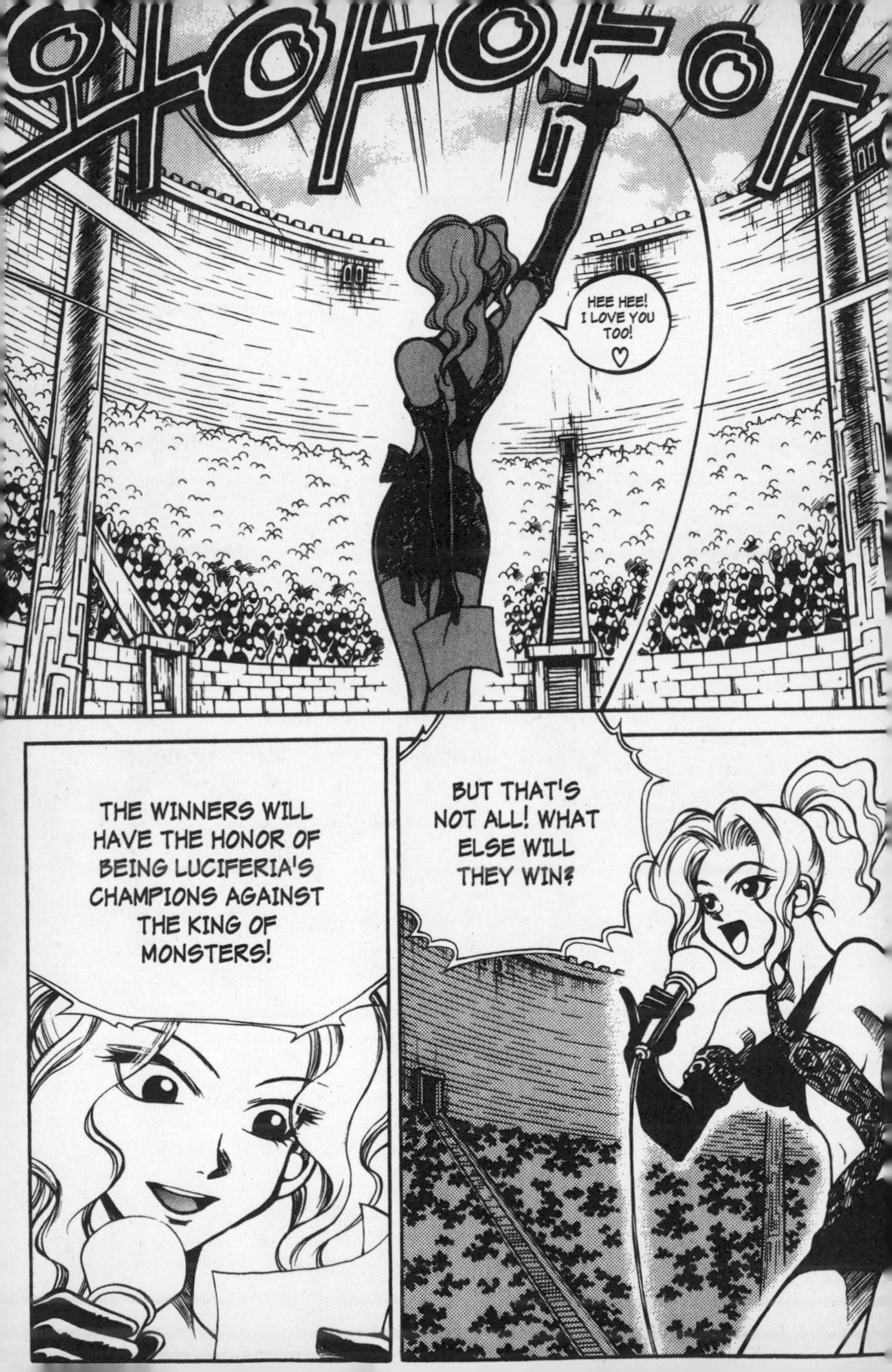
HEE HEE! I LOVE YOU TOO! ♡
THE WINNERS WILL HAVE THE HONOR OF BEING LUCIFERIA'S CHAMPIONS AGAINST THE KING OF MONSTERS!
BUT THAT'S NOT ALL! WHAT ELSE WILL THEY WIN?

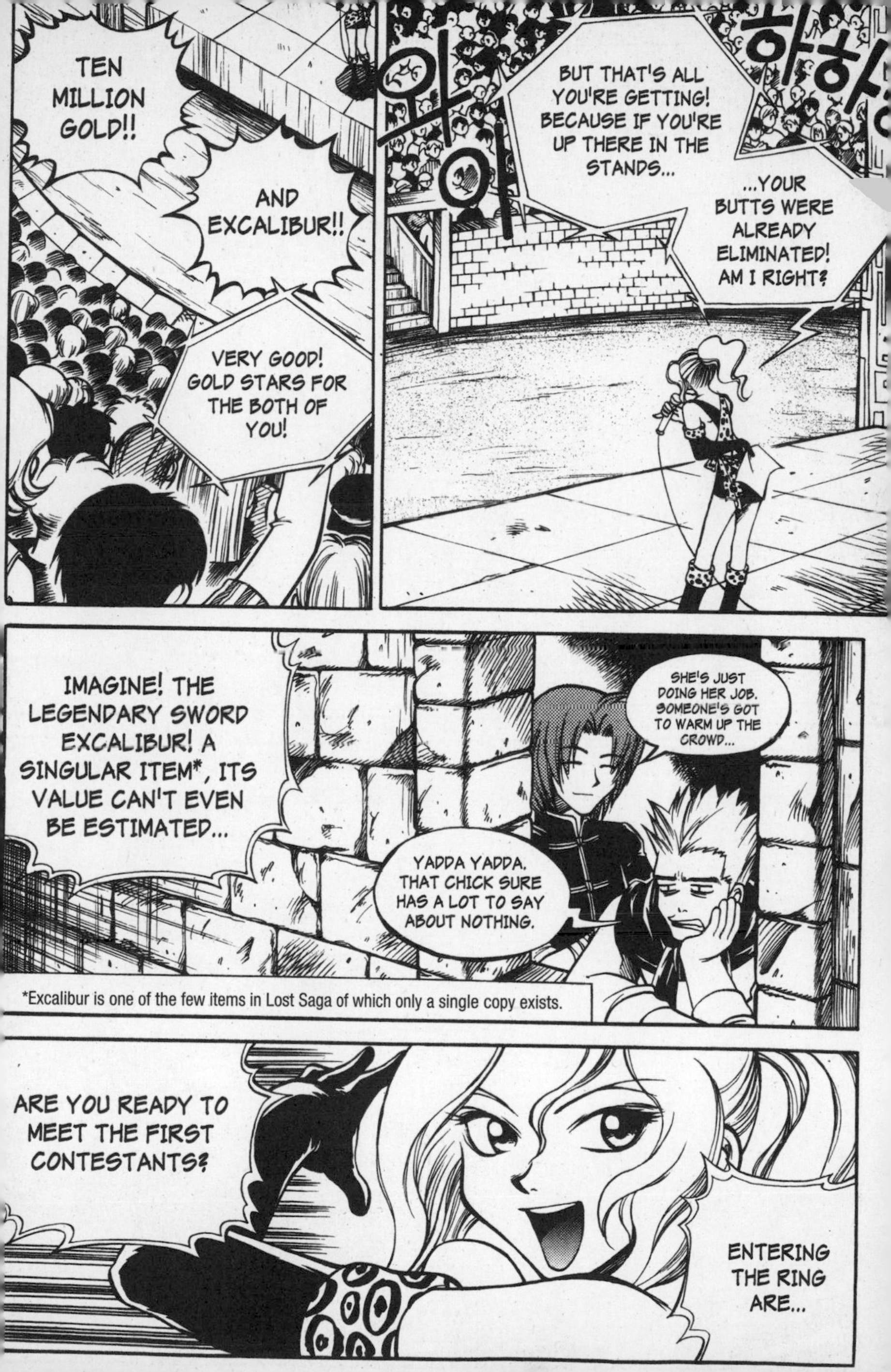
TEN MILLION GOLD!!
AND EXCALIBUR!!
VERY GOOD! GOLD STARS FOR THE BOTH OF YOU!
BUT THAT'S ALL YOU'RE GETTING! BECAUSE IF YOU'RE UP THERE IN THE STANDS...
...YOUR BUTTS WERE ALREADY ELIMINATED! AM I RIGHT?
IMAGINE! THE LEGENDARY SWORD EXCALIBUR! A SINGULAR ITEM*, ITS VALUE CAN'T EVEN BE ESTIMATED...
SHE'S JUST DOING HER JOB. SOMEONE'S GOT TO WARM UP THE CROWD...
YADDA YADDA. THAT CHICK SURE HAS A LOT TO SAY ABOUT NOTHING.
*Excalibur is one of the few items in Lost Saga of which only a single copy exists.
ARE YOU READY TO MEET THE FIRST CONTESTANTS?
ENTERING THE RING ARE...

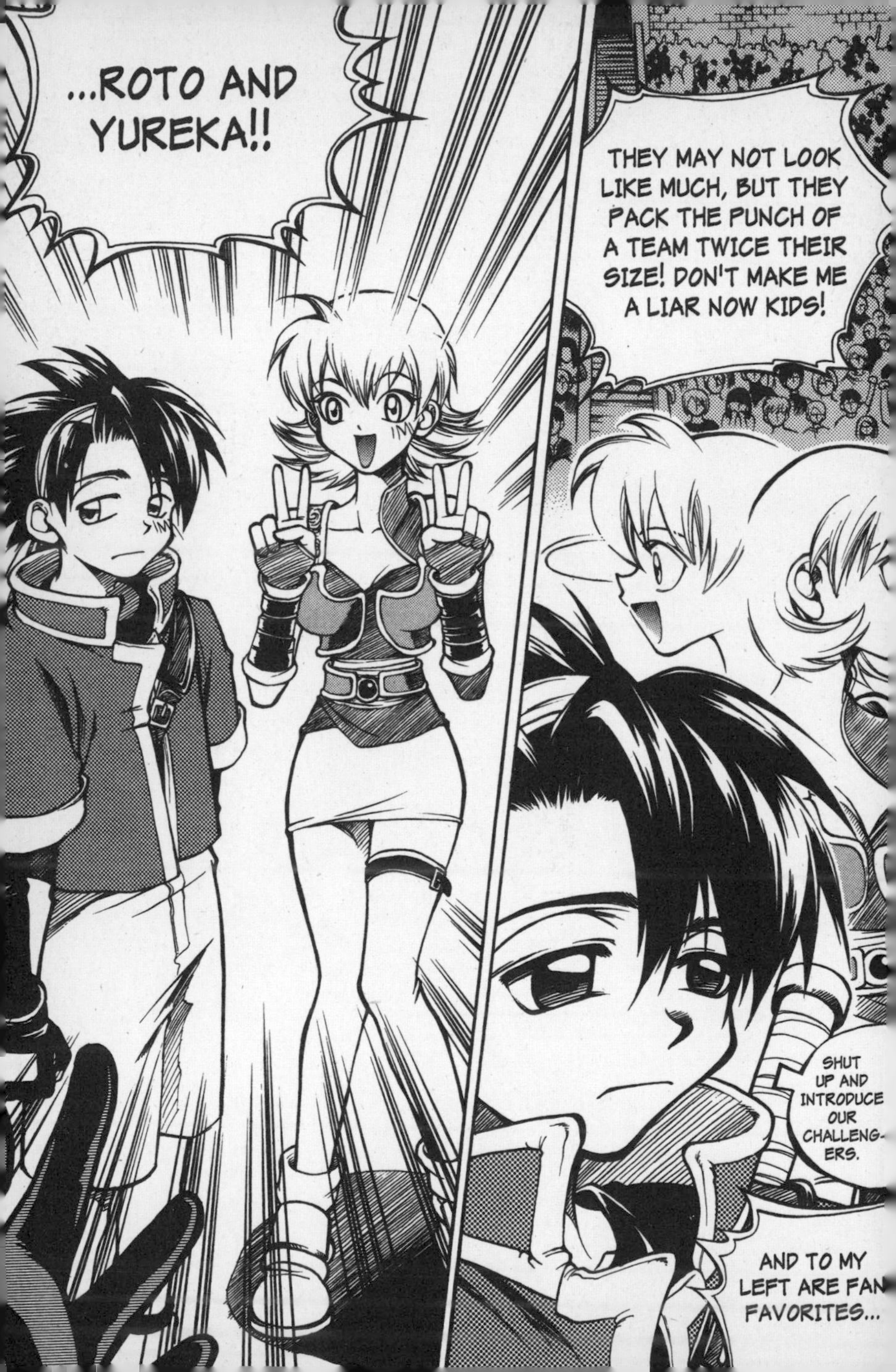
...ROTO AND YUREKA!!
THEY MAY NOT LOOK LIKE MUCH, BUT THEY PACK THE PUNCH OF A TEAM TWICE THEIR SIZE! DON'T MAKE ME A LIAR NOW KIDS!
SHUT UP AND INTRODUCE OUR CHALLENG- ERS.
AND TO MY LEFT ARE FAN FAVORITES...

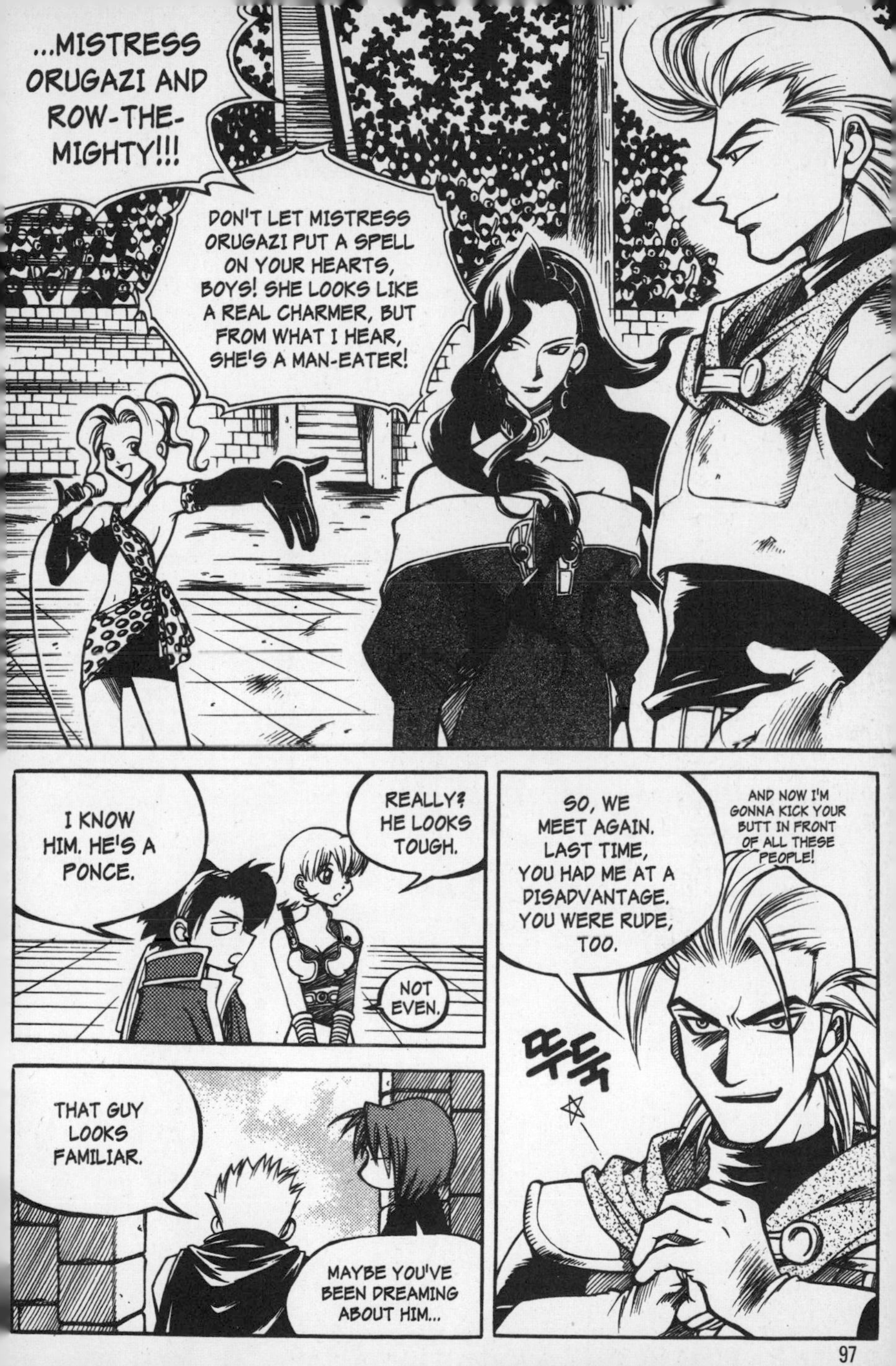
...MISTRESS ORUGAZI AND ROW-THE-MIGHTY!!!
DON'T LET MISTRESS ORUGAZI PUT A SPELL ON YOUR HEARTS, BOYS! SHE LOOKS LIKE A REAL CHARMER, BUT FROM WHAT I HEAR, SHE'S A MAN-EATER!
I KNOW HIM. HE'S A PONCE.
REALLY? HE LOOKS TOUGH.
NOT EVEN.
THAT GUY LOOKS FAMILIAR.
MAYBE YOU'VE BEEN DREAMING ABOUT HIM...
SO, WE MEET AGAIN. LAST TIME, YOU HAD ME AT A DISADVANTAGE. YOU WERE RUDE, TOO.
AND NOW I'M GONNA KICK YOUR BUTT IN FRONT OF ALL THESE PEOPLE!
뚜두둑

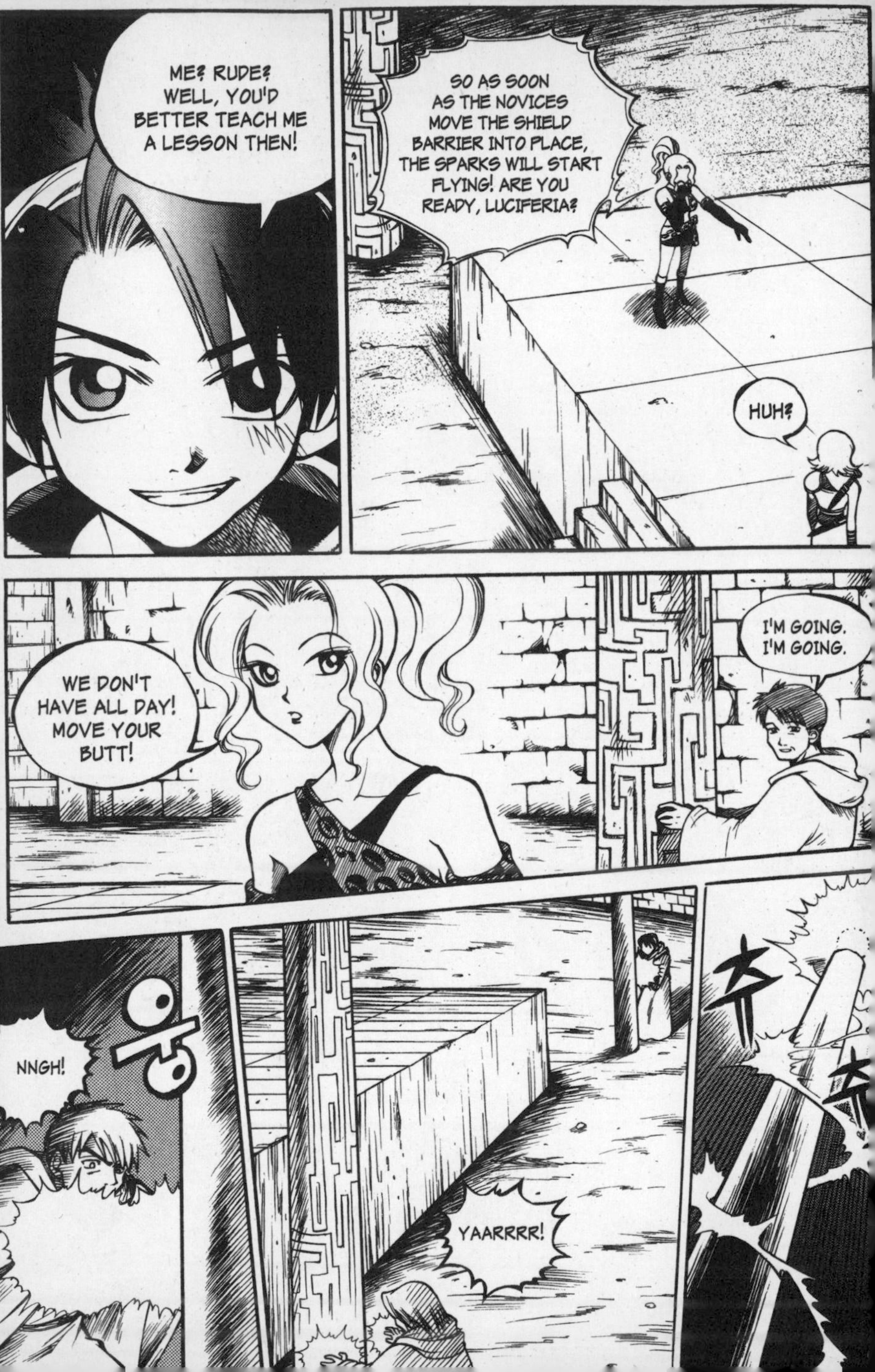
ME? RUDE? WELL, YOU'D BETTER TEACH ME A LESSON THEN!
SO AS SOON AS THE NOVICES MOVE THE SHIELD BARRIER INTO PLACE, THE SPARKS WILL START FLYING! ARE YOU READY, LUCIFERIA?
HUH?
WE DON'T HAVE ALL DAY! MOVE YOUR BUTT!
I'M GOING. I'M GOING.
NNGH!
YAARRRR!

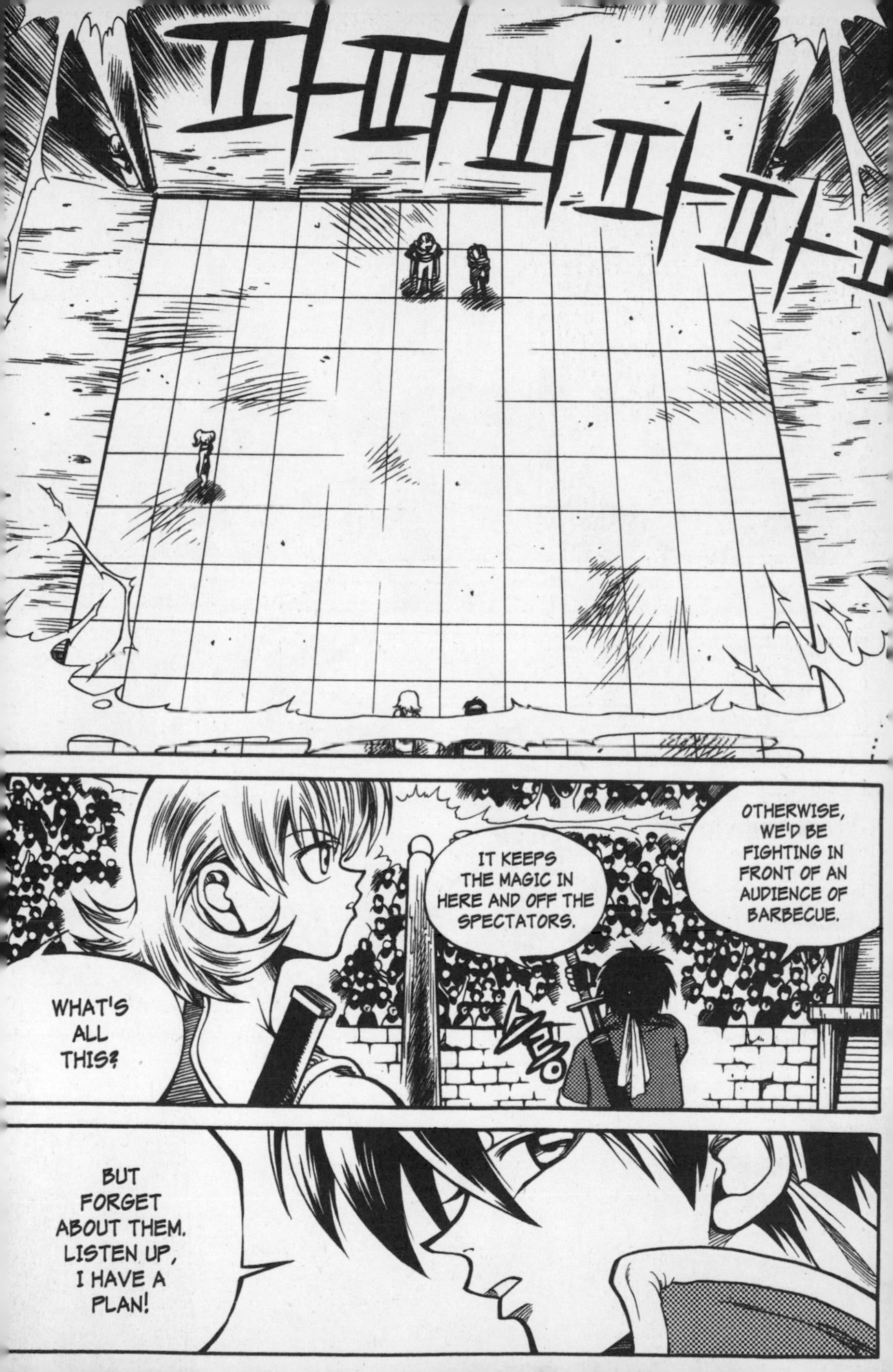
WHAT'S ALL THIS?
IT KEEPS THE MAGIC IN HERE AND OFF THE SPECTATORS.
OTHERWISE, WE'D BE FIGHTING IN FRONT OF AN AUDIENCE OF BARBECUE.
BUT FORGET ABOUT THEM. LISTEN UP, I HAVE A PLAN!

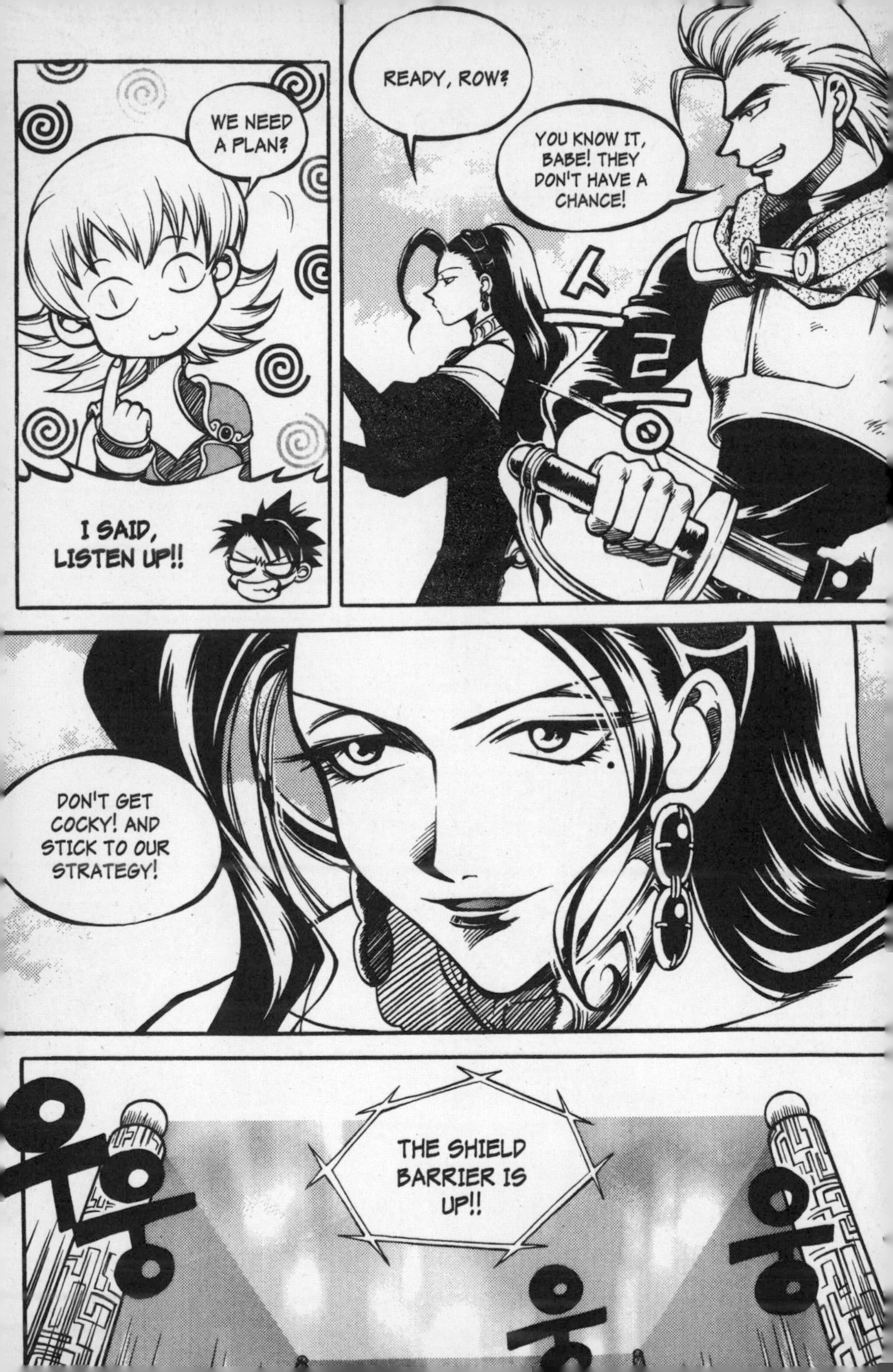
WE NEED A PLAN?
I SAID, LISTEN UP!!
READY, ROW?
YOU KNOW IT, BABE! THEY DON'T HAVE A CHANCE!
DON'T GET COCKY! AND STICK TO OUR STRATEGY!
THE SHIELD BARRIER IS UP!!

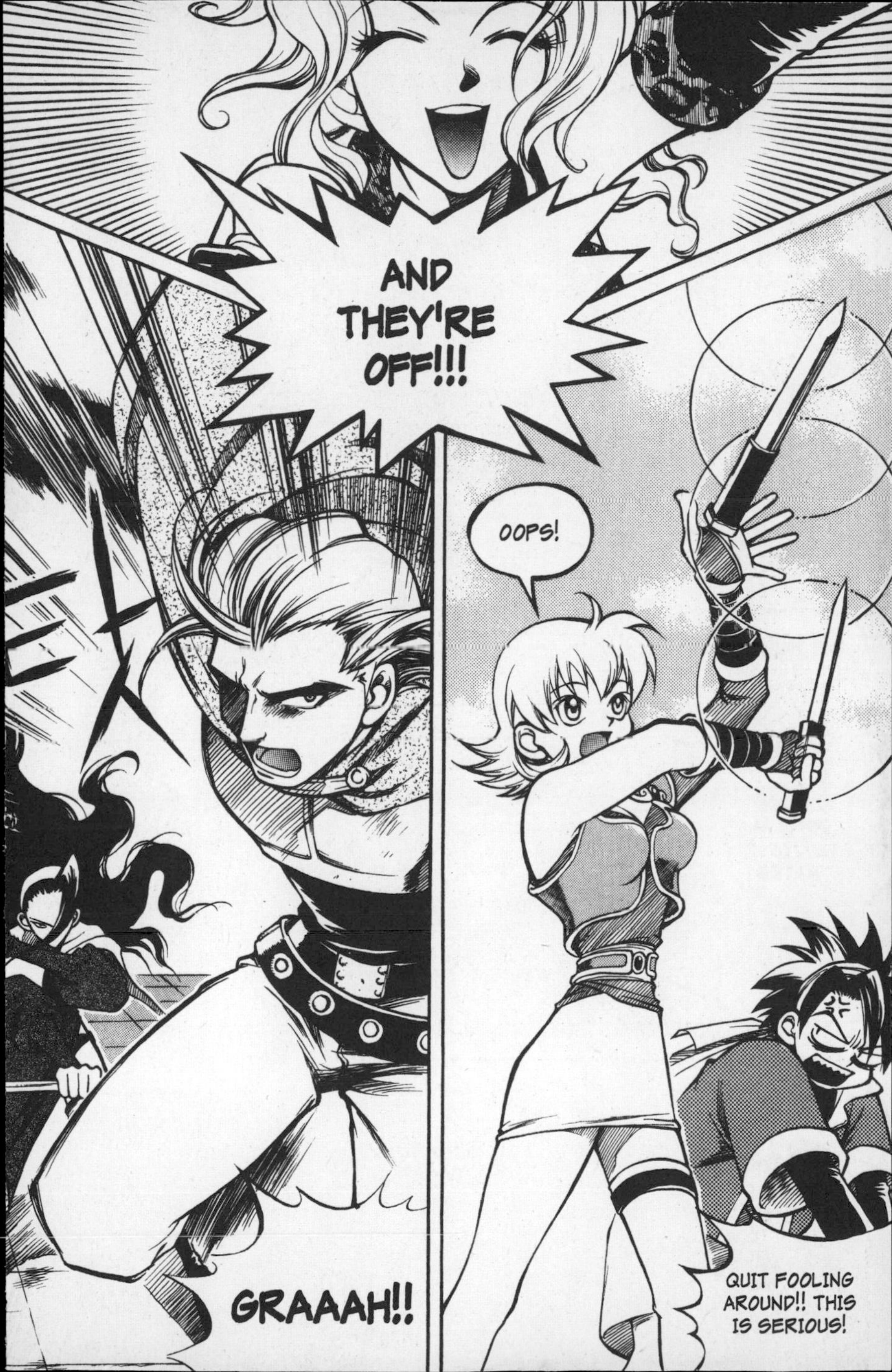
AND THEY'RE OFF!!!
GRAAAH!!
OOPS!
QUIT FOOLING AROUND!! THIS IS SERIOUS!

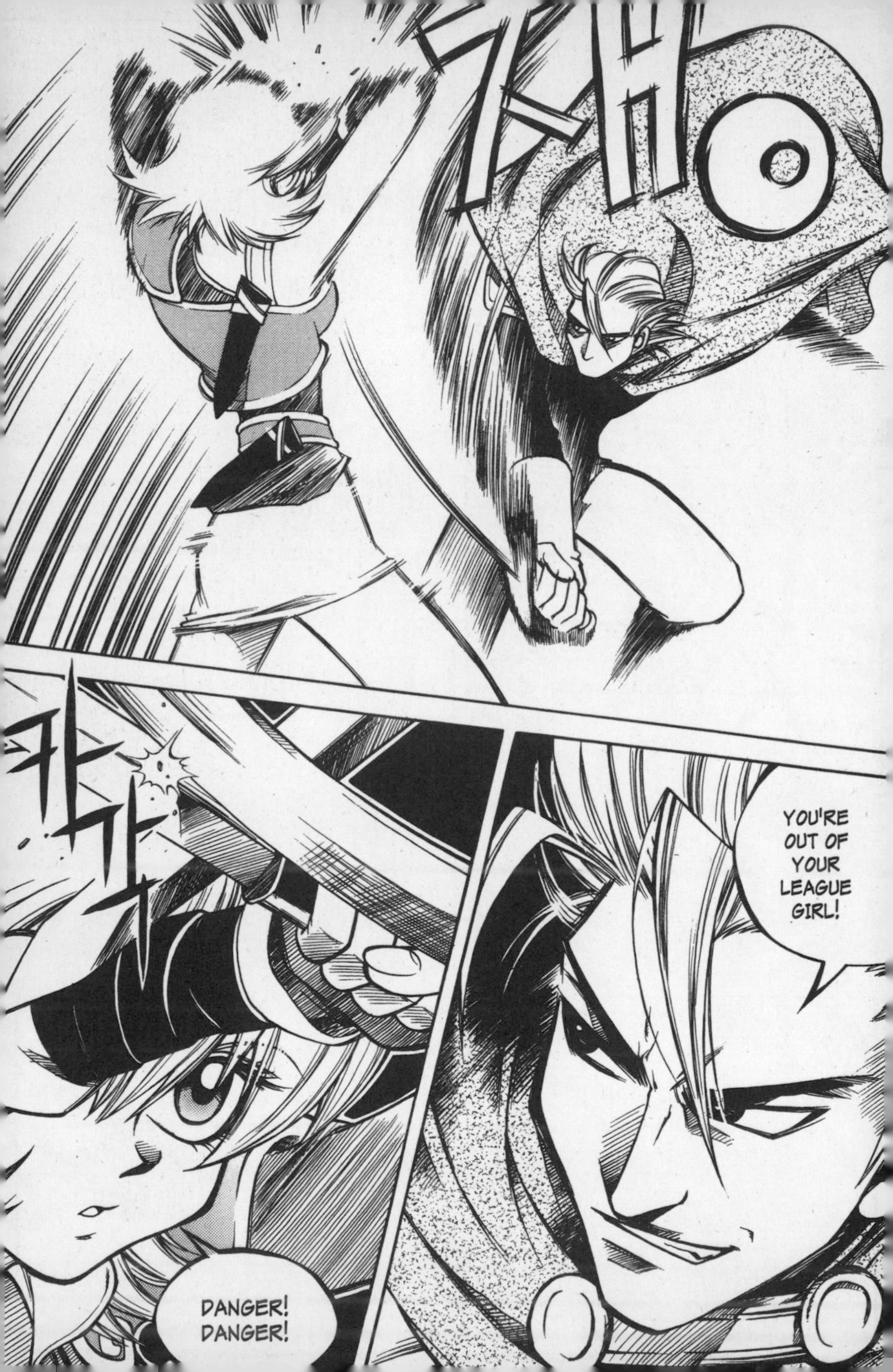
DANGER! DANGER!
YOU'RE OUT OF YOUR LEAGUE GIRL!

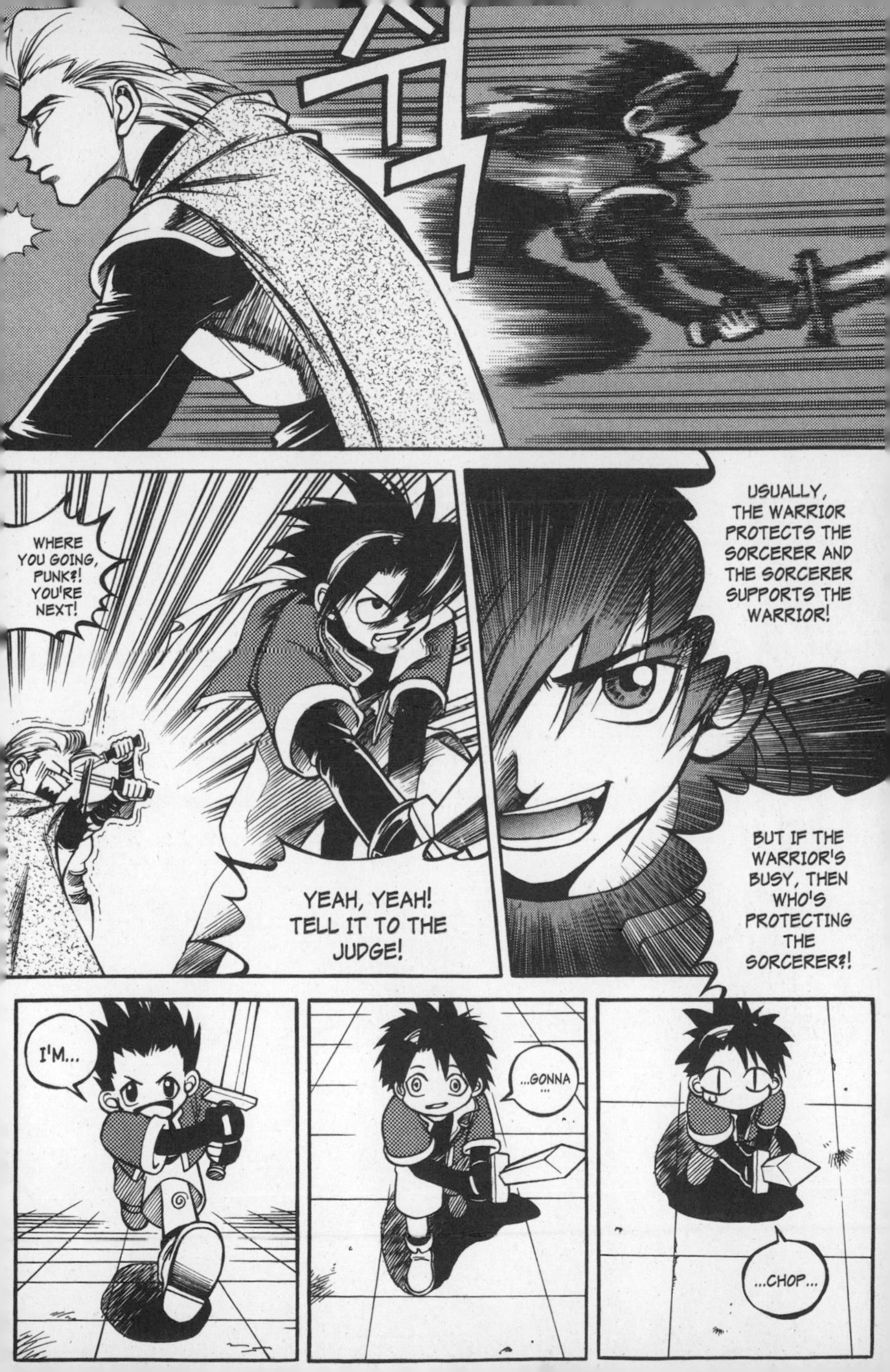
WHERE YOU GOING, PUNK?! YOU'RE NEXT!
YEAH, YEAH! TELL IT TO THE JUDGE!
USUALLY, THE WARRIOR PROTECTS THE SORCERER AND THE SORCERER SUPPORTS THE WARRIOR!
BUT IF THE WARRIOR'S BUSY, THEN WHO'S PROTECTING THE SORCERER?!
I'M...
...GONNA...
...CHOP...

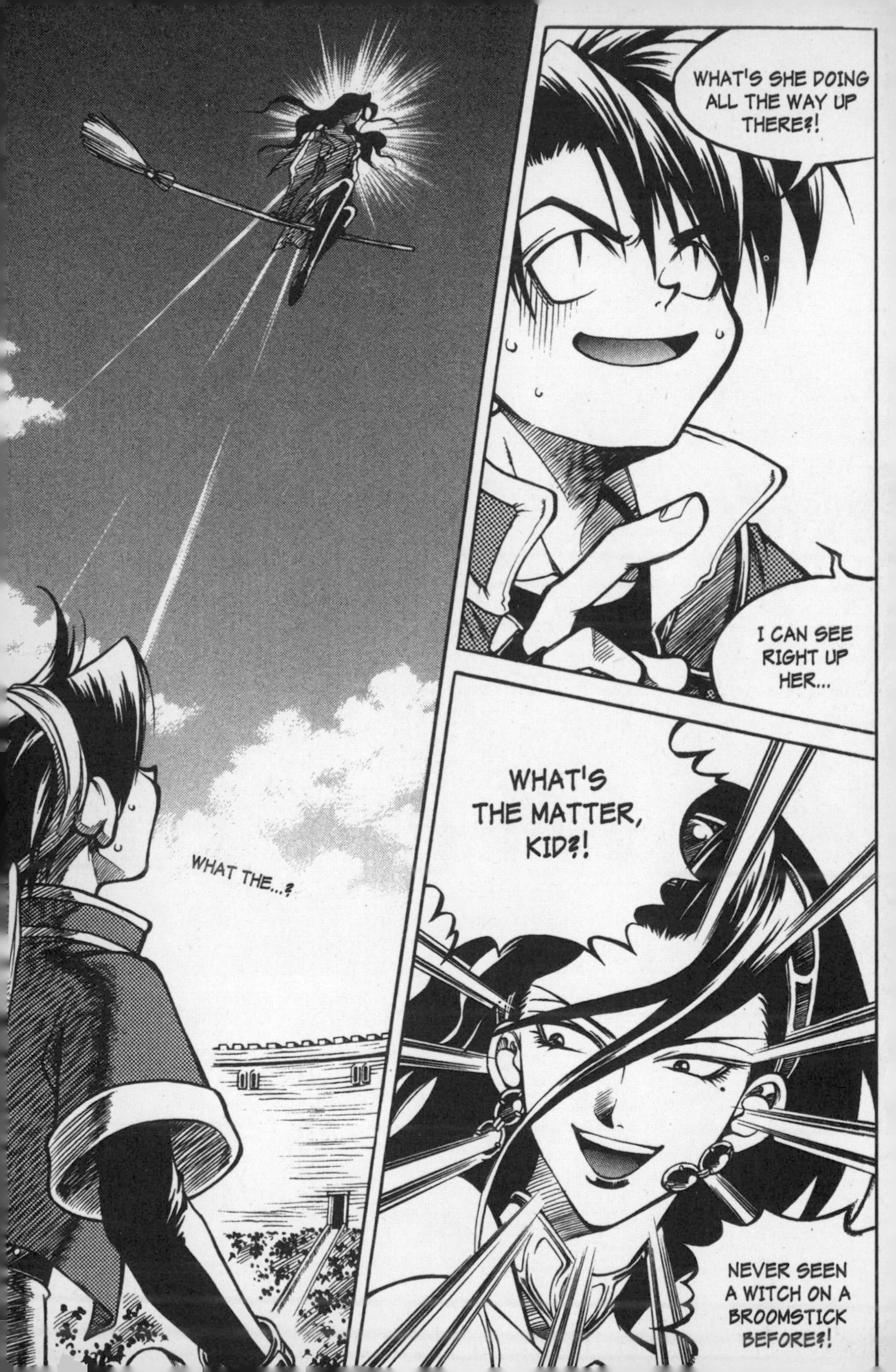
WHAT'S SHE DOING ALL THE WAY UP THERE?!
I CAN SEE RIGHT UP HER...
WHAT'S THE MATTER, KID?!
NEVER SEEN A WITCH ON A BROOMSTICK BEFORE?!
WHAT THE...?

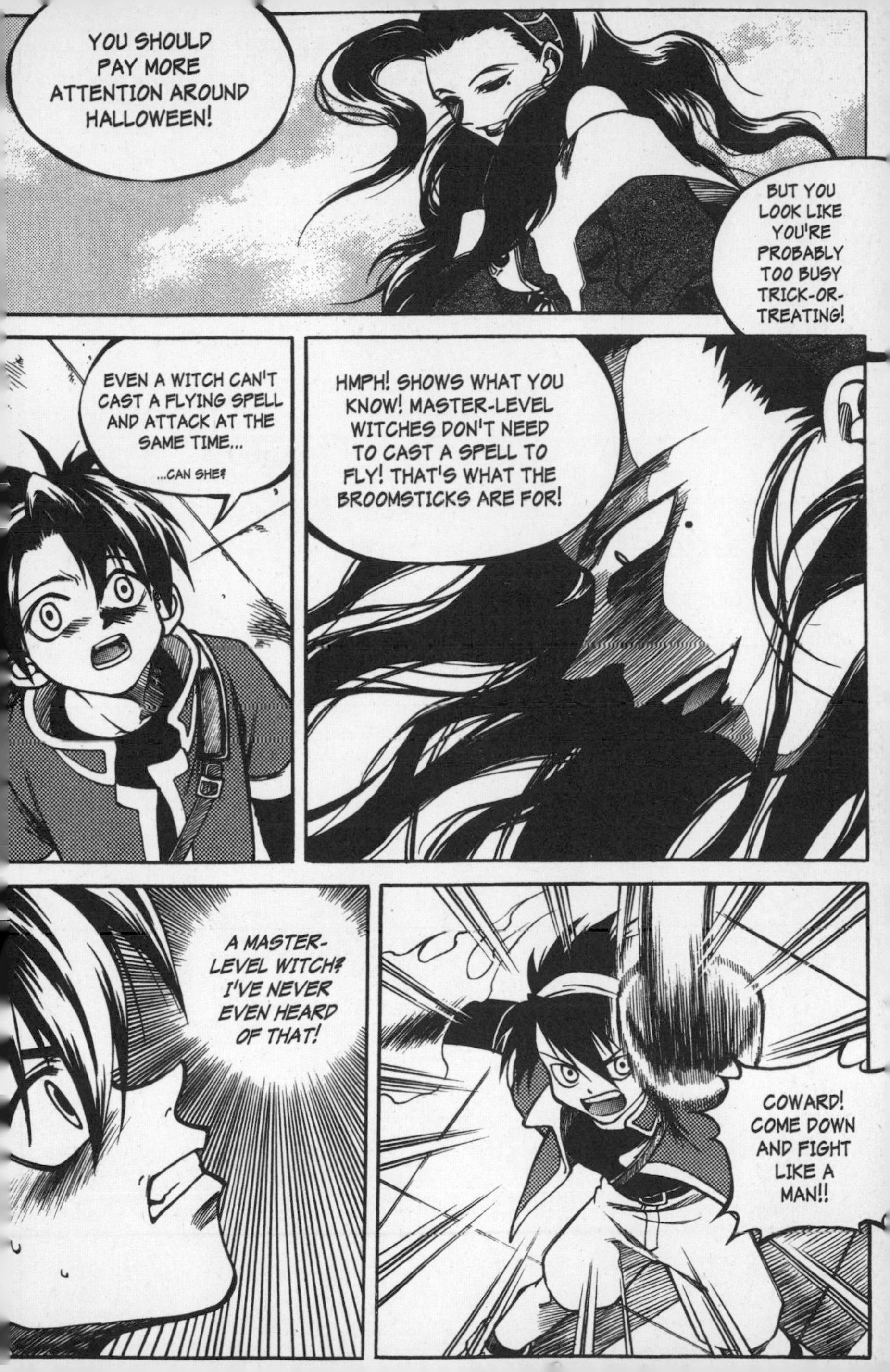
YOU SHOULD PAY MORE ATTENTION AROUND HALLOWEEN!
BUT YOU LOOK LIKE YOU'RE PROBABLY TOO BUSY TRICK-OR-TREATING!
EVEN A WITCH CAN'T CAST A FLYING SPELL AND ATTACK AT THE SAME TIME...
...CAN SHE?
HMPH! SHOWS WHAT YOU KNOW! MASTER-LEVEL WITCHES DON'T NEED TO CAST A SPELL TO FLY! THAT'S WHAT THE BROOMSTICKS ARE FOR!
A MASTER-LEVEL WITCH? I'VE NEVER EVEN HEARD OF THAT!
COWARD! COME DOWN AND FIGHT LIKE A MAN!!

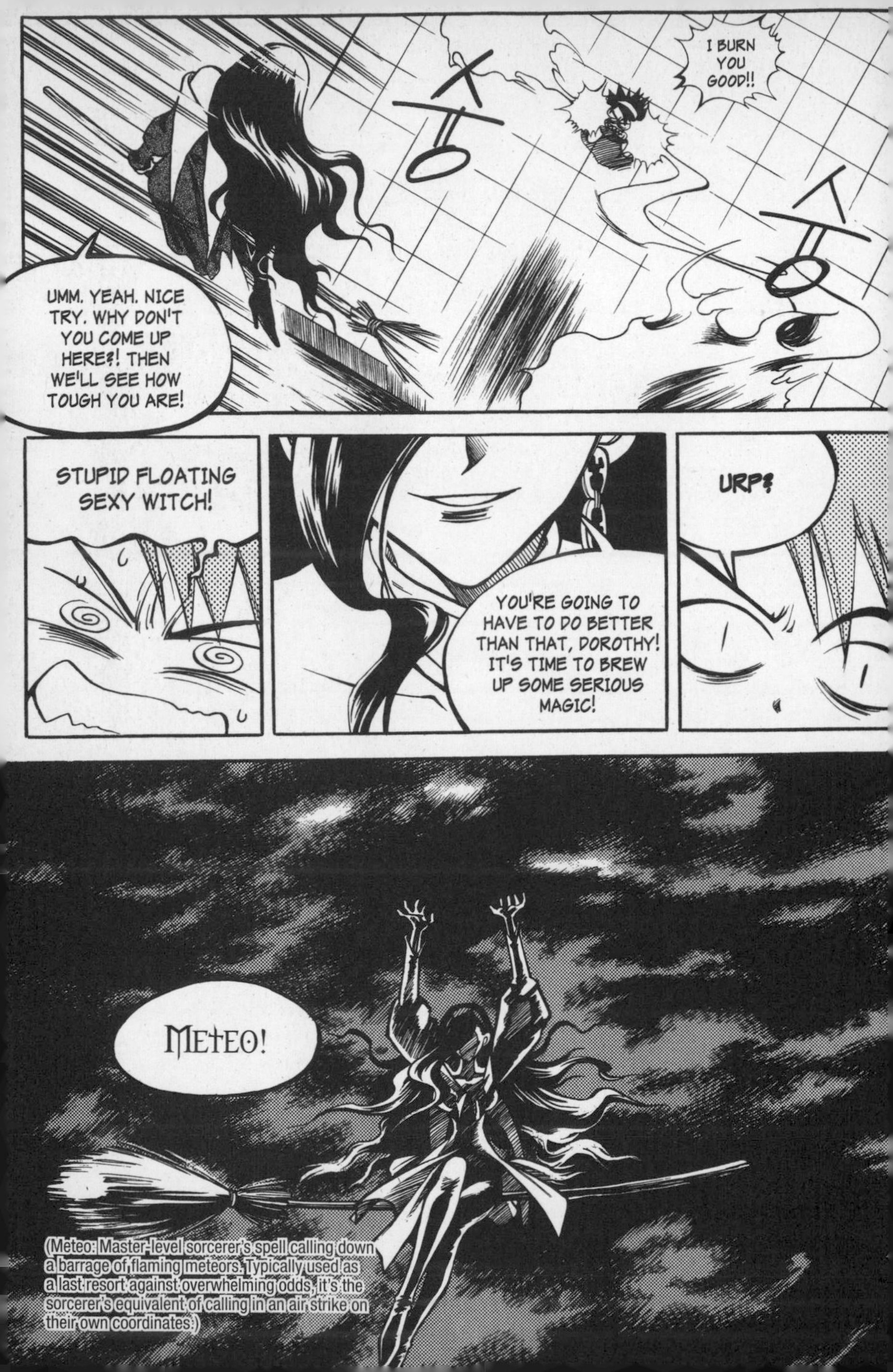
I BURN YOU GOOD!!
UMM. YEAH. NICE TRY. WHY DON'T YOU COME UP HERE?! THEN WE'LL SEE HOW TOUGH YOU ARE!
STUPID FLOATING SEXY WITCH!
YOU'RE GOING TO HAVE TO DO BETTER THAN THAT, DOROTHY! IT'S TIME TO BREW UP SOME SERIOUS MAGIC!
URP?
METEO!
(Meteo: Master-level sorcerer's spell calling down a barrage of flaming meteors. Typically used as a last resort against overwhelming odds, it's the sorcerer's equivalent of calling in an air strike on their own coordinates.)

STAGE 19
PAIR OF DEUCES

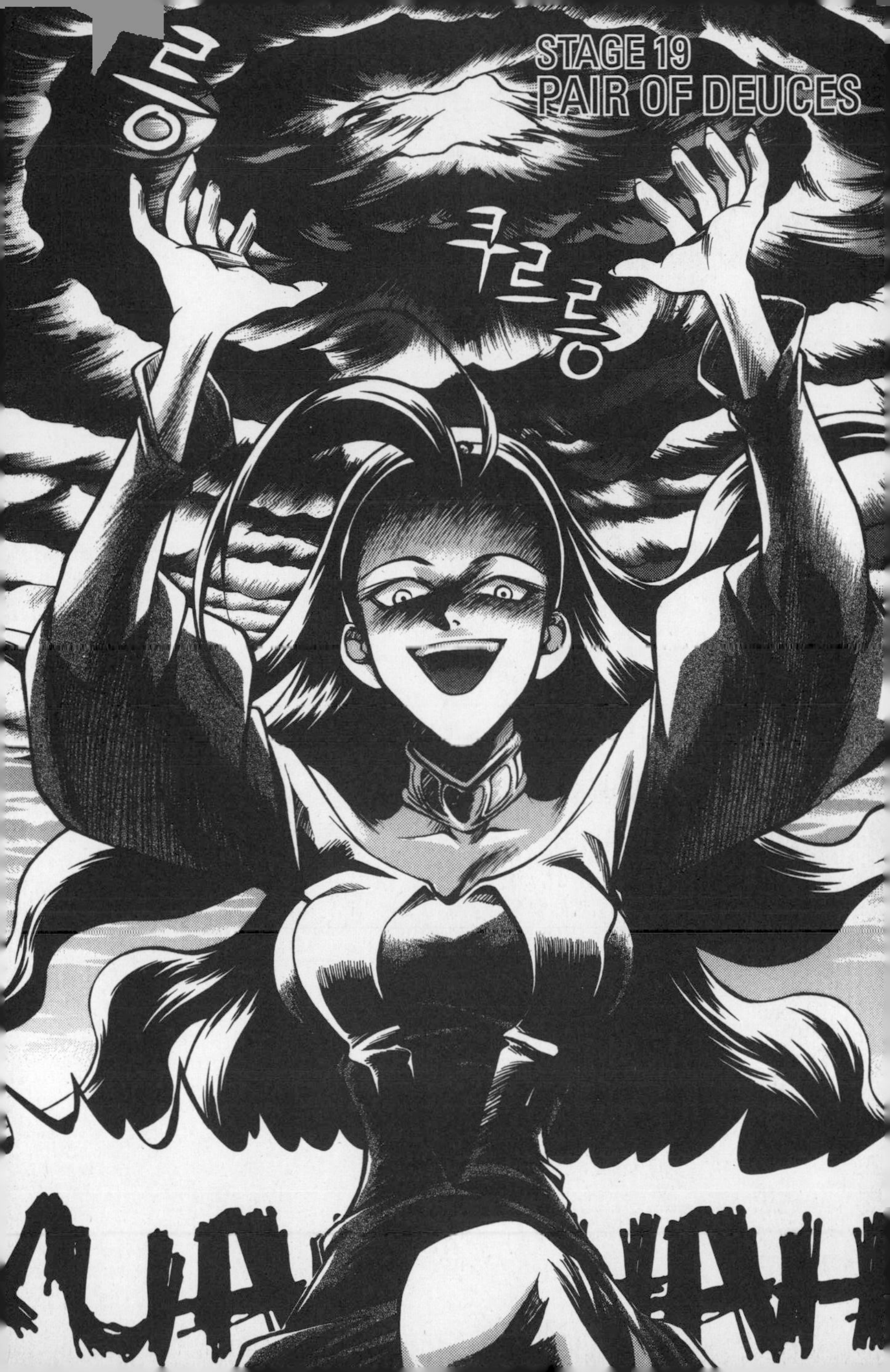
쿠르릉

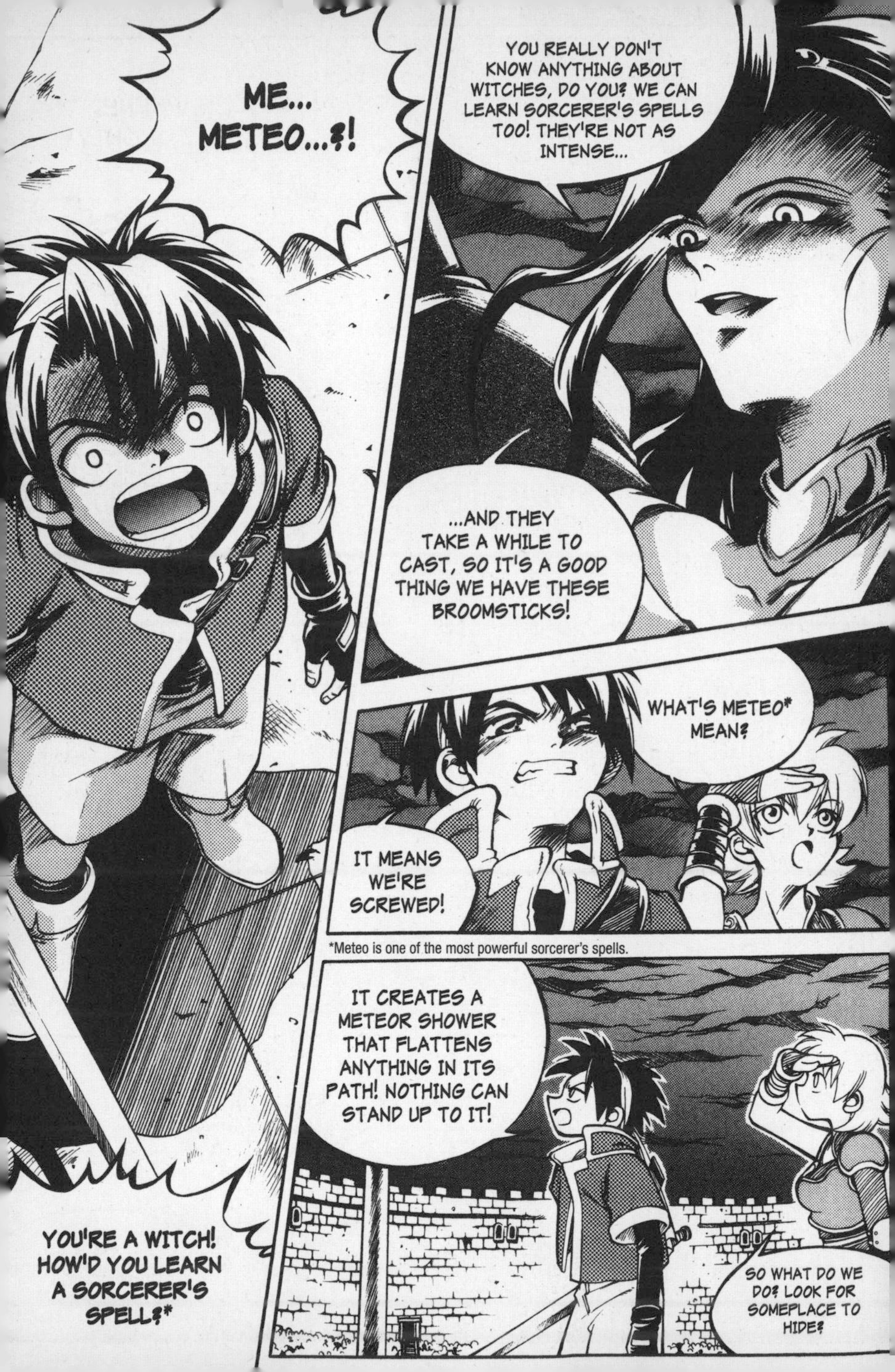
ME... METEO...?!
YOU'RE A WITCH! HOW'D YOU LEARN A SORCERER'S SPELL?*
YOU REALLY DON'T KNOW ANYTHING ABOUT WITCHES, DO YOU? WE CAN LEARN SORCERER'S SPELLS TOO! THEY'RE NOT AS INTENSE...
...AND THEY TAKE A WHILE TO CAST, SO IT'S A GOOD THING WE HAVE THESE BROOMSTICKS!
WHAT'S METEO* MEAN?
IT MEANS WE'RE SCREWED!
IT CREATES A METEOR SHOWER THAT FLATTENS ANYTHING IN ITS PATH! NOTHING CAN STAND UP TO IT!
SO WHAT DO WE DO? LOOK FOR SOMEPLACE TO HIDE?
*Meteo is one of the most powerful sorcerer's spells.

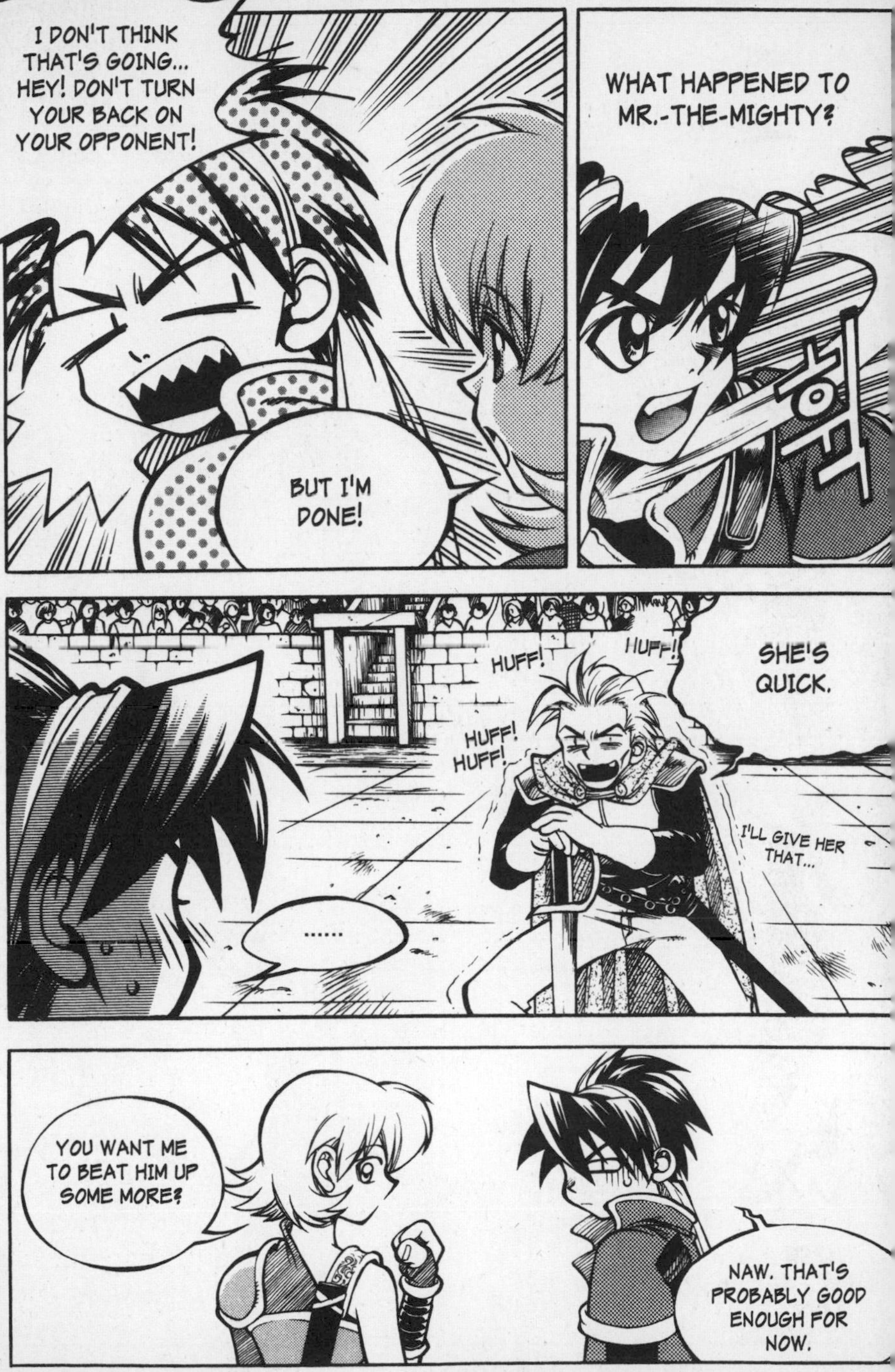
I DON'T THINK THAT'S GOING... HEY! DON'T TURN YOUR BACK ON YOUR OPPONENT!
BUT I'M DONE!
WHAT HAPPENED TO MR.-THE-MIGHTY?
HOFF
HUFF!
HUFF!
HUFF! HUFF!
SHE'S QUICK.
I'LL GIVE HER THAT...
......
YOU WANT ME TO BEAT HIM UP SOME MORE?
NAW. THAT'S PROBABLY GOOD ENOUGH FOR NOW.

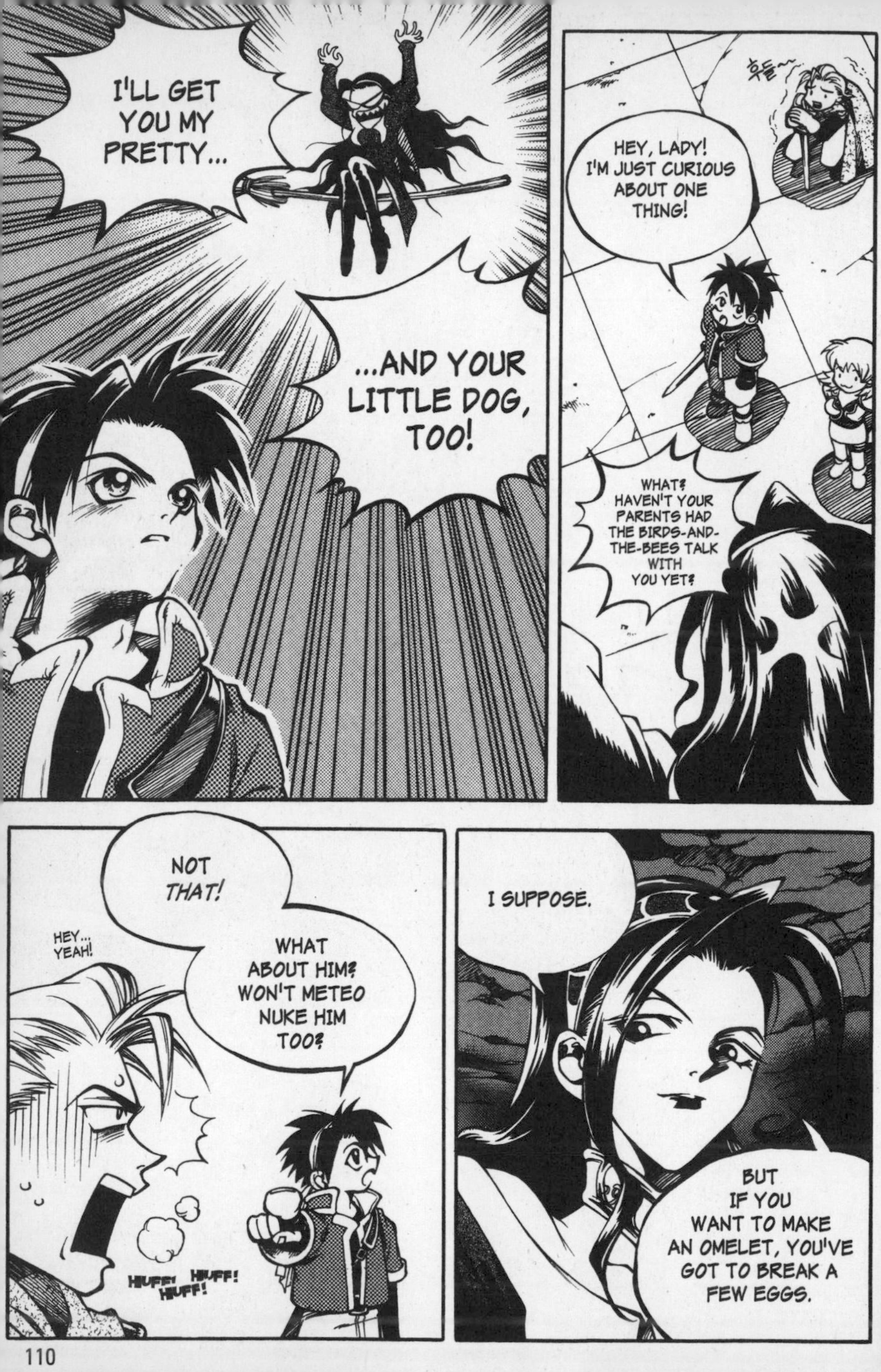
I'LL GET YOU MY PRETTY...
...AND YOUR LITTLE DOG, TOO!
후들~~
HEY, LADY! I'M JUST CURIOUS ABOUT ONE THING!
WHAT? HAVEN'T YOUR PARENTS HAD THE BIRDS-AND-THE-BEES TALK WITH YOU YET?
NOT THAT!
HEY... YEAH!
WHAT ABOUT HIM? WON'T METEO NUKE HIM TOO?
HUFF! HUFF! HUFF!
I SUPPOSE.
BUT IF YOU WANT TO MAKE AN OMELET, YOU'VE GOT TO BREAK A FEW EGGS.

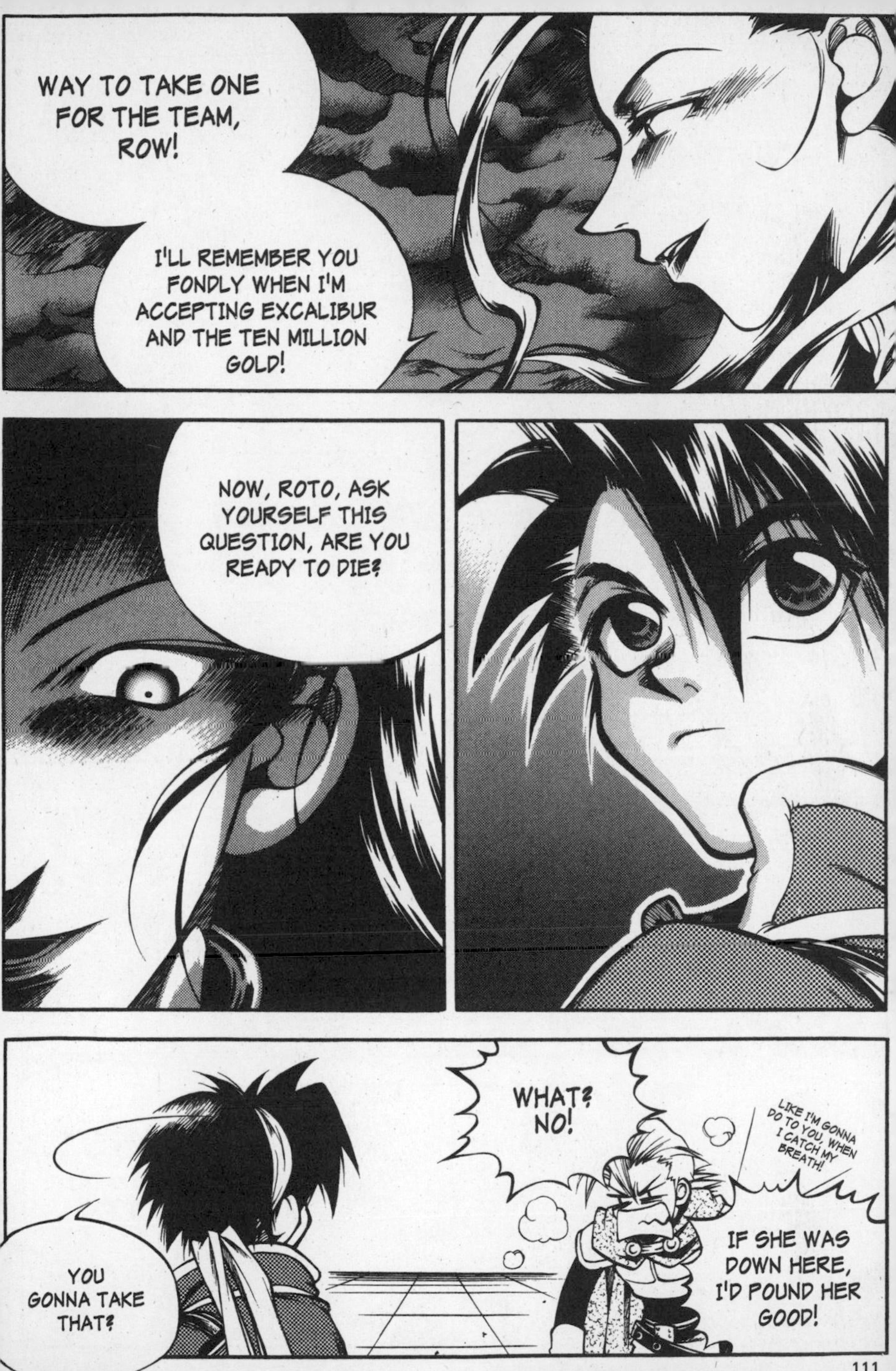

WAY TO TAKE ONE FOR THE TEAM, ROW!
I'LL REMEMBER YOU FONDLY WHEN I'M ACCEPTING EXCALIBUR AND THE TEN MILLION GOLD!
NOW, ROTO, ASK YOURSELF THIS QUESTION, ARE YOU READY TO DIE?
YOU GONNA TAKE THAT?
WHAT? NO!
IF SHE WAS DOWN HERE, I'D POUND HER GOOD!
LIKE I'M GONNA DO TO YOU, WHEN I CATCH MY BREATH!

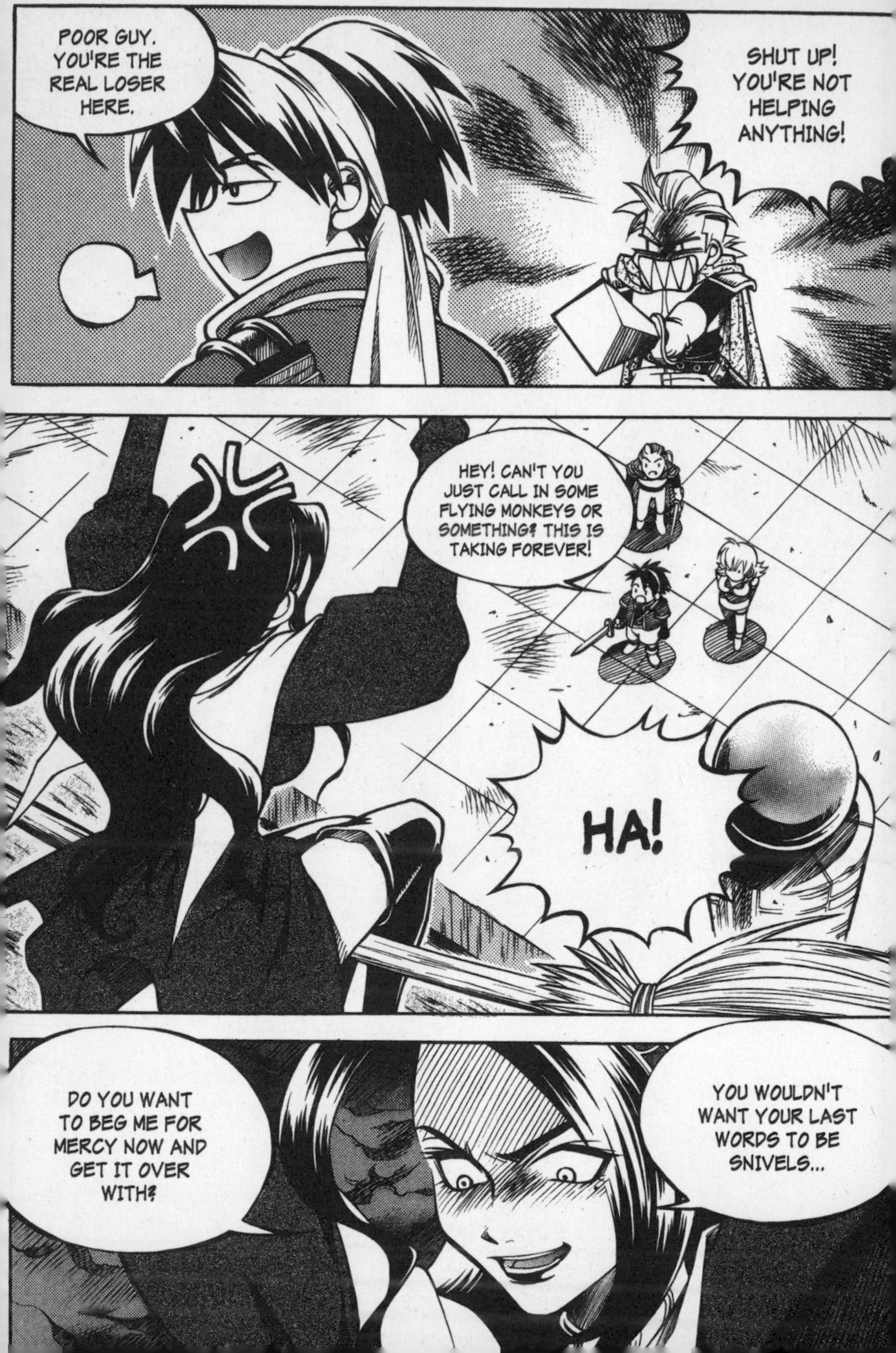
POOR GUY. YOU'RE THE REAL LOSER HERE.
SHUT UP! YOU'RE NOT HELPING ANYTHING!
HEY! CAN'T YOU JUST CALL IN SOME FLYING MONKEYS OR SOMETHING? THIS IS TAKING FOREVER!
HA!
DO YOU WANT TO BEG ME FOR MERCY NOW AND GET IT OVER WITH?
YOU WOULDN'T WANT YOUR LAST WORDS TO BE SNIVELS...

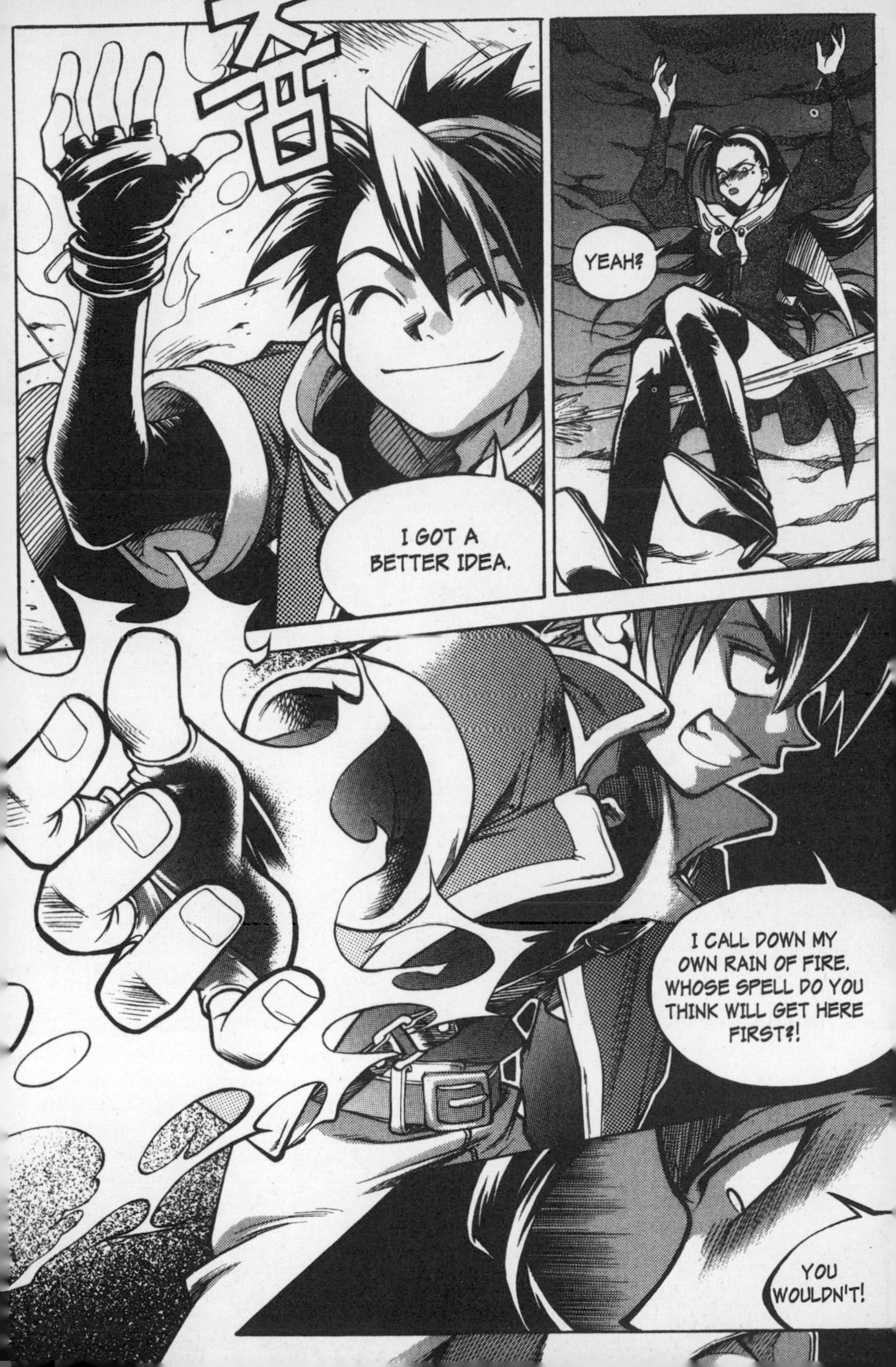
I GOT A BETTER IDEA.
YEAH?
I CALL DOWN MY OWN RAIN OF FIRE. WHOSE SPELL DO YOU THINK WILL GET HERE FIRST?!
YOU WOULDN'T!

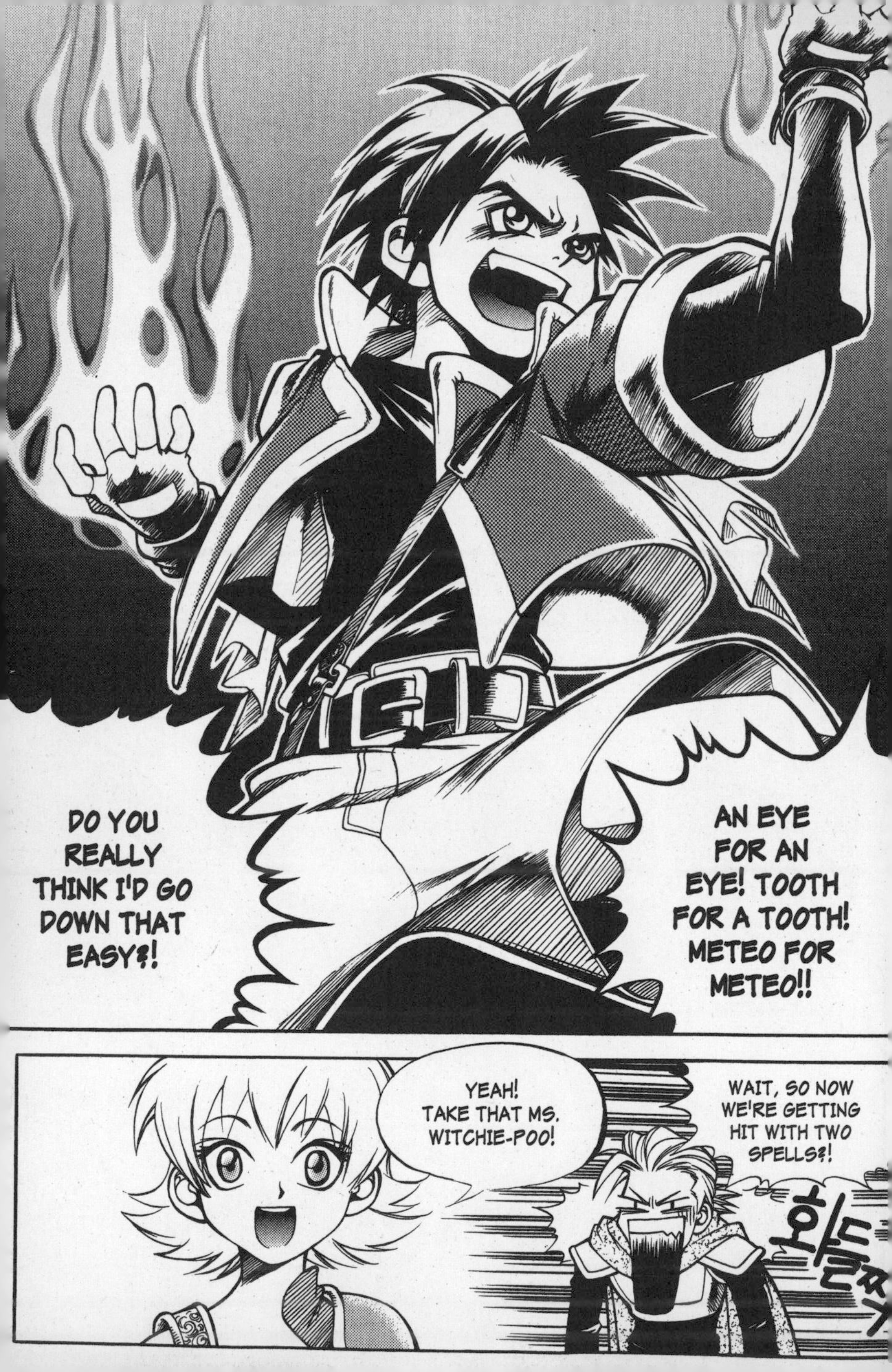
DO YOU REALLY THINK I'D GO DOWN THAT EASY?!
AN EYE FOR AN EYE! TOOTH FOR A TOOTH! METEO FOR METEO!!
YEAH! TAKE THAT MS. WITCHIE-POO!
WAIT, SO NOW WE'RE GETTING HIT WITH TWO SPELLS?!
화들짝

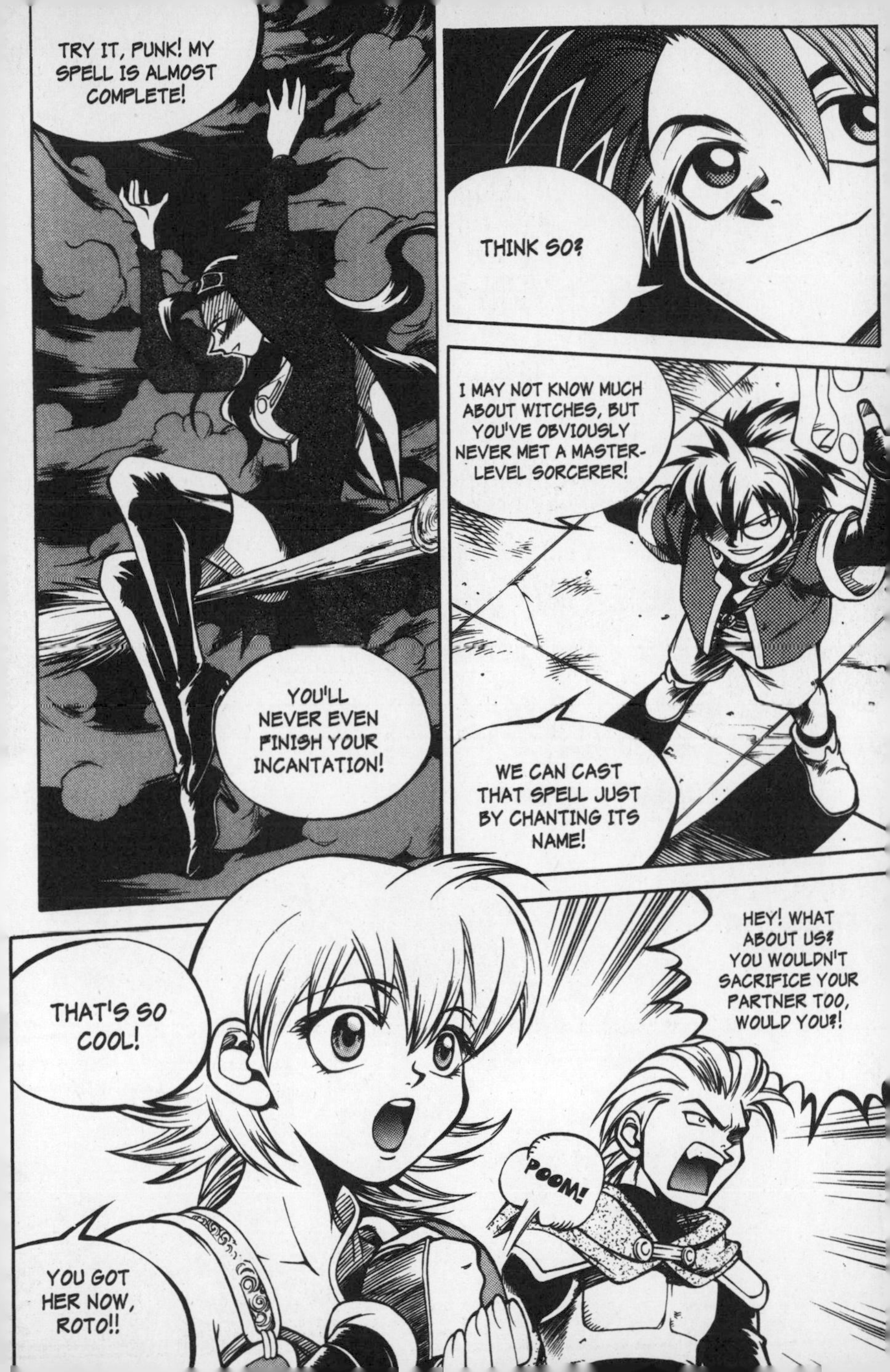
TRY IT, PUNK! MY SPELL IS ALMOST COMPLETE!
YOU'LL NEVER EVEN FINISH YOUR INCANTATION!
THINK SO?
I MAY NOT KNOW MUCH ABOUT WITCHES, BUT YOU'VE OBVIOUSLY NEVER MET A MASTER-LEVEL SORCERER!
WE CAN CAST THAT SPELL JUST BY CHANTING ITS NAME!
THAT'S SO COOL!
YOU GOT HER NOW, ROTO!!
POOM!
HEY! WHAT ABOUT US? YOU WOULDN'T SACRIFICE YOUR PARTNER TOO, WOULD YOU?!

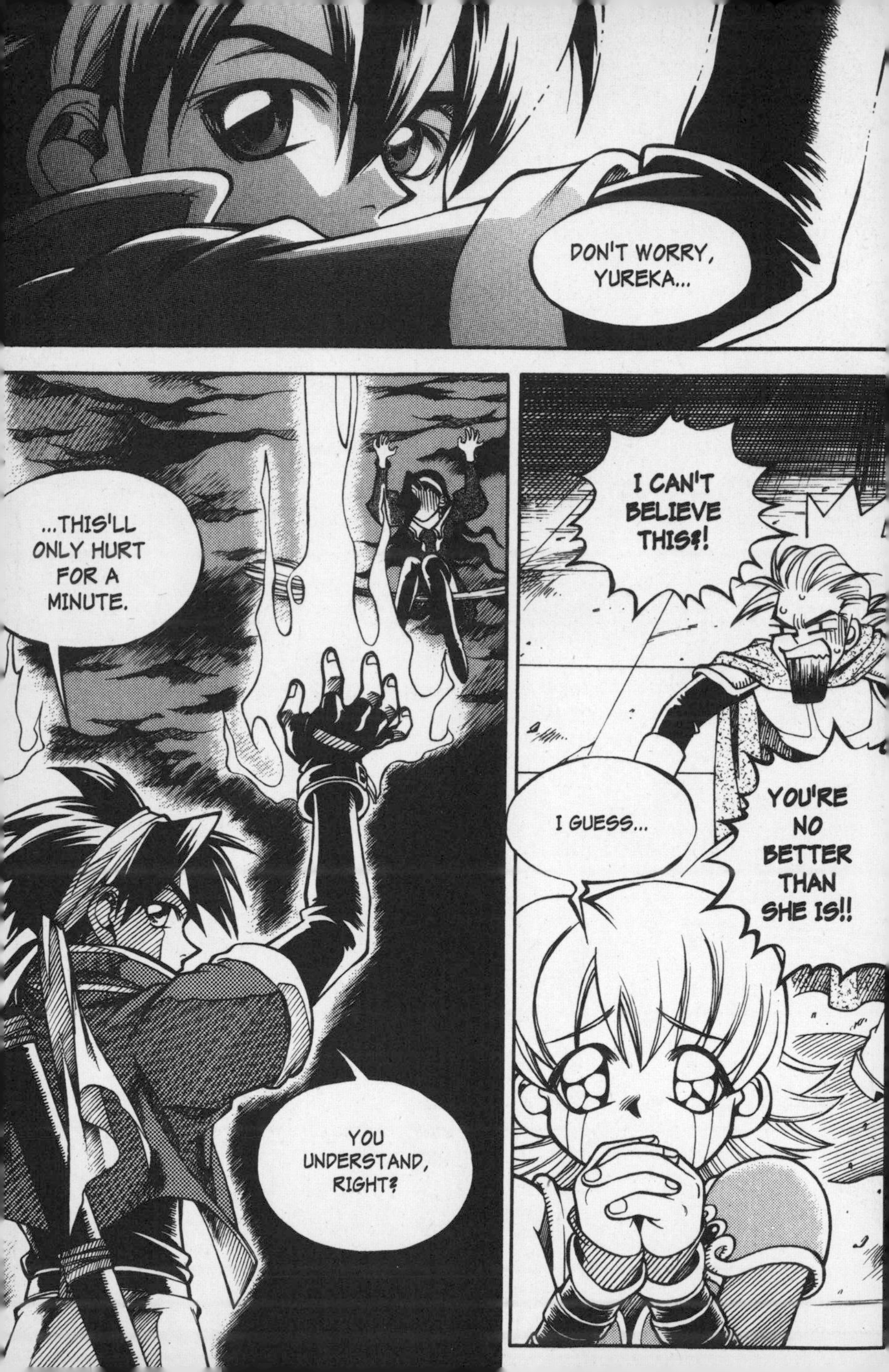
DON'T WORRY, YUREKA...
...THIS'LL ONLY HURT FOR A MINUTE.
YOU UNDERSTAND, RIGHT?
I CAN'T BELIEVE THIS?!
I GUESS...
YOU'RE NO BETTER THAN SHE IS!!

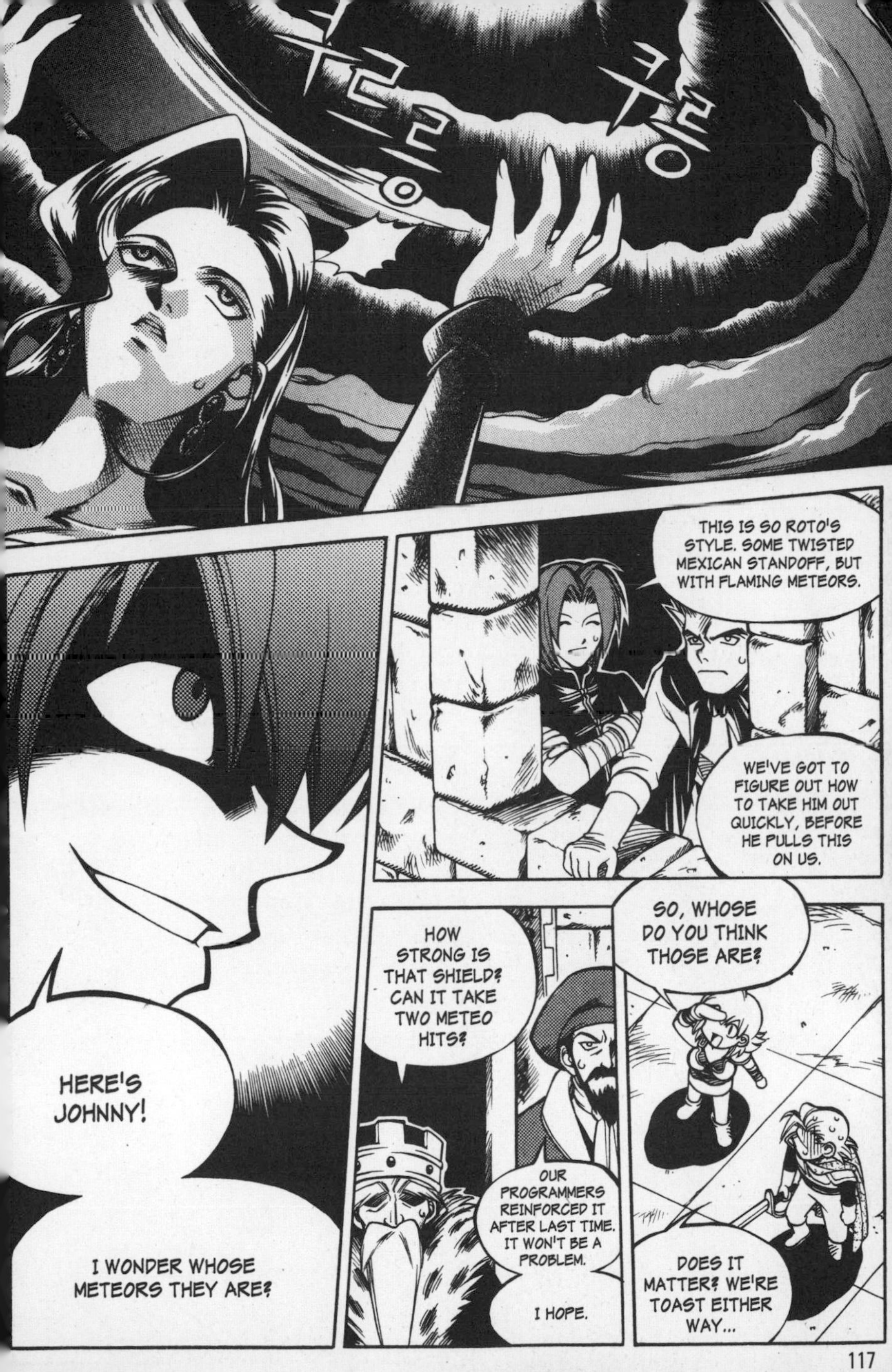
HERE'S JOHNNY!
I WONDER WHOSE METEORS THEY ARE?
THIS IS SO ROTO'S STYLE. SOME TWISTED MEXICAN STANDOFF, BUT WITH FLAMING METEORS.
WE'VE GOT TO FIGURE OUT HOW TO TAKE HIM OUT QUICKLY, BEFORE HE PULLS THIS ON US.
HOW STRONG IS THAT SHIELD? CAN IT TAKE TWO METEO HITS?
OUR PROGRAMMERS REINFORCED IT AFTER LAST TIME. IT WON'T BE A PROBLEM.
I HOPE.
SO, WHOSE DO YOU THINK THOSE ARE?
DOES IT MATTER? WE'RE TOAST EITHER WAY...

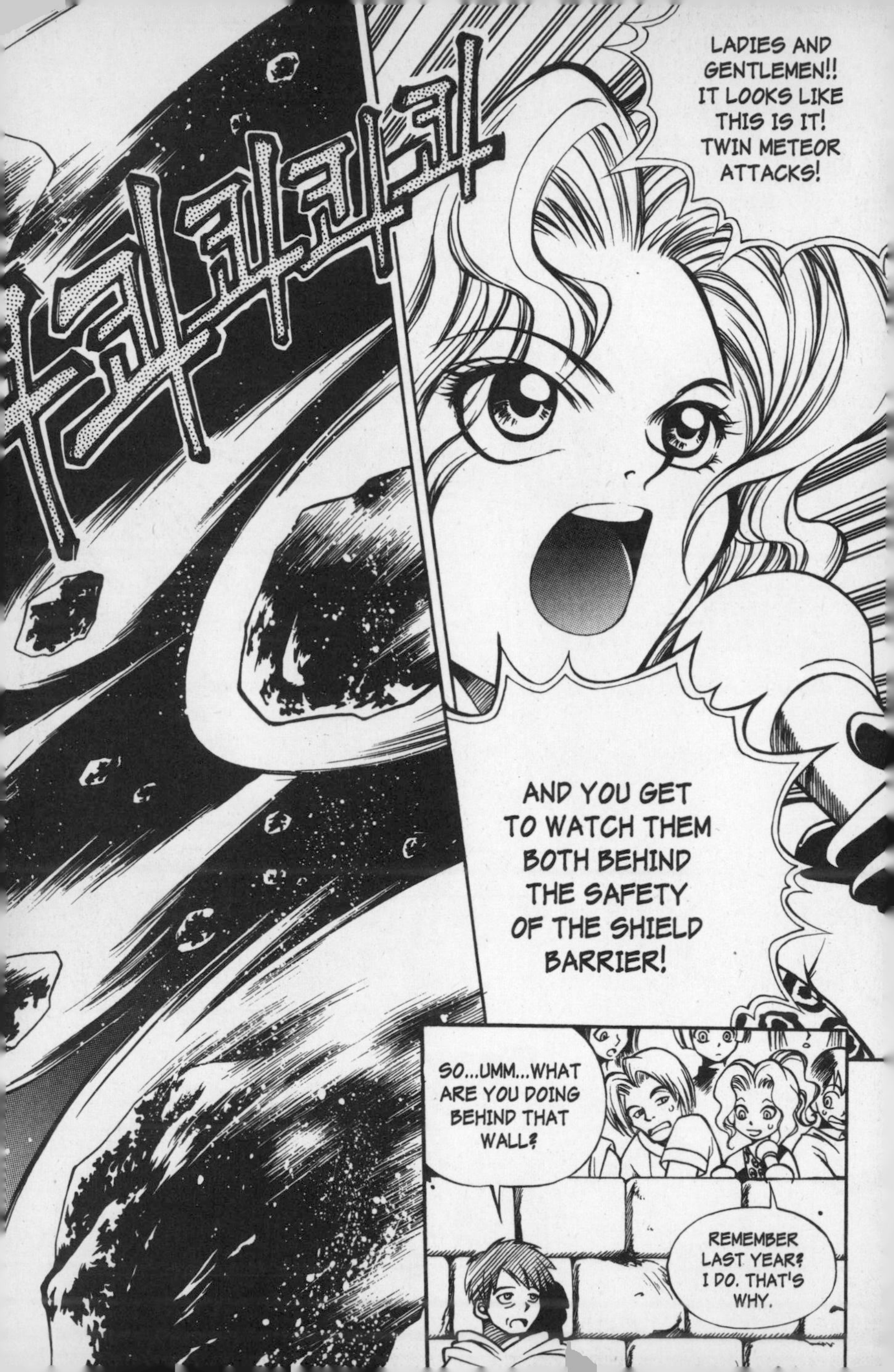
LADIES AND GENTLEMEN!! IT LOOKS LIKE THIS IS IT! TWIN METEOR ATTACKS!
AND YOU GET TO WATCH THEM BOTH BEHIND THE SAFETY OF THE SHIELD BARRIER!
SO...UMM...WHAT ARE YOU DOING BEHIND THAT WALL?
REMEMBER LAST YEAR? I DO. THAT'S WHY.

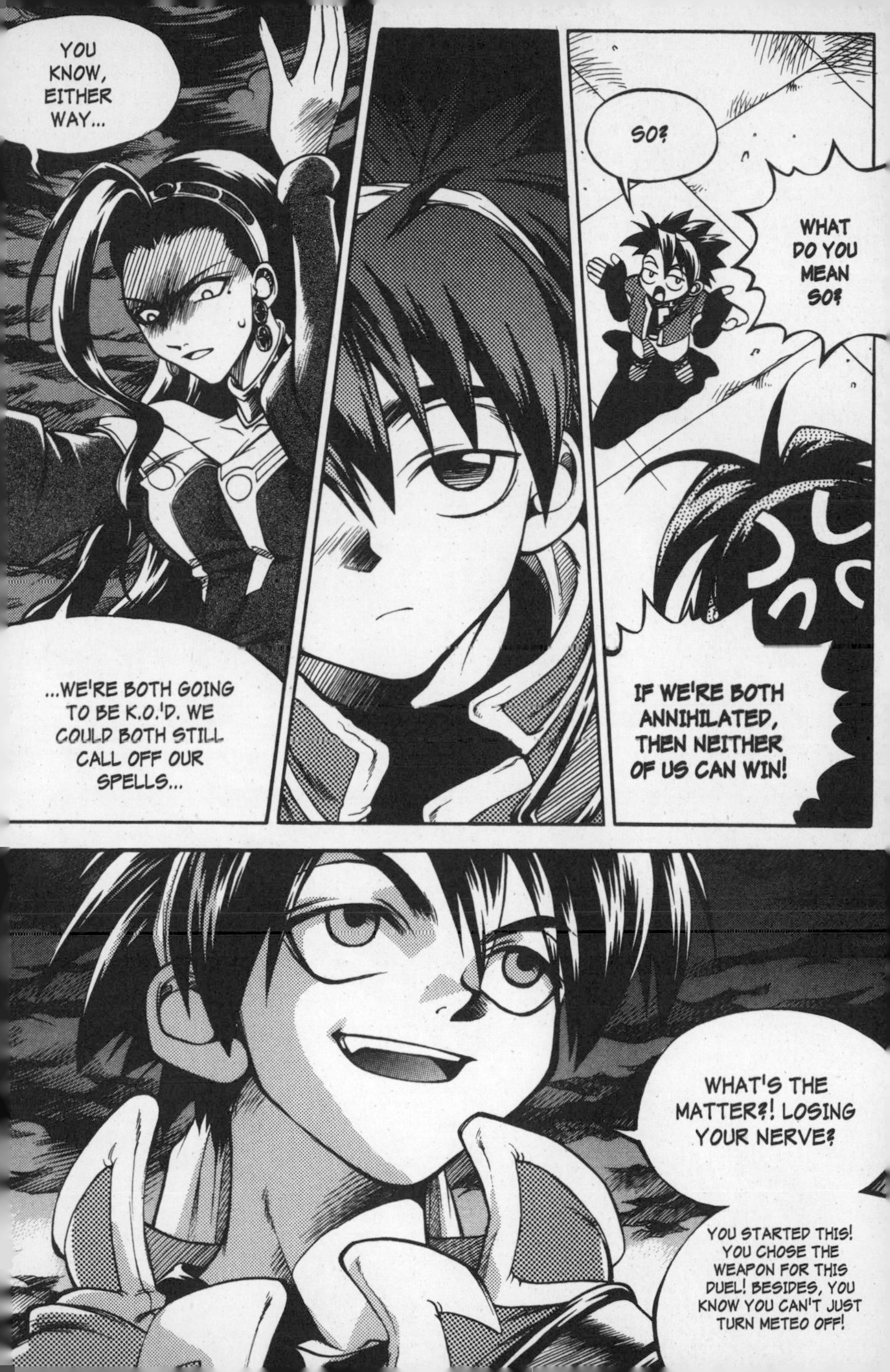
YOU KNOW, EITHER WAY...
...WE'RE BOTH GOING TO BE K.O.'D. WE COULD BOTH STILL CALL OFF OUR SPELLS...
SO?
WHAT DO YOU MEAN SO?
IF WE'RE BOTH ANNIHILATED, THEN NEITHER OF US CAN WIN!
WHAT'S THE MATTER?! LOSING YOUR NERVE?
YOU STARTED THIS! YOU CHOSE THE WEAPON FOR THIS DUEL! BESIDES, YOU KNOW YOU CAN'T JUST TURN METEO OFF!

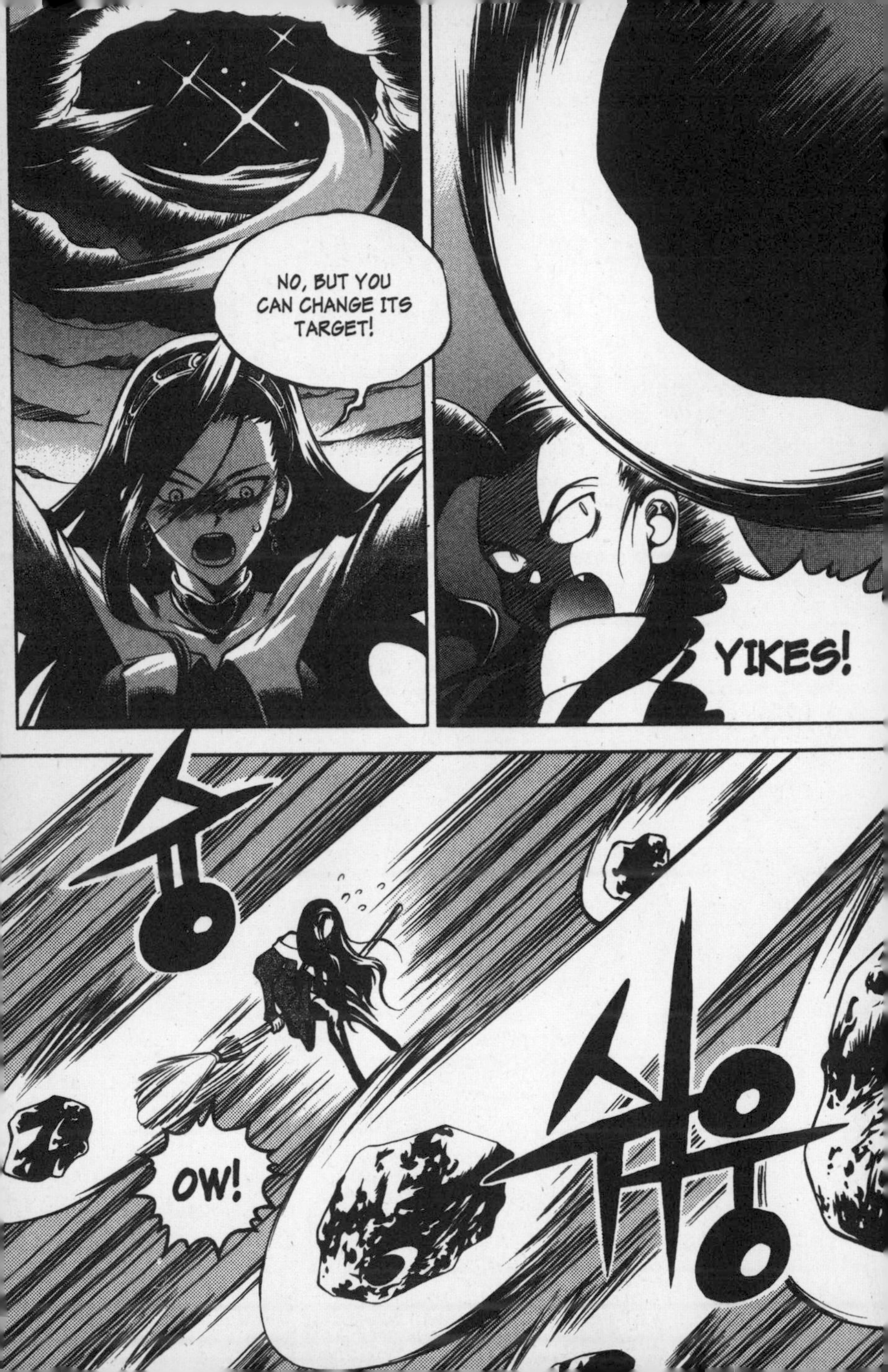
NO, BUT YOU CAN CHANGE ITS TARGET!
YIKES!
OW!

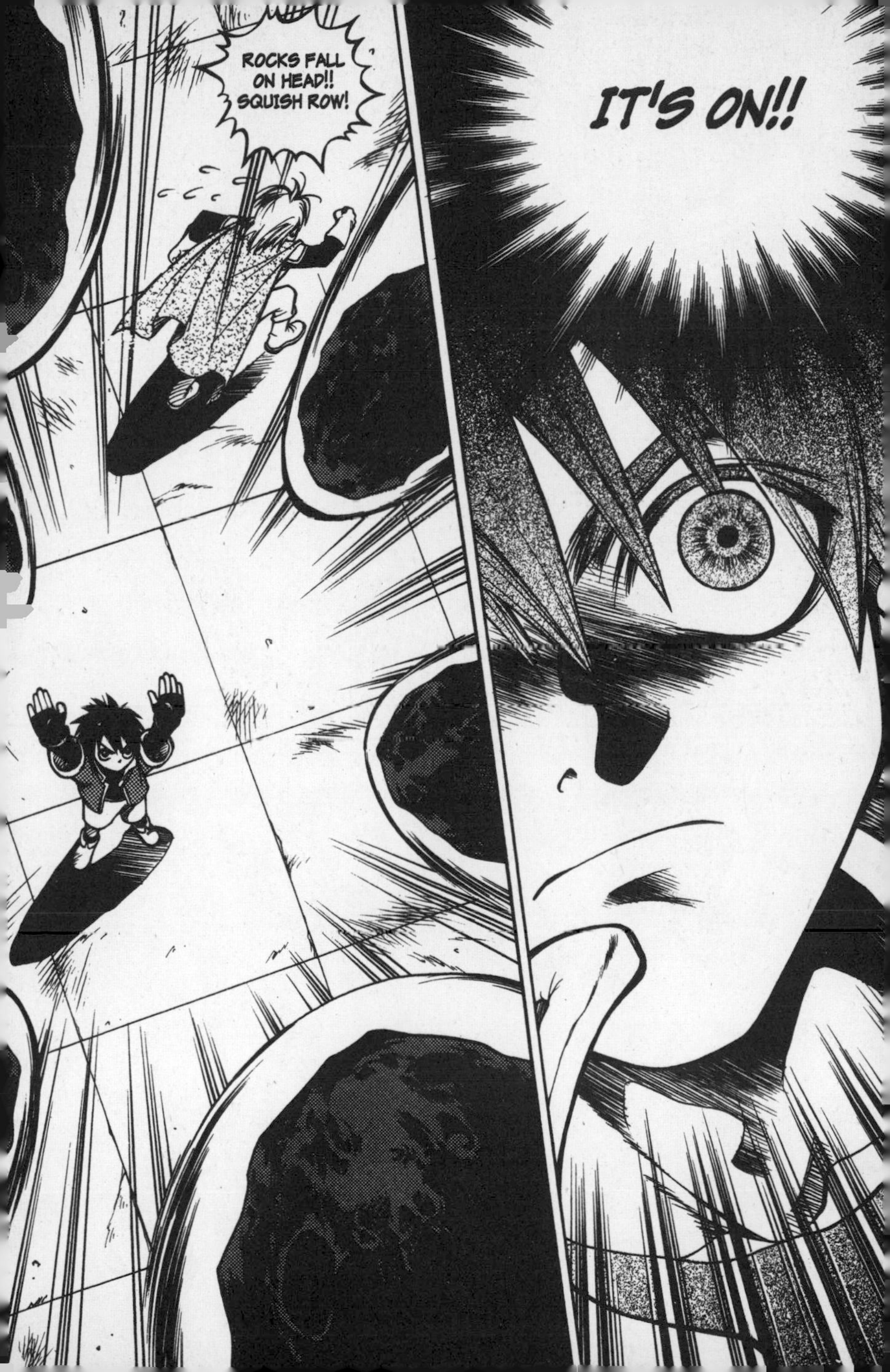
IT'S ON!!
ROCKS FALL ON HEAD!! SQUISH ROW!

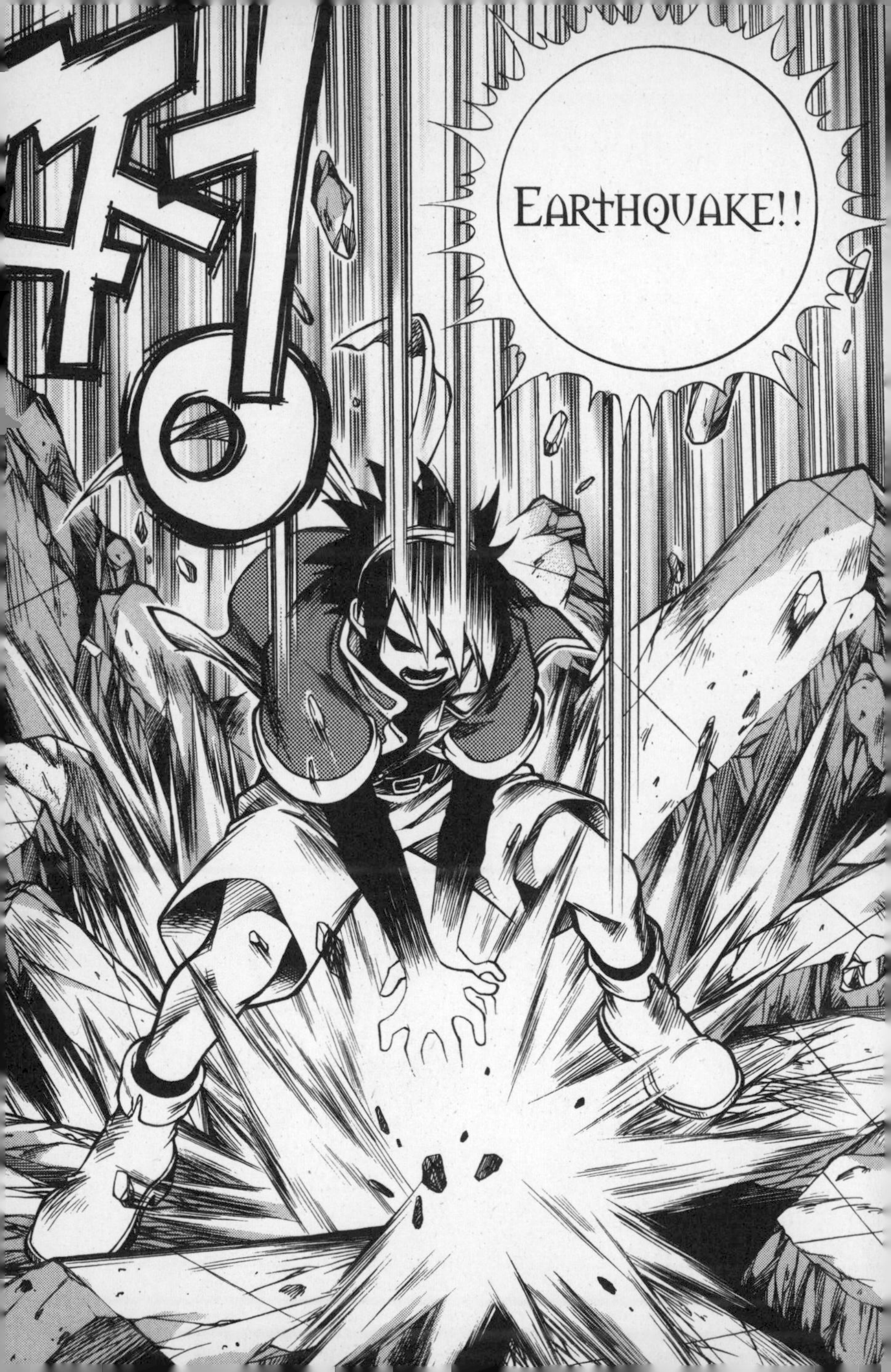
EARTHQUAKE!!

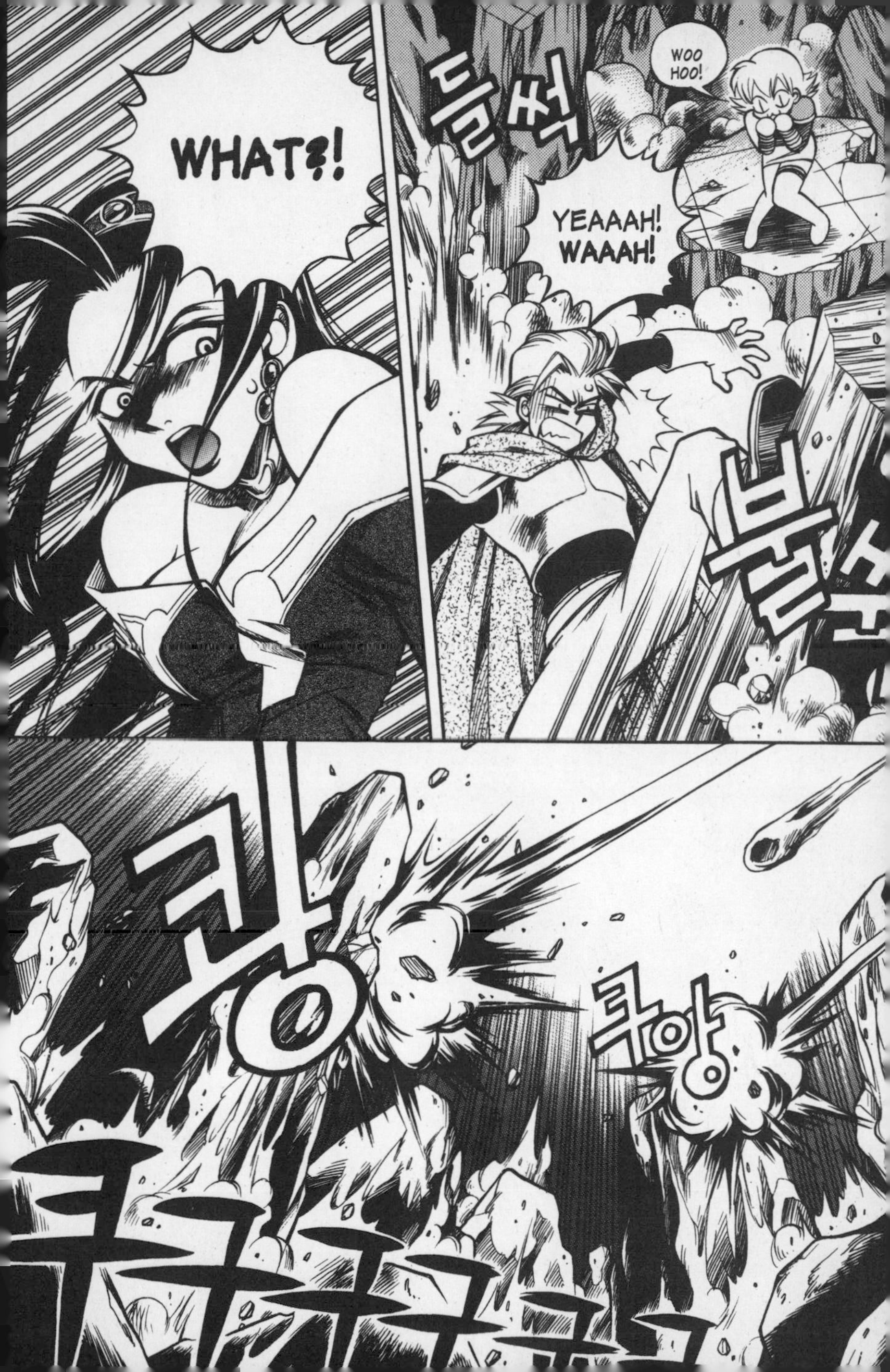

WHAT?!
들썩
WOO HOO!
YEAAAH! WAAAH!

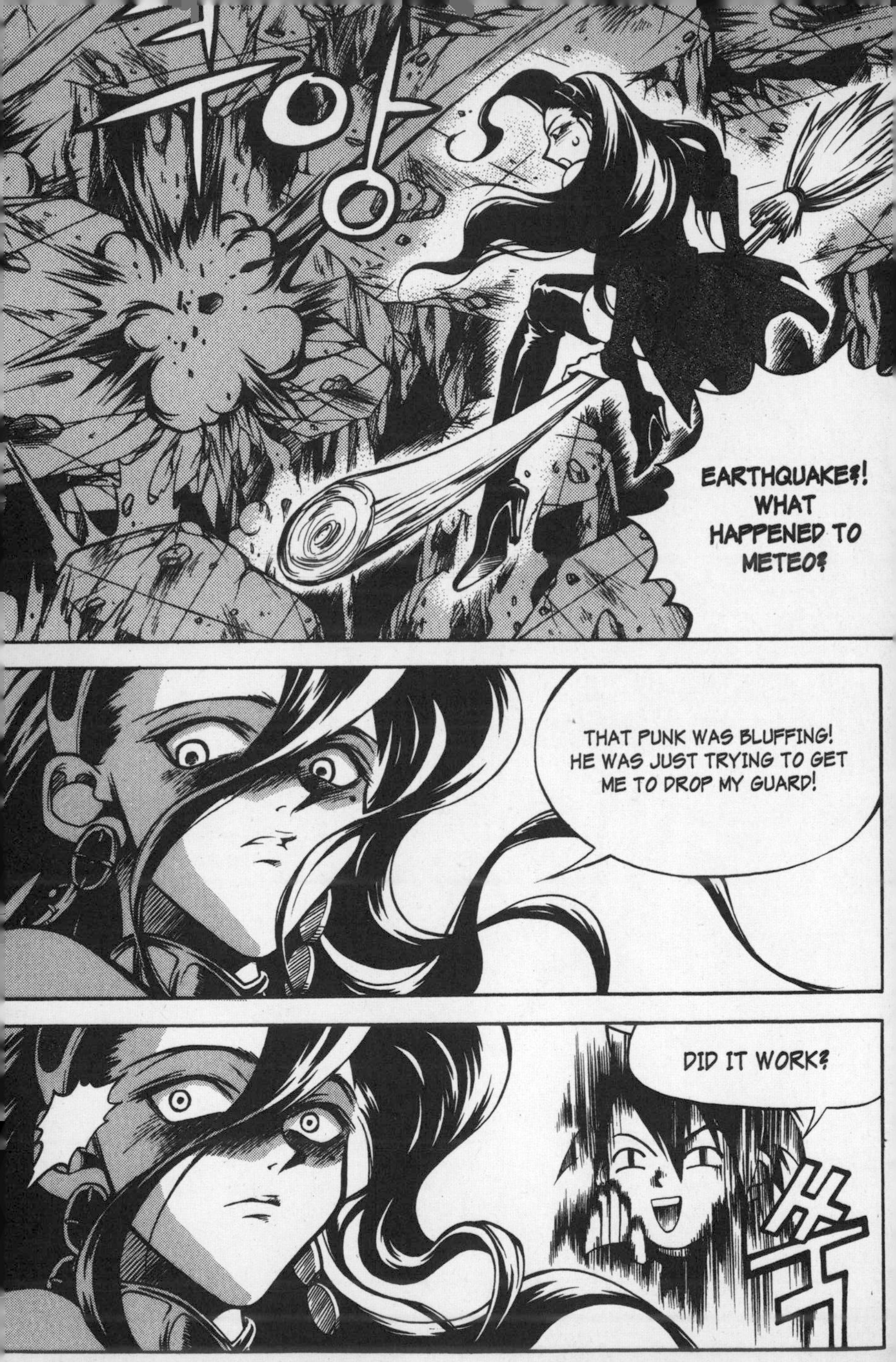
EARTHQUAKE?! WHAT HAPPENED TO METEO?
THAT PUNK WAS BLUFFING! HE WAS JUST TRYING TO GET ME TO DROP MY GUARD!
DID IT WORK?

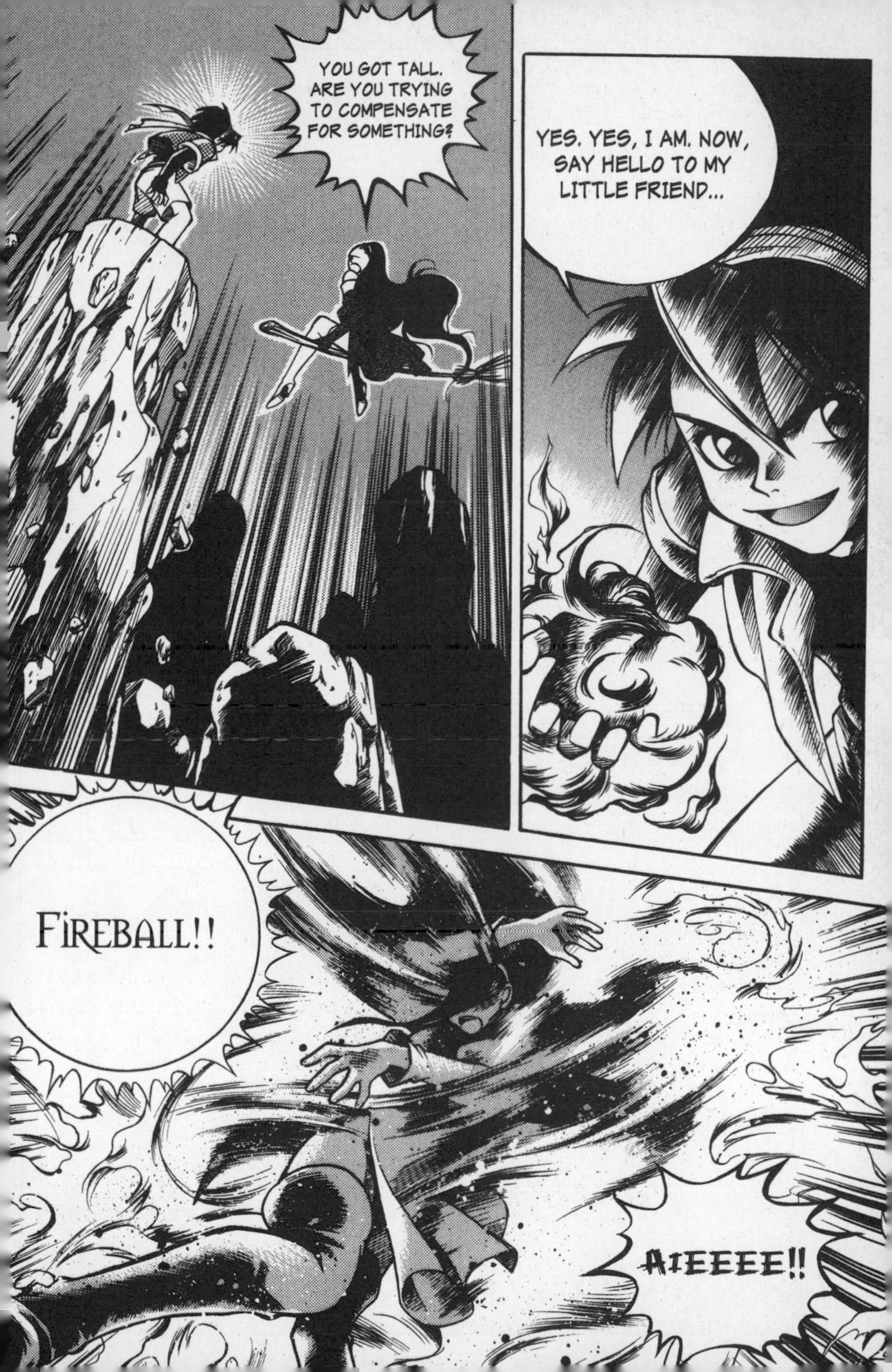
YOU GOT TALL. ARE YOU TRYING TO COMPENSATE FOR SOMETHING?
YES. YES, I AM. NOW, SAY HELLO TO MY LITTLE FRIEND...
FIREBALL!!
AIEEEE!!

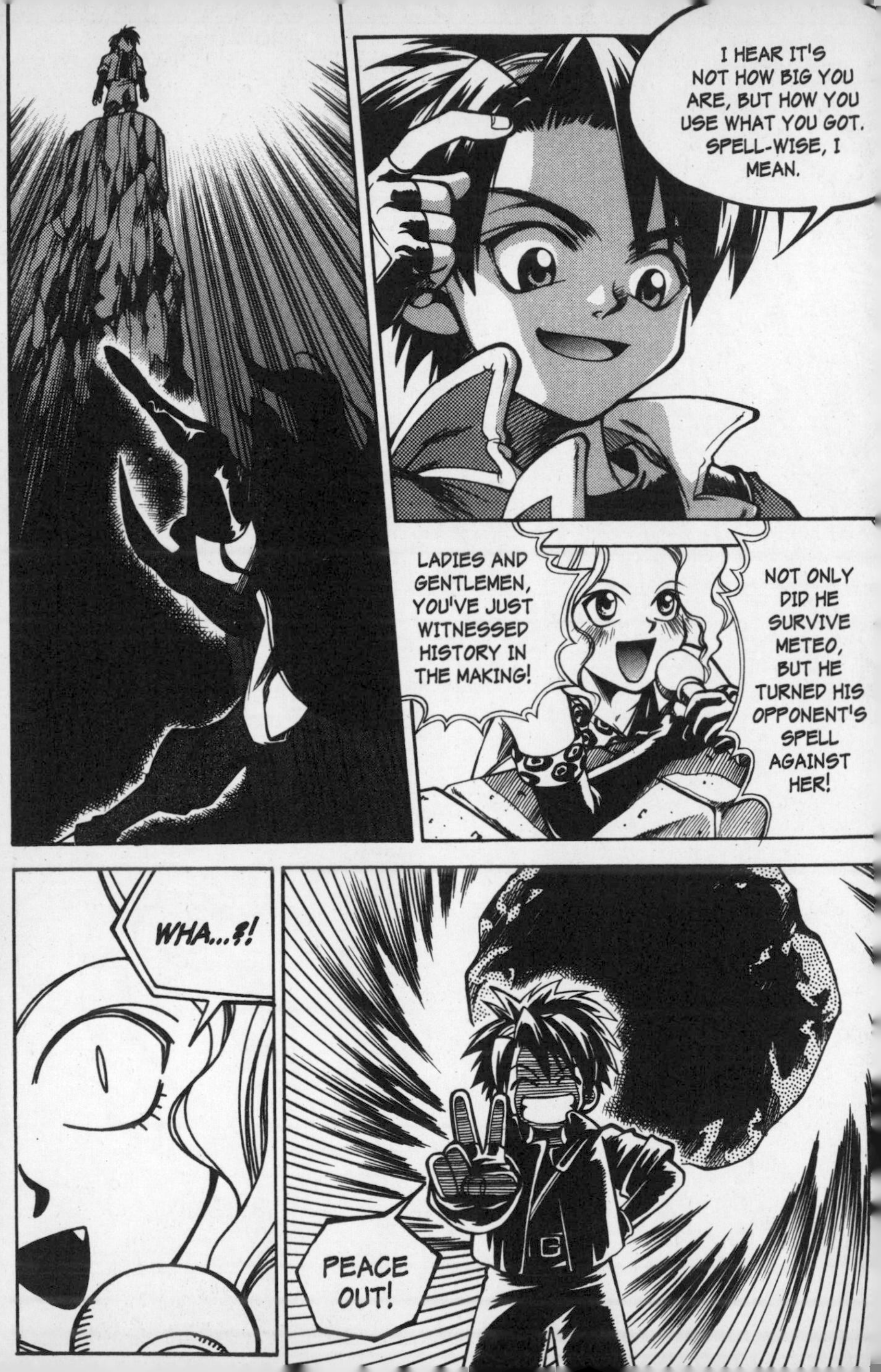
I HEAR IT'S NOT HOW BIG YOU ARE, BUT HOW YOU USE WHAT YOU GOT. SPELL-WISE, I MEAN.
LADIES AND GENTLEMEN, YOU'VE JUST WITNESSED HISTORY IN THE MAKING!
NOT ONLY DID HE SURVIVE METEO, BUT HE TURNED HIS OPPONENT'S SPELL AGAINST HER!
WHA...?!
PEACE OUT!

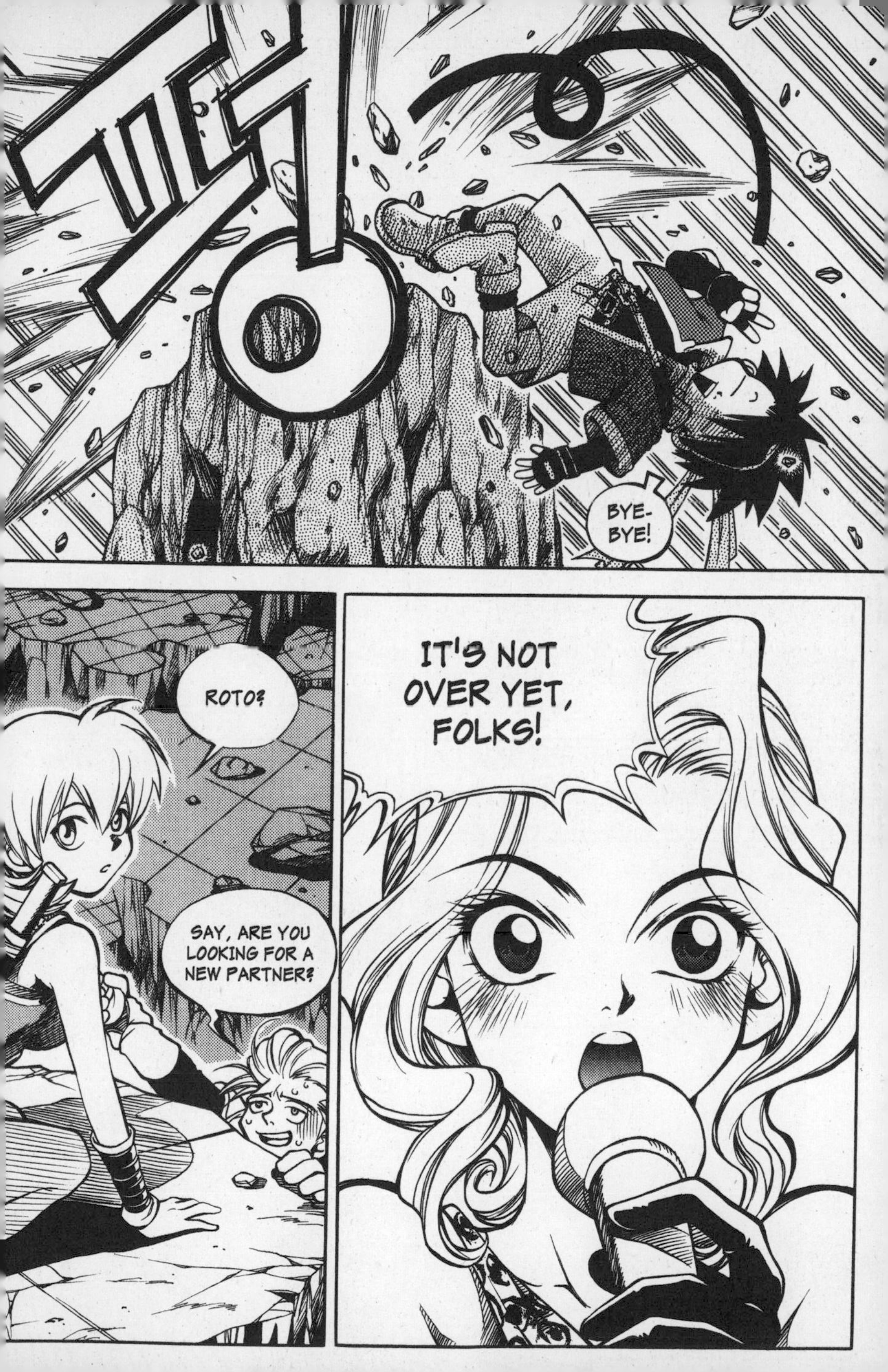
BYE-BYE!
ROTO?
SAY, ARE YOU LOOKING FOR A NEW PARTNER?
IT'S NOT OVER YET, FOLKS!

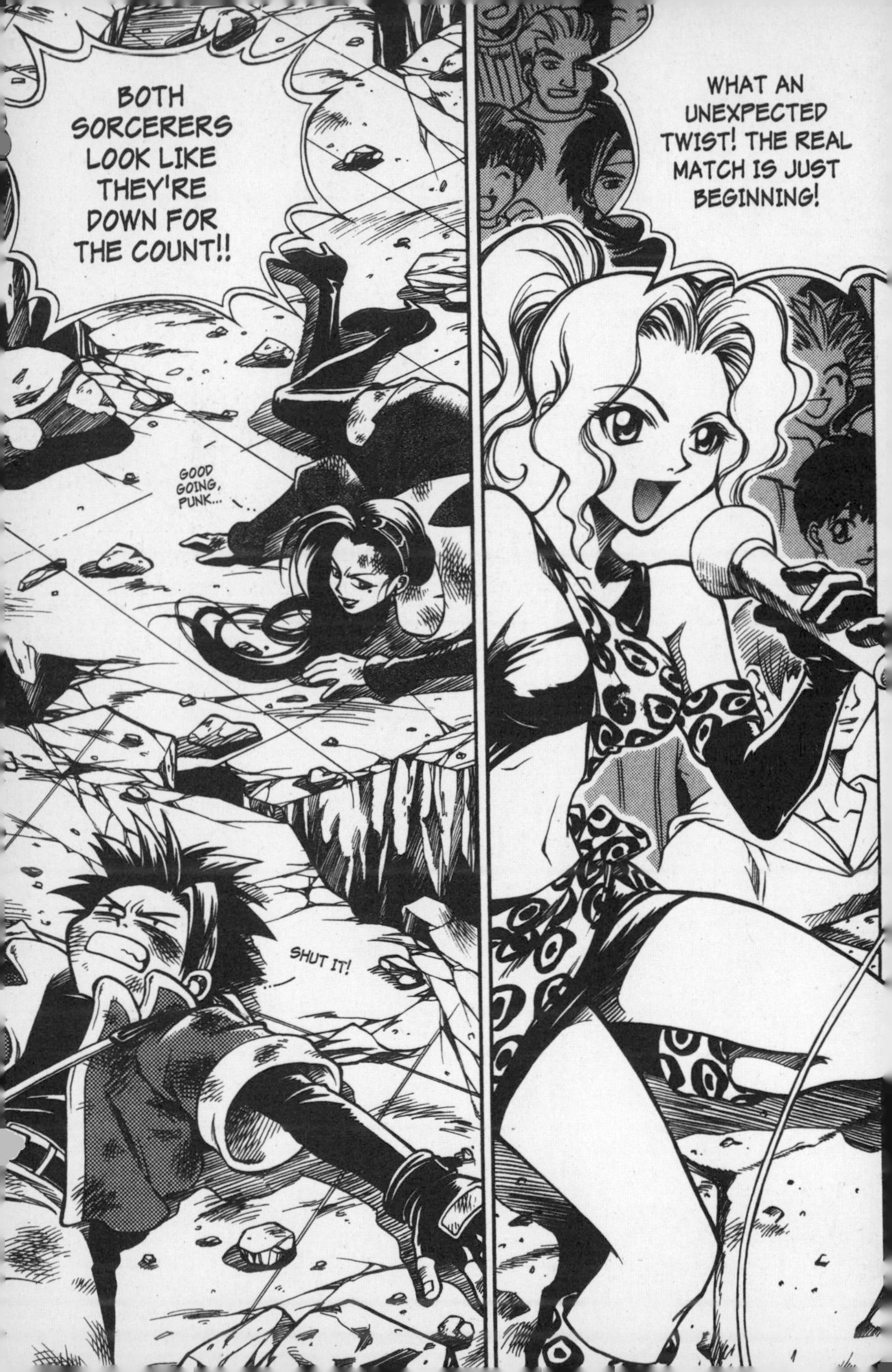
BOTH SORCERERS LOOK LIKE THEY'RE DOWN FOR THE COUNT!!
GOOD GOING, PUNK...
SHUT IT!
WHAT AN UNEXPECTED TWIST! THE REAL MATCH IS JUST BEGINNING!

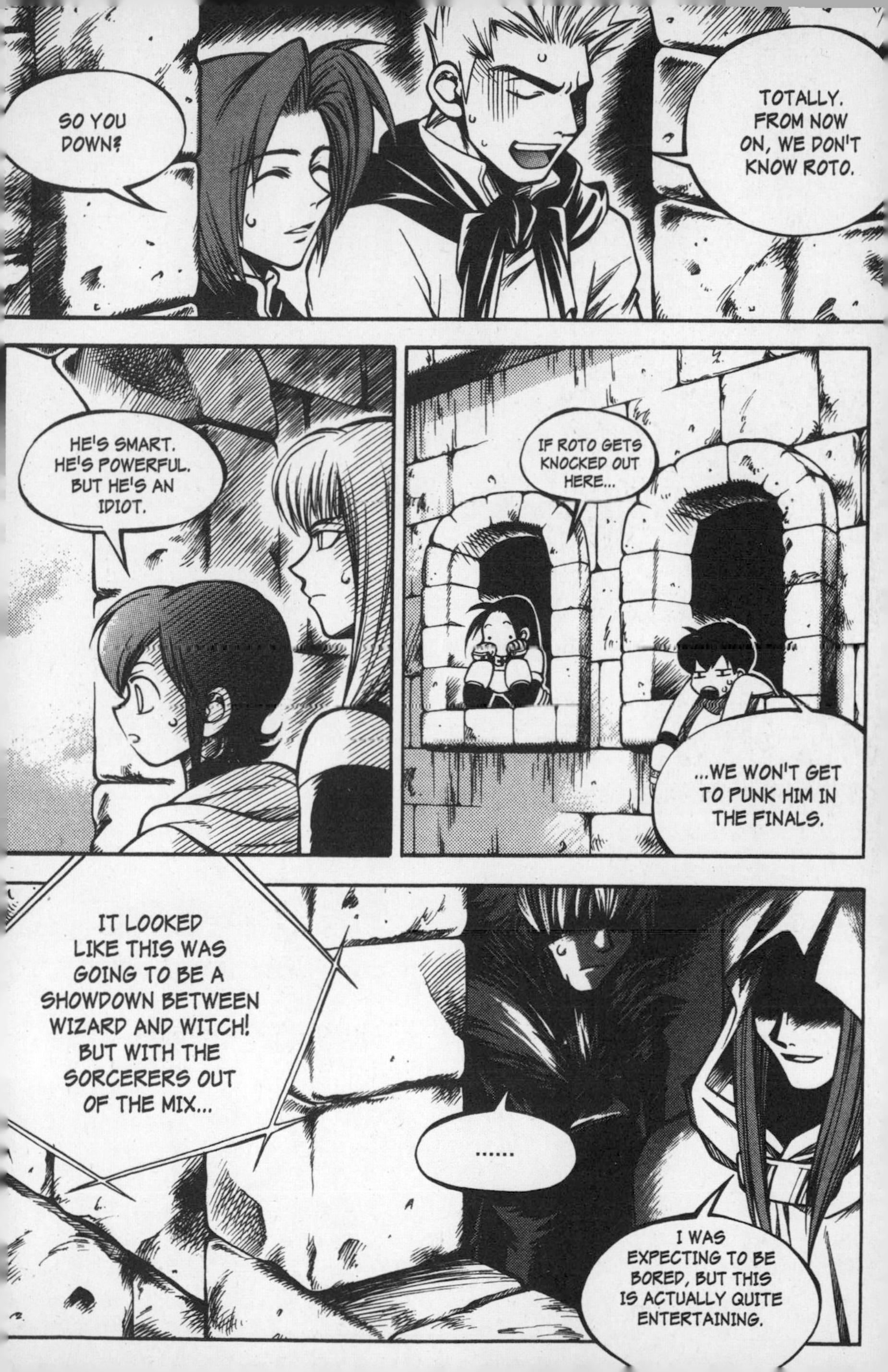
SO YOU DOWN?
TOTALLY. FROM NOW ON, WE DON'T KNOW ROTO.
HE'S SMART. HE'S POWERFUL. BUT HE'S AN IDIOT.
IF ROTO GETS KNOCKED OUT HERE...
...WE WON'T GET TO PUNK HIM IN THE FINALS.
IT LOOKED LIKE THIS WAS GOING TO BE A SHOWDOWN BETWEEN WIZARD AND WITCH! BUT WITH THE SORCERERS OUT OF THE MIX...
......
I WAS EXPECTING TO BE BORED, BUT THIS IS ACTUALLY QUITE ENTERTAINING.

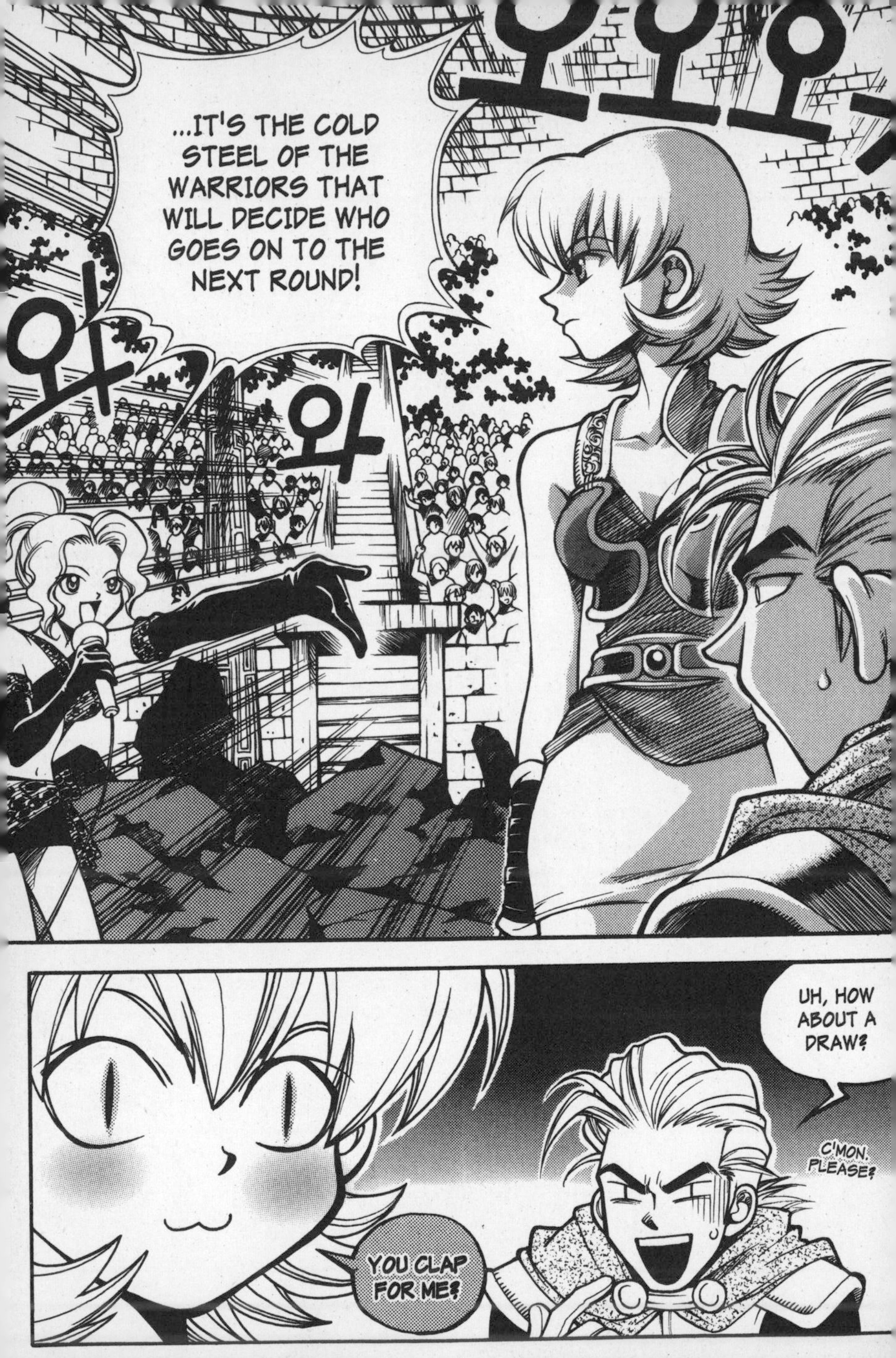

오오오
...IT'S THE COLD STEEL OF THE WARRIORS THAT WILL DECIDE WHO GOES ON TO THE NEXT ROUND!
와
와
UH, HOW ABOUT A DRAW?
C'MON. PLEASE?
YOU CLAP FOR ME?

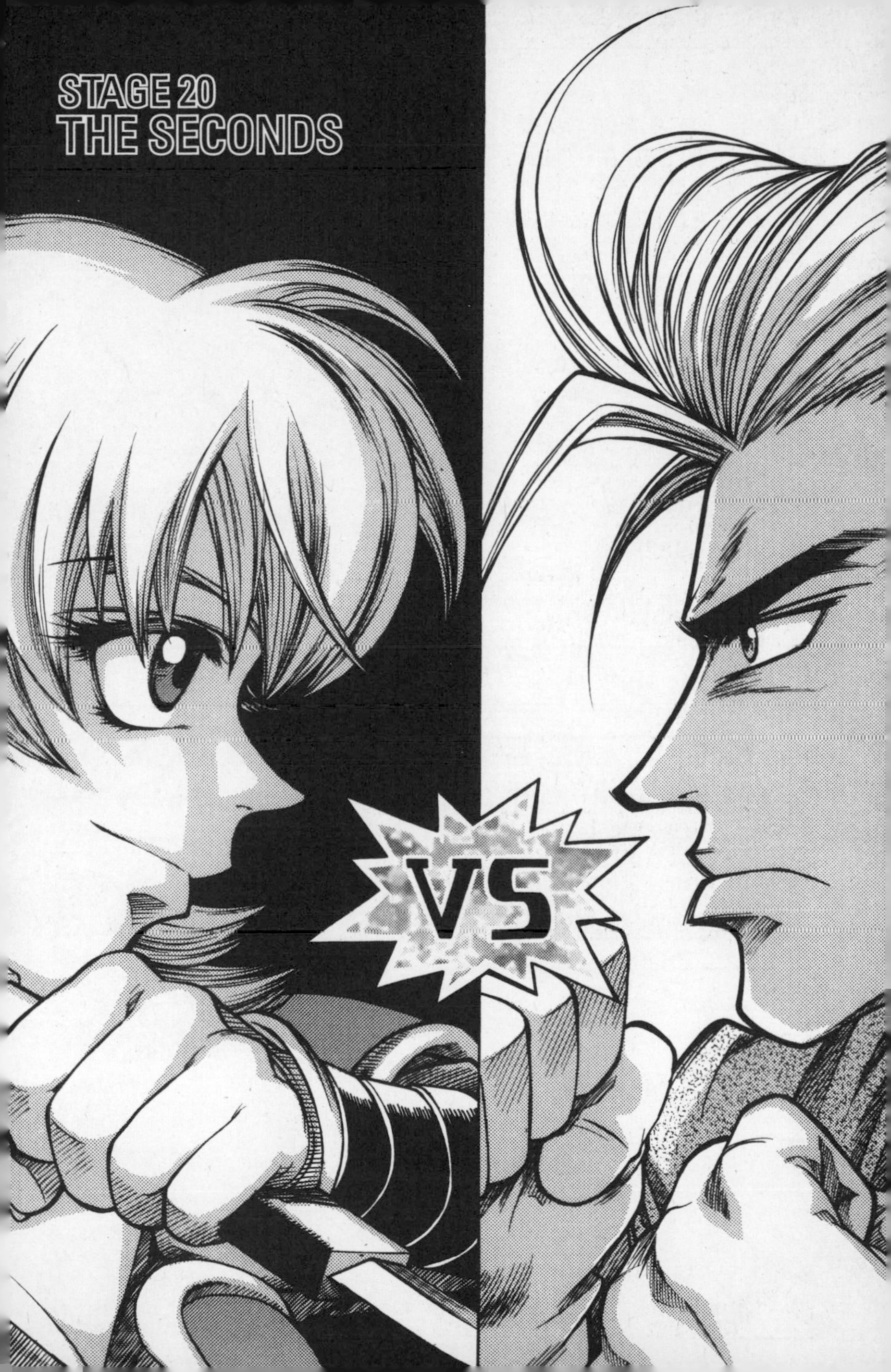
STAGE 20
THE SECONDS
VS

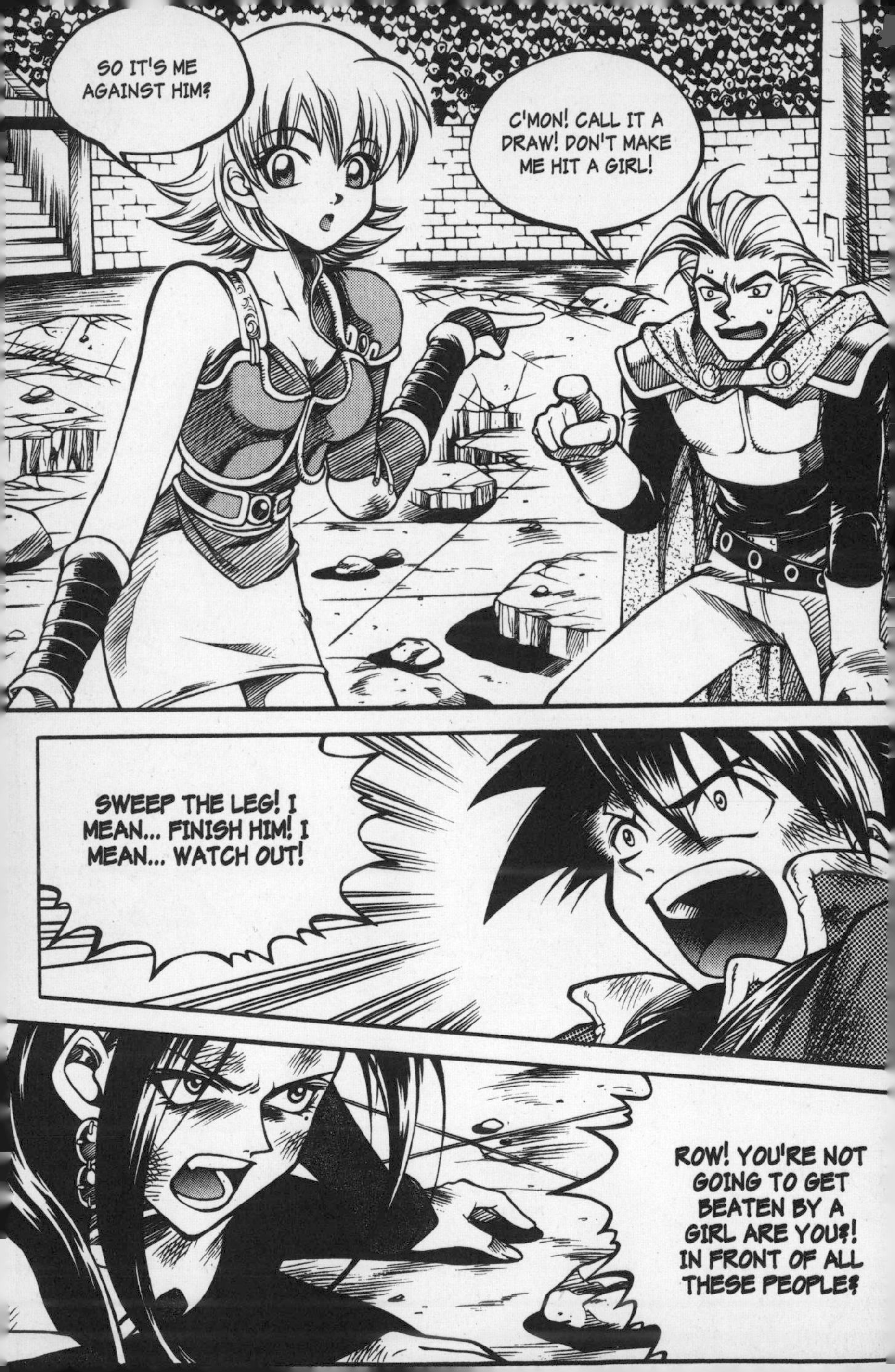

SO IT'S ME AGAINST HIM?
C'MON! CALL IT A DRAW! DON'T MAKE ME HIT A GIRL!
SWEEP THE LEG! I MEAN... FINISH HIM! I MEAN... WATCH OUT!
ROW! YOU'RE NOT GOING TO GET BEATEN BY A GIRL ARE YOU?! IN FRONT OF ALL THESE PEOPLE?

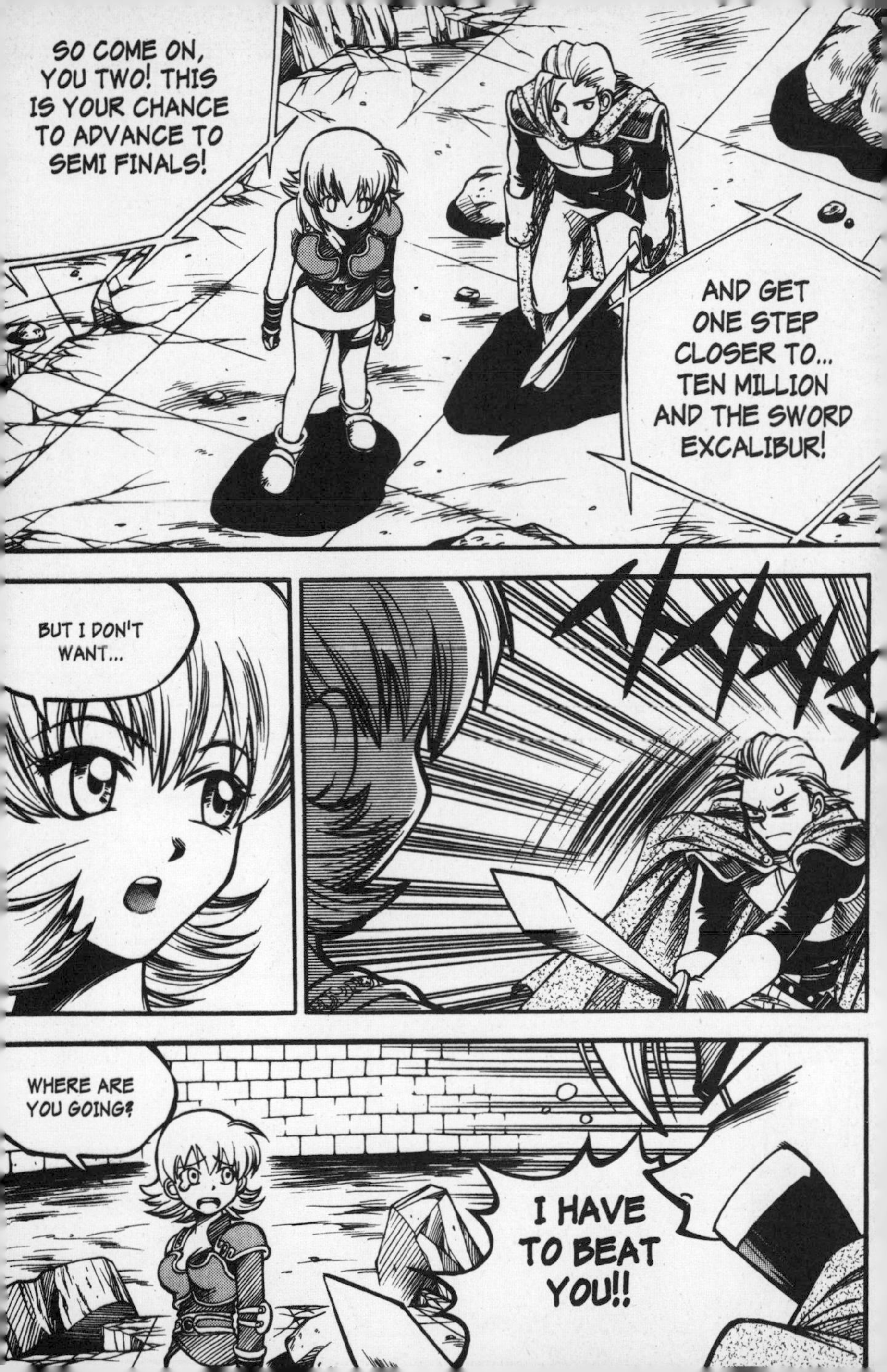
SO COME ON, YOU TWO! THIS IS YOUR CHANCE TO ADVANCE TO SEMI FINALS!
AND GET ONE STEP CLOSER TO... TEN MILLION AND THE SWORD EXCALIBUR!
BUT I DON'T WANT...
WHERE ARE YOU GOING?
I HAVE TO BEAT YOU!!

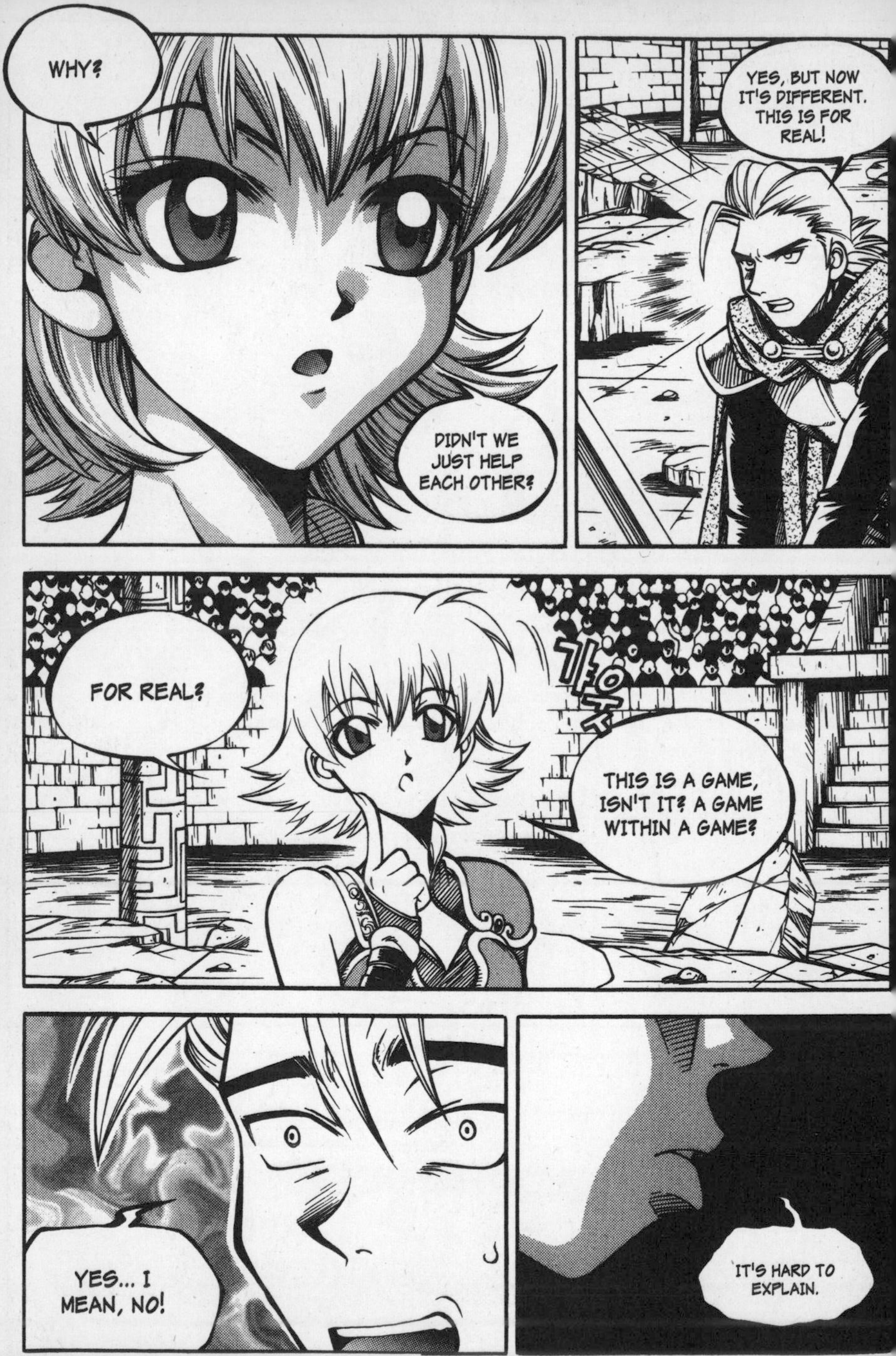
WHY?
DIDN'T WE JUST HELP EACH OTHER?
YES, BUT NOW IT'S DIFFERENT. THIS IS FOR REAL!
FOR REAL?
THIS IS A GAME, ISN'T IT? A GAME WITHIN A GAME?
YES... I MEAN, NO!
IT'S HARD TO EXPLAIN.

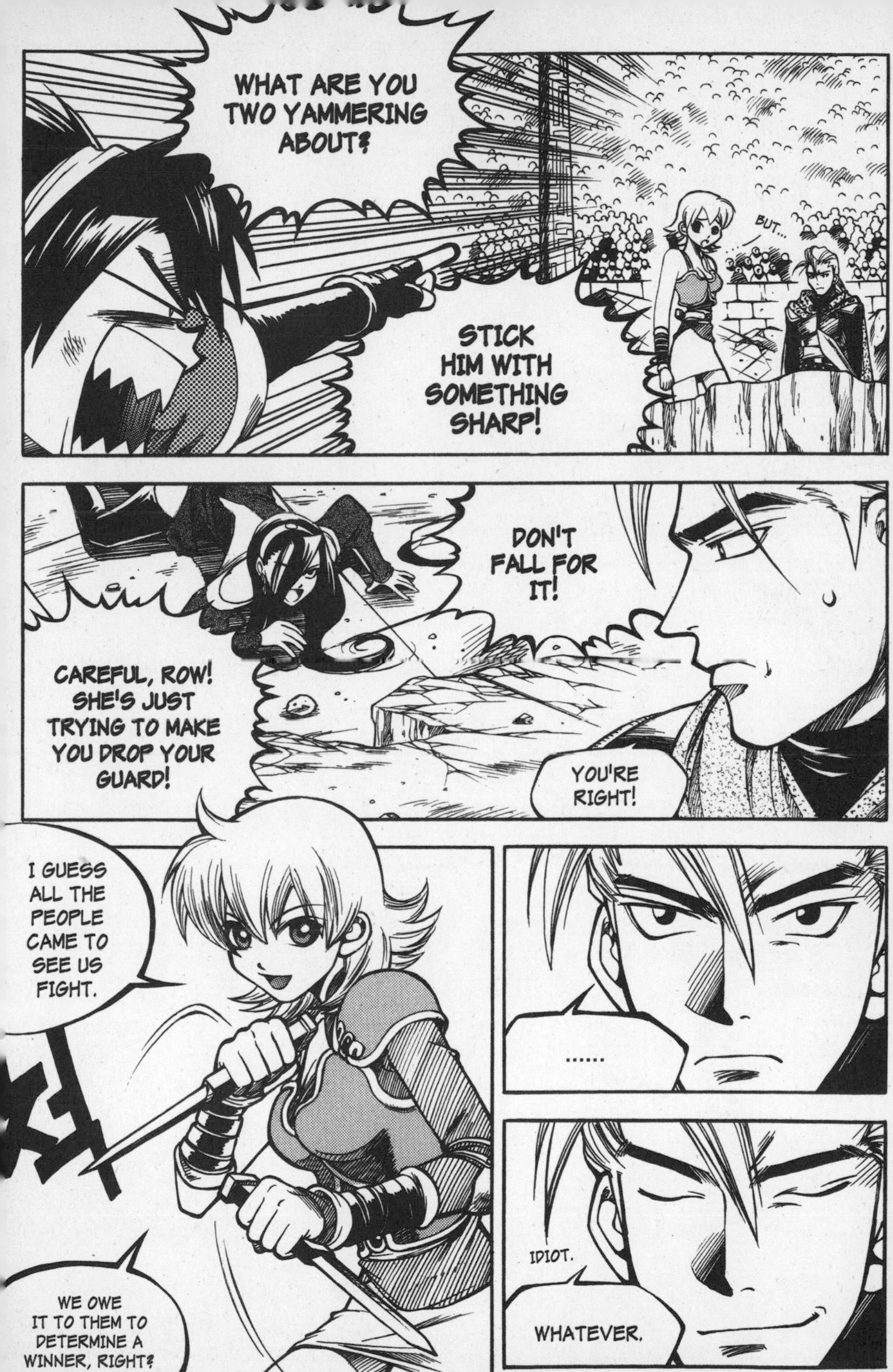

WHAT ARE YOU TWO YAMMERING ABOUT?
STICK HIM WITH SOMETHING SHARP!
BUT...
CAREFUL, ROW! SHE'S JUST TRYING TO MAKE YOU DROP YOUR GUARD!
DON'T FALL FOR IT!
YOU'RE RIGHT!
I GUESS ALL THE PEOPLE CAME TO SEE US FIGHT.
WE OWE IT TO THEM TO DETERMINE A WINNER, RIGHT?
......
IDIOT.
WHATEVER.

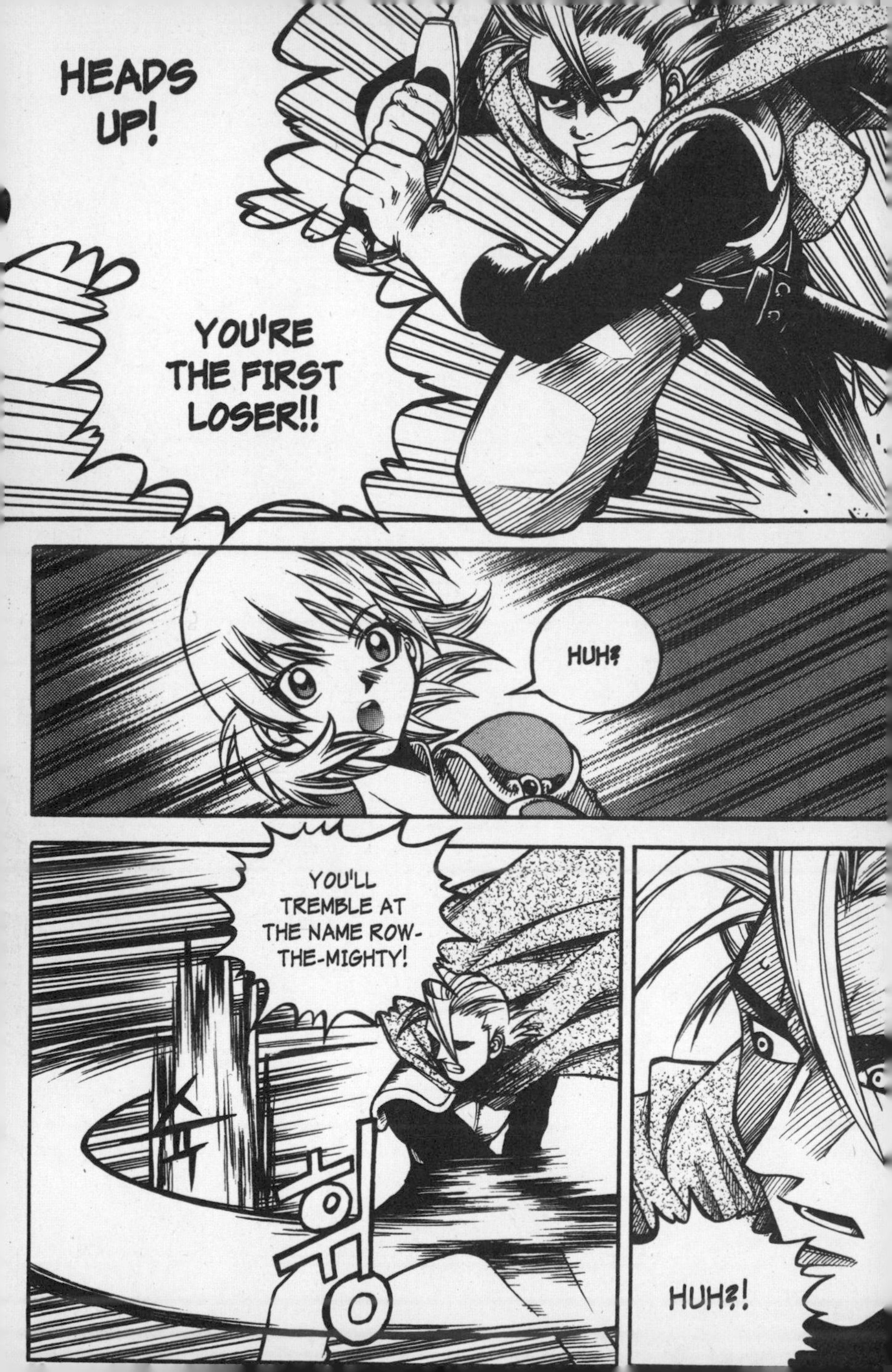

HEADS UP!
YOU'RE THE FIRST LOSER!!
HUH?
YOU'LL TREMBLE AT THE NAME ROW-THE-MIGHTY!
HUH?!

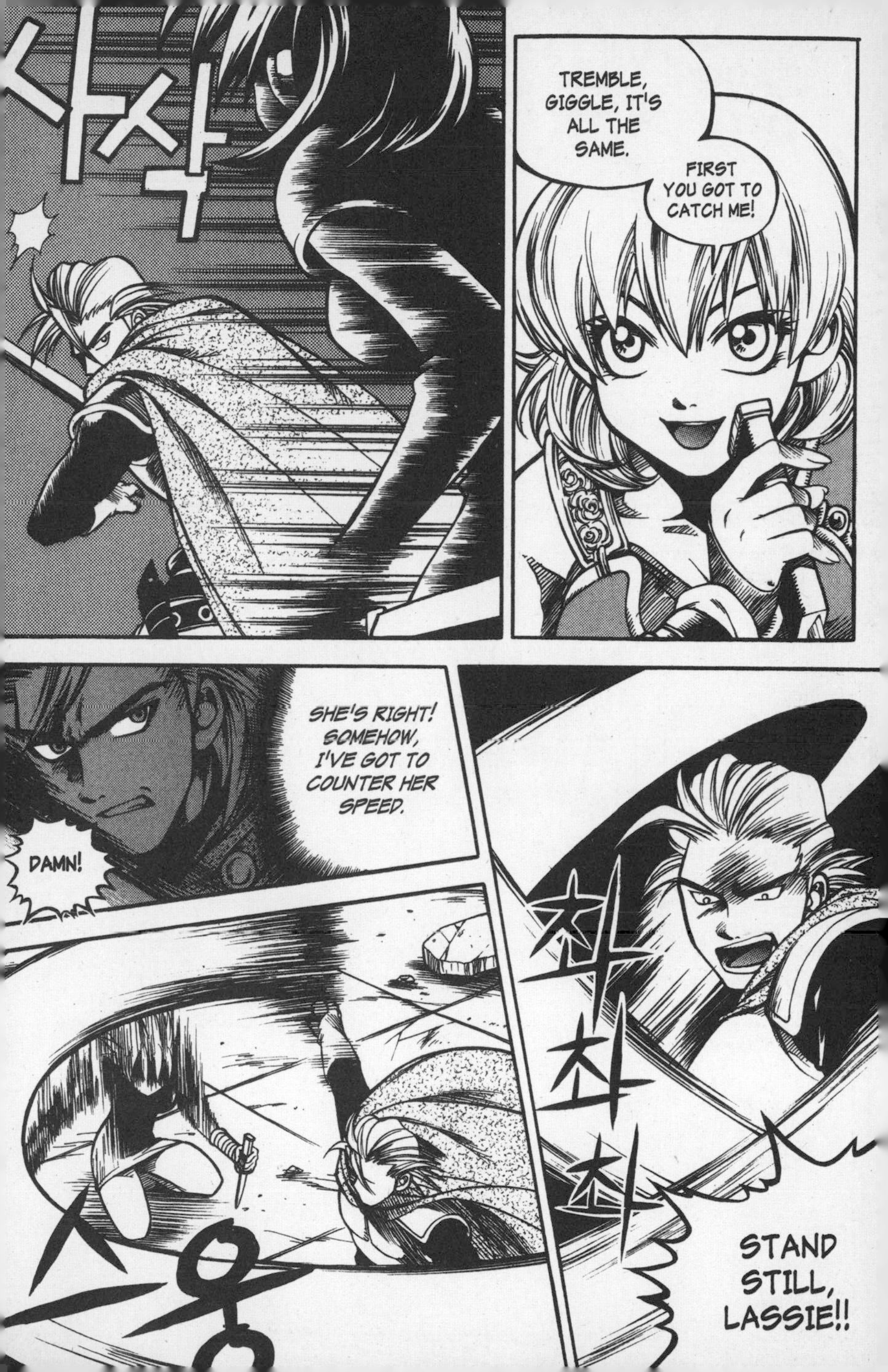
TREMBLE, GIGGLE, IT'S ALL THE SAME.
FIRST YOU GOT TO CATCH ME!
SHE'S RIGHT! SOMEHOW, I'VE GOT TO COUNTER HER SPEED.
DAMN!
STAND STILL, LASSIE!!

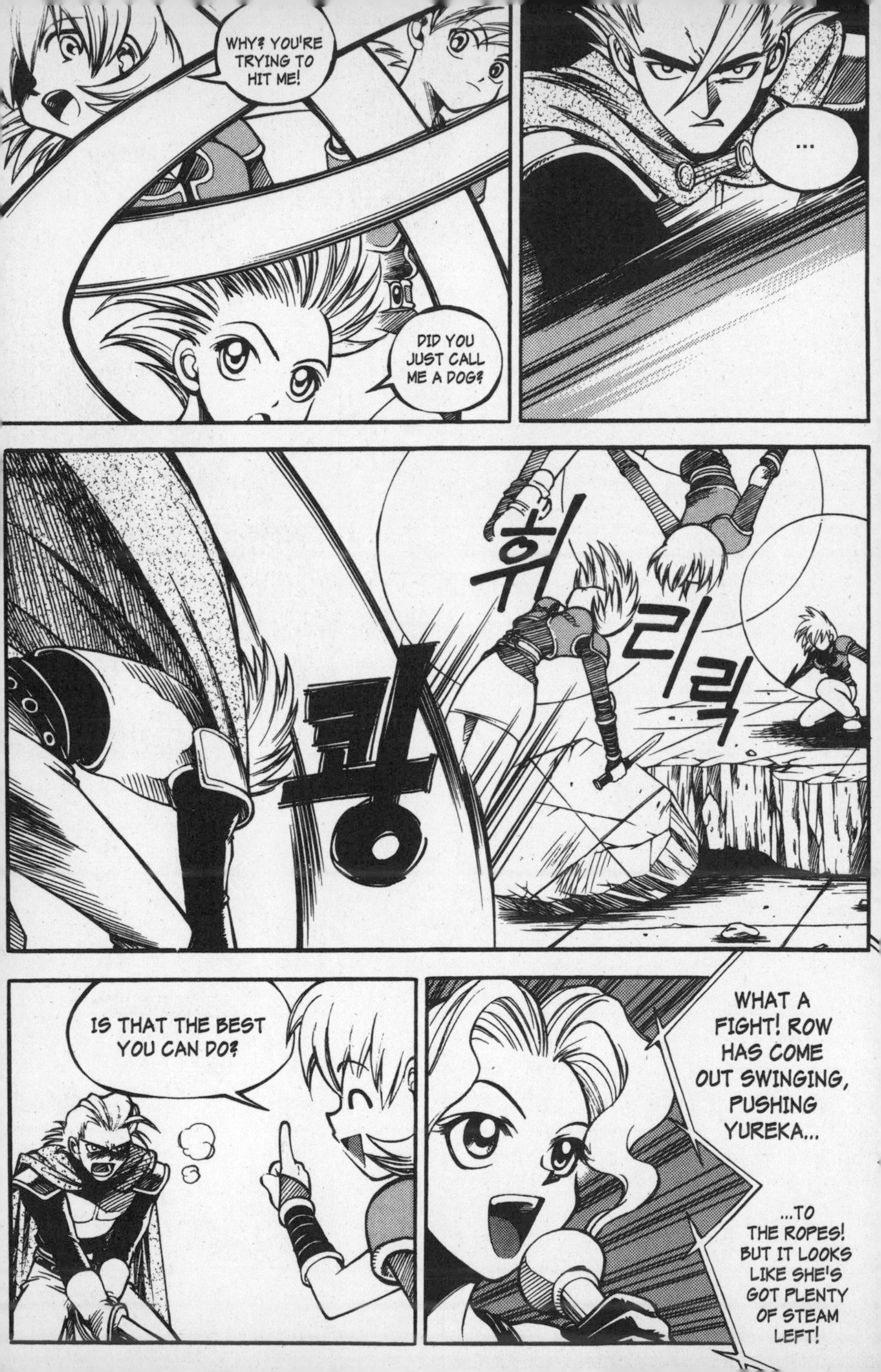

WHY? YOU'RE TRYING TO HIT ME!
DID YOU JUST CALL ME A DOG?
...
쾅
휘리릭
IS THAT THE BEST YOU CAN DO?
WHAT A FIGHT! ROW HAS COME OUT SWINGING, PUSHING YUREKA...
...TO THE ROPES! BUT IT LOOKS LIKE SHE'S GOT PLENTY OF STEAM LEFT!

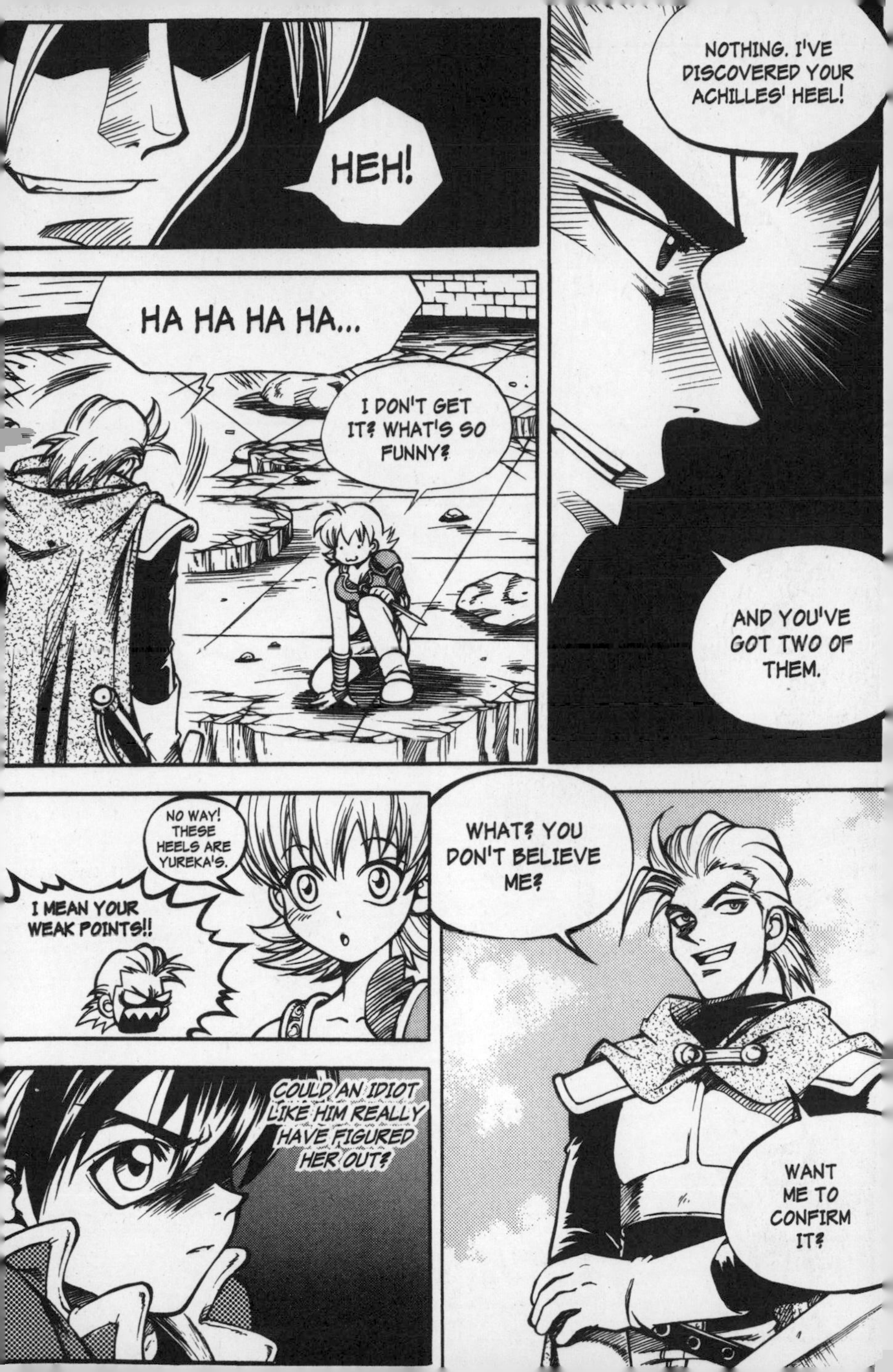
HEH!
HA HA HA HA...
I DON'T GET IT? WHAT'S SO FUNNY?
NOTHING. I'VE DISCOVERED YOUR ACHILLES' HEEL!
AND YOU'VE GOT TWO OF THEM.
NO WAY! THESE HEELS ARE YUREKA'S.
I MEAN YOUR WEAK POINTS!!
COULD AN IDIOT LIKE HIM REALLY HAVE FIGURED HER OUT?
WHAT? YOU DON'T BELIEVE ME?
WANT ME TO CONFIRM IT?

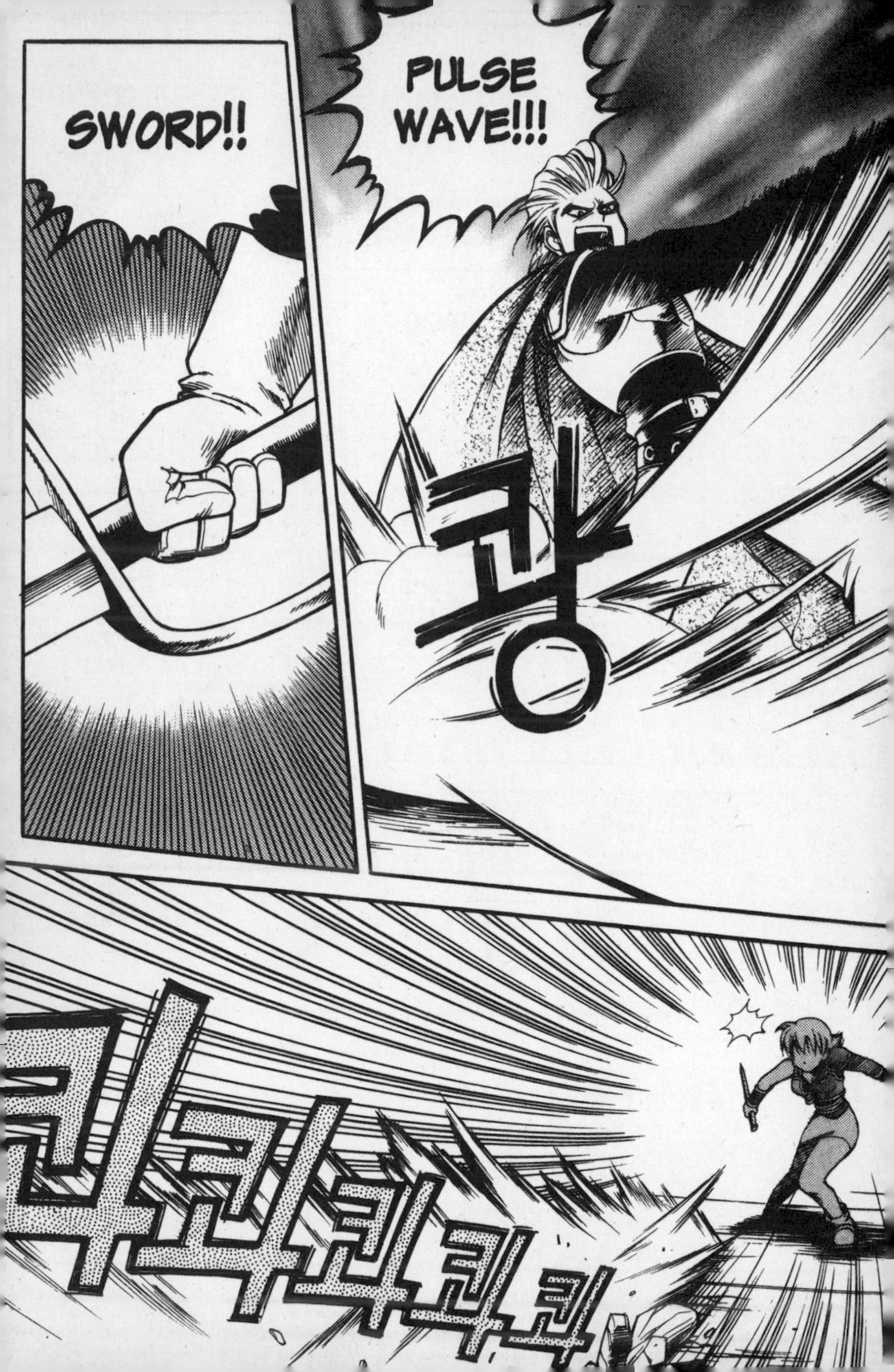
SWORD!!
PULSE WAVE!!!

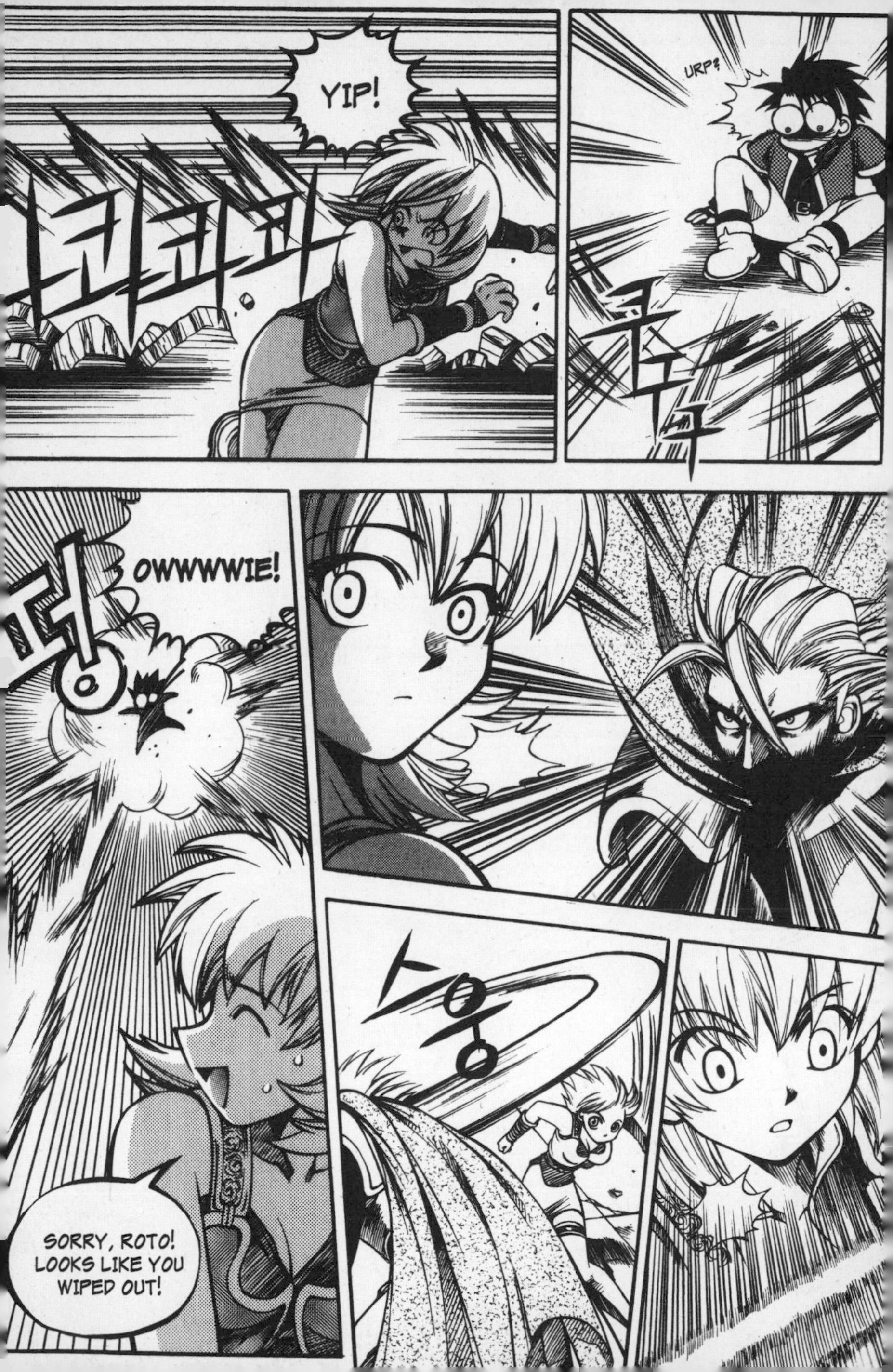
YIP!
URP?
OWWWWIE!
SORRY, ROTO! LOOKS LIKE YOU WIPED OUT!

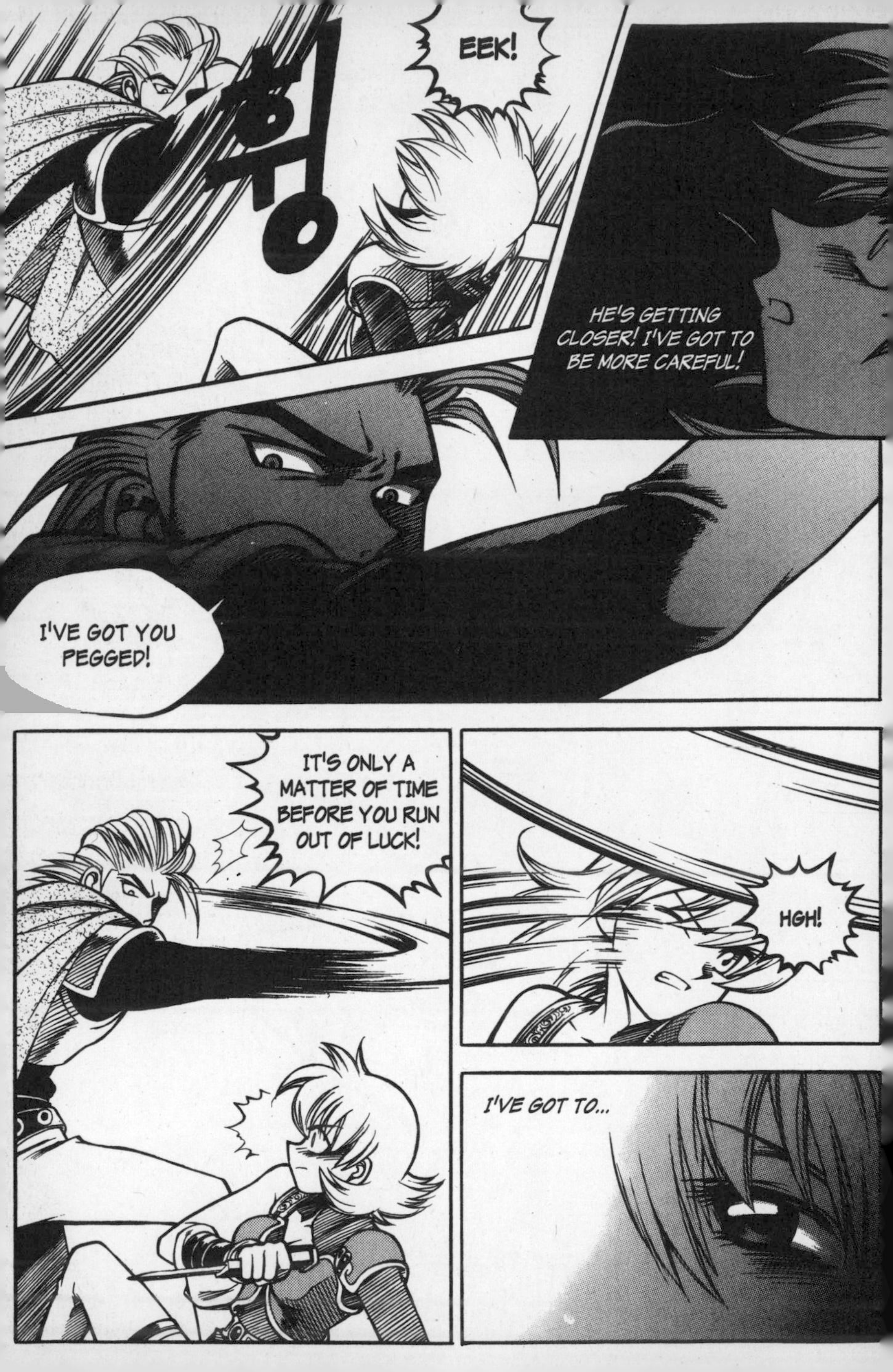
EEK!
HE'S GETTING CLOSER! I'VE GOT TO BE MORE CAREFUL!
I'VE GOT YOU PEGGED!
IT'S ONLY A MATTER OF TIME BEFORE YOU RUN OUT OF LUCK!
HGH!
I'VE GOT TO...

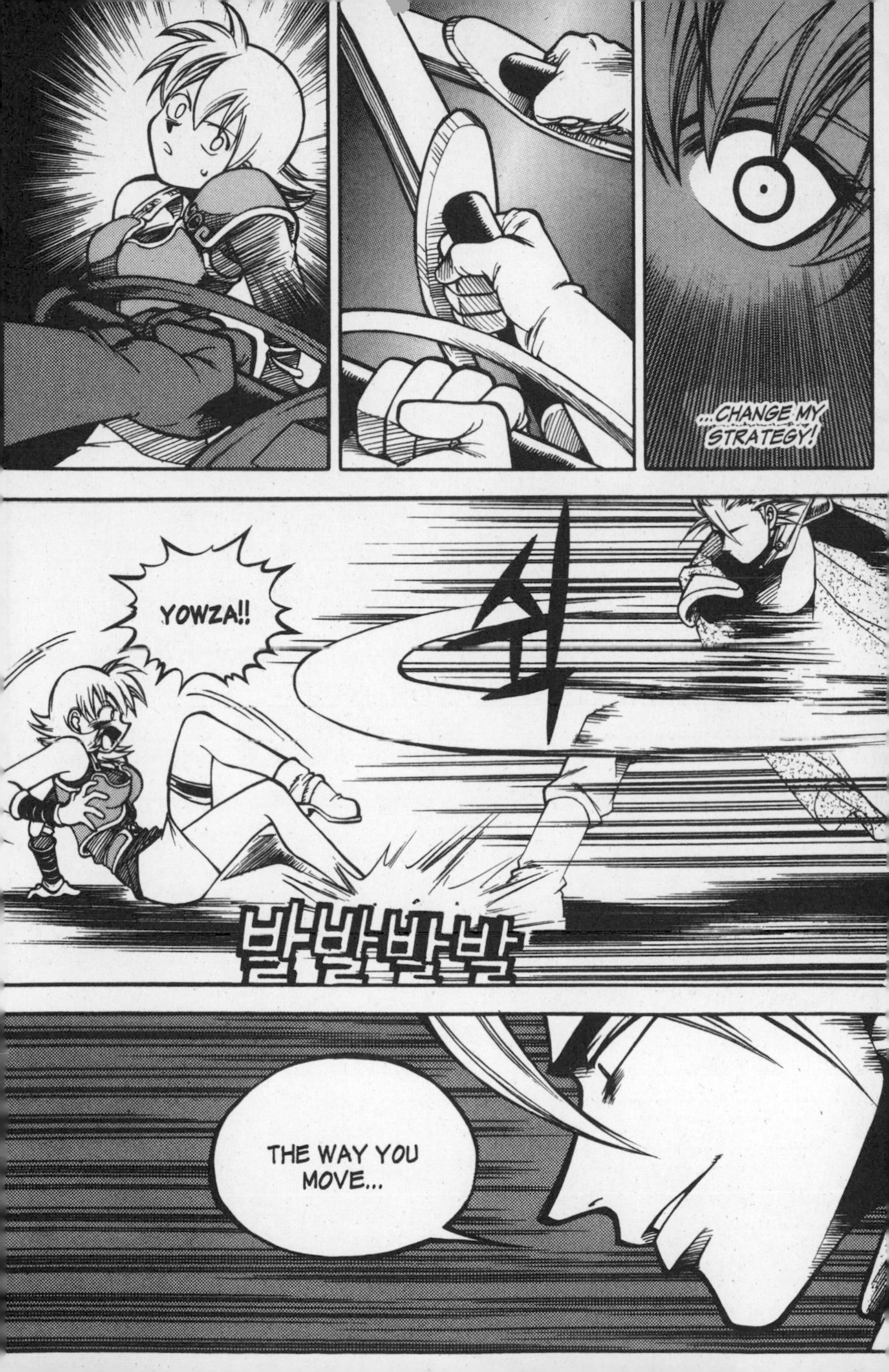
...CHANGE MY STRATEGY!
YOWZA!!
THE WAY YOU MOVE...

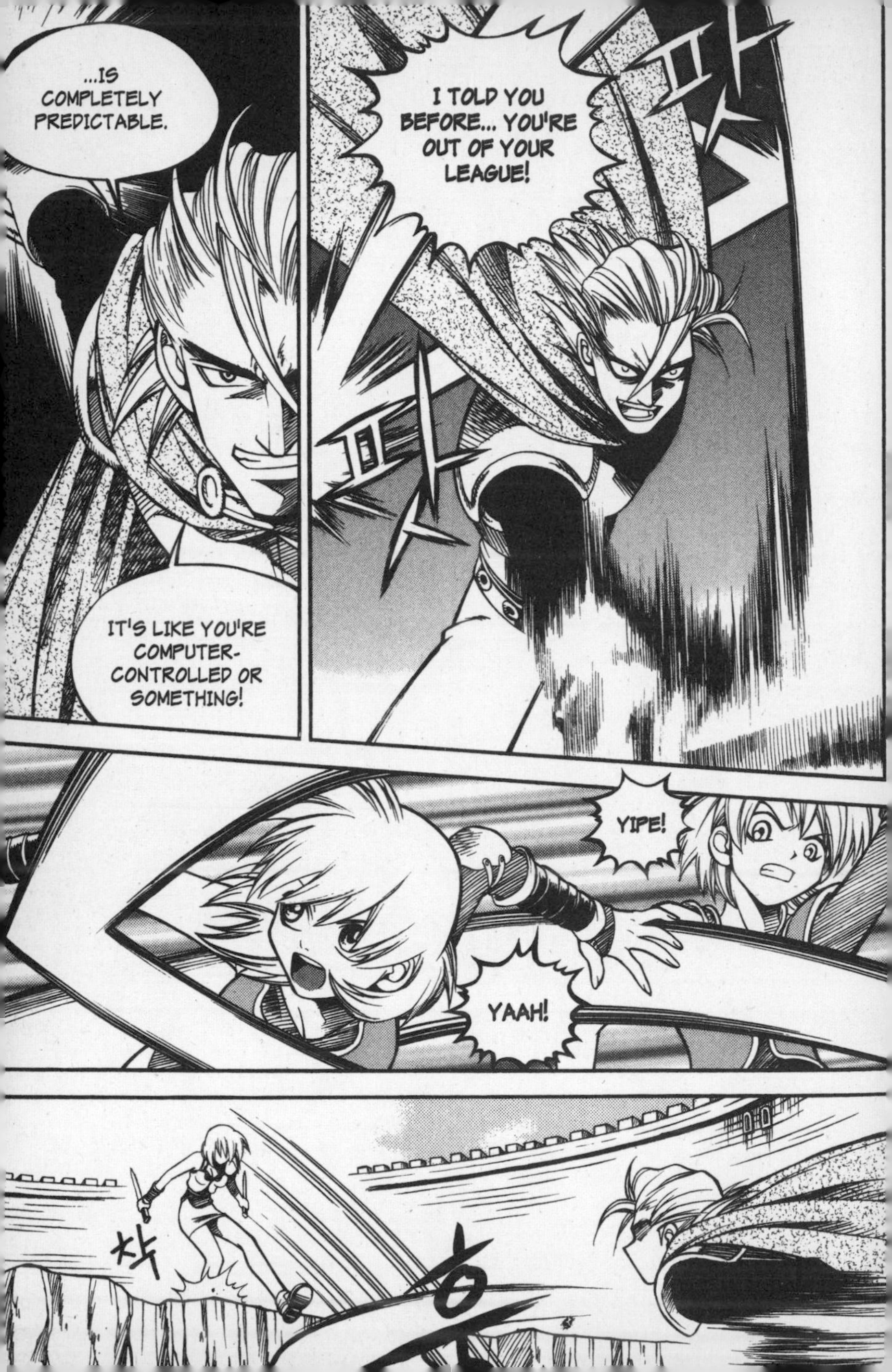
...IS COMPLETELY PREDICTABLE.
IT'S LIKE YOU'RE COMPUTER-CONTROLLED OR SOMETHING!
I TOLD YOU BEFORE... YOU'RE OUT OF YOUR LEAGUE!
YIPE!
YAAH!

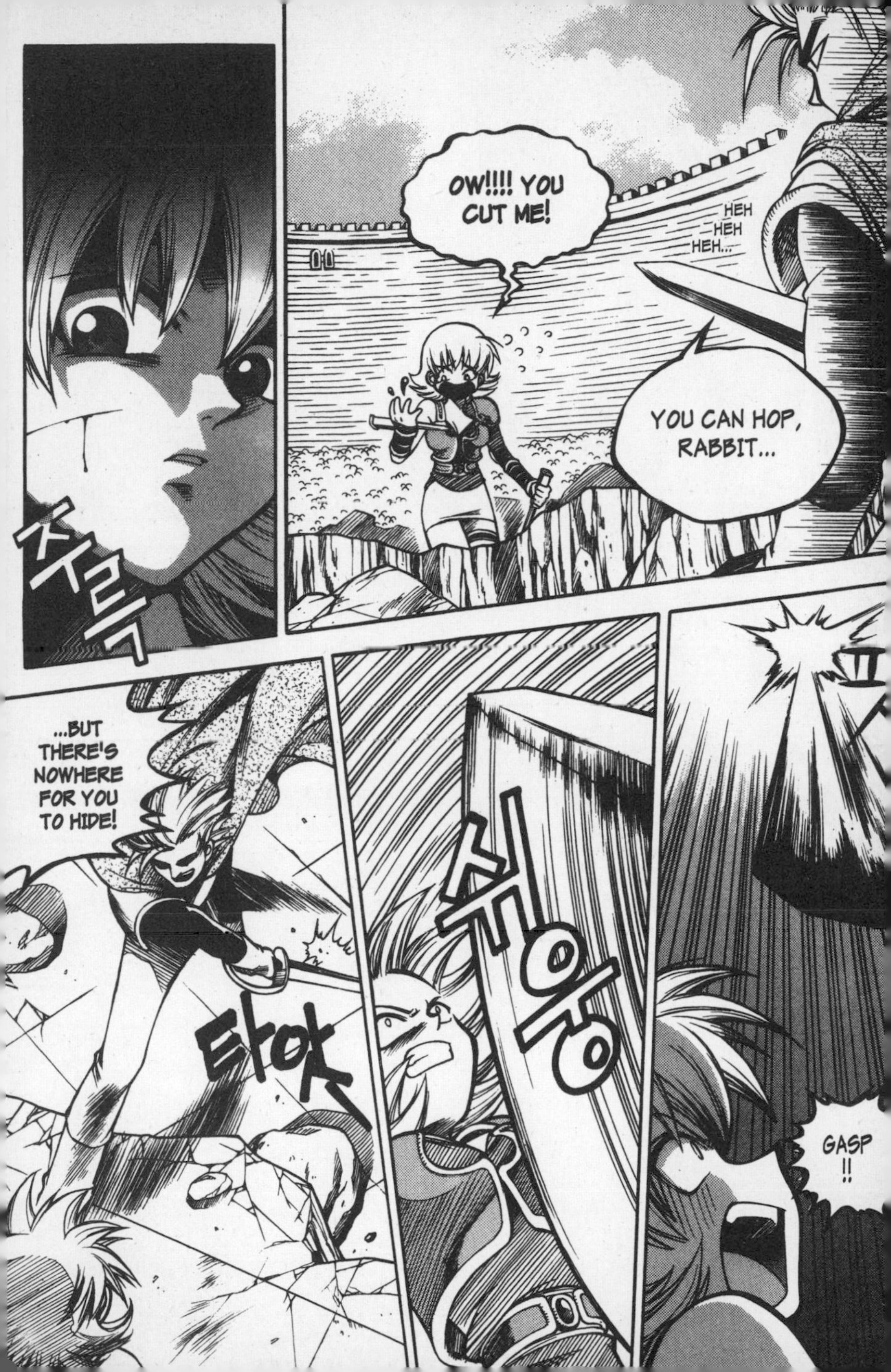
OW!!!! YOU CUT ME!
HEH HEH HEH...
YOU CAN HOP, RABBIT...
...BUT THERE'S NOWHERE FOR YOU TO HIDE!
GASP !!

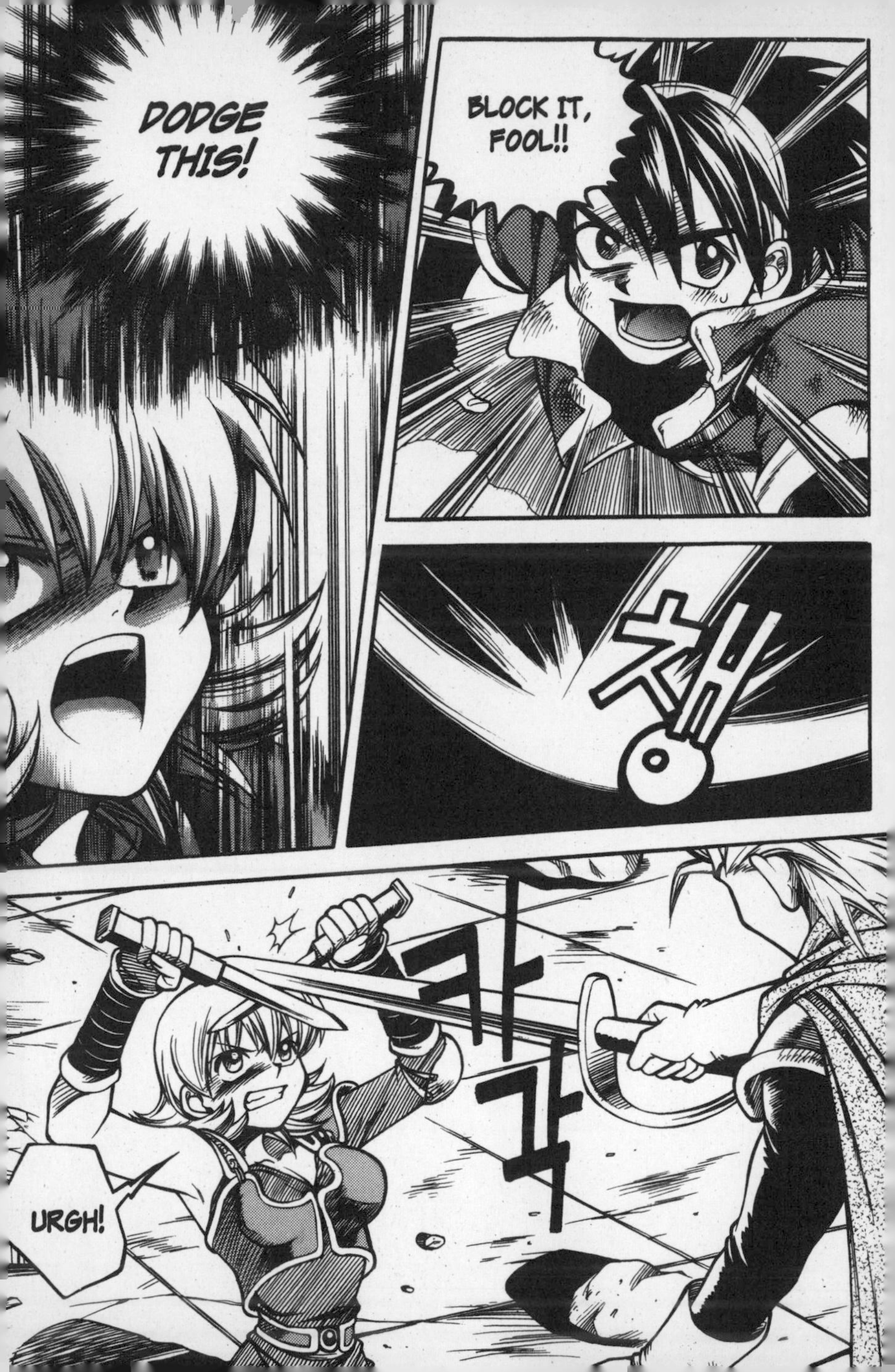
DODGE THIS!
BLOCK IT, FOOL!!
URGH!

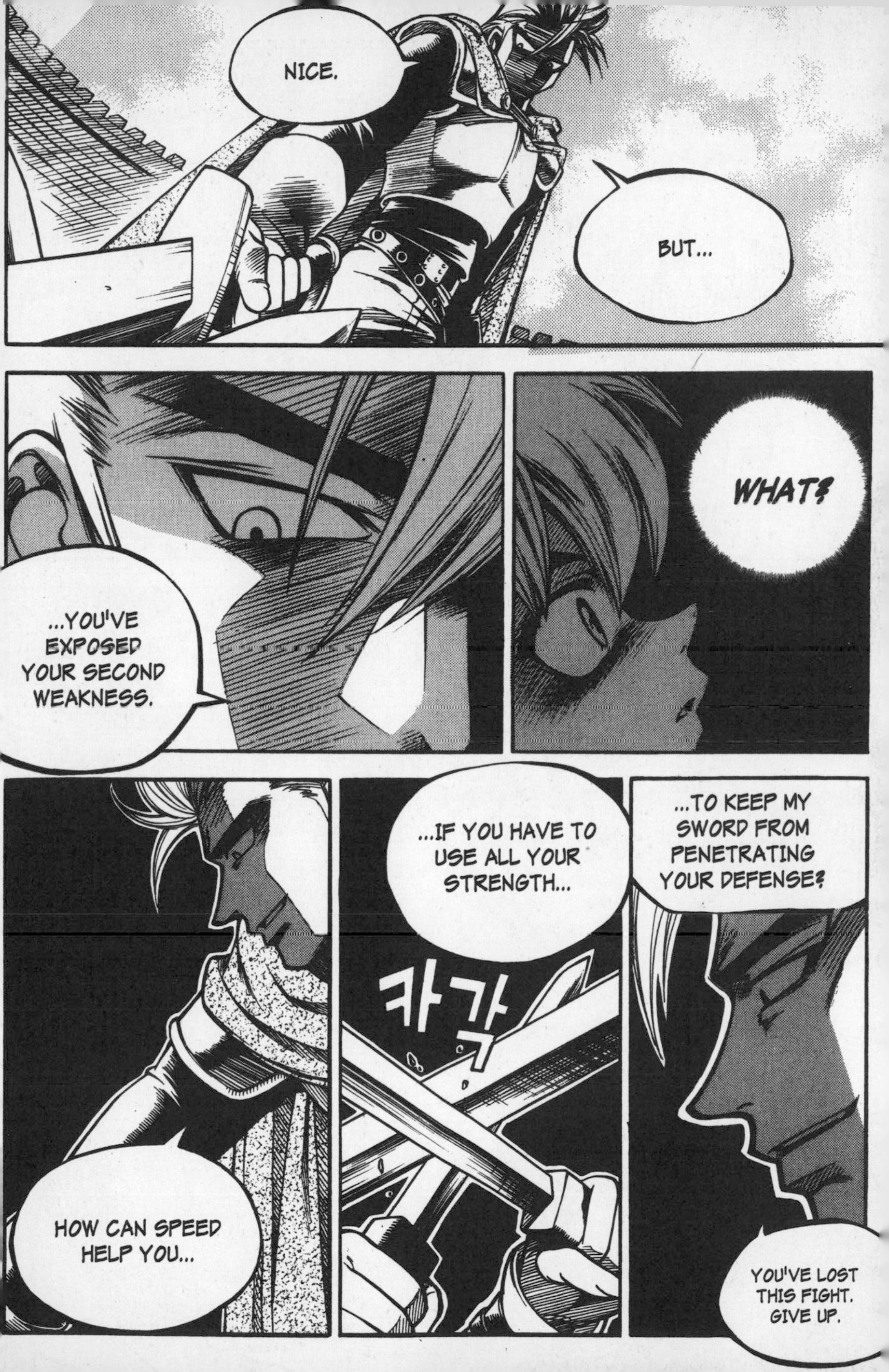
NICE.
BUT...
...YOU'VE EXPOSED YOUR SECOND WEAKNESS.
WHAT?
HOW CAN SPEED HELP YOU...
...IF YOU HAVE TO USE ALL YOUR STRENGTH...
카각
...TO KEEP MY SWORD FROM PENETRATING YOUR DEFENSE?
YOU'VE LOST THIS FIGHT. GIVE UP.

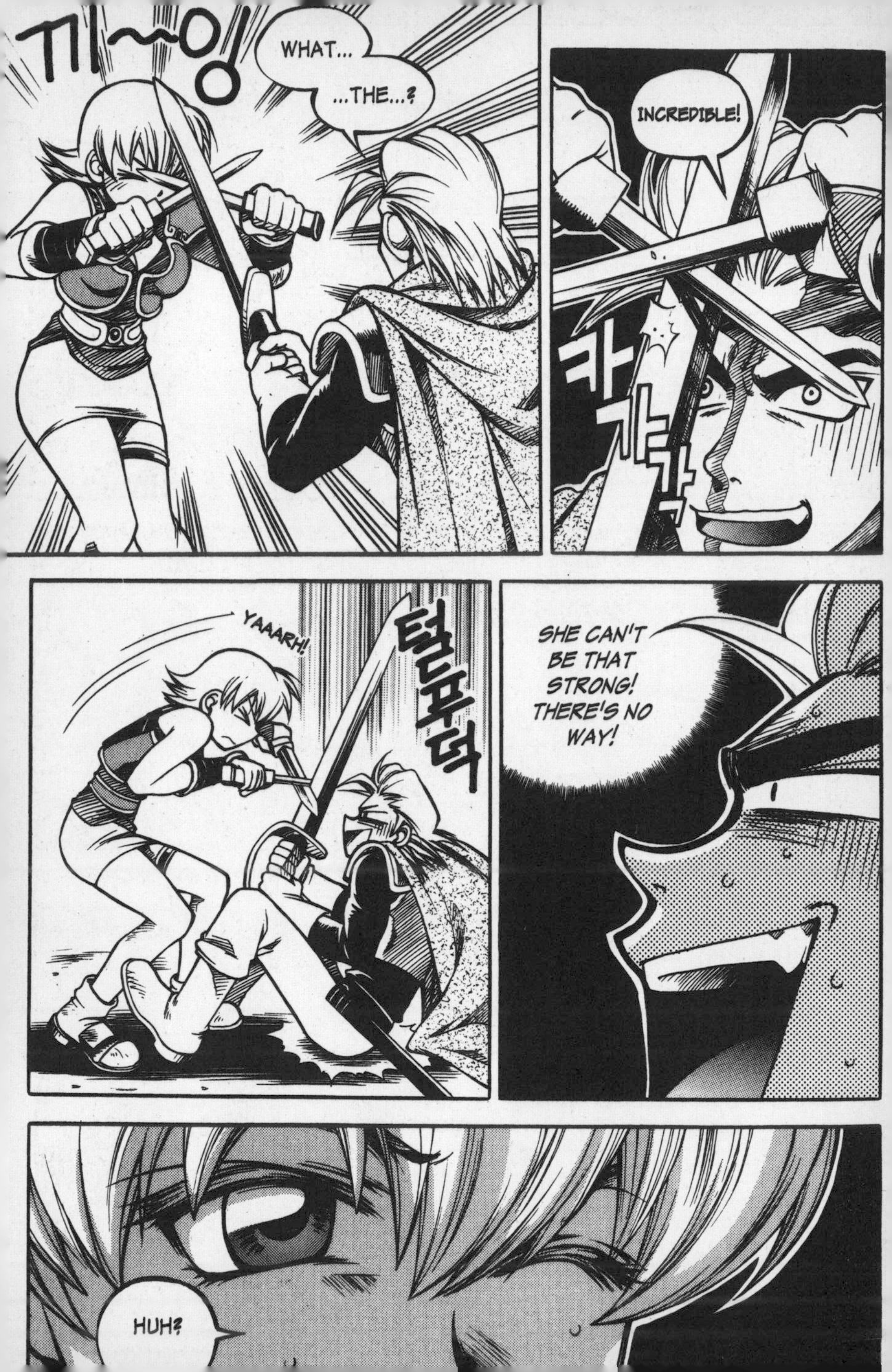
WHAT...
...THE...?
INCREDIBLE!
YAAARH!
SHE CAN'T BE THAT STRONG! THERE'S NO WAY!
HUH?

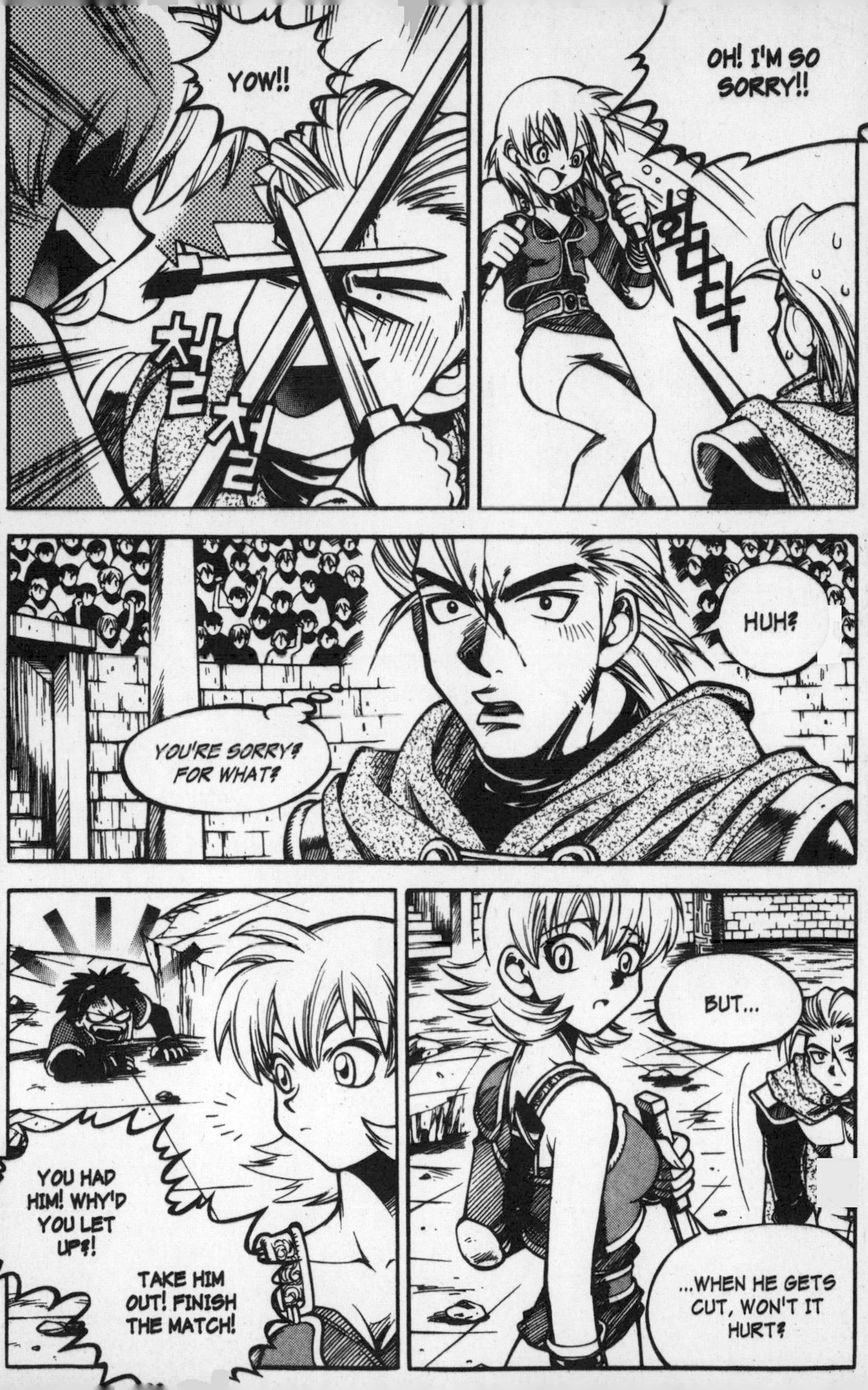
YOW!!
OH! I'M SO SORRY!!
HUH?
YOU'RE SORRY? FOR WHAT?
YOU HAD HIM! WHY'D YOU LET UP?!
TAKE HIM OUT! FINISH THE MATCH!
BUT...
...WHEN HE GETS CUT, WON'T IT HURT?

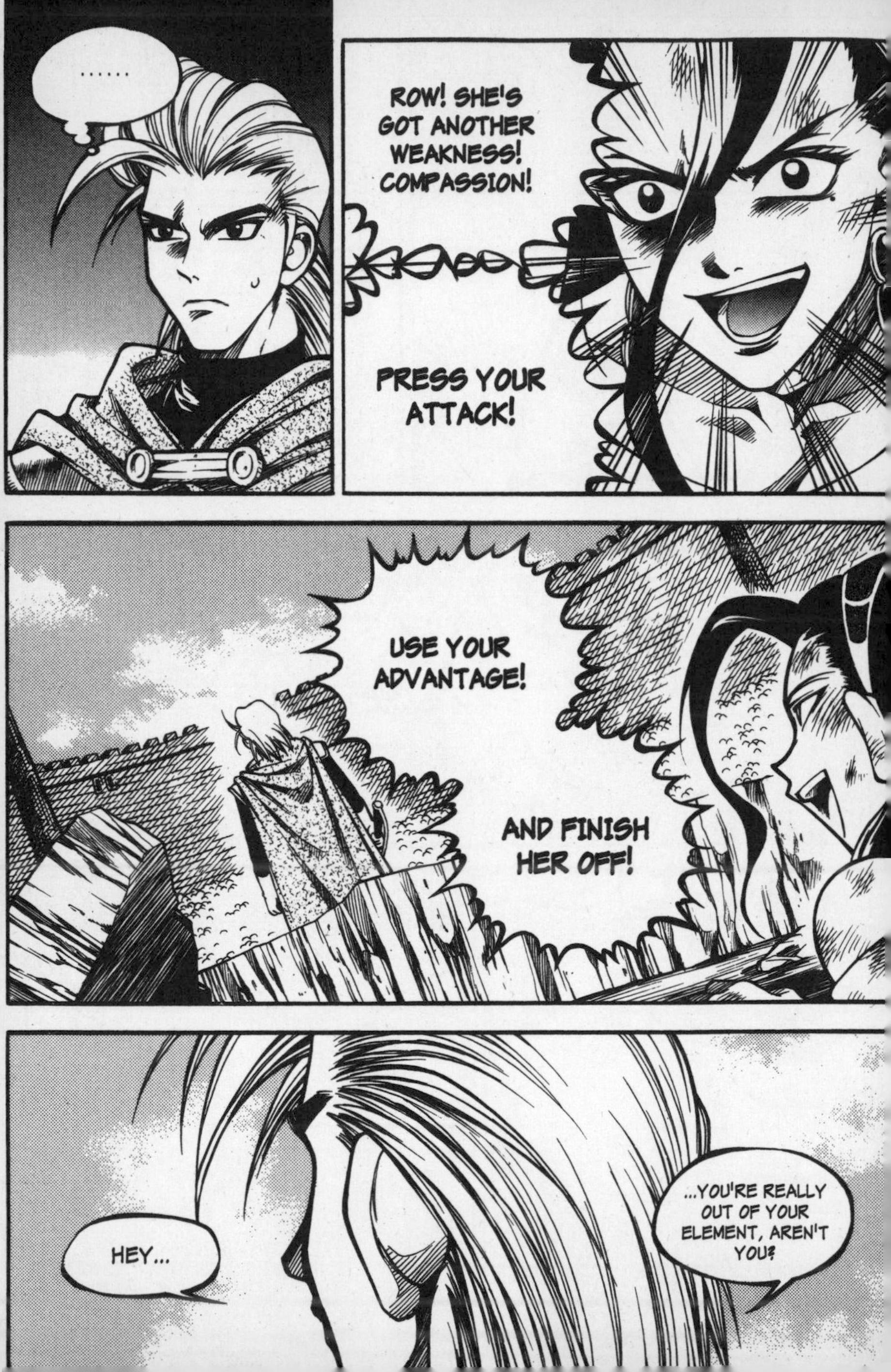
......
ROW! SHE'S GOT ANOTHER WEAKNESS! COMPASSION!
PRESS YOUR ATTACK!
USE YOUR ADVANTAGE!
AND FINISH HER OFF!
HEY...
...YOU'RE REALLY OUT OF YOUR ELEMENT, AREN'T YOU?

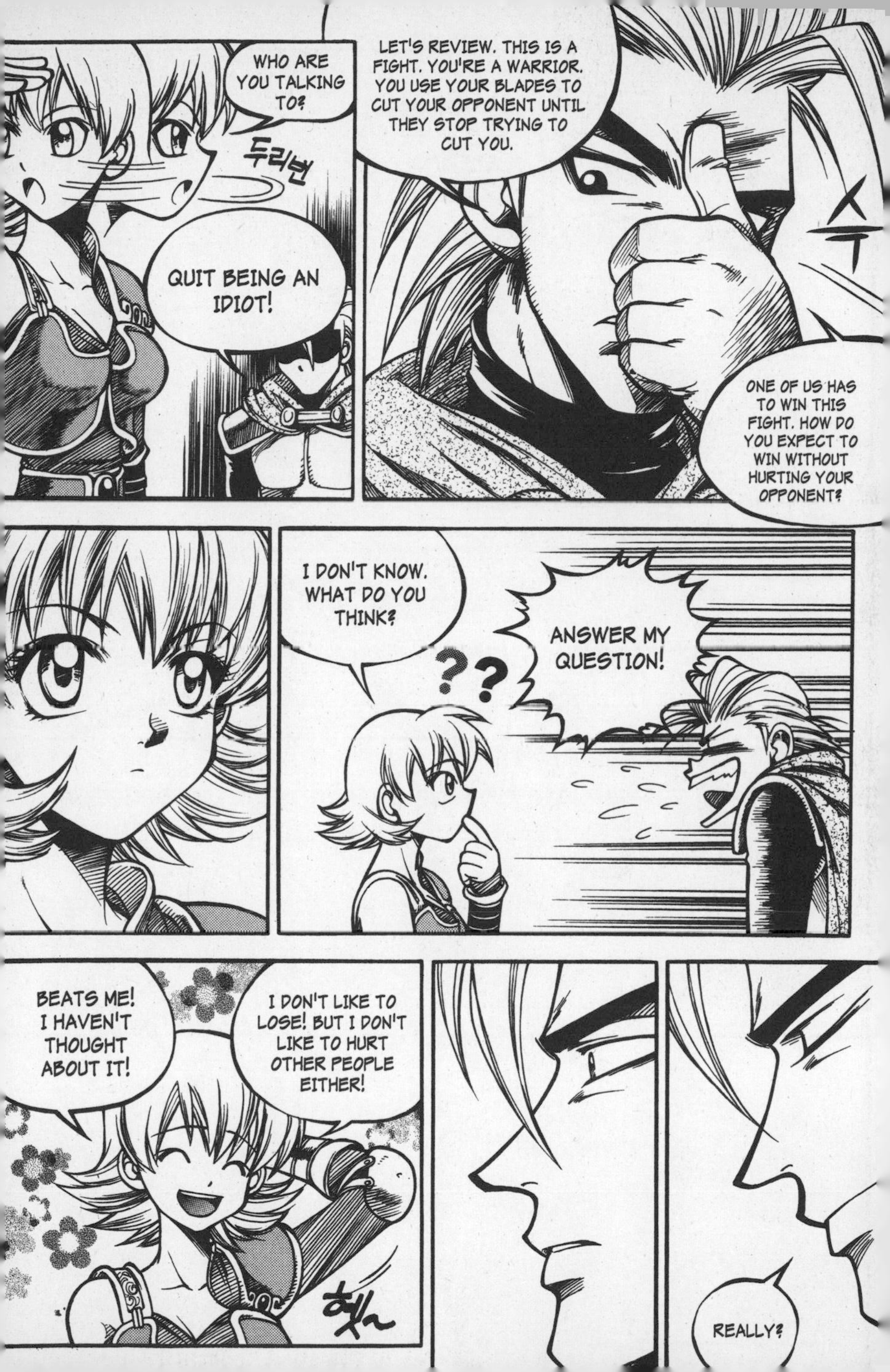
WHO ARE YOU TALKING TO?
두리번
QUIT BEING AN IDIOT!
LET'S REVIEW. THIS IS A FIGHT. YOU'RE A WARRIOR. YOU USE YOUR BLADES TO CUT YOUR OPPONENT UNTIL THEY STOP TRYING TO CUT YOU.
ONE OF US HAS TO WIN THIS FIGHT. HOW DO YOU EXPECT TO WIN WITHOUT HURTING YOUR OPPONENT?
I DON'T KNOW. WHAT DO YOU THINK?
??
ANSWER MY QUESTION!
BEATS ME! I HAVEN'T THOUGHT ABOUT IT!
I DON'T LIKE TO LOSE! BUT I DON'T LIKE TO HURT OTHER PEOPLE EITHER!
REALLY?

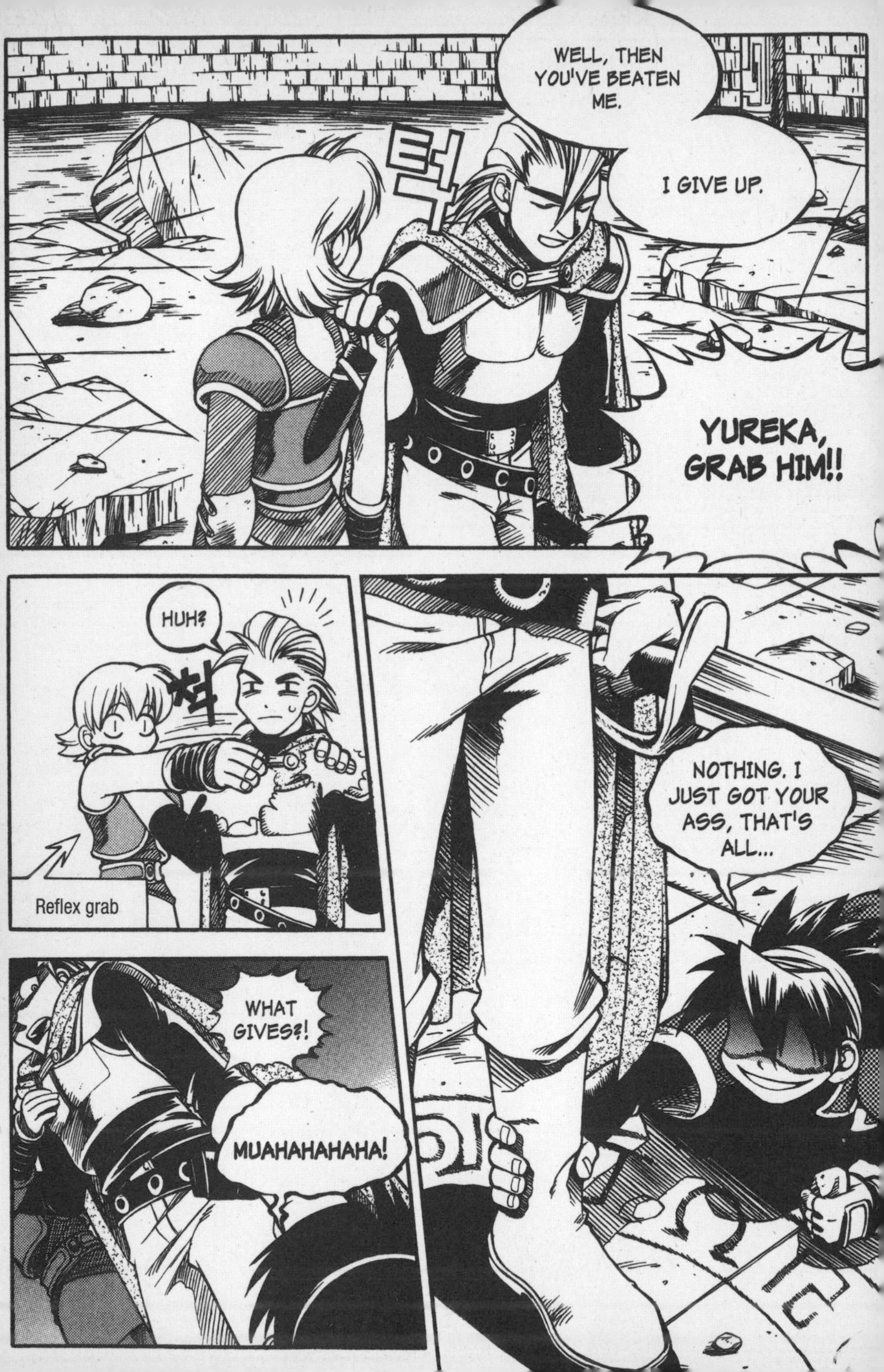
WELL, THEN YOU'VE BEATEN ME.
턱
I GIVE UP.
YUREKA, GRAB HIM!!
HUH?
척
Reflex grab
WHAT GIVES?!
MUAHAHAHAHA!
NOTHING. I JUST GOT YOUR ASS, THAT'S ALL...

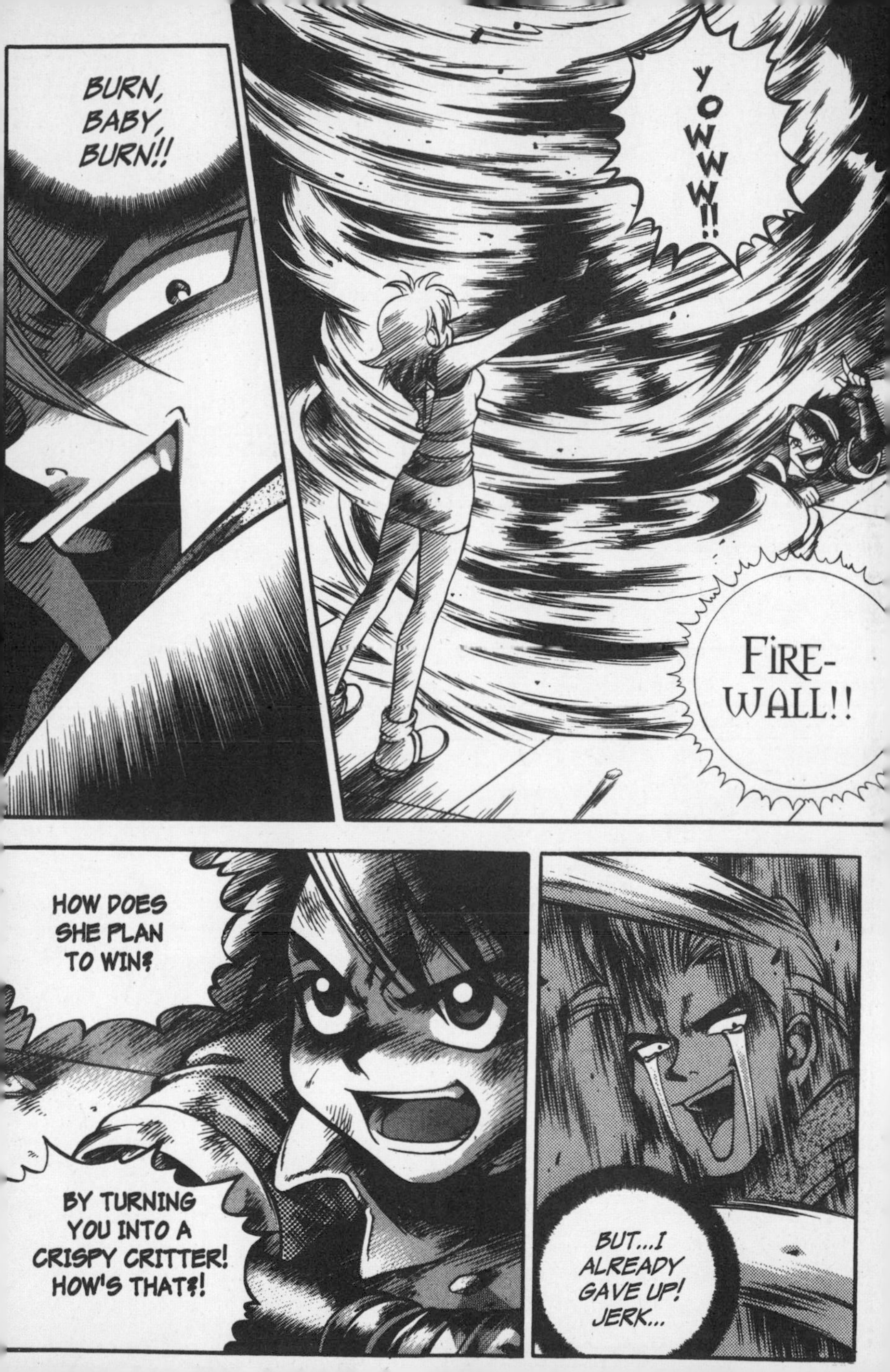
BURN, BABY, BURN!!
YOWWW!!
FIRE-WALL!!
HOW DOES SHE PLAN TO WIN?
BY TURNING YOU INTO A CRISPY CRITTER! HOW'S THAT?!
BUT...I ALREADY GAVE UP! JERK...

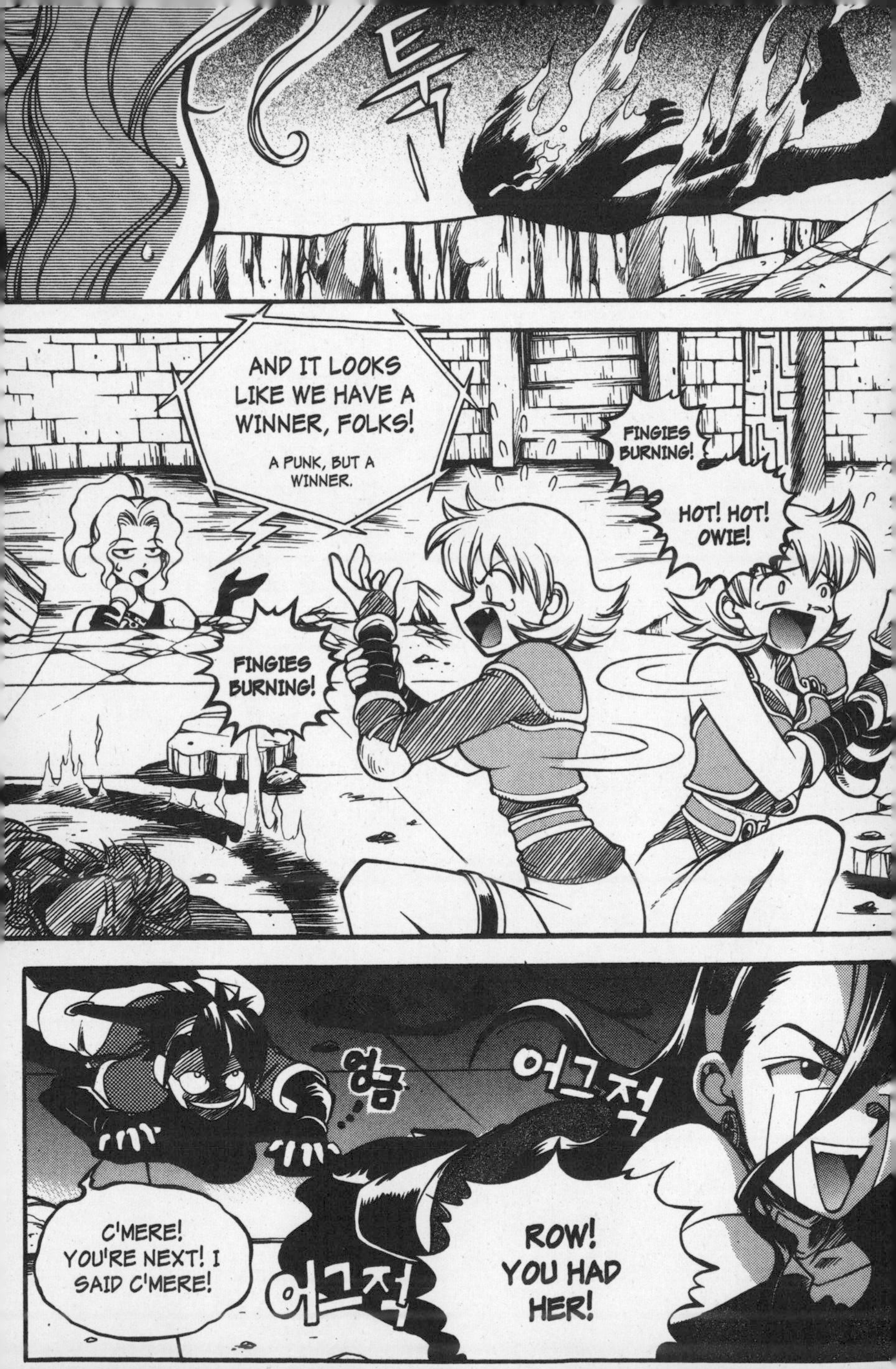

툭
AND IT LOOKS LIKE WE HAVE A WINNER, FOLKS!
A PUNK, BUT A WINNER.
FINGIES BURNING!
HOT! HOT! OWIE!
FINGIES BURNING!
엉금
어그적
C'MERE! YOU'RE NEXT! I SAID C'MERE!
어그적
ROW! YOU HAD HER!

STAGE 21
YOU WERE SAYING?

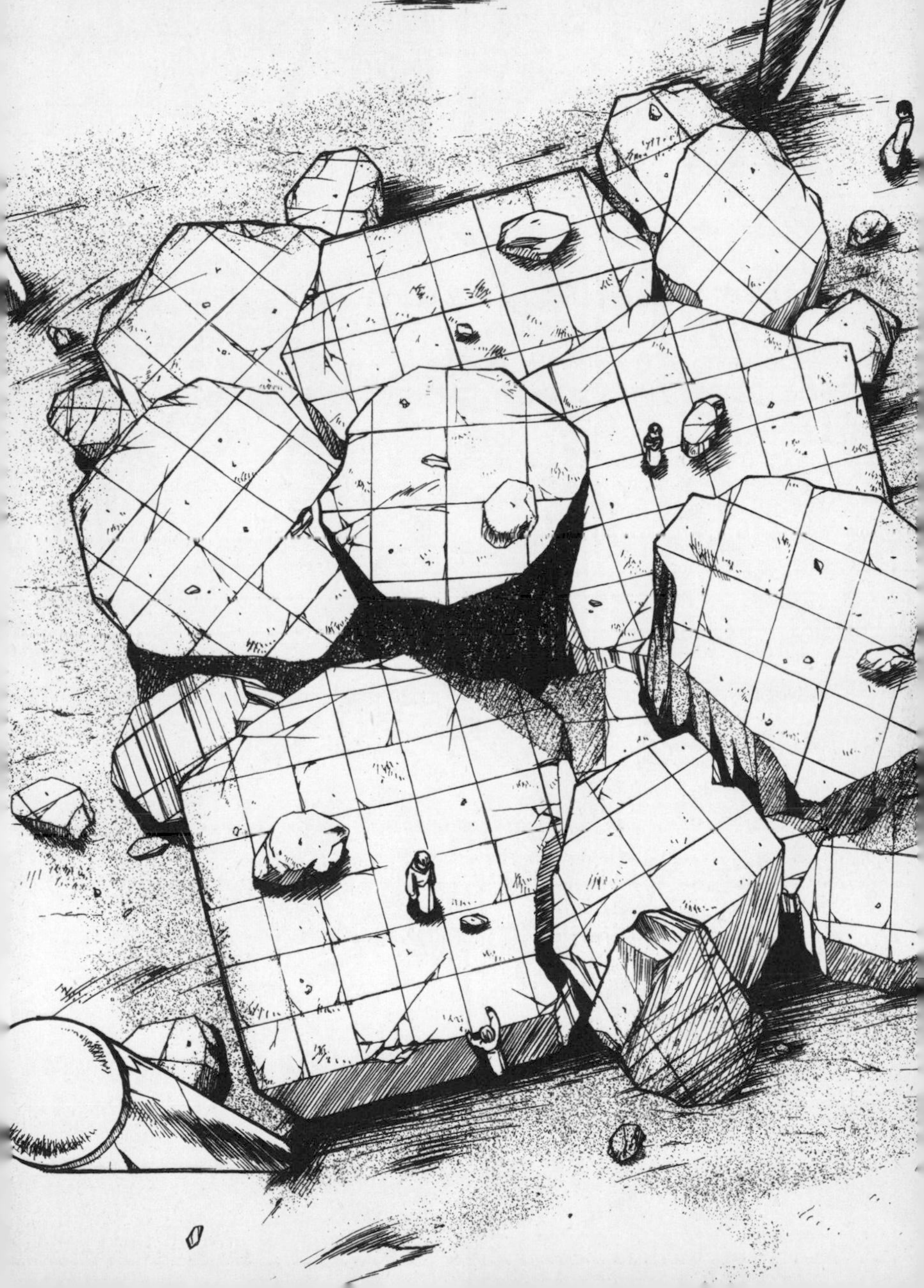

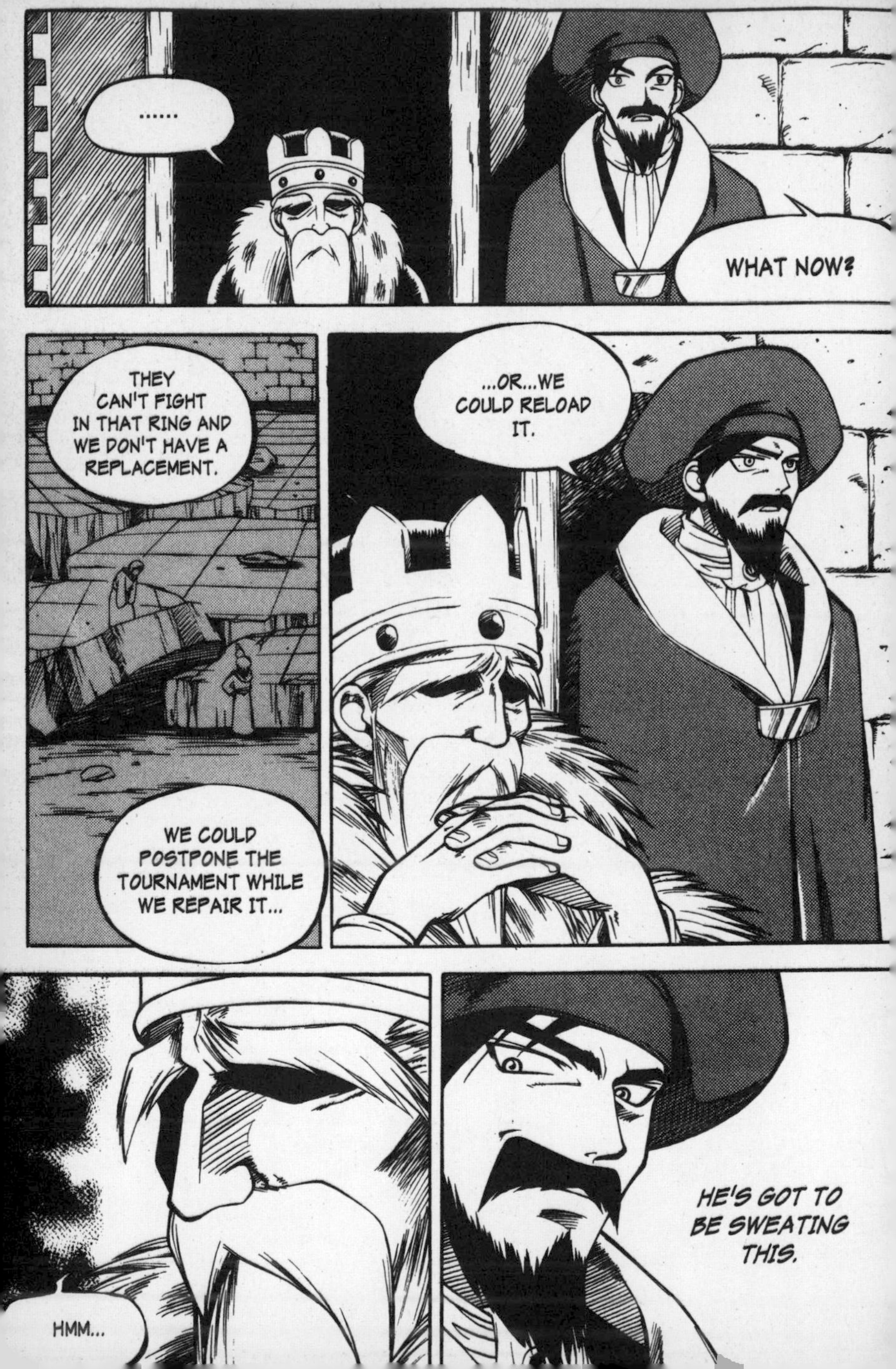

......
WHAT NOW?
THEY CAN'T FIGHT IN THAT RING AND WE DON'T HAVE A REPLACEMENT.
WE COULD POSTPONE THE TOURNAMENT WHILE WE REPAIR IT...
...OR...WE COULD RELOAD IT.
HMM...
HE'S GOT TO BE SWEATING THIS.

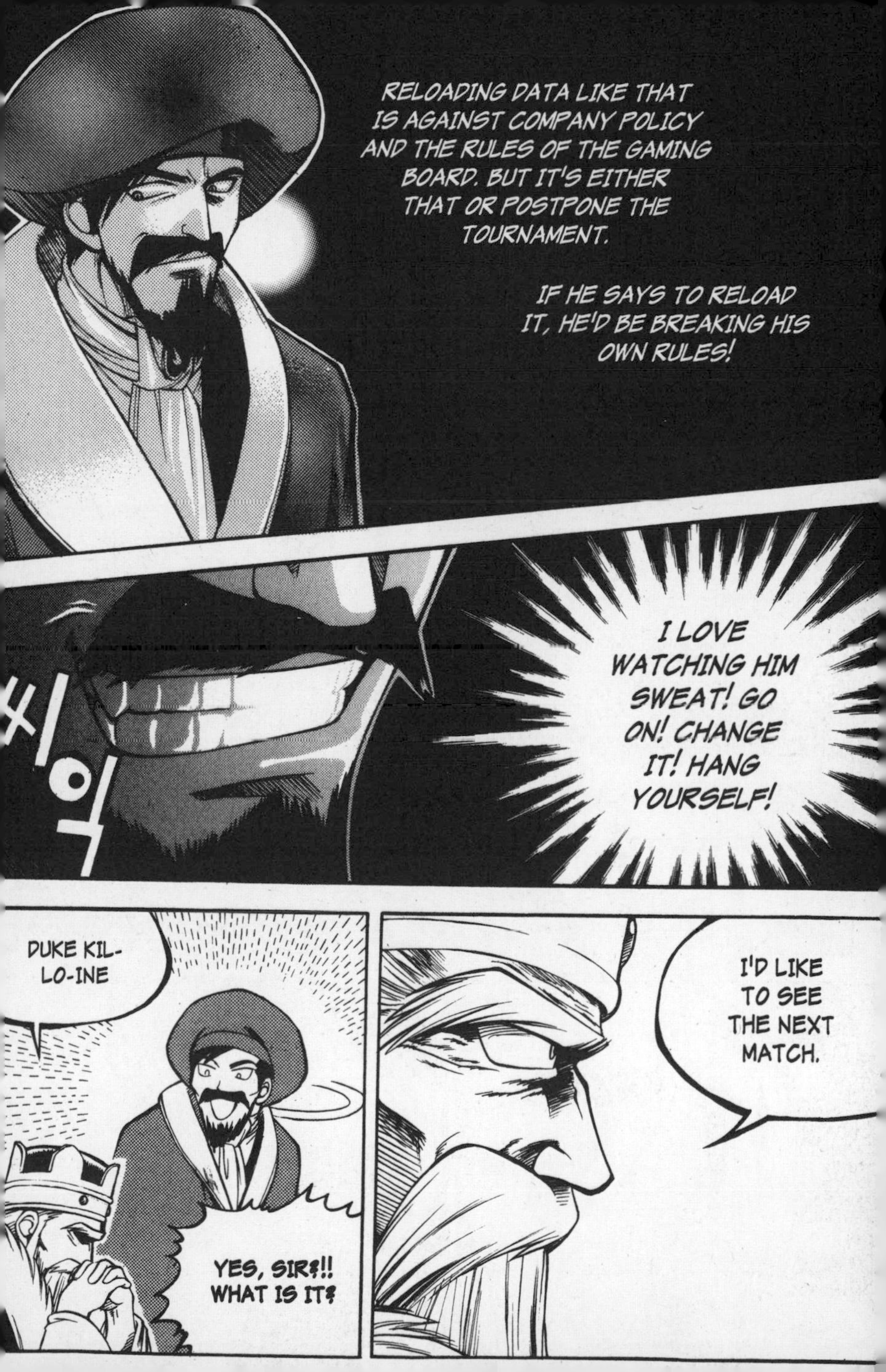
RELOADING DATA LIKE THAT IS AGAINST COMPANY POLICY AND THE RULES OF THE GAMING BOARD. BUT IT'S EITHER THAT OR POSTPONE THE TOURNAMENT.
IF HE SAYS TO RELOAD IT, HE'D BE BREAKING HIS OWN RULES!
I LOVE WATCHING HIM SWEAT! GO ON! CHANGE IT! HANG YOURSELF!
DUKE KIL-LO-INE
YES, SIR?!! WHAT IS IT?
I'D LIKE TO SEE THE NEXT MATCH.

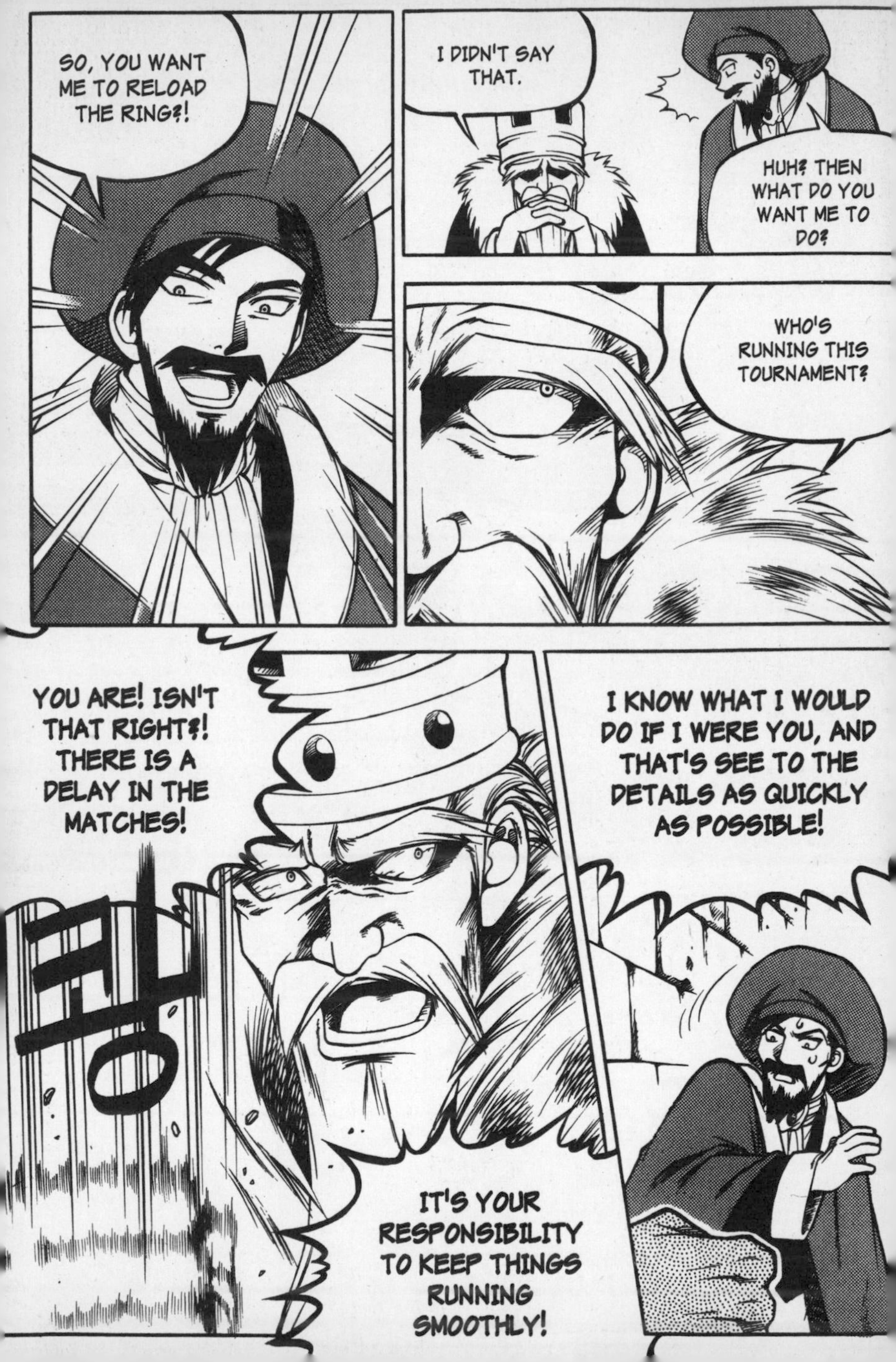
SO, YOU WANT ME TO RELOAD THE RING?!
I DIDN'T SAY THAT.
HUH? THEN WHAT DO YOU WANT ME TO DO?
WHO'S RUNNING THIS TOURNAMENT?
YOU ARE! ISN'T THAT RIGHT?! THERE IS A DELAY IN THE MATCHES!
IT'S YOUR RESPONSIBILITY TO KEEP THINGS RUNNING SMOOTHLY!
I KNOW WHAT I WOULD DO IF I WERE YOU, AND THAT'S SEE TO THE DETAILS AS QUICKLY AS POSSIBLE!

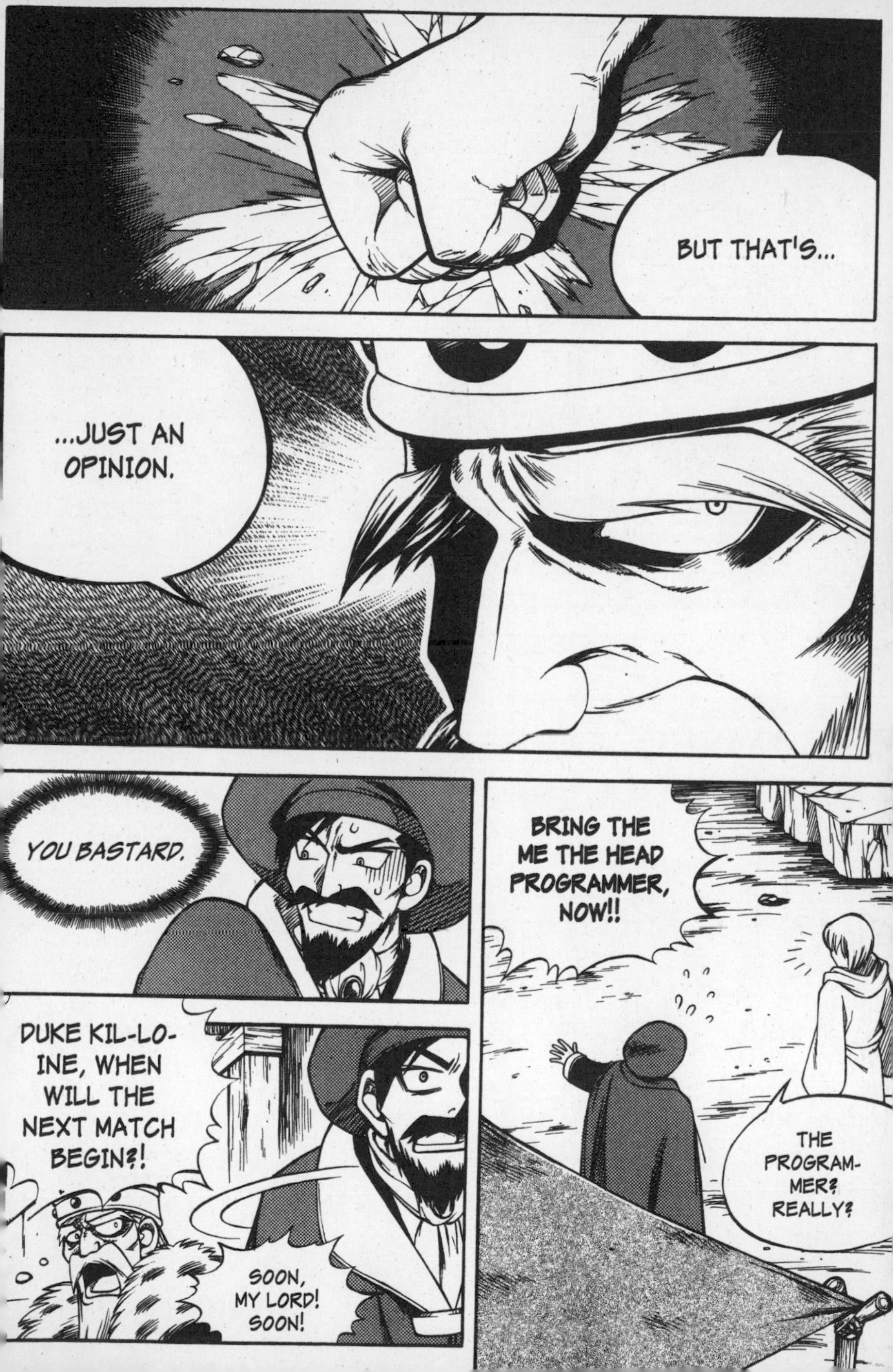
BUT THAT'S...
...JUST AN OPINION.
YOU BASTARD.
DUKE KIL-LO-INE, WHEN WILL THE NEXT MATCH BEGIN?!
SOON, MY LORD! SOON!
BRING THE ME THE HEAD PROGRAMMER, NOW!!
THE PROGRAM-MER? REALLY?

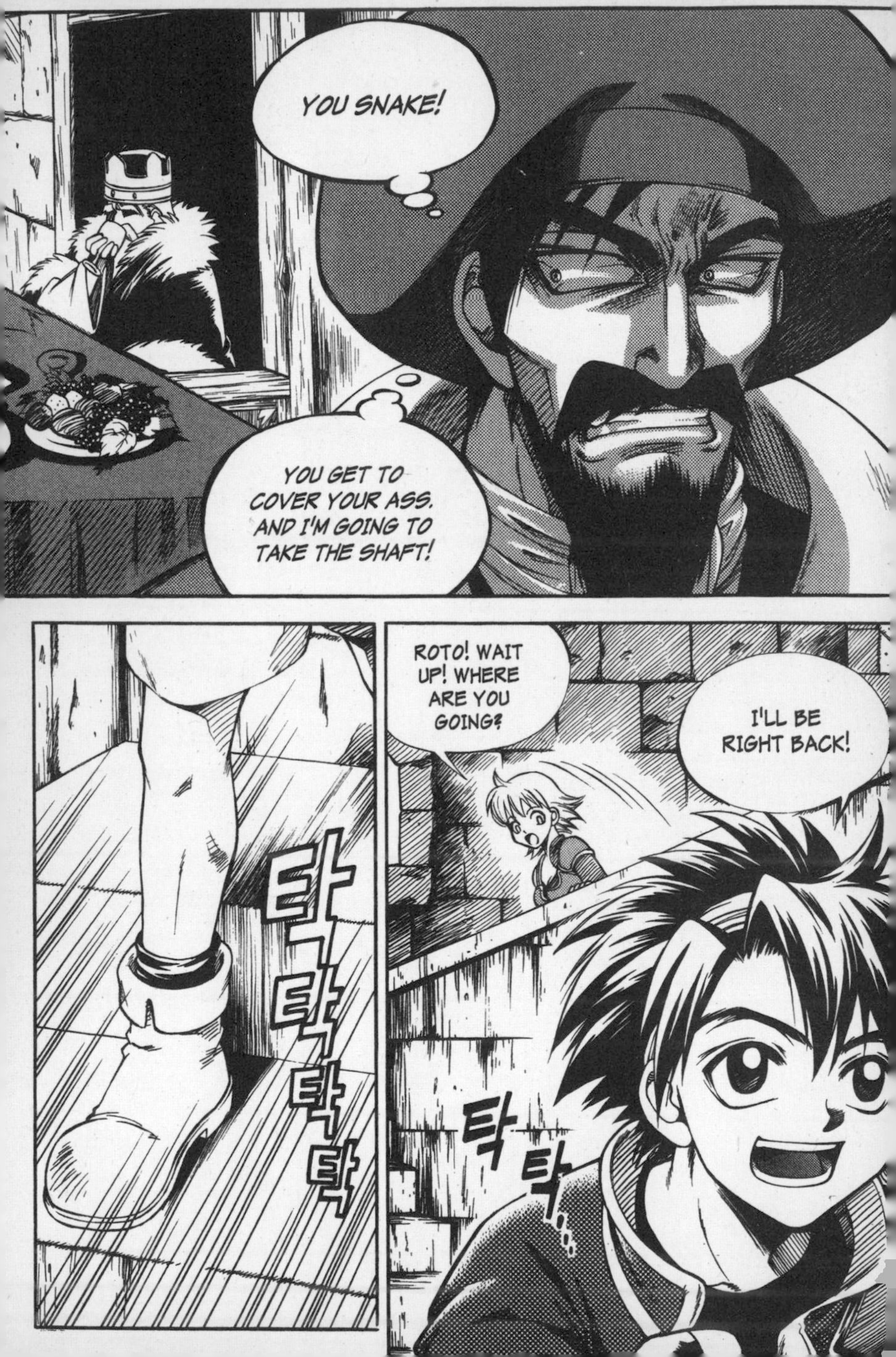
YOU SNAKE!
YOU GET TO COVER YOUR ASS. AND I'M GOING TO TAKE THE SHAFT!
타
탁
타
탁
ROTO! WAIT UP! WHERE ARE YOU GOING?
I'LL BE RIGHT BACK!
타
타

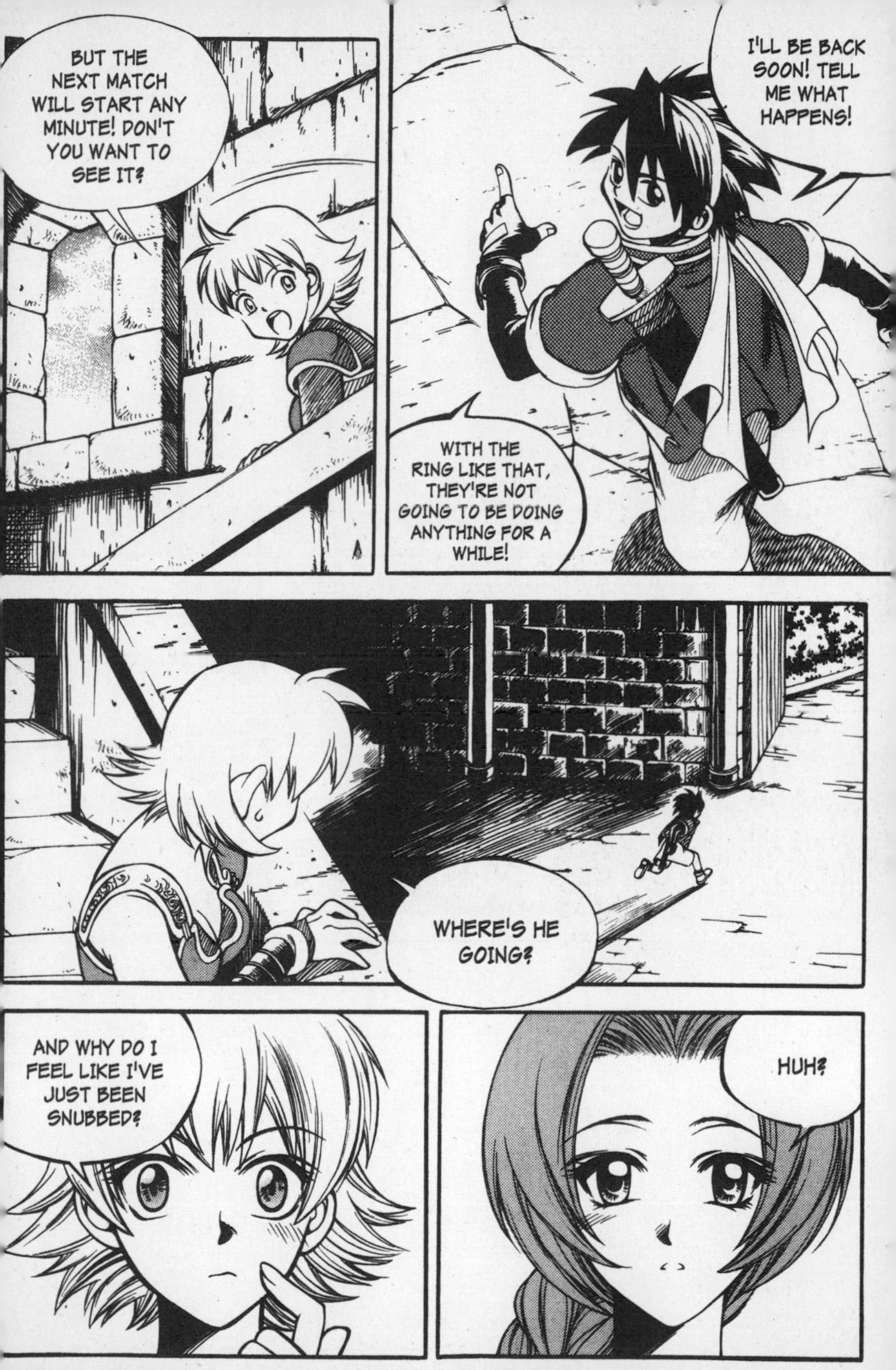
BUT THE NEXT MATCH WILL START ANY MINUTE! DON'T YOU WANT TO SEE IT?
I'LL BE BACK SOON! TELL ME WHAT HAPPENS!
WITH THE RING LIKE THAT, THEY'RE NOT GOING TO BE DOING ANYTHING FOR A WHILE!
WHERE'S HE GOING?
AND WHY DO I FEEL LIKE I'VE JUST BEEN SNUBBED?
HUH?

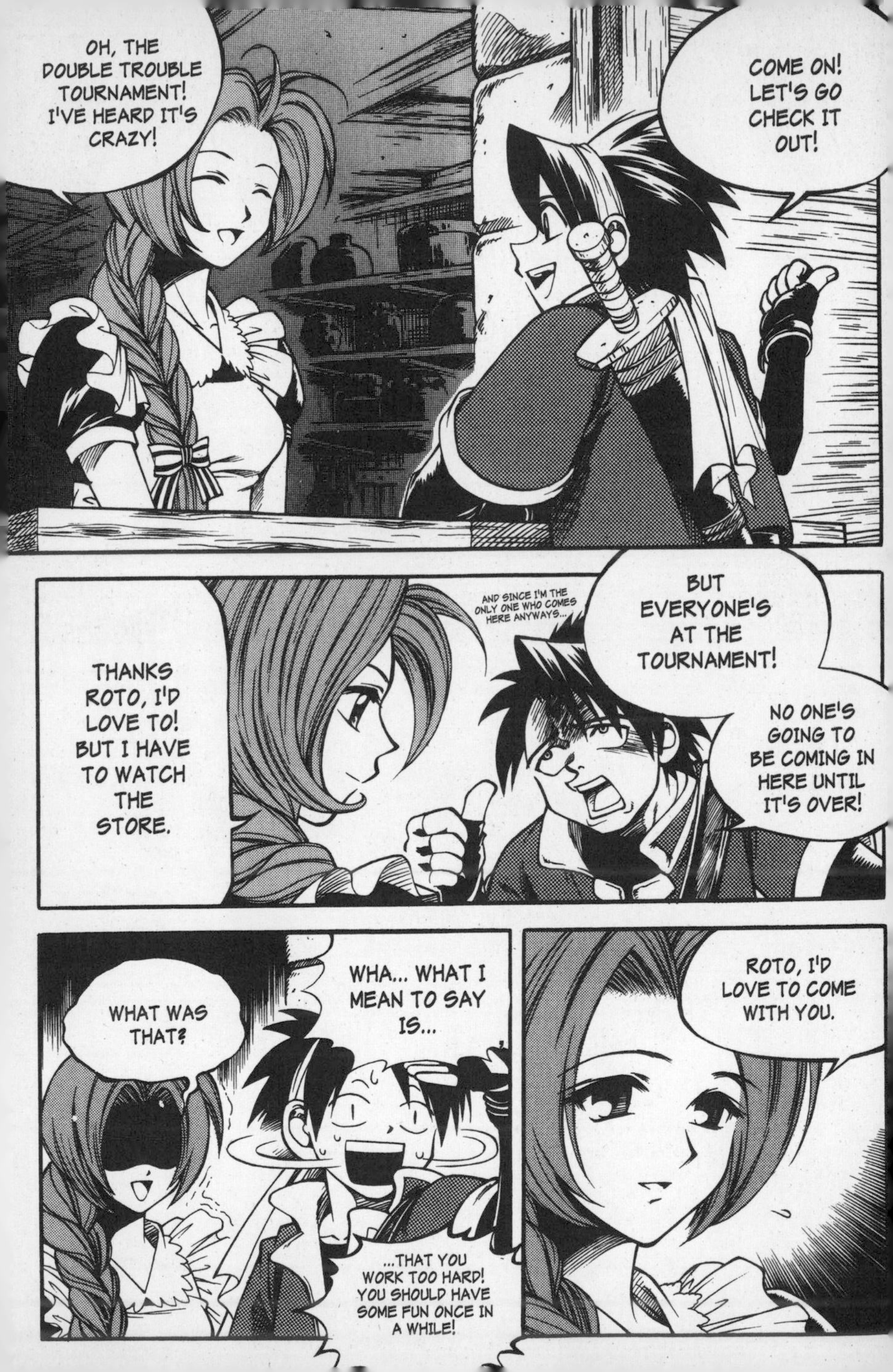
OH, THE DOUBLE TROUBLE TOURNAMENT! I'VE HEARD IT'S CRAZY!
COME ON! LET'S GO CHECK IT OUT!
THANKS ROTO, I'D LOVE TO! BUT I HAVE TO WATCH THE STORE.
BUT EVERYONE'S AT THE TOURNAMENT!
NO ONE'S GOING TO BE COMING IN HERE UNTIL IT'S OVER!
AND SINCE I'M THE ONLY ONE WHO COMES HERE ANYWAYS...
WHAT WAS THAT?
WHA... WHAT I MEAN TO SAY IS...
...THAT YOU WORK TOO HARD! YOU SHOULD HAVE SOME FUN ONCE IN A WHILE!
ROTO, I'D LOVE TO COME WITH YOU.

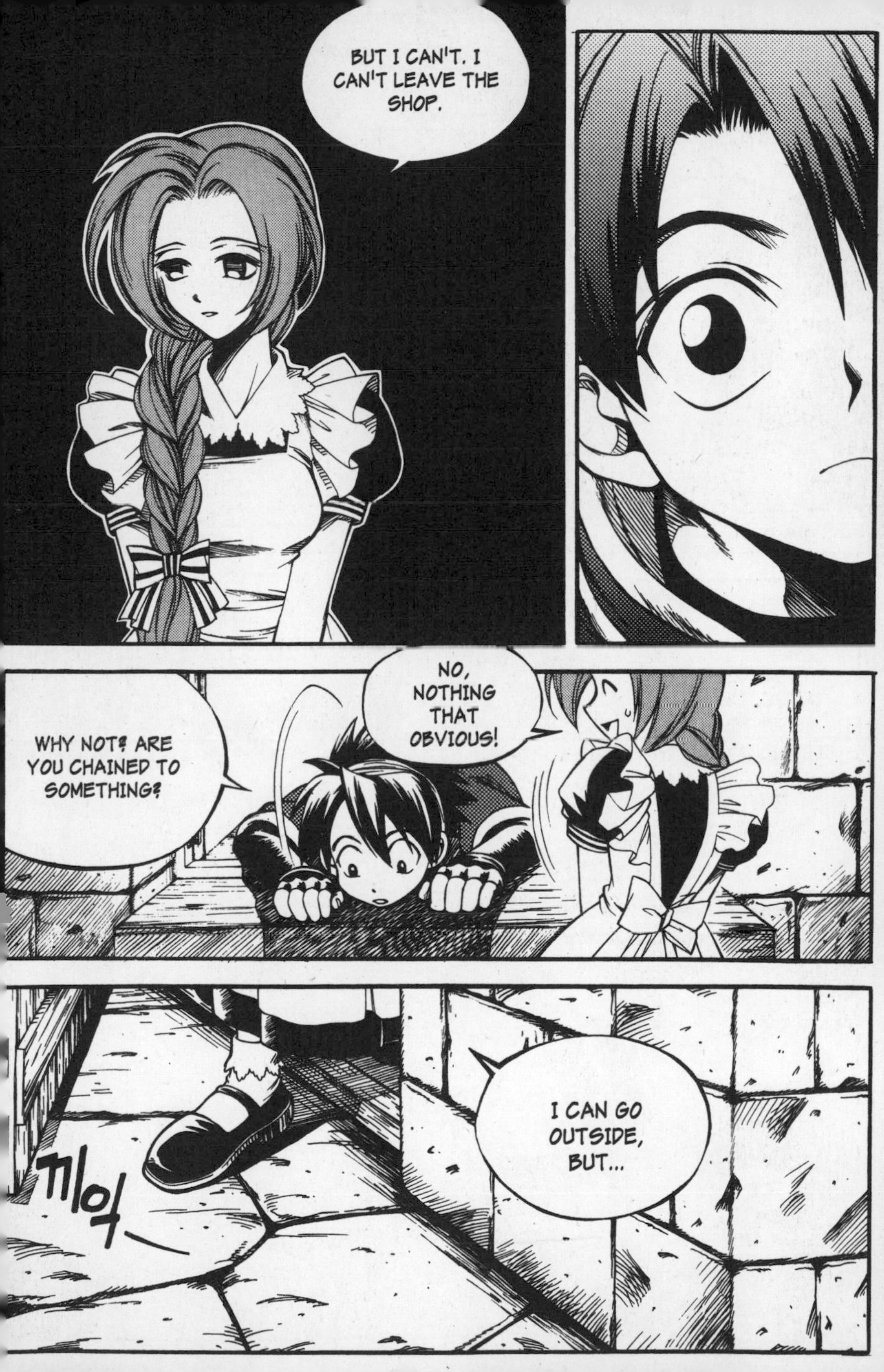
BUT I CAN'T. I CAN'T LEAVE THE SHOP.
WHY NOT? ARE YOU CHAINED TO SOMETHING?
NO, NOTHING THAT OBVIOUS!
I CAN GO OUTSIDE, BUT...

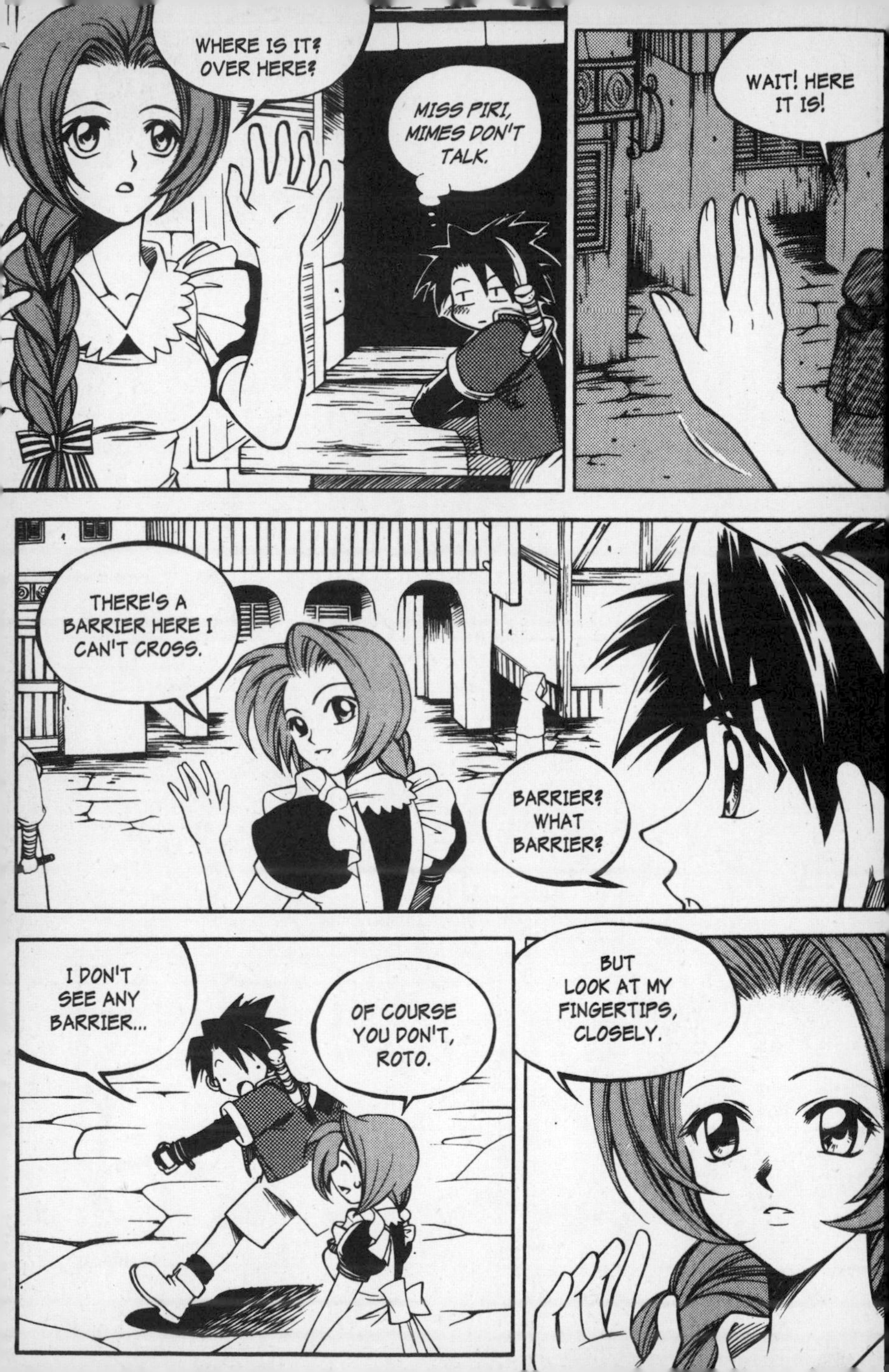
WHERE IS IT? OVER HERE?
MISS PIRI, MIMES DON'T TALK.
WAIT! HERE IT IS!
THERE'S A BARRIER HERE I CAN'T CROSS.
BARRIER? WHAT BARRIER?
I DON'T SEE ANY BARRIER...
OF COURSE YOU DON'T, ROTO.
BUT LOOK AT MY FINGERTIPS, CLOSELY.

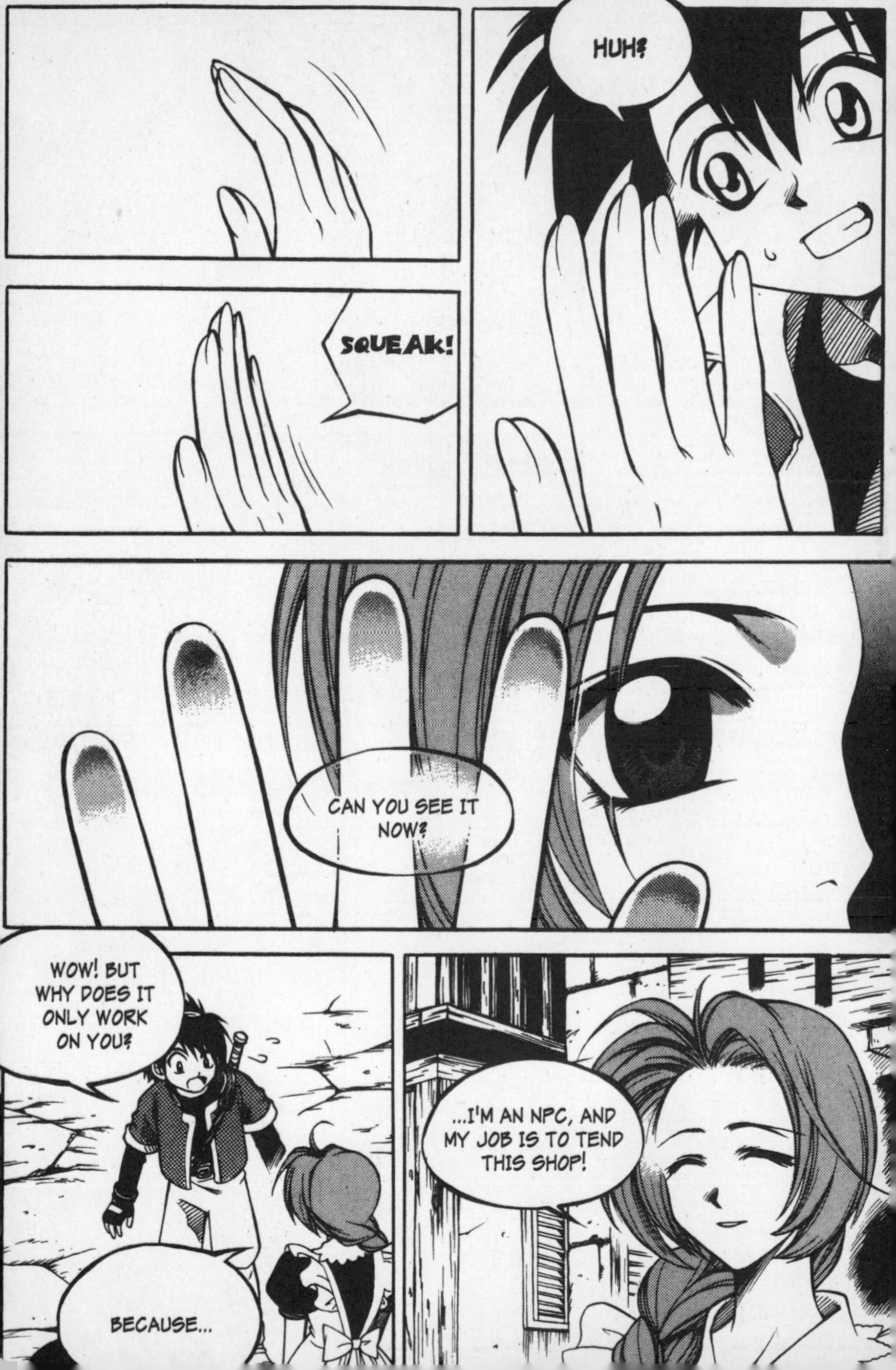
SQUEAK!
HUH?
CAN YOU SEE IT NOW?
WOW! BUT WHY DOES IT ONLY WORK ON YOU?
BECAUSE...
...I'M AN NPC, AND MY JOB IS TO TEND THIS SHOP!

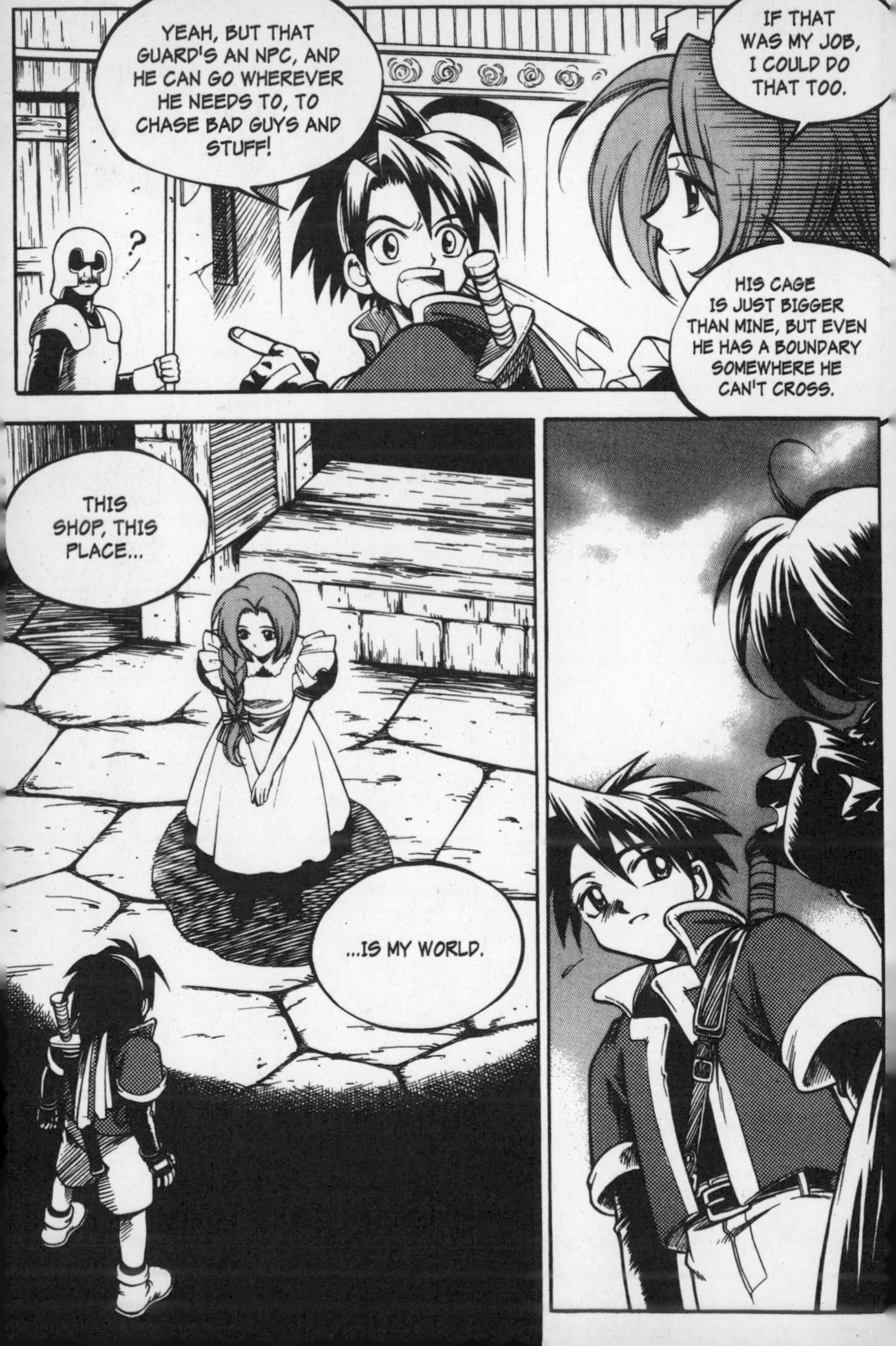
YEAH, BUT THAT GUARD'S AN NPC, AND HE CAN GO WHEREVER HE NEEDS TO, TO CHASE BAD GUYS AND STUFF!
?
IF THAT WAS MY JOB, I COULD DO THAT TOO.
HIS CAGE IS JUST BIGGER THAN MINE, BUT EVEN HE HAS A BOUNDARY SOMEWHERE HE CAN'T CROSS.
THIS SHOP, THIS PLACE...
...IS MY WORLD.

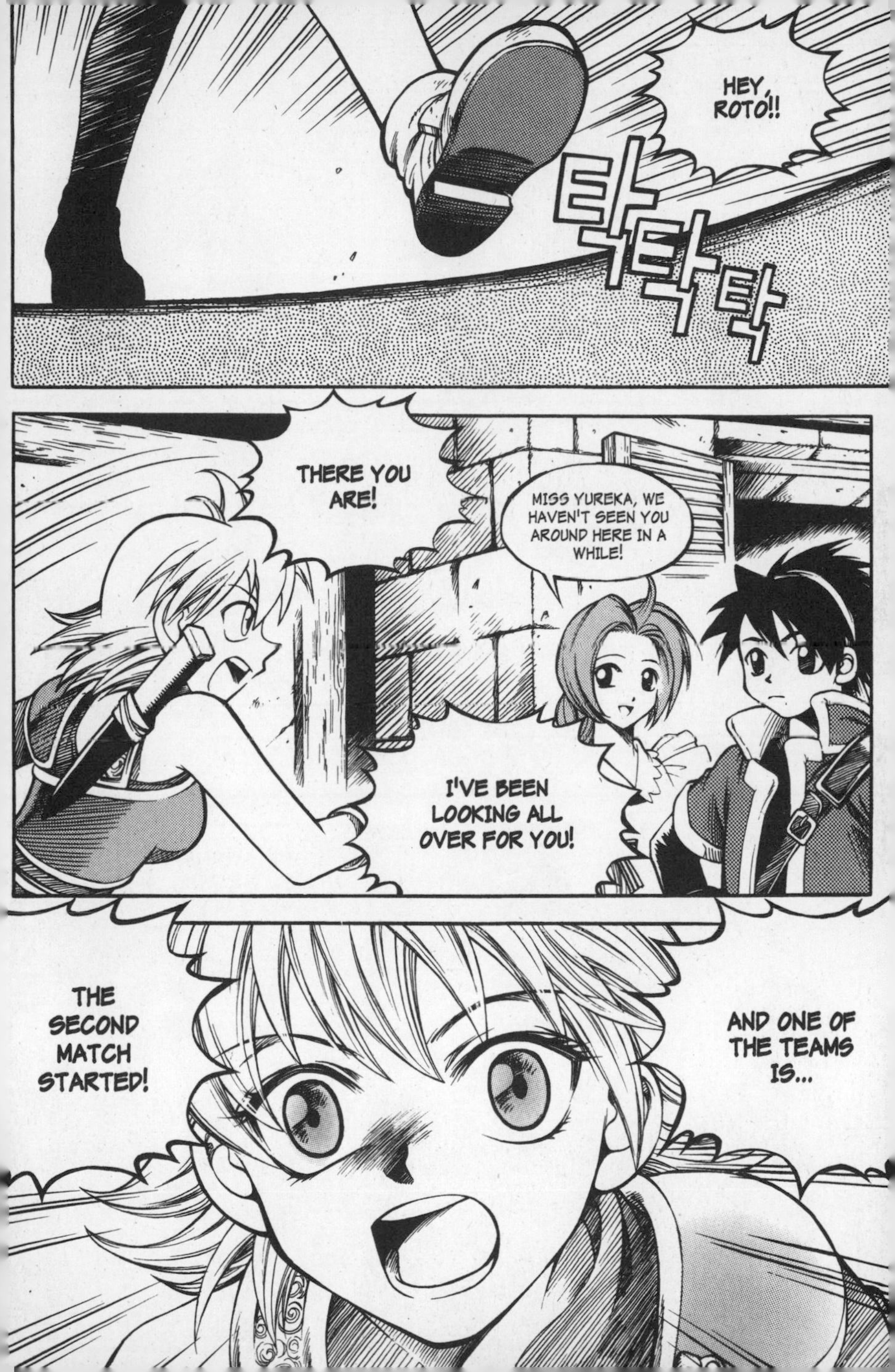
HEY, ROTO!!
탁탁탁
THERE YOU ARE!
MISS YUREKA, WE HAVEN'T SEEN YOU AROUND HERE IN A WHILE!
I'VE BEEN LOOKING ALL OVER FOR YOU!
THE SECOND MATCH STARTED!
AND ONE OF THE TEAMS IS...

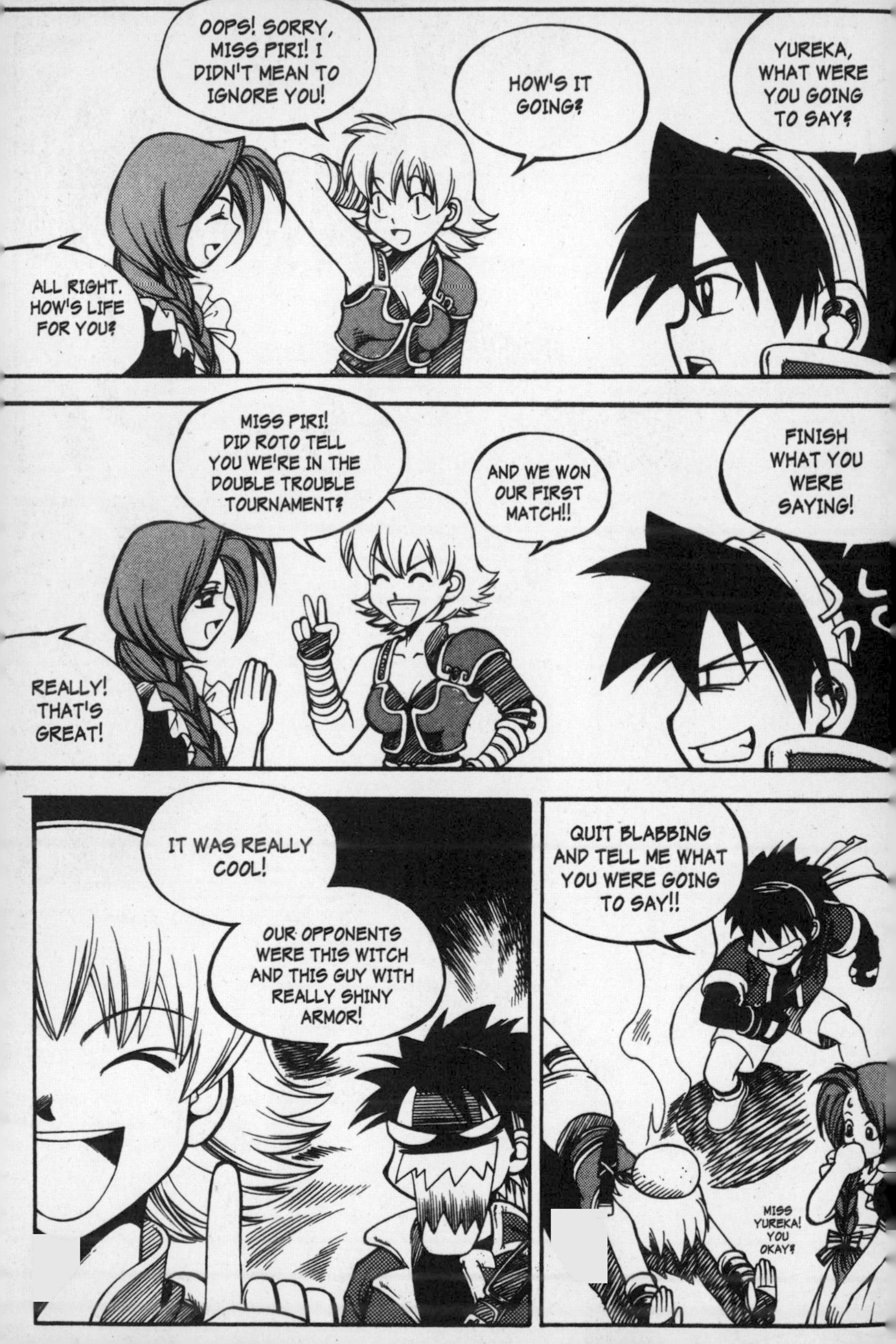
OOPS! SORRY, MISS PIRI! I DIDN'T MEAN TO IGNORE YOU!
HOW'S IT GOING?
ALL RIGHT. HOW'S LIFE FOR YOU?
YUREKA, WHAT WERE YOU GOING TO SAY?
MISS PIRI! DID ROTO TELL YOU WE'RE IN THE DOUBLE TROUBLE TOURNAMENT?
AND WE WON OUR FIRST MATCH!!
REALLY! THAT'S GREAT!
FINISH WHAT YOU WERE SAYING!
IT WAS REALLY COOL!
OUR OPPONENTS WERE THIS WITCH AND THIS GUY WITH REALLY SHINY ARMOR!
QUIT BLABBING AND TELL ME WHAT YOU WERE GOING TO SAY!!
MISS YUREKA! YOU OKAY?

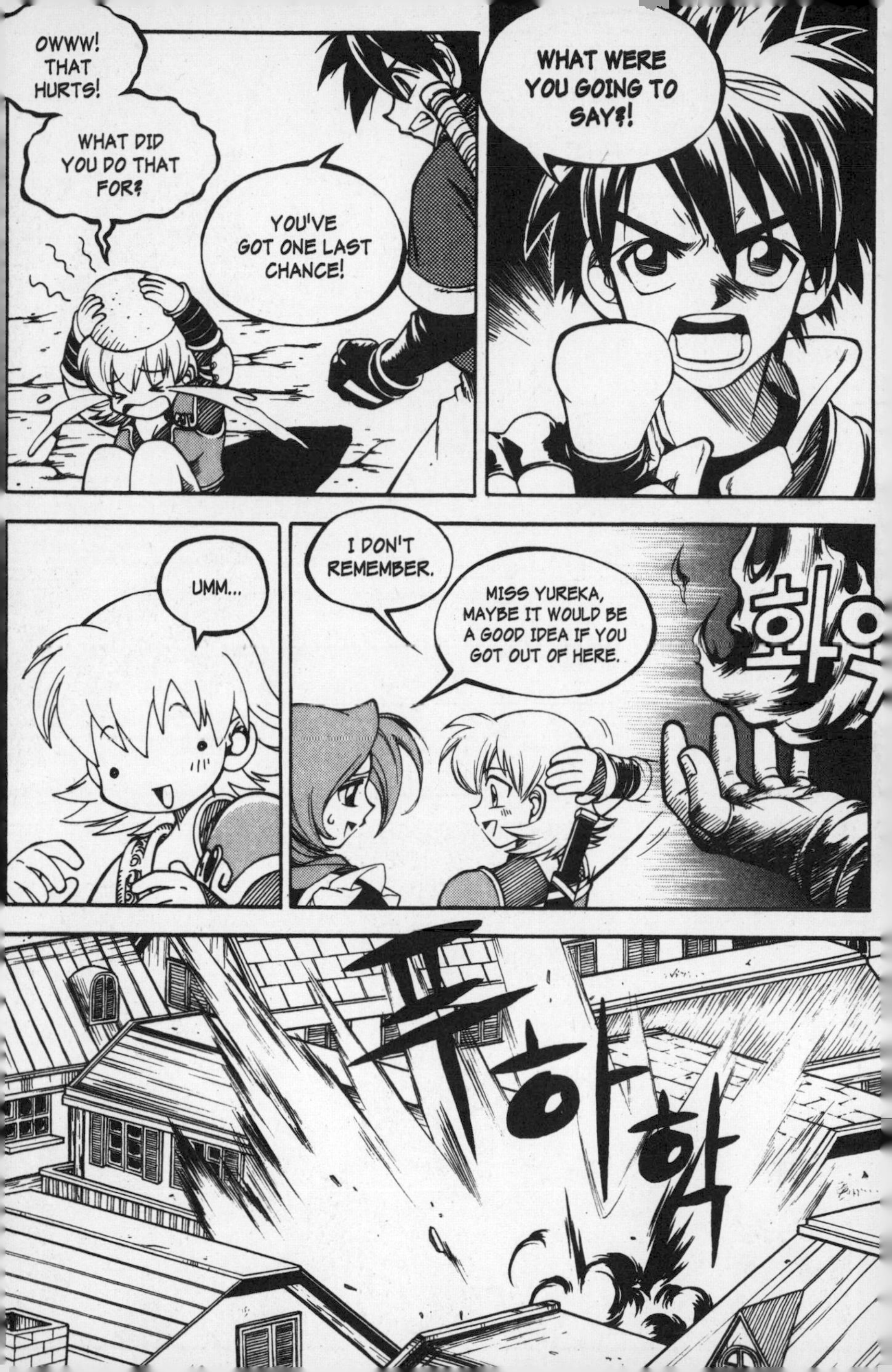
OWWW! THAT HURTS!
WHAT DID YOU DO THAT FOR?
YOU'VE GOT ONE LAST CHANCE!
WHAT WERE YOU GOING TO SAY?!
UMM...
I DON'T REMEMBER.
MISS YUREKA, MAYBE IT WOULD BE A GOOD IDEA IF YOU GOT OUT OF HERE.
푸하하

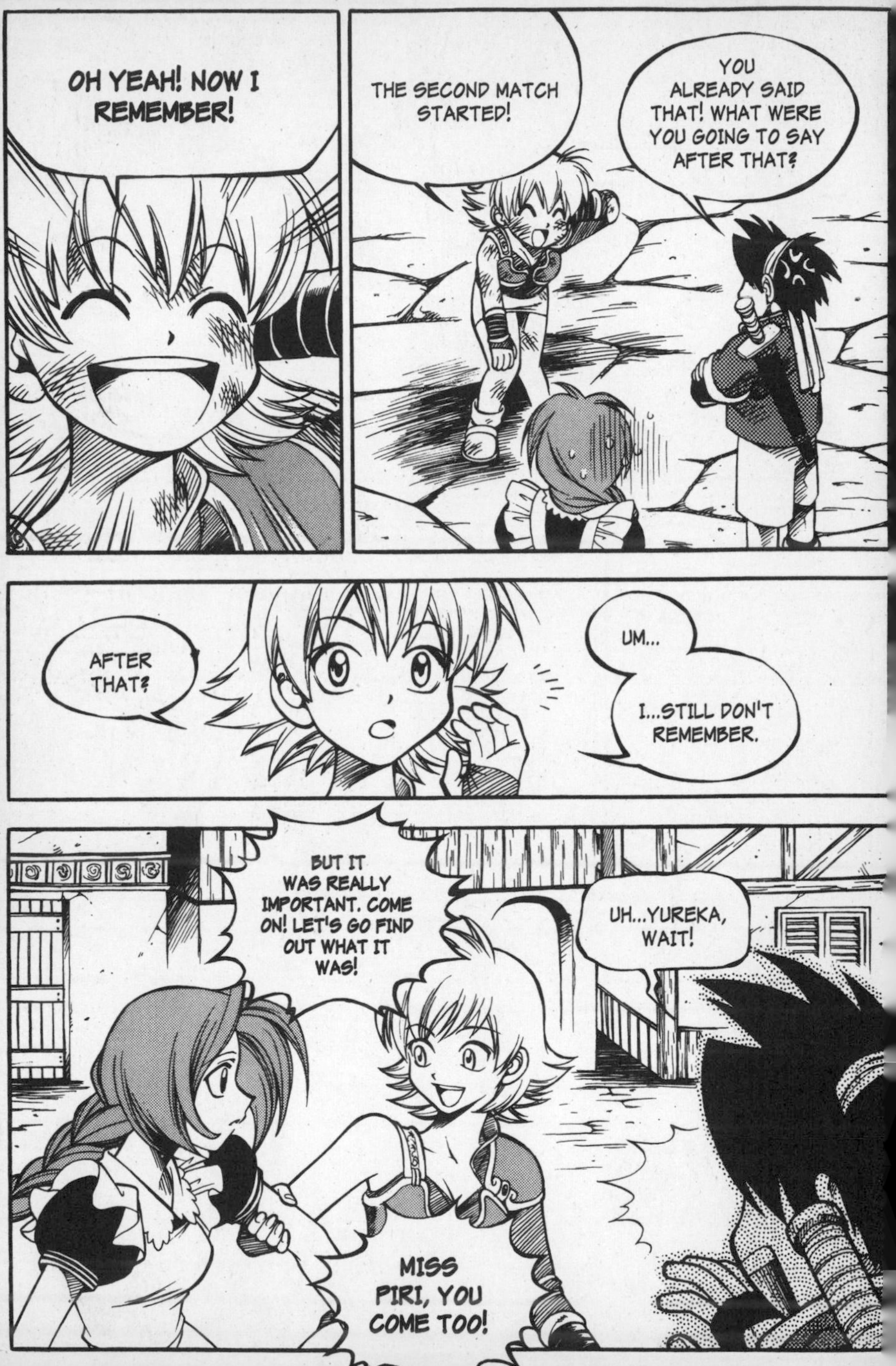
OH YEAH! NOW I REMEMBER!
THE SECOND MATCH STARTED!
YOU ALREADY SAID THAT! WHAT WERE YOU GOING TO SAY AFTER THAT?
AFTER THAT?
UM...
I...STILL DON'T REMEMBER.
BUT IT WAS REALLY IMPORTANT. COME ON! LET'S GO FIND OUT WHAT IT WAS!
UH...YUREKA, WAIT!
MISS PIRI, YOU COME TOO!

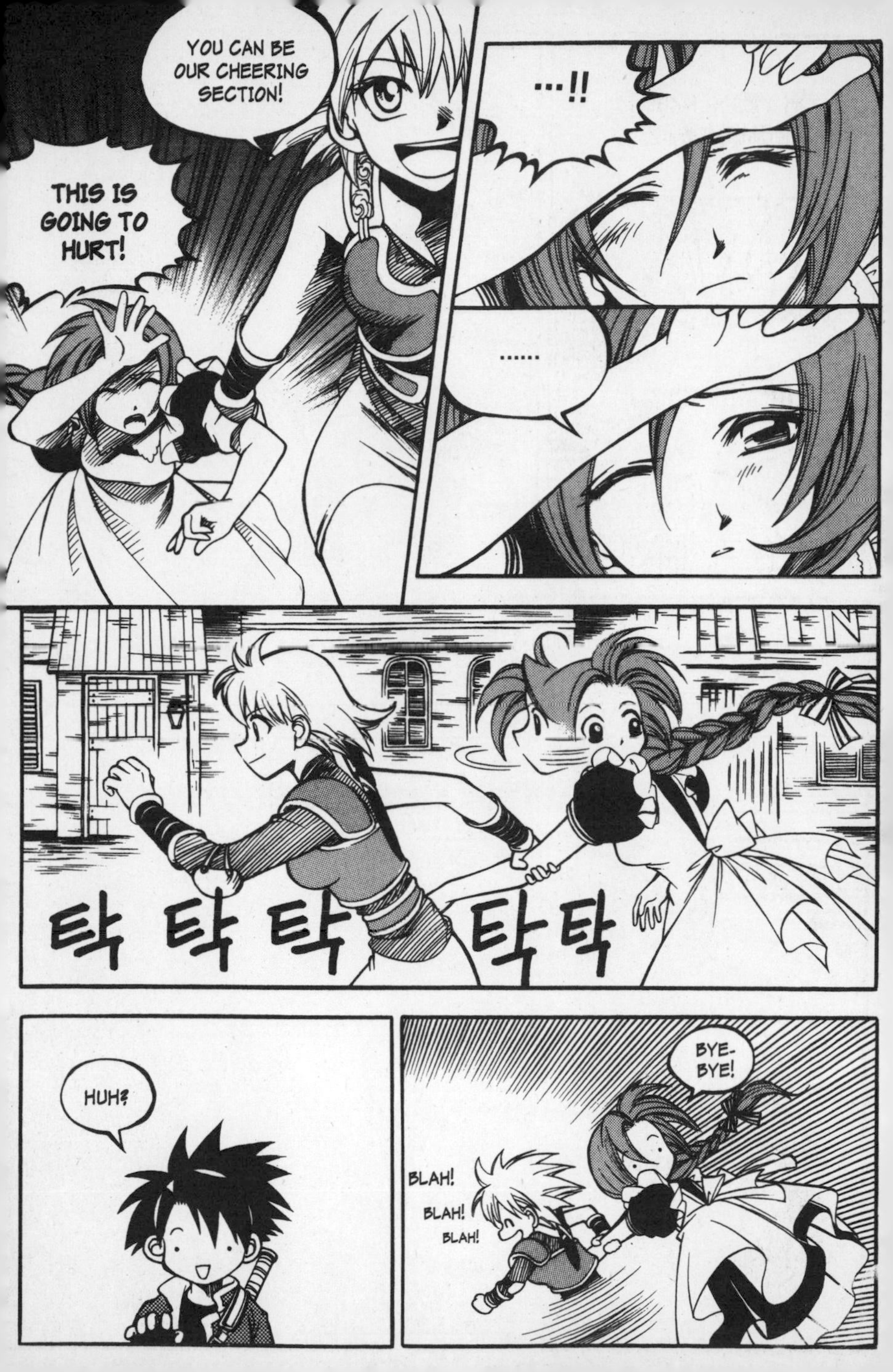
YOU CAN BE OUR CHEERING SECTION!
THIS IS GOING TO HURT!
...!!
......
탁 탁 탁
타탁
HUH?
BYE-BYE!
BLAH!
BLAH!
BLAH!

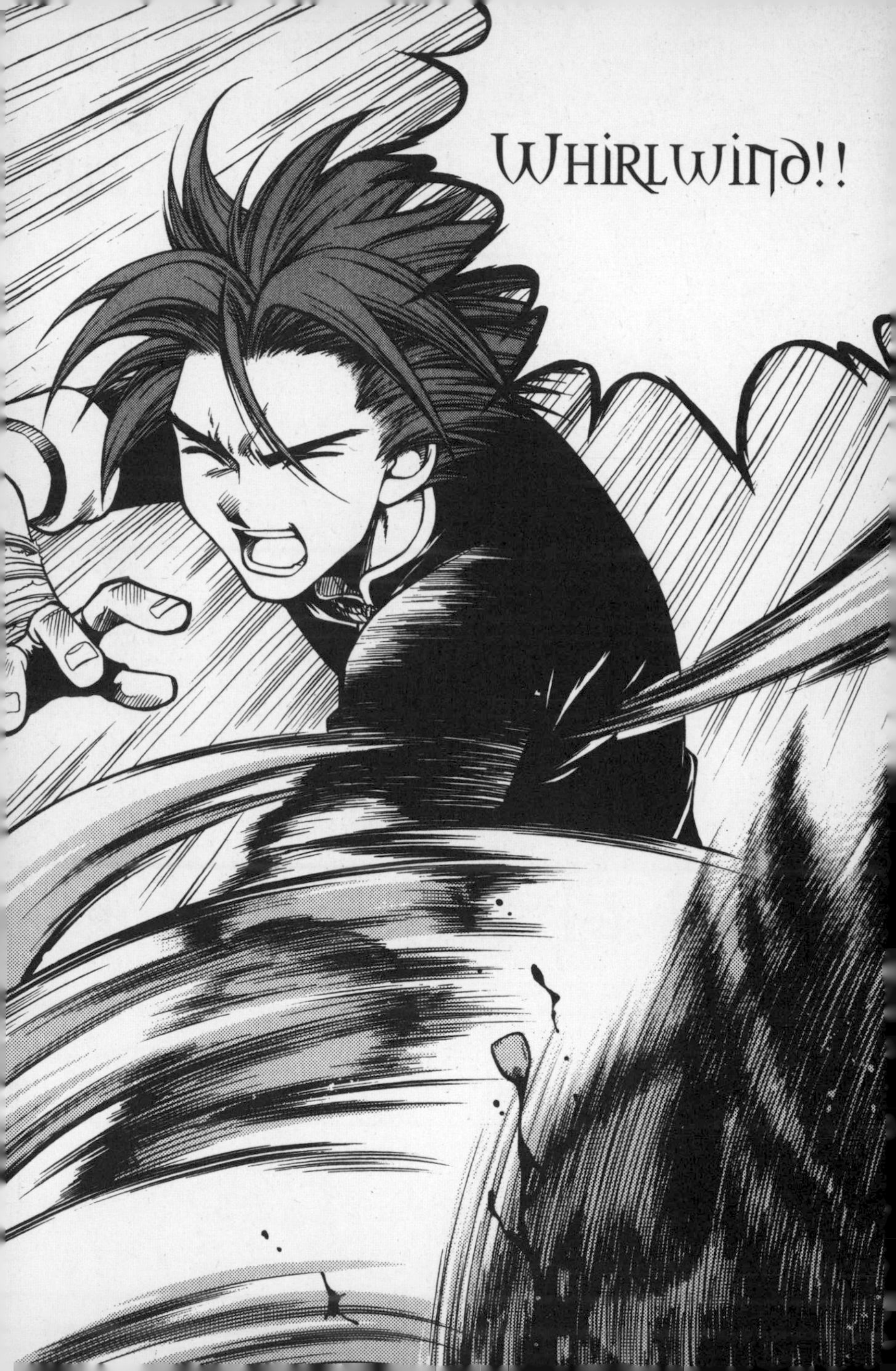
WHIRLWIND!!

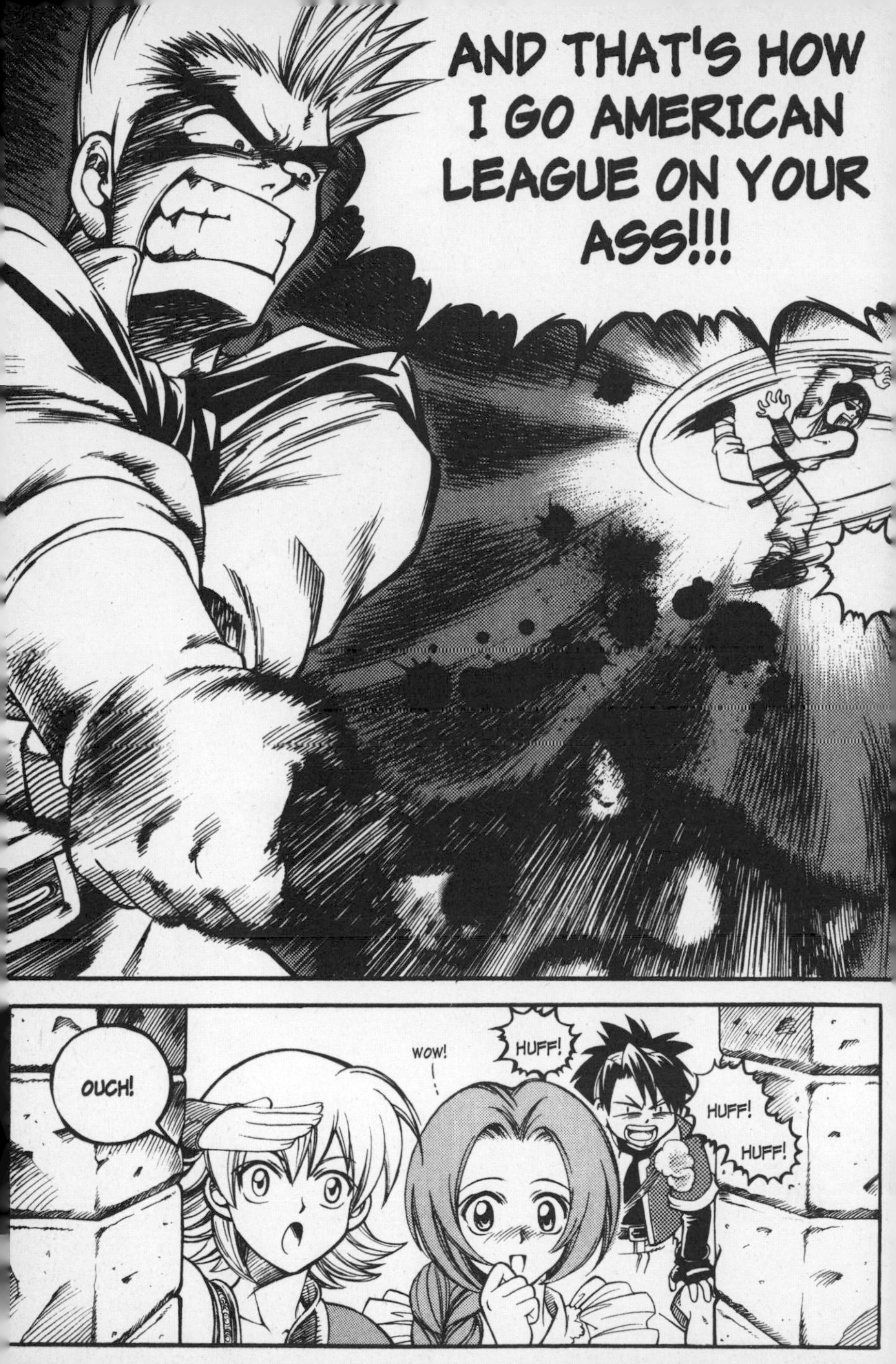
AND THAT'S HOW I GO AMERICAN LEAGUE ON YOUR ASS!!!
OUCH!
WOW!
HUFF!
HUFF!
HUFF!

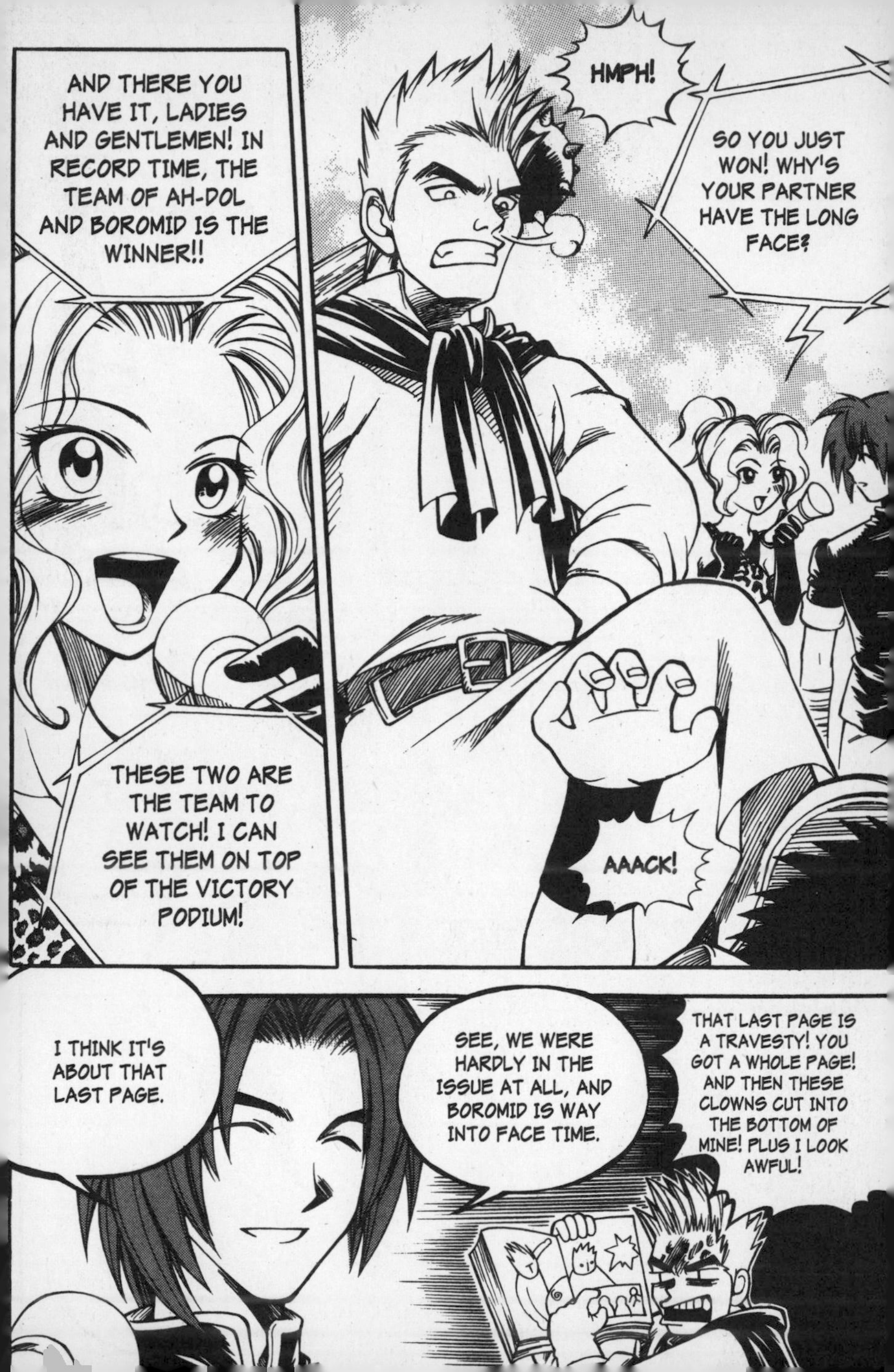
AND THERE YOU HAVE IT, LADIES AND GENTLEMEN! IN RECORD TIME, THE TEAM OF AH-DOL AND BOROMID IS THE WINNER!!
THESE TWO ARE THE TEAM TO WATCH! I CAN SEE THEM ON TOP OF THE VICTORY PODIUM!
HMPH!
SO YOU JUST WON! WHY'S YOUR PARTNER HAVE THE LONG FACE?
AAACK!
I THINK IT'S ABOUT THAT LAST PAGE.
SEE, WE WERE HARDLY IN THE ISSUE AT ALL, AND BOROMID IS WAY INTO FACE TIME.
THAT LAST PAGE IS A TRAVESTY! YOU GOT A WHOLE PAGE! AND THEN THESE CLOWNS CUT INTO THE BOTTOM OF MINE! PLUS I LOOK AWFUL!

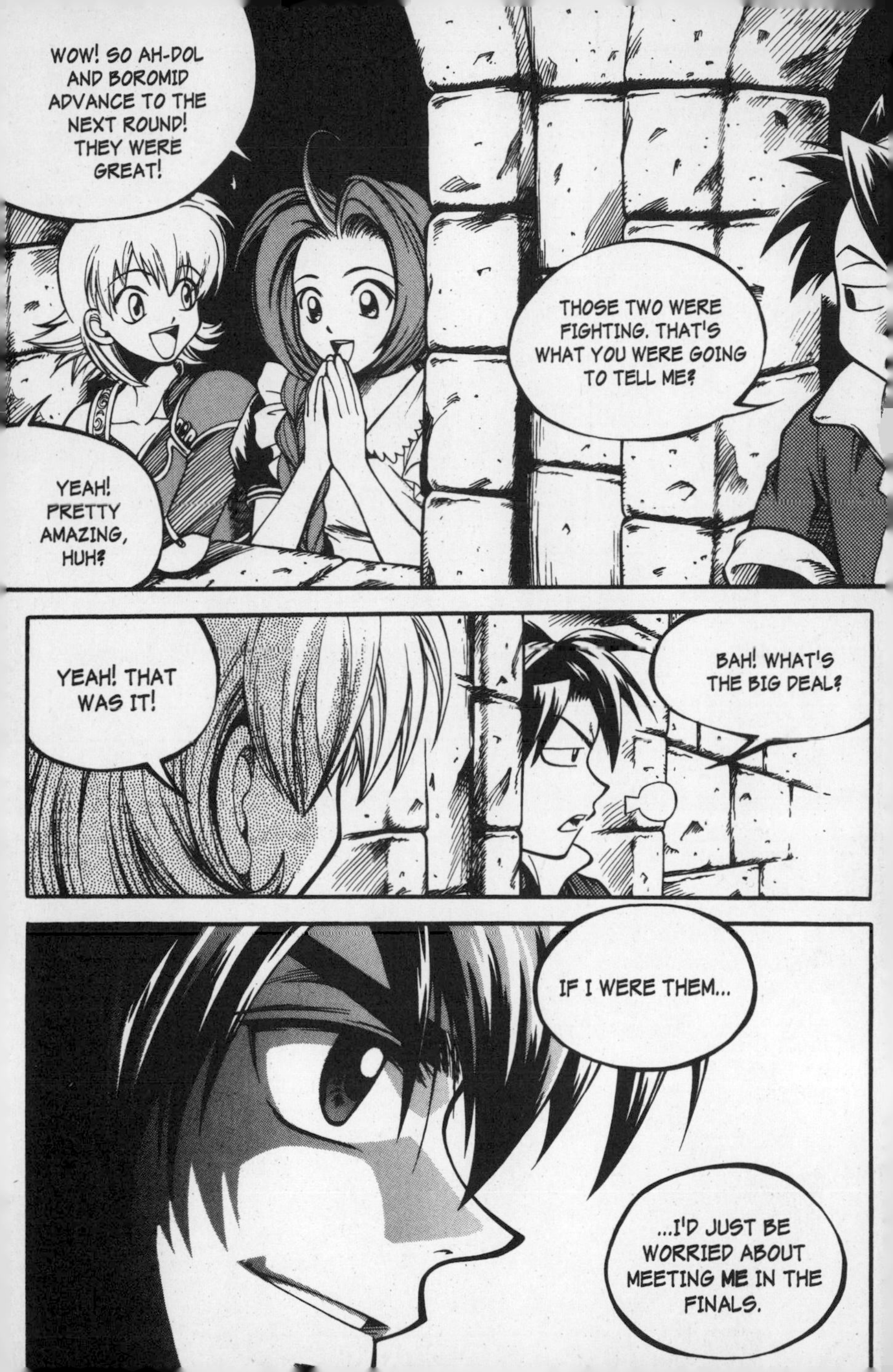
WOW! SO AH-DOL AND BOROMID ADVANCE TO THE NEXT ROUND! THEY WERE GREAT!
YEAH! PRETTY AMAZING, HUH?
THOSE TWO WERE FIGHTING. THAT'S WHAT YOU WERE GOING TO TELL ME?
YEAH! THAT WAS IT!
BAH! WHAT'S THE BIG DEAL?
IF I WERE THEM...
...I'D JUST BE WORRIED ABOUT MEETING ME IN THE FINALS.

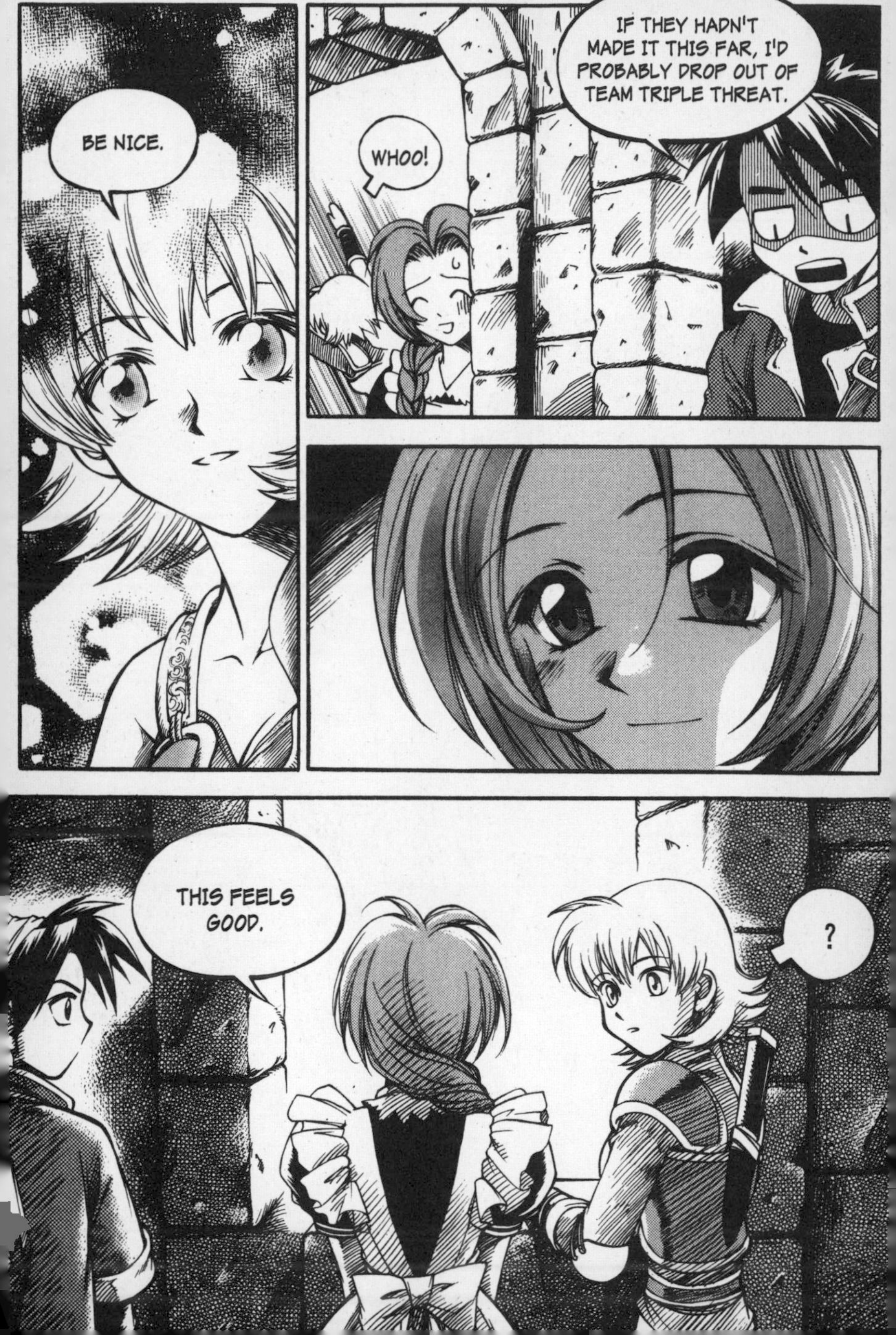
BE NICE.
WHOO!
IF THEY HADN'T MADE IT THIS FAR, I'D PROBABLY DROP OUT OF TEAM TRIPLE THREAT.
THIS FEELS GOOD.
?

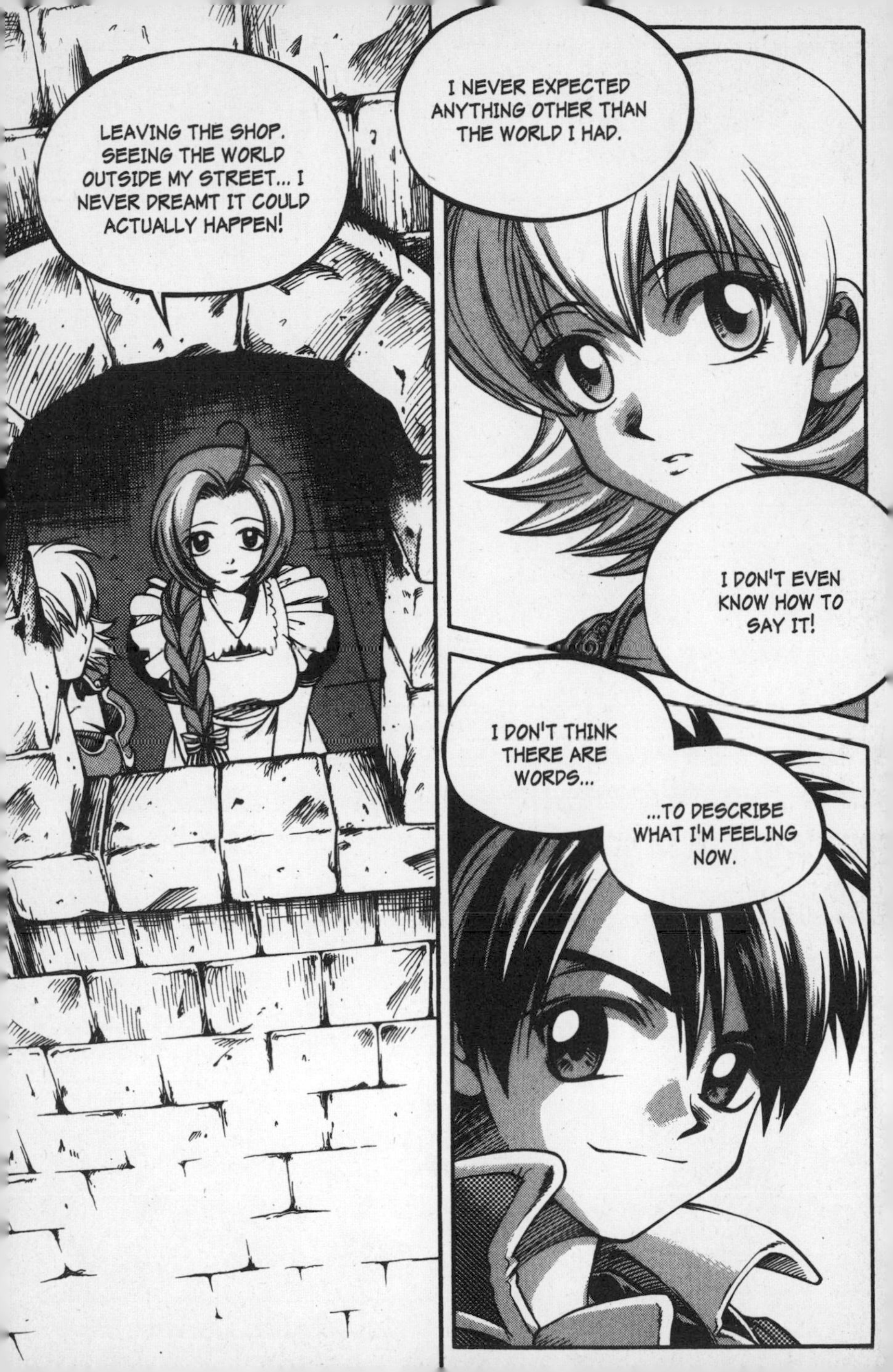

LEAVING THE SHOP. SEEING THE WORLD OUTSIDE MY STREET... I NEVER DREAMT IT COULD ACTUALLY HAPPEN!
I NEVER EXPECTED ANYTHING OTHER THAN THE WORLD I HAD.
I DON'T EVEN KNOW HOW TO SAY IT!
I DON'T THINK THERE ARE WORDS...
...TO DESCRIBE WHAT I'M FEELING NOW.

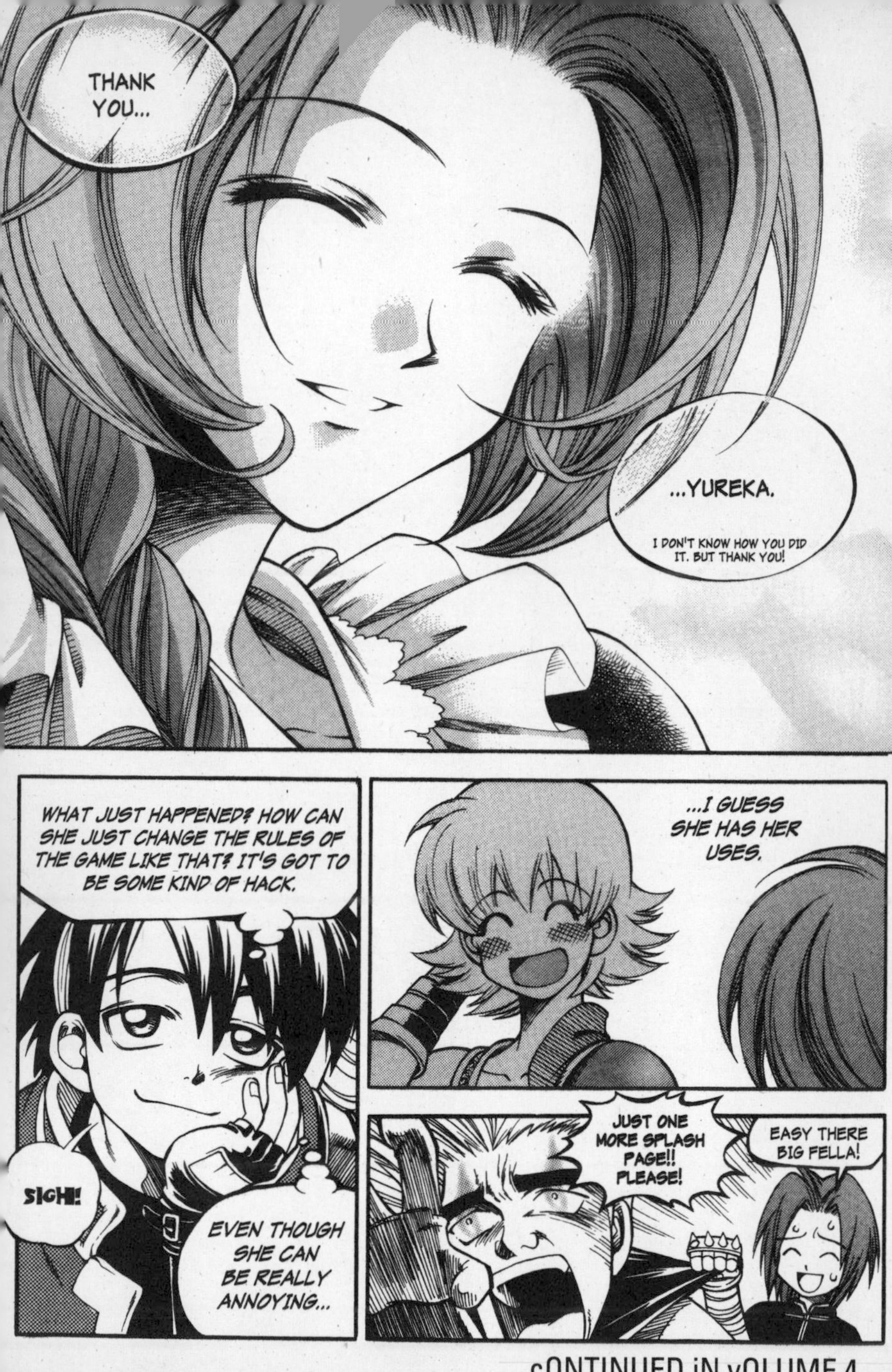
THANK YOU...
...YUREKA.
I DON'T KNOW HOW YOU DID IT. BUT THANK YOU!
WHAT JUST HAPPENED? HOW CAN SHE JUST CHANGE THE RULES OF THE GAME LIKE THAT? IT'S GOT TO BE SOME KIND OF HACK.
SIGH!
EVEN THOUGH SHE CAN BE REALLY ANNOYING...
...I GUESS SHE HAS HER USES.
JUST ONE MORE SPLASH PAGE!! PLEASE!
EASY THERE BIG FELLA!

cONTINUED iN vOLUME 4_

>>LEXICON

Band-aids: Healing prayers that renew a player's health. The ability to use band-aids makes a healer a vital member of a character party.

Bandwidth: The capacity of an Internet connection.

Brick: The kind of warrior a less-powerful character would prefer to be behind when faced with a particularly nasty group of monsters.

Bounty: A reward for completion of a specific deed. In *Lost Saga*, usually the apprehension or killing of a rule-breaking character.

Boss: A high-level monster at the end of a quest or campaign.

Character, ID: A player's identity in the Game.

Debugger: A Dexon employee who assumes an online identity to resolve errors or "bugs" in the *Lost Saga* environment.

Dexon: The software company that created and maintains the *Lost Saga* game.

Dial-up: A slow, old-fashioned internet connection relying on telephone technology.

Dream-mode: A method of playing *Lost Saga* that allows players to control their characters while asleep.

Dungeon chickens: Generic term for relatively harmless monsters that offer little challenge to higher-level players.

Experience: Rewards for success in combat, the accumulation of which allows characters to advance in level, which in turn rewards the character with greater abilities.

Freeze, Frozen: When a player character stops moving, because of a connection error or having been forcibly logged out.

Frag: To kill, especially another player character.

Force quit: To be logged out of the Game by external forces.

Game, the Game: *Lost Saga*, a virtual-reality environment, developed by the Dexon corporation, where players can battle monsters, search for treasure and role-play fantasy-genre characters.

Gamer: Someone for whom playing computer games is a primary leisure-time activity.

Gauntlet: A quarter-crunching mid-'80s arcade game based around seemingly endless mazes populated by teeming masses of easily-killed monsters.

Gib: To kill with gusto, reducing one's opponent to giblet-sized pieces.

Gold: Generic name for Game currency.

Hack: An illegal Game modification.

Healer: A priest-character able to heal other characters by using spell-like prayers.

High-ping bastard (HPB): A player with such a bad connection that he's often frozen, offering no help as a teammate and not much challenge as an opponent.

High priest: A high-level priest character.

Level, level-up: For a character to increase in level through the accumulation of experience.

Live-mode: Playing *Lost Saga* while fully conscious.

Log on, Log in, Drop in: To enter the Game.

Log off, Log out, Quit: To leave the Game.

Lost Saga: The fantasy-genre virtual-reality online game favored by Team Triple Threat.

Low-ping bastard (or LPB): A player who has a really fast Internet connection and low "ping" times to the game server, giving him an advantage over (better) players with slower connections.

Items: Weapons or tools that enhance a character's abilities or otherwise help them to succeed in the Game.

Kicked: To be banned from the Game.

Kill: A defeated enemy.

Medicine: A healing substance allowing characters to instantly recover from damage.

Master-level players: An elite group of players who've logged a minimum of 6,000 hours in the Game and reached a pre-determined level.

Mobs, Monsters: Computer-controlled "mobile objects" that exist solely to be killed by player characters.

Multi-channel: Using a single connection Internet connection for more than one user.

Newbie, Noob: A novice gamer.

Non-player character (NPC): A computer-controlled character.

Offline: The world outside of *Lost Saga*. For players, the "real" world, where things like school, homework and parents get in the way of Game time.

Party: A group of characters who join together to accomplish a common goal.

Patch: A legal modification of the Game.

Player characters: A character controlled by a living, breathing player, as distinguished from a computer-controlled character.

Player killer: A player character who makes a habit of killing other players to steal their items. In *Lost Saga*, this is illegal, and can result in a bounty being placed on the character.

Prayer: An invitation for divine intervention made by a priest-character with results approximating those of a magical spell.

Priest: A character with the ability to use spell-like prayers.

Power player: A player whose only goal is to advance in level as quickly as possible.

Silent step: A stealth-movement technique practiced by thief characters.

Sorcerer: A character with the ability to cast spells.

Spawn: The act of a character or monster entering the Game environment.

Spawn point: The point where a character or monster enters the Game.

Spirit master: A sorcerer adept at calling forth magical beings to do their bidding.

Sun-Bae: A Korean term used by a younger person to indicate an older colleague.

Sword master: A character with extremely high-level swordsmanship skills.

Thief: A character emphasizing dexterity, stealth and guile to succeed in the Game.

Warrior: A character relying on physical skills for success in combat.

iN tHE nEXT vOLUME oF

iDENTITY™

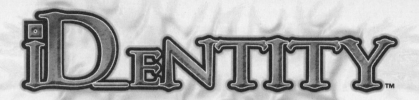

PASSWORD RECOGNIZED...

IDENTITY CONFIRMED...

ACCESSING VOLUME 4 FILE...

The fighting is frenzied and furious as the tournament rolls on, and with the stakes (and the egos) growing bigger with each match, the fighters are pulling out all the stops! Team Aradon, Team Rapha and Team Roto have all lasted this long, and they're not about to back down now. Roto's certain he has the chops to gain the upper hand and bring his team to victory, but with such a wildcard of a partner, there's no telling what might result. And when squaring off against a couple of powerhouses like Rapha and John, that uncertainty can prove to be a liability—a deadly one.

TRANSMISSION COMPLETE...

LOGGING OFF...

vOLUME 4 oN sALE iN dECEMBER

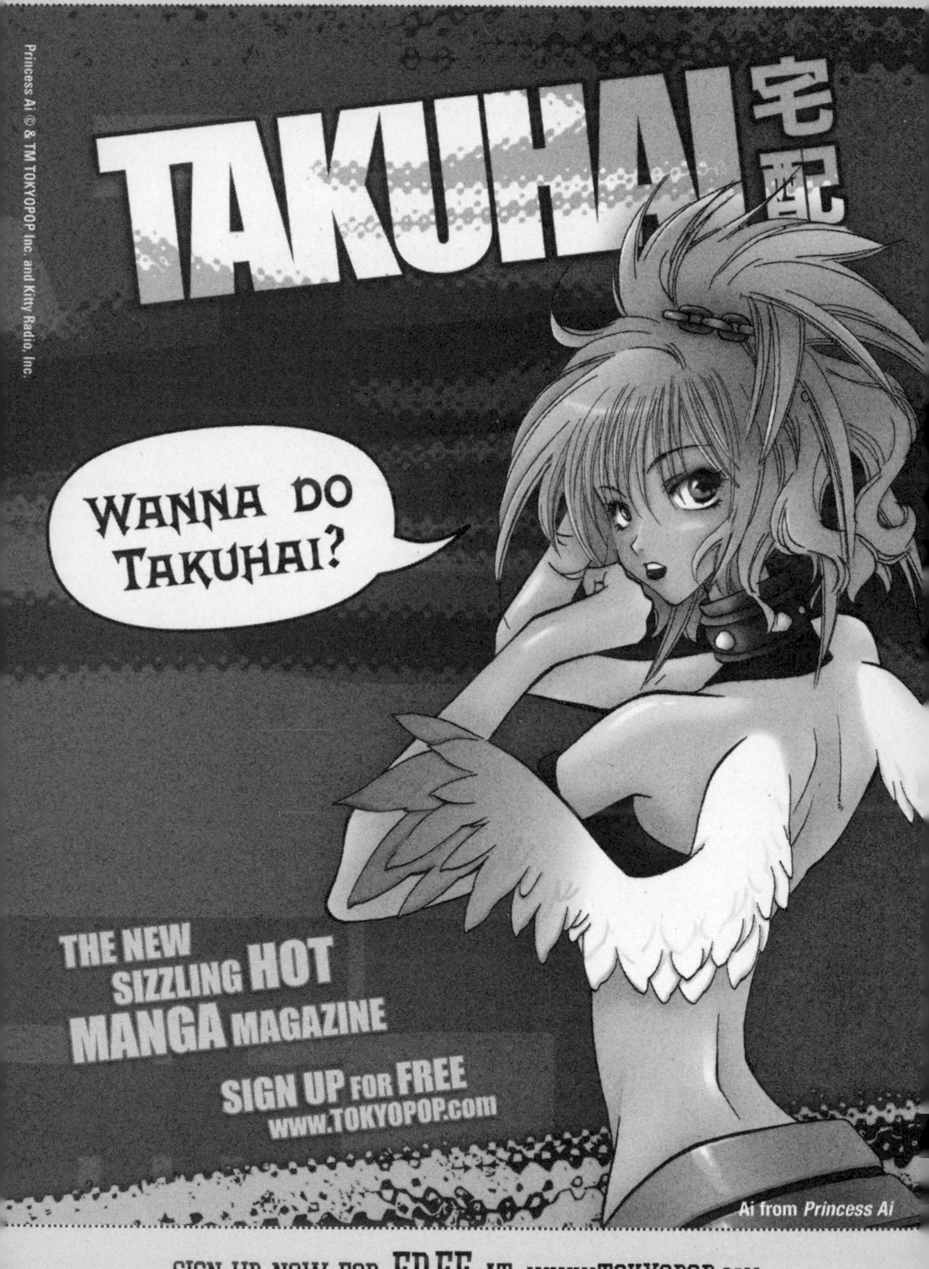
Princess Ai © & TM TOKYOPOP Inc. and Kitty Radio, Inc.
TAKUHAI 宅配
WANNA DO TAKUHAI?
THE NEW SIZZLING HOT MANGA MAGAZINE
SIGN UP FOR FREE
WWW.TOKYOPOP.com
Ai from *Princess Ai*

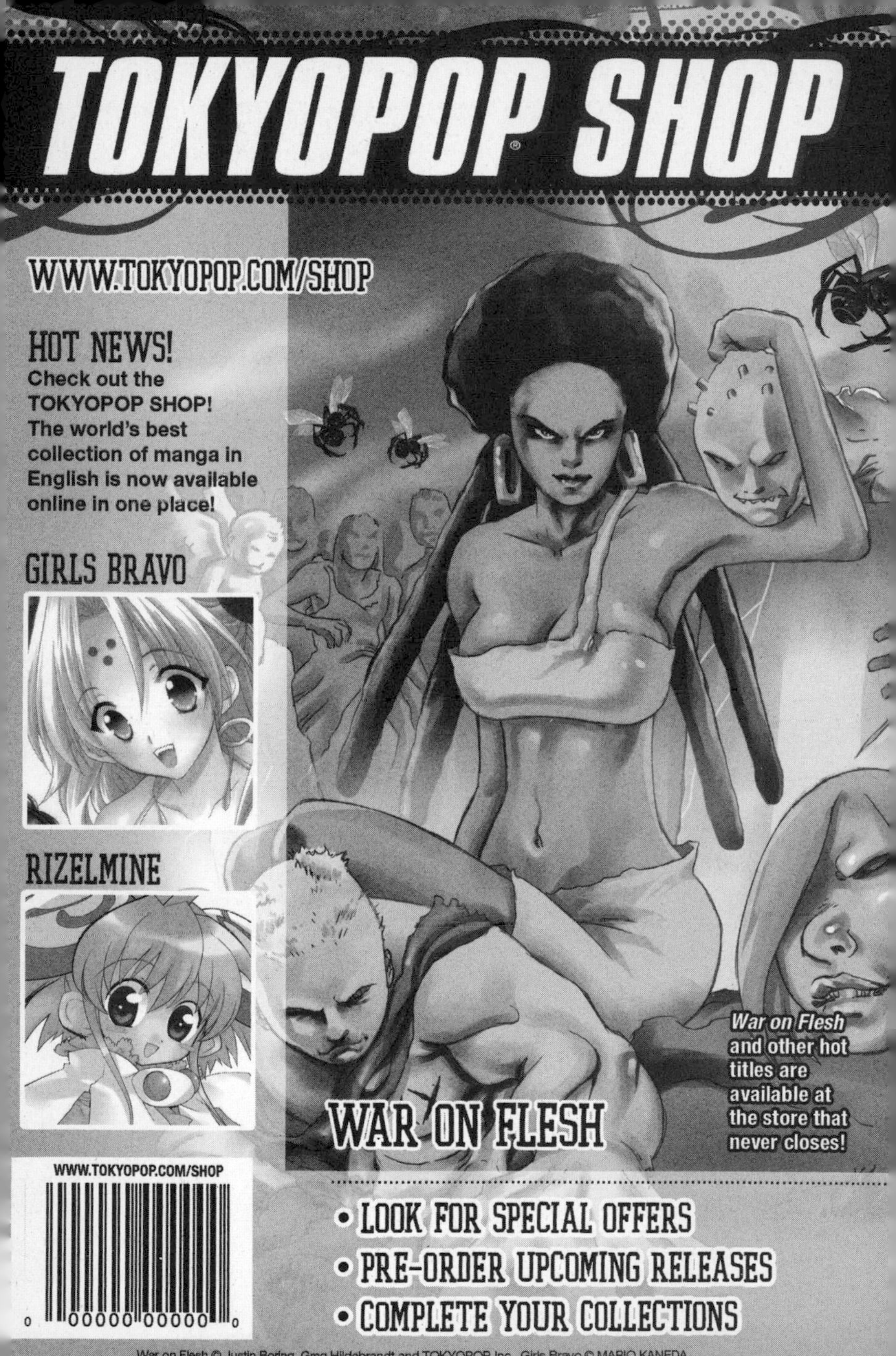
TOKYOPOP® SHOP
WWW.TOKYOPOP.COM/SHOP
HOT NEWS!
Check out the TOKYOPOP SHOP! The world's best collection of manga in English is now available online in one place!
GIRLS BRAVO
RIZELMINE
WWW.TOKYOPOP.COM/SHOP
WAR ON FLESH
War on Flesh and other hot titles are available at the store that never closes!
• LOOK FOR SPECIAL OFFERS
• PRE-ORDER UPCOMING RELEASES
• COMPLETE YOUR COLLECTIONS

I LUV HALLOWEEN

Written by Keith Giffen, comic book pro and English language adapter of *Battle Royale* and *Battle Vixens*.

Join the misadventures of a group of particularly disturbing trick-or-treaters as they go about their macabre business on Halloween night. Blaming the apples they got from the first house of the evening for the bad candy they've been receiving all night, the kids plot revenge on the old bag who handed out the funky fruit. Riotously funny and always wickedly shocking—who doesn't *love* Halloween?

OT
OLDER TEEN
AGE 16+

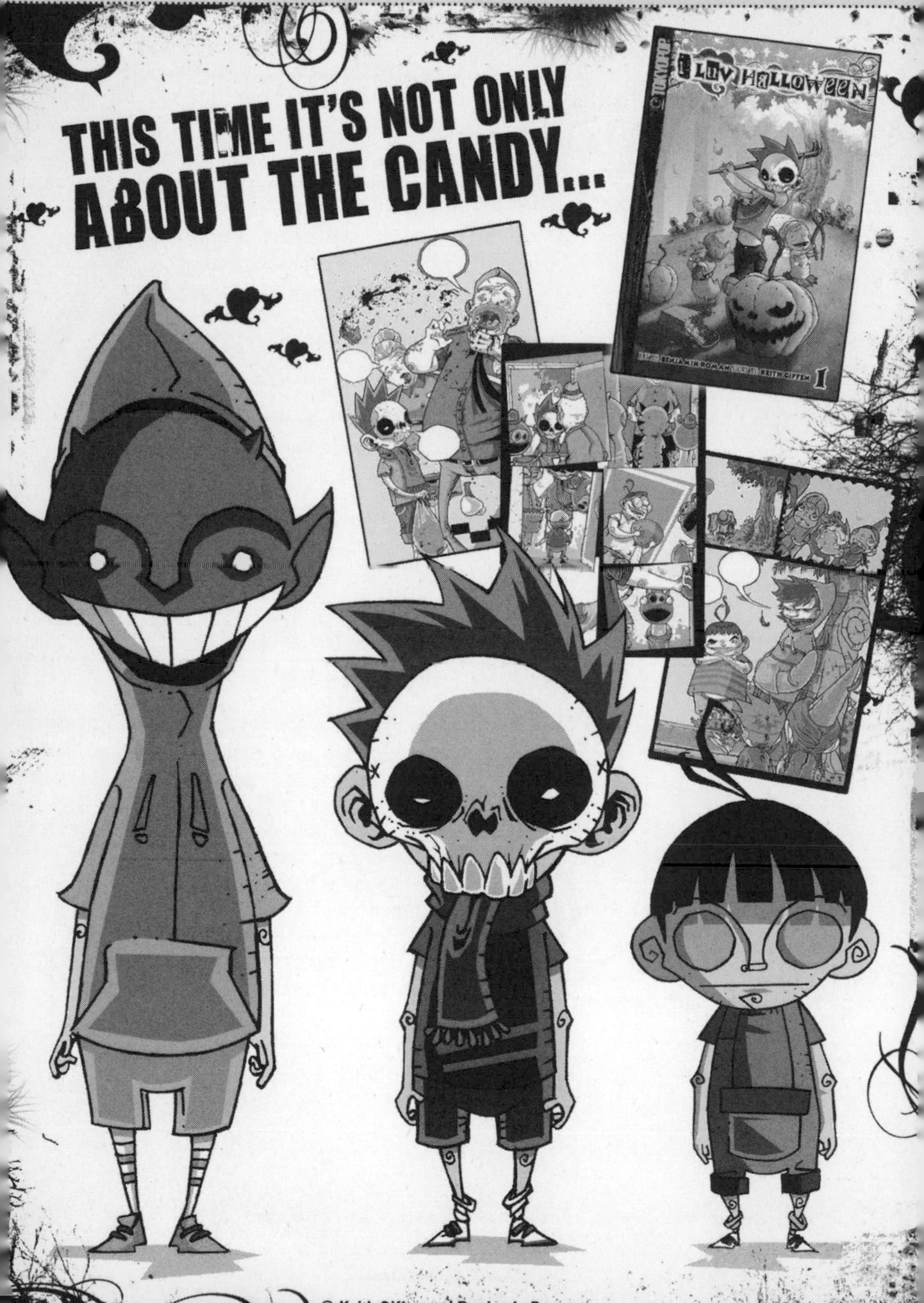
THIS TIME IT'S NOT ONLY
ABOUT THE CANDY...
I LUV HALLOWEEN
1

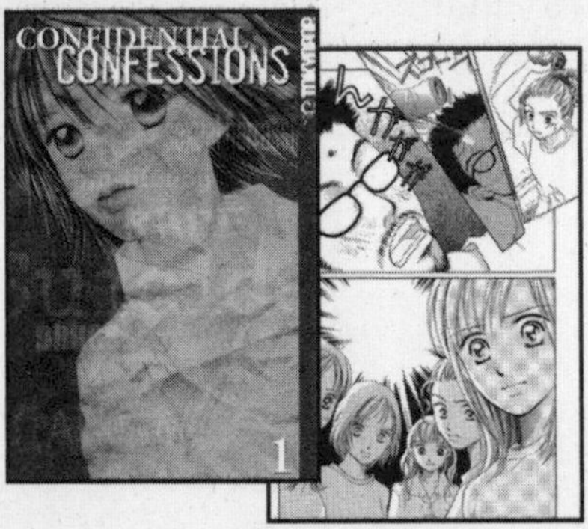
CONFIDENTIAL
CONFESSIONS
1

BY REIKO MOMOCHI

CONFIDENTIAL CONFESSIONS

If you're looking for a happy, rosy, zit-free look at high school life, skip this manga. But if you're jonesing for a real-life view of what high school's truly like, *Confidential Confessions* offers a gritty, unflinching look at what really happens in those hallowed halls. Rape, sexual harassment, anorexia, cutting, suicide...no subject is too hardcore for *Confidential Confessions*. While you're at it, don't expect a happy ending.

~Julie Taylor, Sr. Editor

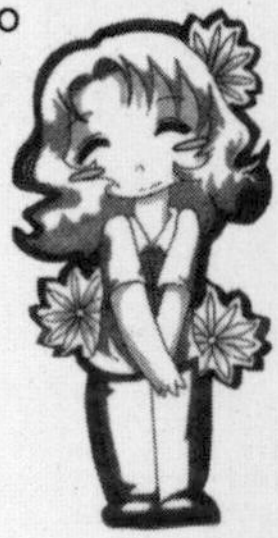

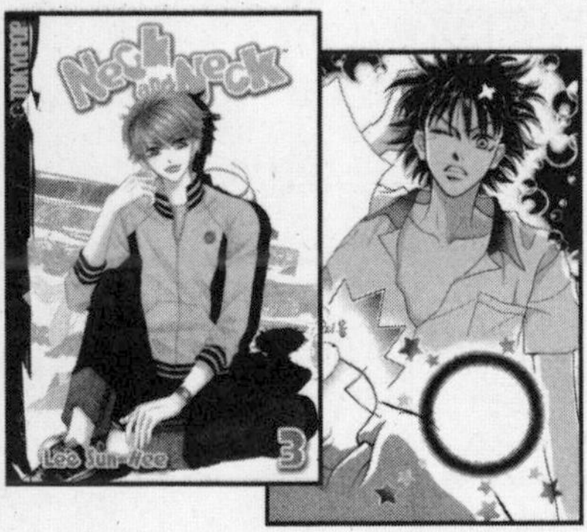
Neck and Neck
TOKYOPOP
Lee Sun-Hee
3

BY LEE SUN-HEE

NECK AND NECK

Competition can bring out the best or the worst in people...but in *Neck and Neck*, it does both! Dabin Choi and Shihu Myoung are both high school students, both children of mob bosses, and each is out to totally humiliate the other. Dabin and Shihu are very creative in their mutual tortures and there's more than a hint of romantic tension behind their attacks. This book's art may look somewhat shojo, but I found the story to be very accessible and very entertaining!

~Rob Tokar, Sr. Editor

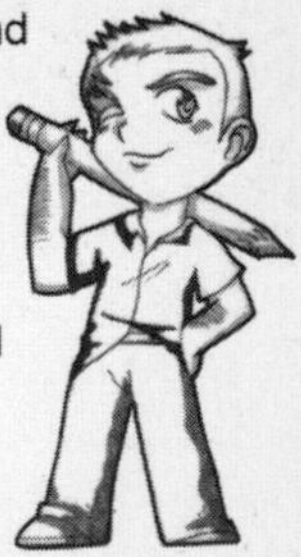

Suikoden
III
幻想水滸伝
Aki Shimizu

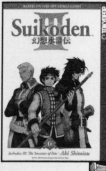

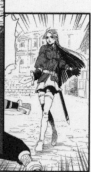

BY AKI SHIMIZU

SUIKODEN III

I'm one of those people who likes to watch others play video games (I tend to run into walls and get stuck), so here comes the perfect manga for me! All the neat plot of a great RPG game, without any effort on my part! Aki Shimizu, creator of the delightful series *Qwan*, has done a lovely, lovely job of bringing the world of Suikoden to life. There are great creatures (Fighting ducks! Giant lizard people!), great character designs, and an engaging story full of conflict, drama and intrigue. I picked up one volume while I was eating lunch at my desk one day, and was totally hooked. I can't wait for the next one to come out!

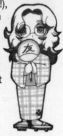

~Lillian Diaz-Przybyl, Editor

Tow Nakazaki Nº FIVE

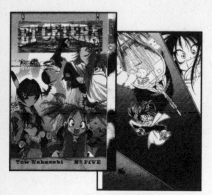

BY TOW NAKAZAKI

ET CETERA

Meet Mingchao, an energetic girl from China who now travels the deserts of the old west. She dreams of becoming a star in Hollywood, eager for fame and fortune. She was given the Eto Gun—a magical weapon that fires bullets with properties of the 12 zodiac signs—as a keepsake from her grandfather before he died. On her journey to Hollywood, she meets a number of zany characters...some who want to help, and others who are after the power of the Eto Gun. Chock full of gun fights, train hijackings, collapsing mineshafts...this East-meets-wild-West tale has it all!

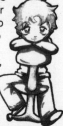

~Aaron Suhr, Sr. Editor